Voice Lessons

THE NEW CULTURAL HISTORY OF MUSIC

SERIES EDITOR **Jane F. Fulcher**

SERIES BOARD Celia Applegate
Philip Bohlman
Kate van Orden
Michael P. Steinberg

Enlightenment Orpheus:
The Power of Music in Other Worlds
Vanessa Agnew

Voice Lessons:
French Mélodie in the Belle Epoque
Katherine Bergeron

KATHERINE
BERGERON

Voice Lessons

French Mélodie in the

Belle Epoque

UNIVERSITY PRESS

2010

OXFORD
UNIVERSITY PRESS

Oxford University Press, Inc., publishes works that further
Oxford University's objective of excellence
in research, scholarship, and education.

Oxford   New York
Auckland   Cape Town   Dar es Salaam   Hong Kong   Karachi
Kuala Lumpur   Madrid   Melbourne   Mexico City   Nairobi
New Delhi   Shanghai   Taipei   Toronto

With offices in
Argentina   Austria   Brazil   Chile   Czech Republic   France   Greece
Guatemala   Hungary   Italy   Japan   Poland   Portugal   Singapore
South Korea   Switzerland   Thailand   Turkey   Ukraine   Vietnam

Published by Oxford University Press, Inc.
198 Madison Avenue, New York, New York 10016

www.oup.com

Oxford is a registered trademark of Oxford University Press.

Library of Congress Cataloging-in-Publication Data
Bergeron, Katherine.
Voice lessons : French mélodie in the belle epoque / Katherine Bergeron.
   p. cm. — (The new cultural history of music series)
Includes bibliographical references.
ISBN 978-0-19-533705-1
1. Songs—France—19th century—History and criticism.   2. Songs—France—20th century—History and
criticism.   3. Singing—France—History—19th century.   4. Singing—France—History—20th century.
I. Title.
ML2827.B47 2009
782.421680944—dc22   2009003948

Recorded audio tracks (marked in text with ◗) are available online at
www.oup.com/us/voicelessons

Access with username Music1 and password Book5983

9 8 7 6 5 4 3 2 1

Printed in the United States of America
on acid-free paper

To the memory of my father
Edward Henry Bergeron (1927–2007)

The ideas in this book first took shape in 1995, in a course I taught with a colleague from the French department at the University of California at Berkeley. The course was a seminar with a simple premise: a study of music and literature taught by a musicologist with an attraction to French poetry and a literary critic with musical training. My colleague was Ann Smock, a specialist in twentieth-century French theory who was also a talented violinist and a friend, in fact, the daughter of William Austin, one of my important teachers at Cornell. Because 1995 was an anniversary year for the composer Gabriel Fauré, we made Fauré our subject, pairing him with a much more famous literary figure from the same social milieu, Marcel Proust. The idea was to use our twin disciplinary perspectives to approach writer and musician differently, in effect, to look at Fauré and listen to Proust with fresh eyes and ears.

With graduate students from different backgrounds, our task became more difficult. Discussions of Fauré, at least, had to steer a careful course, engaging those who knew music and those who did not. And so we experimented. We scrutinized the violin sonata in search of the *petite phrase* of Vinteuil. We roamed the vast surface of the Ballade. We squinted at the songs, pausing over one of Proust's favorites—a melody from 1897 called "Le Parfum impérissable"—that inspired the only fan letter Proust ever wrote to the composer, not to mention a memorable recording by Proust's first lover, the composer Reynaldo Hahn. As a diversion, we even tried listening over the telephone, as Proust had once done, to a scene from Debussy's opera *Pelléas et Mélisande*. Our semester ended with a return to Fauré and a symposium on his extraordinary 1910 song cycle, *La Chanson d'Eve*.

Overall, the experiments proved useful. The mixed audience had made us find unusual ways to listen, and, perhaps for that reason, an unusual set of values came into view. I began to appreciate one aspect of Fauré that had until then remained obscure, a quality that made his music somewhat resistant to analysis. We could call it reticence. It is a hard thing to describe; by nature, it refuses to call attention to itself. I found it in the tendency of Fauré's instrumental music to hide its complexity and in the reserve of some vocal melodies, with their shy and often forgettable tunes. And yet because the seminar had deliberately shifted the focus, I experienced this reserve differently, not as a lack but as a gain, even as the source of Fauré's elusive charm. By the time we reached semester's end, it was a hard thing to miss, especially in the context of a song cycle like *La Chanson d'Eve*, where restraint appeared as the ultimate goal. In the final song, the singer invokes death to silence her, and a nearly motionless melody tells us that her prayer has been answered. Vladimir Jankélévitch called this tendency the "inexpressive 'expressivo'" of French music, without ever saying why.[1] That question persisted for me, long after our seminar had ended, to become the starting point for this book.

My focus now is not Fauré or Proust, although both do play a role in the history I am about to tell. The subject of this book is song, in particular, the art of extreme nuance and discretion that Proust admired, Hahn performed, and Fauré developed over his long musical career—an art the French call, simply, "melody" (*la mélodie*). The history of this art remains obscure, in many ways as discreet as its unforthcoming music. As a repertory, it encompasses a large body of songs created by the poets and composers of the Belle Epoque, and yet it remains virtually absent from standard histories of music. Its performance gave rise to a new class of French singers, and yet the practice nearly died out with those who brought it into prominence. It coincided with France's most enduring modern political regime, the so-called Third Republic, and yet its aims were hardly political. Indeed, by comparison with the more pointed chansons of the boulevards or the Left Bank cabarets, this was a repertoire that appeared to have almost nothing to say. The French composers and performers who created songs for the salons of the Parisian bourgeoisie were concerned less, one might say, with the message than with the medium—with how French words should sound through melody.

The story I tell in these pages is, in a sense, all about that French sound, both what it was and how it got that way. Throughout, I have tried to find the set of critical terms, and a critical approach, that might do it justice. The task has been challenging, to say the least. A musical repertory based on ideals of delicacy and restraint can all too easily produce not criticism but self-congratulation, where the urge to acknowledge a work's value becomes a mere reflection of good taste. This is a tendency I have tried to work against, by dealing with sound not only as an aesthetic and a poetic condition but also as a historical object. It may be impossible to hear music from the past in the way its original audience knew it, but by approaching the *mélodie* from many oblique angles, I try to suggest, at least, what it meant to those who first enjoyed it—and, more important, why it mattered. My goal is not only to seek out the historical perspectives that may allow us to catch the salience of French melody in the years around 1900 but also to show how a study of song might itself offer a new angle on our approach to telling history.

One of those angles has to do with the history of the French language itself—or, perhaps I should say, the history of the idea of the French language, since it was the heyday of the *mélodie*, the period between 1880 and 1920, that saw the greatest advance in the understanding of the material and physical properties of the French tongue. That advance, however, had a bearing on an even more influential development, pushed through by the new republican government, that would have enormous repercussions for the future of France and French national identity. This was the influential series of laws, passed in 1882, that transformed the French public school. The new legislation, which I discuss in chapter 2, established a modern, national, and secular curriculum for all French children and taught them but one language: French. The laws were as practical as they were ideological. By 1880, a percentage of the population in France still spoke only the dialects or patois of their local regions. The new curriculum effectively banished dialects from the school and forced peasant children to accept *la langue française* (a language they did not learn at home) as their true mother tongue.

It was an episode that would, in practical terms, transform the meaning of French for future generations, and, by 1890, it had stimulated a whole new field of language studies. My exposition reaches into this field, as well, to consider a broader range of historical witnesses, from Ferdinand Buisson, who produced in the 1880s a huge "pedagogical dictionary" for the use of the nation's teachers, to the great historian Ferdinand Brunot, who began writing his own massive history of the French language in 1900. But there are other, more surprising texts. Take, for example, a French dictionary from 1897, written entirely in phonetic notation, with words listed not in alphabetical order but in the order of their pronunciation. Its author, Paul Passy, had published a popular book on French phonetics ten years earlier, while spearheading a movement to reform French spelling. There was also the playwright Ernest Legouvé who pushed a course on the "Art of Reading Aloud" into the new standard curriculum. And Paul Koschwitz studied this art in 1891 by making meticulous phonetic transcriptions of Parisian artists, writers, and civic leaders reading their own prose or verse. Alongside them, I muse over the inventor of experimental phonetics, Abbé Rousselot, who began measuring the nuances of the spoken tongue in his laboratory at the Collège de France, and the even more curious Dr. Marage of the Sorbonne, who in 1910 succeeded in making a series of machines capable of phonating the French vowels.

Together, these sources offer evidence of a remarkable new awareness of French sound at the very moment the state was requiring its citizens to learn the language well. A few reformers even dreamed of establishing a latter-day *Académie française*, one that would monitor speech as strictly as the old academy had sought to regulate writing. Such controls would ensure, they thought, the continuity of the spoken language, along with the values of the elite culture that had formerly sustained it—the speech habits of "the best Parisian society," as Rousselot put it. The new language sciences, in other words, appeared as a canny response to what could be described as an emerging bourgeois anxiety: a concern about what would become of the beautiful French language when all French citizens, including peasants and indigents, were required to speak it. Grasping this concern, I argue, is one way of explaining the unusual display of French speech that distinguishes the modern *mélodie*.

It is a truism of music history, of course, to acknowledge the increasingly realistic, speechlike character of French vocal music at the end of the nineteenth century. That observation should take on new meaning in the context of the language history I am outlining here. In chapter 3, I explore the connection further by considering the practice of modern French poets and musicians. In many ways, the poets of the 1890s—the young followers of Verlaine and Mallarmé—tell the other side of the story. These were writers like Gustave Kahn and Camille Mauclair, among many others, who formed a kind of republican counterculture, standing on the side of universal suffrage and showing their solidarity through poetry. If these poets had one anxiety, it was not about the accent of the people invading the beautiful French language; it was about bourgeois values destroying the beautiful accent of the people. They disdained the establishment, dismissed academic poetry as "literature," and developed their own noisy brand of verse—earthy and physical—which they called "free." We could think of them as France's Woodstock generation.

Literary histories have, unfortunately, blunted the edge of these poets by collecting them under one of the more familiar isms of the period: *symbolism*. The term was as vexing in its time as it is in our own, evoking a cult of mystical dreamers, writers of precious and difficult verses, who were either oblivious or downright contemptuous of their audience. I make an effort to reverse this view by following the lead of more than one outspoken apologist of the period, and by taking time to read a few poems quite closely. It may be more useful, as I suggest, to think of these writers not as symbolists but as *realists* in the broadest sense. What they were trying to capture in their back-to-nature verse was a kind of physical reality: the concrete sensations of language. I trace their quest for a truer French accent, as they mined folk poetry for its irregular rhythms and marveled at the clangorous impression of words—the unique aural stamp known (in French) as *timbre*. The much-discussed "music" of the symbolists needs to be understood in these terms, not as a poetic dream but as a phonetic reality, surprisingly in sync with language science of the same period. Indeed, the search for the truest representation of French even inspired a few of these poets to find their way into the laboratories of the Collège de France.

French composers of the 1890s may not have gone to such extremes, but their ears were developing in similar ways. At the end of chapter 3, I make the case by turning to songs by Debussy and Fauré and to one by Ernest Chausson as well, although others could tell the same story. Here the evidence lies in the musical notation, capturing a more and more exact likeness of spoken French. What emerges, over time, is a striking shift in musical values: as the French accent becomes more and more central, the melodic line has less and less to "say." A song like Debussy's "C'est l'extase l'amoureuse," from 1887, looks and sounds overheated next to the cool recitations of "La Flûte," from the *Chansons de Bilitis*, a decade later. Likewise, the plainspoken austerity of Fauré's 1897 "Parfum impérissable" can make the lushness of an early Fauré song like "Après un rêve" seem in bad taste. Unlike the poets, the composers tell us almost nothing about their change of heart, or the change in their art. But other witnesses are more forthcoming, a group whose language training could and did affect the sound the composers were now imagining. I am speaking of French performers. A good part of the story of the *mélodie* belongs to them, and so I have sought out their voices, too: to heed their advice and to hear their extraordinary accents.

I should also confess that one of the ways I have tried listening to these voices is by learning to sing myself. Evidence of my own voice lessons may not be immediately obvious in the pages that follow, but the experience of singing has afforded me a unique perspective on my subject. Among other things, it has given me a new appreciation for a certain type of historical document: the recordings made by singers who were active during the era of the *mélodie*. Not exactly household names today, the singers include Claire Croiza, Charles Panzéra, Mary Garden, Maggie Teye, and Hector Dufranne—

all of whom played roles in *Pelléas* during Debussy's lifetime. There was also Jane Bathori, known for her premieres of Ravel, and the aforementioned Reynaldo Hahn, admired not only by Proust but also by Fauré.

Before my lessons, I'll admit, I had trouble hearing what made these singers great. It was difficult to identify with the sound of their recordings, diminished as they are by the audible patina of time. Singing made me more physically aware of French resonance, and that sensation tuned my ear, in turn, making the historic voices ring truer. The most thrilling quality I began to hear was also, in some ways, the most alien: an impeccable feeling for diction. This is not just a technique. On these recordings, the sound of French has invaded the tone of the singing voice so completely as to produce a wholly new oral object. The sound is almost unheard of today, and hearing it, I developed a different sense of the *mélodie*—a sense that, at first, I tasted more than understood. But it has become central to the history I am trying to tell in this book. The sound, in effect, *is* the history.

Chapter 4 follows that sound, surveying the rich culture of performance that sustained the *mélodie* between 1880 and 1920. I consider not only singers but also actors, and not only sound recordings but also written records: the treatises, memoirs, self-help manuals, and musical scores that offer another angle on the object of performance. Here I am interested as much in what the historical performers were doing, as in what they said *about* what they were doing or, to put it another way, in what their training might reveal about their culture. And as it turns out, it reveals quite a lot. The treatises of both singers and actors of the period expose an almost uncanny tendency among the lyric arts—what the French called the *arts de dire*—to merge into one another, the actor's recitations becoming songlike, and the songs like recitations. This formal reciprocity offers another telling context for the modern *mélodie*, whose newer forms clearly depended on this new concept of performance, one whose true object was French itself.

Like the language scientists of the same period, French performers examined this object in all its facets, but their conclusions had more to do with beauty than with science. As they extolled the virtues of this or that French consonant or vowel, they affirmed not the material quantities but the affective qualities of French letters—what some liked to call their "impressionistic value." This was a value recognized by even savvier witnesses. A treatise by the formidable French linguist Maurice Grammont observed with great solemnity how the letter *r* in its French pronunciation produced an essential rumbling that evoked fear, and how the *l*, embodying liquidity, signaled flow. Singers and actors reinforced the point by advising that the most meaningful performances consisted not in interpreting but simply pronouncing the words: drawing out the feeling of what was already there, within the sounds themselves.

This advice may help to explain the uncommon taste for diction one hears on historic recordings from the first part of the twentieth century. But the idea that the best performance should consist in doing nothing—or nothing more than savoring the letters of the language—may also tell us something about the quality of reserve we find in the melodies themselves. Singers were praised for keeping still, for barely moving their lips, for quelling their desire to act. Once again, the sensibility followed the sound. It was as if an ideal of comportment were being dictated by the most French sound of all, the central timbre of tongue known in French as *l'e muet*: the "mute" *e*. This is a letter about which the historical sources have much to say, and I have tried to listen closely. What emerges from the accounts is an unusual sort of chiasmic relationship between timbre and temperament, where the character of the French sign seems to become, for a moment, a sign of the French character.

The music of the period reflected the same character, suggesting that composers were attuned to the same ideals. Chapter 4 features a variety of examples along the way, including songs and declamations by Hahn, Massenet, Debussy, and others. At the end of the chapter, I turn to Debussy's opera *Pelléas et Mélisande*, presenting it as a kind of *summa lyrica*, in order to examine the range of French expression he puts on stage and how he represents that range in music. By lingering over several scenes, and by listening closely to performances by Croiza, Panzéra, and Garden, I show how Debussy's meticulous attention to the language in performance illuminates the character not only of the drama but also of the different lyric forms themselves. In the context, the *mélodie* emerges as a special case, a music that appears to meld the melodic purity of the rustic chanson with the formal clarity of theatrical declamation. Nor will this be the last angle on our subject. In chapter 5, I trace the fate of the *mélodie* through the first decades of the twentieth century. Song cycles by Debussy, Ravel, and Fauré confirm the increasingly special case of this uncompromising art, now burdened by the awareness of its own idealism.

And at this point, my story has circled back to where it started. In fact, the first and most extensive exposition of French song occurs not at the end but at the very beginning of this book, in chapter 1, where I take up that extraordinary song cycle I encountered so many years before in my seminar on Fauré and Proust: *La Chanson d'Eve*. As a work that marked an important turning point in Fauré's professional life, it offers a unique view on the art he did so much to cultivate throughout his long career. I approach the cycle from this perspective, reading it as an allegory—a kind of Ovidian myth about the origins of *mélodie*—where the story of Creation and the Fall, told now from a fresh perspective, becomes a vehicle for instructing about the past, present, and future of French song. Indeed, the story of the first woman-child savoring her first taste of speech on the first morning of the world prepares us for much of the history in the ensuing chapters: the history of French language instruction, the history of French poetry, and the history of French performance.

My opening chapter, though, seeks to make another kind of point, as well. Because this book is about a musical practice, I want to make the music as central as the history, and so, in chapter 1, the song cycle itself becomes the main event. If a critical argument about *mélodie* emerges from the story of *La Chanson d'Eve,* a critical approach emerges, too. I try to find a way of speaking about this music that will keep the image—and the feeling—of its ten remarkable songs in view, which means taking the time to linger over the phrases, to delight in the musical details as one might in performance. The task could be called close reading, but the term does not quite catch the spirit of the challenge. I would rather call it slow reading or, better yet, slow listening, to acknowledge the temporality of the sung texts that are my real subject. In any case, it is the approach I take in every chapter: treating songs and poems not simply as examples but as experiences in their own right. Reading in this way ends up affording one final, salient angle on the *mélodie française.* A musical practice that belongs to the French art of speaking, the *art de dire,* has an even more nuanced tale to tell, simply in the way its words are spoken (*dit*). *Dire l'histoire,* to tell the story of that sound, requires us to hear, above all, what these melodies might be saying about themselves. And that, as I discovered, turns out to be the most telling history of all.

———

A book that has evolved over ten years, two continents, and three different universities has required the support of many people, and I want to end the story of my project by acknowledging their generosity. Much of this book was conceived during a leave supported by two fellowships: the President's Fellowship from the University of California Board of Regents in 2002 and the Frederick Burkhardt Fellowship from the American Council of Learned Societies in 2003. I am extremely grateful to both institutions for the interest they showed in this project and for providing me with the means to think and write without interruption. I was, in fact, a visiting scholar at the University of North Texas when the first few chapters were drafted. The high plains of Denton turned out to be an opportune place to think about a repertory of melodies that held flatness as an ideal, and I remain indebted to Mary Anne Venner and the staff of the interlibrary loan department, and to Mark McKnight and Andrew Justice in the Music Library, for helping me obtain the materials I needed. Additional fellowship support from the Harry Ransom Research Center at the University of Texas at Austin allowed me access to their own marvelous collection of letters and first editions of modern French writers, as well as to some autograph manuscripts of Fauré and Debussy.

I was fortunate to present some of the arguments in this book at meetings of the American Musicological Association in Toronto (2000) and Seattle (2004), as well as in conferences and colloquia at Berkeley, Brandeis, Brown, Columbia, Cambridge, Cornell, Duke, Eastman, Florida State, Keele University, Leiden University, the National Humanities Center, Penn, Stanford, UCLA, the University of North Texas, the University of Warwick, and Yale. The generous response of the audiences at all these events enriched my thinking enormously. Many colleagues read portions of the manuscript and offered commentary at different stages of the writing. I want to express my gratitude to Wendy Allanbrook, Ernst van Alphen, Mieke Bal, Jane Bernstein, Carol Clover, David Copenhafer, Jean Day, Emma Dillon, William Fitzgerald, Carla Hesse, Joseph Kerman, Thomas Lacqueur, Celeste Langan, Roger Parker, Celeste Schenck, Arman Schwartz, David Schwarz, Mary Ann Smart, Ann Smock, Anya Suschitzky, Alan Tansman, Richard Taruskin, Ann Wagner, and Richard Winslow. Heartfelt thanks also go to Gregory Bloch, Roger Moseley, Anna Nisnevich, David Paul, and Heather Wiebe, the graduate students in my Berkeley seminar "In search of the *mélodie française*." By now, they have all embarked on their own careers, but the semester we spent together pondering this elusive music is one I will never forget, standing as a model of the kind of synergy that results when teachers and students set their minds to the same task.

Other people contributed to this book in less direct ways. Lillian Loran—my octogenarian voice teacher in Berkeley and one of the more remarkable women I have known—taught me about the sensibility of the *mélodie* through a unique pedagogy based on the resonance of the speaking voice. Her focus on the *voix parlée*, I later realized, had much in common with the teachings of Claire Croiza, Jean de Reszké, Reynaldo Hahn, and Jane Bathori and thus offered me an invaluable reality check, a physical sensation by which to gauge their historical testimonies. The French contralto Marion Kilcher tuned my ear in a different way when I had the good fortune to perform with her in Paris a decade ago. More recently, I have benefited from conversations with the American mezzo Lucy Shelton, who tested the limits of my critical approach by offering a singer's insight on these readings. My Brown colleague Dana Gooley helped put my readings to the test more directly, when he and I prepared Fauré's *Chanson d'Eve* for live performance in 2008 and again for a recording in 2009. I remain ever grateful for Dana's extraordinary musicianship and for his keen sensitivity to Fauré's declamatory rhythms. In the preparation of the recording, we were ably assisted by James Moses, the technical manager of Brown's music department. And if it seems like poetic justice that our recording of this biblical cycle should take place in Providence, aided by a man called Moses, I am nevertheless indebted to him for the patience and the perfectionism he brought to that project, which is included on the companion Web site to this book.

It has been rewarding for me to work through the last stages of this book with the support of Oxford University Press, especially series editor Jane Fulcher and my Brown colleague Michael Steinberg. Chris and Donna Wilson offered expert assistance in producing the musical examples, and my wonderful student Hannah Lewis oversaw many details of the manuscript preparation with grace and professionalism. I cannot end, though, without mentioning the debt I owe my family, who indulged me in more conversations about French song than they ever needed or deserved. My husband, Butch Rovan, believed in this project from the first sentence to the last, listened to many drafts, and served as a dedicated and talented vocal coach as I worked my way through these extraordinary songs over the past ten years. But it is perhaps to my father, the late Edward Bergeron, that I owe the greatest thanks. I can hardly remember a conversation in the last decade of his life when he did not ask, "How's the book?" The encouragement he showed at every stage of my professional development—both as a musician and as a musicologist—was an unimaginable gift, and I dedicate this book to his memory.

CONTENTS

Because the argument of *Voice Lessons* features close readings of songs and poems, the companion Web site offers a number of recordings as a supplement to the reading. In addition to more recent performances, I include historic recordings by certain well-known French singers and *diseurs* of the Belle Epoque: Claire Croiza, Jane Bathori, Reynaldo Hahn, and Sarah Bernhardt herself. Their readings, and their diction, will afford readers a window onto the rich culture of the voice that informed the French mélodie at the turn of the twentieth century. Where such recordings have been featured, an icon appears in the text alongside the relevant musical example.

The tracks on this Web site are listen-only files. Readers who would like to download a copy of the 2009 recording of Fauré's *La Chanson d'Eve* prepared for this publication may find the files at http://www.soundidea.org/voicelessons.

Recordings on the Companion Web Site

TRACKS 1–10. Gabriel Fauré, *La Chanson d'Eve* (poems by Charles van Lerberghe). Katherine Bergeron, voice. Dana Gooley, piano. Recorded in Grant Recital Hall, Brown University, June 2009.
Paradis
Prima Verba
Roses ardentes
Comme Dieu rayonne
L'Aube blanche

L'Eau vivante

Veilles-tu, ma senteur de soleil

Dans un parfum de roses blanches

Crépuscule

O Mort, poussière d'étoiles

TRACK 11. Ascending scale of vowels. Demonstration reproduced from Paul Passy, *Les Sons du français*, 1887.

TRACK 12. Claude Debussy, "La Flute de Pan," from *Chansons de Bilitis* (prose poems by Pierre Louÿs). As performed on a 1929 recording by Jane Bathori. Reproduced with permission.

TRACK 13. Gabriel Fauré, "Le Parfum impérissable" (poem by Charles-Marie-Réné Leconte de Lisle). From a 1930 recording by Reynaldo Hahn. Reproduced with permission.

TRACK 14. François Coppée, "Un Evangile" (excerpt). From a performance by Sarah Bernhardt recorded by French Gramophone in 1903.

TRACK 15. François Coppée, "Un Evangile" as an imaginary *mélodie*. Sarah Bernhardt, voice. Katherine Bergeron, piano.

TRACK 16. Claude Debussy, *Pelléas et Mélisande*, Act I, ii (The Letter Scene), from a 1927 recording featuring Claire Croiza in the role of Geneviève. Reproduced with permission.

TRACK 17. Claude Debussy, "Colloque sentimental," from the second set of *Fêtes galantes* (poems by Paul Verlaine). As performed on a 1929 recording by Jane Bathori. Reproduced with permission.

TRACK 18. Maurice Ravel, "Le Martin-Pêcheur," fourth song from *Histoires naturelles* (prose poems by Jules Renard). As performed on a 1929 recording by Jane Bathori. Reproduced with permission.

TRACK 19. Guillaume Apollinaire reading "Le Pont Mirabeau," from *Alcools*. As performed by the poet in 1913.

Voice Lessons

CHAPTER ONE

Eve Sings, an Origin Story

I N August 1905, two months before assuming his post as director of the Paris Conservatoire, Gabriel Fauré announced a first, ambitious goal: to reform French instruction in singing. Reacting to complaints about declining musical standards, he went to the heart of the curriculum to find a solution. Voice teachers, he said, should change their ways. To make "true artists" of France's future singers, vocal training would have to go beyond technique, and beyond the opera house, to include a nobler repertoire: "the admirable lieder of Schubert and Schumann."[1] The advice worked. A year later, in 1906, first prize in the women's vocal competition went to a young student who dared to sing *Gretchen am Spinnrade.* Pierre Lalo hailed the event in an enthusiastic review for *Le Temps,* calling it "almost a revolution."[2] Fauré acknowledged the victory more modestly. That same year—a year of fresh beginnings for the most conservative of musical institutions—he was at work on a new cycle of modern French "lieder," his first in more than ten years. The collection he eventually completed would itself be a song of beginnings, celebrating the original murmur of creation and its very first singer: *La Chanson d'Eve.*

It is with this singularly French tale of origins that I choose to begin my own story, divining from Fauré's Eve the complex ethos of an art that defines a unique moment in the history of French music, an art that would later renounce its German roots and come to be known more literally—and, no doubt, more patriotically—as *la mélodie française.* There is a certain justice in inaugurating my history with Fauré. Contemporary critics judged him almost single-handedly responsible for transplanting the foreign genre of the lied onto French soil. The musicologist Henri Fellot, wondering in 1904 how this music of "Germanic and Nordic origins" managed to take root in France, proclaimed Fauré its "Master and incontestable creator" and "the most exquisite of our modern Minnesingers."[3] A few years later, the journalist Robert Brussel echoed the sentiment, when he granted Fauré all the credit for "restoring if not inventing" the belated genre of the lied in France.[4] Fauré's former student Charles Koechlin went further, seeing in the evolution of his teacher's long musical career not only a perfect analogy for the genre's development but also a spectacularly Darwinian vision of the survival of this rare musical species. Already in some of Fauré's earliest songs, Koechlin said, we can see "a 'new organism' being born. The *mélodie*, once upon a time a simple strophic form, is about to become a whole . . . like a living being now supplied with a central nervous system."[5]

Not surprisingly, it was Fauré's representation of the first living being in *La Chanson d'Eve* that Koechlin would praise as the highest realization of the species.[6] But how exactly did this new life-form emerge? When did the little French parlor song—the strophic form known as *romance*—give way to the more colorful and meaningful forms of *mélodie*? Before turning to Fauré, it may be useful to consider some of the ways critics over the last century have attempted to answer.

Melody

Most historical accounts have looked considerably beyond Fauré, to Berlioz and Schubert, in fact, to find the origins of the art.[7] We hear about the craze for Schubert songs that in the 1830s gave rise to a spate of French-language versions known conveniently as *mélodies*. Berlioz, however, is usually given credit for the first use of the term, in the 1830 collection *Neuf mélodies imitées de l'anglais*—his Gallic response to another popular foreign import, the *Irish Melodies* of Thomas Moore.[8] Both phenomena signal the emergence of a new genre (or the idea of a new genre) rising from the dust of the old *romance*.[9] At least a few modern musicologists have cautioned against such lexical determinism. Marie-Claire Beltrando has observed, for example, that the *romance* never really disappeared, remaining a staple of bourgeois music making throughout the nineteenth century.[10] Still, it is clear that in the 1830s something called *mélodie* began to take its place, and one might wonder what this term—a near neologism—meant for those who first employed it. Why did French composers begin speaking of song, simply, as "melody"? Frits Noske long ago attempted to trace the origins of the usage, but his historical account only partly answers the question. I want to consider not just the origins but also the ethics of the name, to begin to understand how melody mattered.

Let us not forget that, as Berlioz used it, *mélodie* was essentially a foreign word, a direct transliteration of English. When he chose to dub his imitation Irish songs "melodies," he self-consciously evoked Moore's more famous anthology and all its vicarious music. Moore had designed his poems, after all, to fit with a collection of well-known Irish airs. The deliberate anglicism of Berlioz's title was thus calculated to speak in two directions. It obviously drew on the novelty of Moore's musical verses. But the sweet music wafting through that poetry carried another message. More than a set of tunes, the Irish air was also, for Moore, a guarantor of authenticity, the breath of life that would make his verse ring true. Berlioz hoped to breathe the same, and so he used these English poems (now in French translation) in much the same way that Moore had traded on the Irish, as a means to writing a more authentic modern song. By all accounts, he achieved his goal in *Elégie en prose*, the last song of his new collection. The plain, declamatory vocal line and through-composed setting represented, in many ways, a surprising stylistic departure. With its freer prose rhythms, its earnest accents, the voice of this *mélodie* did seem more genuine. The irony was that such pure music came only by way of a foreign muse. For both Moore and Berlioz, an imaginary Ireland was the catalyst—and "melody" the symbol—of a new, more direct expression. Like a brisk northerly wind, its cleansing foreign air conveyed a new idea of truth.[11]

The air of Schubert had an equally bracing effect. The same foreign charm and the same powerful aura of authenticity hovered around the lieder that circulated in Parisian salons of the 1830s and 1840s. At least, this is what we learn from Adolphe Nourrit, the singer who eventually became Schubert's most devoted French interpreter. Nourrit's biographer tells of the first time the tenor heard Liszt performing a Schubert song, in piano transcription, at the home of a wealthy Hungarian patron. Ravished, Nourrit requested a repeat performance. Liszt demurred; he wanted Nourrit to sing instead. No, it was impossible; Nourrit knew no German. And so it went until, after a bit more coaxing, the singer finally rose to the challenge, following along without any words at all.[12] One can almost imagine the eerie effect, as Nourrit cooed his tentative vocalise. The effect of this foreign music must have been all the more uncanny: what he sang was nothing more (and nothing less) than the purest *"mélodie" de Schubert*.

The Parisian publishers who issued new editions of Schubert songs in the 1830s capitalized on this purity. They, too, were anxious to give their clientele authentic Schubert melodies, fitting them out, in the fashion of

Moore's Irish *airs*, with new French words by popular salon poets. Thus the 1833 edition brought out by Richault was titled *"Six mélodies célèbres avec paroles françaises par M. Bélanger de Fr. Schubert."* It hardly mattered that the charming French rhymes of Bélanger had little to do with the texts that had served as Schubert's inspiration. (Bélanger, as it happens, also knew no German.) What mattered were those famous melodies. The German air evidently had the power to elevate the mundane poetry and transform the song into something far more affecting than a simple French *romance*. This was melody with a difference. Here again the term appeared to carry a dual meaning, both literal and metaphorical, referring to an actual melody by Schubert that was at the same time a mysterious and compelling source of artistic inspiration. Antoine Romagnesi hinted at this difference a decade later in his *L'Art de chanter les romances* (1846). He invented a special category for those songs that had been influenced by German lieder, calling them "dreamy and solemn melodies" (*mélodies rêveuses et graves*).[13] The more serious German tone distinguished them from the conventional *romance*, whose song was charming but forgettable. Indeed, one might say that a foreign accent had actually made the "melody" of the *romance* audible—and therefore thinkable—as an aesthetic category. Ernest Legouvé put it succinctly in 1885: Schubert, he said, had "killed romance and created melody."[14]

What these early accounts show is not so much the birth of a genre as the birth of an ethos, a new expressive value. The Gallicized lieder of Schubert, like the Irish airs of Berlioz, appealed to their Romantic audience through an elusive quality of difference, a character conveniently evoked by the double-edged term *mélodie*. Noske long ago pointed out, with some dismay, that no reputable nineteenth-century French lexicon seemed willing to recognize the generic meaning that we now take to be commonplace,[15] yet one could say that such omissions simply show that French "melody" meant something else: not a "type of vocal piece," as Noske would have it, but a vague and captivating quality of voice. Even if the dictionary of the Academy failed to acknowledge the existence of *la mélodie française* in 1835, it nonetheless acknowledged this other, more evocative sense of the term. "In speaking of poetry or prose," it noted, *mélodie* referred to a property within "a sequence of words or phrases suitable to charm the ear."[16] The duplicity of the definition recalled the twin meanings of the Greek root from which it sprang, for *melos* was also a two-faced term standing for both music and poetry. Berlioz, Nourrit, and the nineteenth-century musicians who followed seemed to understand French "melody" in the same, intriguingly mixed terms—the musical dimension of poetry becoming the poetic condition for a new kind of music. To enhance this evocative dimension of their art, to charm the ears of listeners, they transposed French in a new key. Embracing a rare foreign muse, they learned to speak with a different accent.

This kind of origin story is, of course, not the usual stuff of genre history, whose narrative relies on straighter lines. No real evolution could be tied to such elusive beginnings, no generic development assigned to a music that was never, in fact, conceived as a genre. That is why most accounts of French song have simply avoided the problem, moving swiftly, and with reassuring directness, from the beginning of the century to its end. Accepting the *mélodie* as a foregone conclusion, critics have typically treated Berlioz's early and admittedly awkward experiments as a natural precursor to the more polished songs of Gounod ("the first *mélodie* composer of genius")[17] and Massenet (who "delivered the *mélodie* from the yoke of the square phrase"),[18] before arriving at Duparc (who would "raise the French *mélodie*" higher still),[19] and his glorious aftermath in the celebrated songs of Fauré and Debussy.

Not forgetting, of course, all the ones who came between: the sensuous Bizet and the subtle Chausson, the inspiring pedagogues Franck and Saint-Saens, Charles Bordes and Vincent d'Indy, and some of their less significant pupils, including a few that even the nonpartisan Koechlin would call undesirable. The sheer quantity of names invoked in such surveys seems calculated to overwhelm, as if to debunk with numbers the long-held view, reaching back to Rousseau, that French was a language ill suited to singing, "a throaty idiom without prosody," as Théophile Gautier once wrote, that "disturbs all music."[20]

The heroes who emerge in such histories are, of course, those who worked hardest to advance the cause of their native song. Gounod, well known for his experiments in prosody,[21] was praised by Koechlin for having invented a "sort of melodic recitative with an extreme variety of contour and accompaniment."[22] Massenet, despite some regrettable lapses of taste, showed real ingenuity in the early song cycle *Poème d'Avril* (1866), which featured a novel mixture of recitation and song. Duparc's relatively slim contribution to the repertory was overlooked in light of his far more notable achievement in the 1870s, as the first composer to make a successful setting of Baudelaire. Indeed, with this discovery of great poetry—the moment when French composers, in effect, found their Goethe—we reach the final evolution of the genre and, in Noske's words, "the epoch when the *mélodie* becomes a preferred medium for the greatest French composers, who confide to it their most intimate and profound inspirations."[23] We reach, in other words, the era of Gabriel Fauré.

But this triumphalist view of French song moving inexorably toward its destiny, the glorious apogee of *la mélodie française*, nonetheless conceals a more potent irony: French composers and critics at the end of the century were just as likely to think of the *mélodie*, their "preferred medium," as a form of lied. Koechlin was especially troubled by the tendency, and in 1925 he argued that, despite the persistence of the foreign term, French song was different. He was the one who insisted that his colleagues give up the German word and call this genre by its properly French name.[24] Most twentieth-century accounts have followed suit, mentioning the German *lied* only to ban it from further discussion or, in what amounts to the same thing, to prove how special French song really was. Yet all such terminological jingoism misses the point. The foreignness of the word *lied* only made explicit what had been implicit, as I have been arguing, in the idea of *mélodie* all along—a quality of difference, a charming accent, a feeling for nuance and shading. If the specter of the lied haunted the modern French idea of song, making "melody" audible in a new way, then to use the foreign word was to acknowledge, by a kind of reverse logic, the Frenchness of the modern form.

A sense of this logic can be glimpsed in a telling remark from Robert Brussel's 1909 essay on Fauré. In France, Brussel commented, the word *lied* meant something different, referring not to song in a more global sense, as it did in Germany, but to a distinct intonation: "a particular nuance of 'melody'" (*une nuance particulière de la "mélodie"*), as he suggestively put it.[25] This shade of meaning was evidently harder to pin down. "What is this nuance?" he goes on to ask, and then replies: "it's almost sentimental, and yet not quite that; misty, imprecise, perhaps; in any case subtle."[26] The impossible description only confirmed that the lied—in the French conception, at least—was not so much a form to be copied as a principle to be exalted, not a thing but an idea.

———

At the risk of terminological confusion, I want to pursue this idea of the lied for just a bit longer. As an idea, it gathers together a number of salient values informing French music and poetry of our period, values that by 1900 had become a good deal more potent. The significance of the lied can be seen not only in the musical reforms proposed by Fauré at the Conservatoire but also in the poetic reforms championed by certain prominent writers. One in particular, a poet, novelist, and essayist from Mallarmé's circle known pseudonymously as Camille Mauclair, offers us the most instructive view. In an essay from his 1909 collection, *La Religion de la Musique*, he attempted to clarify the meaning of the lied for the young poets of his generation.[27] A poet himself, Mauclair naturally addressed the question of song from the opposite perspective, stimulated by the writerly concern of how to make a musical poem or, better yet, a poem suitable for setting to music.[28] Lingering over his remarks will allow us to enlarge our own "sense of the lied" and, more generally, to gauge the importance of song for French artists and intellectuals at century's end.

But Mauclair is interesting to consider in another respect. Self-styled anarchist and passionate advocate for poetic freedom, he experimented as a young man with the new "free" verse (*vers libre*, although he never liked the term). His poetic habits reflected his libertarian concerns, and his idea of the lied intersected with both. As the purest and freest form of verse, the lied represented for Mauclair a kind of Ur-music, the origin of all true poetry. It had nothing to do with the "literary poetry" of the Academy, as he sneeringly called it, those verses "served up by famous men . . . ratified by them all . . . so that they appear such an integral part of the language that its pontiffs would excommunicate anyone daring to oppose them." No, the lied sprang from a very different source. "Ordinary people" had invented it. An "expression of anonymous individuals," this "free and polymorphous poetry" belonged to no one in particular and thus belonged to all.[29]

It was, in short, a supremely democratic art. Its primitive cry could be heard not only at the origins of French poetry but also in the verse of many other ancient cultures—Oriental, Jewish, Chinese. "The admirable haikus of Japan" were, after all, not so distant in spirit from the little airs of Verlaine, whose poetic sensibility resonated with many a truth from the seventeenth-century Basho. All these poems, "from the medieval lay to the Verlainian *romance*, from Japanese tercets to Slovak song, from the Persian *rubaiyat* to Catalan improvisation to the sighs of the German people—all these poems were nurtured by a spontaneous, irregular, polyrhythmic spirit, their cadence and their feeling mutually engendered outside every literary precept."[30] Standing "on the border between music and poetry," the lied thus ratified the "polyrhythmic spirit" of those modern French poets who had chosen to write free verse, for it alone stood for freedom. "The sense of the lied," Mauclair declared, was "the sense of liberty in art."[31]

The dramatic conclusion should give us pause, for it offers a rather different view of the role of song in turn-of-the-century France. Far from a self-indulgent or disposable art of the salon, Mauclair presented this musical poetry as a kind of manifesto, imbuing its forms with unexpected political significance. The barely concealed republicanism lurking between the lines of his account suggested that the democratic music of the lied was to be understood as a specifically French birthright—a sign, in Mauclair's words, of "the genius of our race."[32] This freedom was not to be found in grand gestures but, as Brussel had put it, in its nuances. For Mauclair, that meant rhythmic nuances, details of poetry so spontaneous and free they became impossible to pin down.

But where had this new poetic music come from? More than one critic had begun to speculate. Henri Fellot offered one explanation in 1904, in what would be a whole series of essays on the proponents of the modern French "lied." He traced the emergence of this nuanced music ("fusion of pure melody, sung poem and popular song") to a kind of geological shift, in his words, a "colossal evolution that, some thirty years earlier, [had] swept away the well worn forms of French music."[33] For Fellot, there was no doubt that the principal force behind such an evolution was not the belated influence of a Schubert or a Schumann but the more totalizing impact of Wagner.[34]

Mauclair saw it in much the same way. In an essay from 1908, he had ascribed the late flowering of the lied in France largely to literary developments, around 1890, that had drawn composers toward good poetry, and poets toward the musical possibilities of their art.[35] Standing over this evolution was the figure of Wagner, whose music had stimulated a new sense of aesthetic freedom, "turning all souls," as Mauclair put it, "toward the dream of fusing word and song in search of expressing the most delicate states of mind." The result was an entente between previously distant factions. "United by their admiration of Wagner, poets and musicians fraternized," he said, and this dialogue had led, on the one hand, to "that polymorphous verse form improperly called *vers libre*" and, on the other, to the "modern school of the lied."[36] A version of this Wagnerian history was repeated, in fact, by many of the period's most serious critics. The arch-Wagnerian and sometime poet Edouard Dujardin, mastermind behind the short-lived *Revue wagnérienne*, wrote that Wagner's example of a "musique libre" had led him to imagine the possibilities of an analogous "poésie libre."[37] The historian André Barre named Wagner as the key force behind the entire *mouvement symboliste*, "the living flag" raised by those idealistic writers seeking an alternative to rationalism and positivism.[38]

Yet Mauclair himself would go on to claim—hyperbolically, to say the least—that the modern French school of song, supposedly born of Wagner's influence, had finally eclipsed the great composer, yielding the true artworks of the future. In his view, the "polyrhythmic lied" in France had realized a subtler fusion of music and letters, creating a "subjective and intimate language" that was already making way for "a new type of theater." The irony of this development was that "what Wagner tried to do in the domain of drama will finally be realized by the old form of the *romance*; and, by a singular return of things, it is modern France that will have taken the decisive step in this German and Nordic form."[39] Replaying the familiar nationalist trope that all great ideas found ultimate expression in the French language,[40] Mauclair saw the modern French lied as the art's logical conclusion, a form so perfect, he announced, that France could now be called the "current Queen of song" (*reine actuelle du lied*).

The social implications of this transformation were considerable. Fellot, too, saw in the lied's development a clear manifestation of the new liberalism of French musical culture, the flourishing of a "more sincere art," as he called it, that spoke of "intimate and eternally human things."[41] The idea of sincerity had long been a watchword of republican ethics and thus a term with unmistakable political resonance. "If the charm of the old regime is to be polite," Ernest Legouvé had once written, "the duty of democracy is to be sincere."[42] Fellot's invocation of this term connected the lied's evident freedom of expression not simply to matters of aesthetics—to the vagaries of Wagnerian melody or the new free verse—but to the very notion of a free society. French music had become "humanized," in Fellot's terms, and one of the clearest signs of this socialization were the human proportions of the lied.

The signs were just as evident in performance. Mauclair, for his part, had remarked on the highly nuanced art of singing that had grown up alongside the modern French lied and called attention to a sophisticated and sensitive group of Parisian performers responsible for its development. He singled out, among others: Jane Bathori and her husband, Emile Engel; Jeanne Raunay; and Lucienne Bréval. They were all intelligent artists who, in indirect opposition to singers of the Opéra, had cultivated a subtler performance practice, adapting their vocal faculties to an entirely new aesthetic purpose, even going so far as to "elaborate the principles of a new kind of diction," as he put it, in order to realize all of the lied's intimate and human emotion, its interior drama.[43]

If the question of performance brings the idea of the lied quickly down to earth, it also leads us back, in a more or less direct way, to Fauré. It was precisely this more intimate, more intelligent, more human art of singing that Fauré had attempted to promote with the reforms he announced on assuming the directorship of the Conservatoire. Through Fauré's influence, the lied crossed the institutional threshold, making what Pierre Lalo called a "victorious entrance" the following year.[44] And as if to mark that public victory, with its vaguely republican undertones, Fauré began to fashion his own response in a cycle of songs devoted to the first Queen of Song. It is time to take this response more seriously, and, in the remainder of this chapter, I intend to do just that. My brief historical exposition of the lied will now yield to another more musical account: the one Fauré has written. I want to begin again, in other words, with the cycle that marked Fauré's new beginning at the Conservatoire, reading the poems closely and listening—one song at a time—to the melodies he fashioned in their image. Attending to music in this way will take time. But it should also tell us more about Fauré's modern vision of the lied and allow us, in the process, to hear a different historical voice: through the song that Eve herself was bound to sing.

Eve Sings

La Chanson d'Eve marked a new beginning in Fauré's career in more than one respect. With its austere writing for both piano and voice, the cycle inaugurated what some critics would call a "new manner" for the composer, one that "stripped the music to its most essential elements."[45] The sense of purity certainly reflected the simplicity that a critic like Mauclair saw as the lied's most valued attribute. It also matched the denuded text Fauré had chosen for his new work, Charles Van Lerberghe's *La Chanson d'Eve*, a book of poems that had appeared in print only two years earlier in 1904. In a review of the book published that same year in the *Mercure de France*, Albert Mockel described the Belgian Van Lerberghe as a "poet of the ineffable," a poet who had fashioned a vocabulary out of "the simplest elements of language," carefully weighing his words to create a "luminous, fluid, ethereal" verse.[46] The critical judgment almost anticipated the kind of music that Fauré would produce for the ten songs he eventually completed, four years after he had begun, in 1910.

Such purity was, of course, entirely in keeping with the poetic theme—the birth of the world and the beginning of human time. How else could a poet imagine that first perfect rhythm except as stillness, or near silence? But Van Lerberghe was improving on the Genesis myth. In the first poem of his chapter "Premières Paroles," he offers an innocent, almost pre-Raphaelite Eden. Eve alone awakes in a mystical dream of Paradise, a "blue garden" in which she answers God's command to read the book of creation. "Go," he says, "and give all beings . . . a word . . . a sound that we might know them by." Half-dreaming, she enters her grove to pick a flower that will bloom on her rosebud lips, a word as animate as the creation around her. A "fugitive thing that breathes and flies," the poem says, it takes wing as soon as Eve opens her mouth to utter the mystery of creation. Through this image of sound in flight, Van Lerberghe recounts the origins of language.

Like Rousseau, who imagined the first languages as "songlike and passionate, before being simple and methodical,"[47] Van Lerberghe presents the first words issuing from the mouth of the first woman-child as an ardent and divine chanson. And yet, as a child, she is no master of what she does. "How *it* sings in my voice," she exclaims indirectly to the "long murmuring soul of forest and fountain." The passive locution is key. Fauré gave the title "Prima Verba" (First Words) to this chanson, underscoring Eve's wonder at language coming to life "in sounds, in flowers" on her lips. Later, she will address those perfumed words more directly, calling them "impassioned roses" (*roses ardentes*) and acknowledging her very existence in the sheer pleasure of uttering them: "it is in you that I sing, and that I am." It is hard to imagine a more fitting symbol for the poet than this orphic representation of Eve, surprised and delighted at her own creation.

Certainly, the picture spoke volumes to the young poets of Van Lerberghe's generation, French and Belgian alike, who embraced the idealistic stance generally subsumed under the rubric of "symbolism." I will have much more to say in chapter 3 about these poets and their beliefs. For now, it is useful to linger on the idea of Eve as a figure of *melos* in Paradise, a key concept that no doubt struck a chord with those who professed to value music, as Verlaine famously put it, "before all things." For Mauclair, the "truly musical verse" of the lied pointed to the very origins of civilization: "when there were no books, when there were no cities, where then was poetry?" he mused, paraphrasing an old English ballad about Adam and Eve. "It was in the lied."[48] Van Lerberghe makes the same kind of allusion in *La Chanson d'Eve*, in a poem not simply about Genesis but about the very first lied in human history.

The purity of the song was ensured by the apparent naturalness of its first singer. As Mockel puts it, Eve "sings like a child, sings without think-ing"[49]—without thinking, that is, of the meaning of what she says, without taking measure of her phrases. She simply sings, struck with wonder at the purely sensual qualities of her words—the sound of her voice, the breath on her lips. This image, too, served to represent something about the ontologi-cal status of the poem for Van Lerberghe's generation. Far from an abstract architectural plan, the poem was to be conceived, as Mauclair explained, only "in the sound of its syllables." Grammar or meaning made little difference when the rhythmic impulse for the poem was a "physiological principle" based on "the arterial beating of the blood, the fullness or constriction of the breath, . . . changing according to the particular emotion."[50] Poetry thus became not a literary art but a performing art, and Eve herself its physical embodiment. In search of such palpable poetry, Van Lerberghe even changed his own performance habits in *La Chanson d'Eve*, casting the world of his naïve protagonist in the liberated, organic cadences of free verse.[51]

Through this free-form singing, the poet would make Eve's music evident at another, more audible level, again not as symbol but as sound. In Van Lerberghe's Paradise, for example, we can hear a whole resonant family of sounds extending from the poem's main character, and the sonorous progression essentially defines her being. As Eve is roused ("*éveillée*"), she sees a beautiful world open before her, a dream ("*rêve*") that she recaptures as words form on her lips ("*lèvres*"). The pale timbre of her name thus sounds as a continuous echo throughout this tiny narrative. Through a kind of oneiric logic, the sequence (*ève, éveillée, rêve, lèvres*) reinforces the significance of the dream within the poem, highlighting a concept that became for the symbolists a poetic imperative: "we must dream, not compose; we must sing, not write."[52]

The dreamy echo sounds just as strong in the final chanson of the cycle, where Van Lerberghe brings out the connection between Eve and her dream more clearly, in a classic couplet that both opens and stands apart from the rest of the poem. Her earthly life now extinguished, Eve has been absorbed into the universe, and, as Van Lerberghe writes, "A pale dawn fills the sad heavens," while "the Dream rises from the earth like a great golden sail." Conspicuously, Eve's fate is mirrored in the material of the verse itself, her fertile name absorbed directly into the rhyme: "Une aube pâle remplit le ciel triste; le Rêve, / Comme un grand voile d'or, de la terre se lève." If these sonic reminiscences connecting *Eve* with her *rêve* thematically suggest the wholeness of creation, the timbral alliance also brings out another, more aesthetic conceit: what we might call the dream of poetry's transcendent language. The verbal echo, through a sort of primitive Cratylism, reveals how not only Eve's language but also the very sound of her name, as a divine creation, carries within itself a deep and primordial resonance.[53] This was the ultimate fusion of sound and sense. The resonant name becomes a generator of poetry, and Eve herself, as the first poet (embodied in the androgynous figure of a woman-child), a representation of the original, corporeal unity of word and music.

This vision of a perfect union of poetry and music was no doubt as inspiring to modern composers as it was evocative for modern poets, suggesting, as it did, the promise of new forms of poetic expression and unheard melodies. Fauré could not have been unaware of the possibilities, for the happy outcome of such fusion was, as Van Lerberghe's cycle implies, a kind of silencing of expression. Early in his book, Van Lerberghe has his naïve singer celebrate the wonder of this poetic condition. Fauré himself will make these the very first words Eve is heard to sing:

Comme elle chante
Dans ma voix

L'âme longtemps murmurante
Des fontaines et des bois!

Air limpide du paradis,
Avec tes grappes de rubis,
Avec tes gerbes de lumière,
Avec tes roses et tes fruits;

Quelle merveille en nous à cette heure!
Des paroles depuis des âges endormis
En des sons, en des fleurs,
Sur mes lèvres enfin prennent vie.

Depuis que mon souffle a dit leur chanson,
Depuis que ma voix les a créées,
Quel silence heureux et profond
Naît de leurs âmes allégées!

(How it sings in my voice / The long murmuring soul / Of springs and forests! / Limpid air of Paradise / With your ruby-red clusters, / Your showers of light, / Your roses and fruits; / Such a marvel within us at this moment! / Words that have slept for ages / Finally come to life in sounds, in flowers, / On my lips. / And since my breath gave voice to their song, / Since my voice created them, / What a deep and contented silence / Is born from their lightened souls!)

The poem ends with a paradox. Just as Eve gives voice to the beauty of creation, the once dormant words she now sings are also silenced.[54] The incantatory rhythms of the poem are an unmistakable sign of her music, apparent in the density of rhyme and the sheer volume of repeated syllables, which form bright clusters in the mouth like the ruby-red fruits of Paradise, so full of sweetness that the poem gushes into a deliciously incomplete thought, a burst of pleasure: "Such a marvel . . . !" And it is in the context of this noise that the poem's conclusion begins to make sense. The "deep and contented silence" of the ending may be the final expression of such happiness, of the "marvel" of Eden, but this condition, as Mockel explains, is difficult to convey in words alone. "Sadness is as varied as life," he says, "but there is only one word for joy. The cry has a thousand modulations; but ecstasy is voiceless" (*l'extase est sans voix*).[55] The chanson, as an idea, conveys this joyous unvoicing of language, the act of singing itself conceived as a kind of poetic liberation. Fauré would, of course, make the chanson far more real when setting Van Lerberghe's poems to music, but the aesthetic effect was the same. Held aloft in melody, the poetic word was unburdened precisely because, as music, it no longer had to "say" anything.

This muting of expression in *melos* is another deeply resonant trope within the book of poems, a theme that finds its archetypal embodiment, once again, in the sound of the protagonist's two-syllable name: *E-ve*. This word, too, ends in a paradoxical silence, the second half disappearing, on the other side of lips and teeth, into a vague and neutral sound, into the vowel the French, in fact, call mute *e*. It is a purely French phoneme, with a fundamentally French attitude. The linguist Albert Dauzat called it the "neutral vowel *par excellence*," the site "where all vowels merge to be silenced."[56] Paul Passy noted more than a half century before Dauzat that the mute *e* is the sound French speakers tend to make "when [they] open their mouths without a very clear intention,"[57] in other words, when they don't intend to say anything at all. Wrapped around a figure that "sings without thinking," the mute *e* of *Eve* could be said, then, to reflect that condition of nonintention—and hence silence—that Van Lerberghe imagined he could hear at the origin of language. The book of creation that Eve read on that first morning of the world remained fundamentally silent, because in its original, musical fullness there was nothing more to express.

———

Of all the poetic cues that Fauré followed in composing his own Song of Eve, it was this paradoxical theme of silence—the muting of expression in Eve's music—that would prompt the most complex response. Like Van Lerberghe, he managed to sketch, in his much-abbreviated cycle of songs, a more or less complete version of the Eden story. From the ninety-six poems at his disposal, he chose just ten, shaping them into a progression that traced the same plot of pleasure, knowledge, sin, and loss that Van Lerberghe himself had borrowed from Genesis and developed over four separate chapters: "Premières Paroles" (First Words), "La Tentation" (Temptation), "La Faute" (Sin), and "Crépuscule" (Dusk).[58]

This grand tale of Paradise lost was not, however, the only plot running through Fauré's collection. Drawing the largest number of poems from Van Lerberghe's first chapter, his cycle would give precedence to the first, more musical origin myth we have already encountered—a story about the birth of language in song. Obviously, this proved most suggestive for France's foremost composer of lieder. Taking up that narrative strand, Fauré appeared in many ways to address his most pressing concerns as an artist, telling a tale in song that not only celebrated the first act of singing but also revealed the noble simplicity of that original act. Indeed, the moral of the story, as we shall see, teaches an unexpected lesson about the expressive burden he assumed as a modern composer. This unusual cycle about history's first singer becomes, then, a surprisingly fruitful place to situate our own history of French song, for in his musical portrait of a bold and reticent Eve, Fauré shows us, perhaps more clearly than any contemporary critic, what *la mélodie française* is all about.

Muteness (Songs 1–2)

As an object lesson in the modern art of melody, it is certainly noteworthy that the opening song, "Paradis," which Fauré finally completed in 1906, is both grander and simpler than any he had previously composed: grander, in the sheer scope of the setting whose extended narrative (of almost 140 measures) explored a much wider range of expressive effects; simpler, in the nakedness of its principal phrase. At the start of the piece, the stillness of creation is conveyed through a static and exposed line for voice and piano. Its pure, white-note modality unfolds in a series of perfect intervals and in an archaically slow (3/2) meter dominated by note forms one could call—using the terms of mensural notation—"perfect" longs. Eve does not speak to us directly in this prehistoric setting, which functions more as a launching tableau than as a true episode in the cycle. The voice is that of an omniscient narrator who surveys the scene but does not break the silence.

The primordial vibration of the spheres is evidently the first sound to be heard on this first morning of the world (Musical Example 1.1). The slowly rising figure will recur through the song as if to remind us of the profound quiescence of Paradise, and it can be heard later as well, becoming one of two prominent unifying themes Fauré weaves into the musical landscape. It tints the beginning of "Comme Dieu rayonne," the fourth chanson of the collection, and appears even more distinctly as a kind of ostinato in the lament near the end of the cycle, the song Fauré called "Crépuscule." Vladimir Jankélévitch called it the Eden theme (*le thème édenique*), for obvious reasons, although the meaning of this musical figure is perhaps best understood not in words but in relation to the other motif Fauré introduced to oppose it.[59]

That second theme, also heard at the beginning of "Paradis," makes a more dramatic entrance, blooming like a strange flower in the setting, just as the narrator begins to describe the marvelous vision of Eden: a blue garden rising, Venus-like, from the sea (*Un jardin bleu s'épanouit*). The initial rising figure anticipates the change, stretched out of shape by the strong pull of the bass, which falls down a whole-tone scale to cadence in the new key of E major. All at once, the atmosphere warms, the glacial tempo of the first phrases yielding to more complex harmonies that spell color, movement, and light. And snaking through the thicket of sound is a naïve and artless melody with apparently nowhere to go (Musical Example 1.2).

EXAMPLE 1.1 Fauré, *La Chanson d'Eve*, "Paradis," mm. 1–11

The sudden shift in tone is audible with the second motif's opening note (D♯), buzzing delightfully over the bass as a bright but benign major seventh. The sonority is like a brush of pleasure, lighting on the measure to accent the harmony, much as the meandering piano line calls attention to melody. Fauré marks the piano line *cantando* to highlight the difference and to point to its source. The garden that blooms before our ears is also a mysterious exhalation, formed (as the poem says) on "the new breath rising from the waves" (*au souffle nouveau qui se lève des ondes*). Eden thus merges with its lone inhabitant—the figure who has herself risen from the froth of the sea,[60] and whose own warm breath will eventually give rise to the splendor that surrounds her, by speaking the long dormant words of creation. Fauré's second theme thus could be called another sort of *thème édenique*, yet this time the vibration is more sensual than symbolic. It is a concrete sign of the girl in the garden, and of the voice that both makes and breaks the silence of Eden.

This voice becomes clearer later in the song, after God commands Eve—imposingly, in a rising chromatic line—to name all the creatures of Paradise ("*Va, fille humaine, / Et donne à tous les êtres / Que j'ai crées, une parole de tes lèvres*"). Eve obeys, and again we hear the melody in the piano, accompanying her acts of verbal creation (Musical Example 1.3a). It occurs one final time, as

EXAMPLE 1.2 Fauré, *La Chanson d'Eve*, "Paradis," mm. 12–23

well, at the end of the song, when night has fallen. Eve herself has fallen asleep, yet the rest of creation awaits the morning star (*Tout demerure en l'attente / Lorsque'avec le lever de l'étoile du soir / Eve chante*). And at the sound of the singing verb, the familiar theme (now marked *dolce*) joins with the final syllable as if returning us directly to Eve's dream (Musical Example 1.3b).

The returning melody has an uncanny effect. If the dreaming Eve indeed "sings without thinking," as Mockel suggested, then Fauré's aimless piano

EXAMPLE I.3A Fauré, *La Chanson d'Eve*, "Paradis," mm. 90–93

EXAMPLE I.3B Fauré, *La Chanson d'Eve*, "Paradis," mm. 133–136

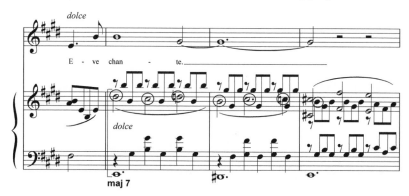

line becomes a perfect representation of that thoughtless music, conveying an image of Eve, this figure of *melos*, through a song she does not yet know she sings. It is this inspired but intentionless melody that we must attend to, for it becomes a key to Fauré's whole cycle. The deliberately voiceless motif (*très peu mélodique*, as Jankélévitch says) not only captures something of the muted ecstasy of Eve's singing but also points, as we shall see, to a more resonant idea—a little allegory about melody—concealed within the plot of *La Chanson d'Eve*.

The idea becomes more resonant with the chanson Fauré would call "Prima Verba," echoing the title of Van Lerberghe's first chapter ("Premières Paroles"). The second *mélodie* in Fauré's collection, "Prima Verba" marks the true beginning of the cycle, where Eve will hear her own voice for the first time, and where she will also *give* voice, as we have already discussed, to the central,

EXAMPLE 1.4 Fauré, *La Chanson d'Eve*, "Prima Verba," mm. 1–12

expressive ideal of the work: the blissful silence lying at the heart of poetry's "music." Fauré's song conveys this value in an unusual way. Eve utters a melody that seems on the surface to say very little, producing a cautious, wayward line that sounds almost improvised in its continuation—as if she does, in effect, "sing without thinking" (Musical Example 1.4).

The naiveté of the music goes neatly with the poetry, whose short and often uneven verses (quoted on pp. 14–15) amble from lines of eight syllables

EXAMPLE 1.4 (Continued)

to six, seven, nine, ten, even twelve. It is exactly the sort of free, "polyrhyth-mic" construction that Mauclair imagined as the essence of natural poetry and the source of a "truly musical verse." Fauré's song captures a similar aura of naturalness, the free-form verses declaimed rather than sung, uttered slowly and deliberately over an aimless chord progression that counts out the irregular phrases while following the vagaries of the line in the manner of

EXAMPLE 1.5 Fauré, *La Chanson d'Eve*, "Prima Verba," last four measures

a plainchant accompaniment. The construction seems to mimic, on a larger scale, the calculated artlessness of the little cantabile theme that earlier introduced Eve's voice in Paradise. Fauré has, in short, made Eve's first chanson, like her aimless motive, *très peu mélodique*, fashioning a *mélodie* without much melody at all.

If this relative tunelessness functions as one way to represent the muting of expression in Eve's song, Fauré underscores the idea in another, more direct way by melodically linking the poem's first and last phrases—indeed, by setting the lines to the very same music (Musical Example 1.5). The "long murmuring soul of springs and forests" (*l'âme longtemps murmurante*) that Eve frees with her singing thus becomes essentially equivalent to the "happy and profound silence" (*quel silence heureux et profound*) of those chanted words. The second phrase serves not only to round out the song's somewhat free form but also to make the paradoxical conclusion follow inevitably from the beginning.

The fuller implications of this silence will be realized, however, only in the song's last gasp, for Fauré holds onto the image of the now "lightened souls" (*âmes allegées*) through a cadence whose unusual declamation leaves the singer suspended, as if in midair, on the last syllable of the final word. Fauré places the rhythmic weight of the song, in other words, on its most ephemeral sound, making the so-called mute *e* (*a-llé-gé-e*) last six long beats. It was a slightly more extreme version of the ending he had crafted for the previous song. In "Paradis," he brought out the impression of Eve's unintentional singing by prolonging the song's final syllable (*E-ve chan-te*) for an unprecedented five beats—long enough, in fact, to accommodate the second, cantabile theme sounding in the piano (see again Music Example 1.3b). In each case, the excess is telling. The prosody enacts the aesthetic limit implied by the poem—the muting of the word in song—but music makes the point more clearly than Van Lerberghe's verses could express it. In the elongated caress of the song's final, silent syllable, we hear "singing" begin: right at the point where there is nothing more to say.

There is a lesson to be learned from Eve's first speech act in "Prima Verba," a lesson that would seem to adhere to the peculiar reticence of its *mélodie*. Graham Johnson said as much in his own impassioned description of the song's form, the distinctly Fauréean type he calls the "chordally accompanied hymn": "The singer floats above the bar-line moving slightly to the left and right, into one key and out of another, permitting us glimpses of undreamed of beauty and then leading us onward through the ether. We do not know the final destination, but this music leads us to the heart of whatever distinguishes French music from that of the rest of the world."[61] These are high stakes, indeed. But it is intriguing to think about a piece like "Prima Verba" pointing the way to a new vision of French music, especially when we remember that Fauré conceived the cycle only after signing on as chief of France's premier music institution. The idea is particularly resonant in the context of *La Chanson d'Eve*, where the chordally accompanied hymn forms a kind of structural foundation for the cycle as a whole. Only one other song shares the somber style of "Prima Verba." It happens to be the last one, the funereal "O mort, poussière d'étoiles."

The path traced between these songs—from first words to last—follows closely the fate of Eve in the garden. Indeed, through Fauré's music, we can watch that plot develop, not so much through his highly original and often baffling sense of harmony as through the very texture of his settings. My discussion will therefore continue to stay close to the musical surface, to account for traits like rhythm and gesture, qualities so crucial to performance yet too often ignored in conventional musical analysis. By tracking these features across the cycle, we not only gain a greater sense of Fauré's melodic imagination but also glimpse, through the situation of that hymnlike form Johnson describes, a greater truth about the limits of *mélodie*, a truth that Eve's destiny will help to make plain.

Oral Pleasures (Songs 3–5)

The three chansons that follow, composed in 1908 and 1909, portray the young Eve awakening to the marvel that she had only dimly acknowledged in "Prima Verba." In "Roses ardentes," she glimpses the power of her voice; in "Comme Dieu rayonne," she ponders the nature of her god; in "L'aube blanche," she thrills at the pleasures stirring in her body. Although the songs are largely independent, Fauré's settings suggest a distinct progression through the changing accompaniments and the evolving relationship between piano and voice.

In "Roses ardentes," Eve calls out to the objects in the garden that she has just named, newly aware of the sound, and the generative potential, of her singing (*Roses ardentes / Dans l'immobile nuit, / C'est en vous que je chante / Et que je suis*). By comparison with "Prima Verba," the perspective is distinctly off-kilter. The E-major tonality of the second Eden theme has returned, although without the seductive cantabile that had once animated it. There is, in fact, an odd misfit between the singing and its support, the chiming chords of the hymnlike "Prima Verba" now fractured into a rootless progression of offbeat triads in the treble register, as Eve herself sings a melody in what sounds like a completely different meter (Musical Example 1.6). One can almost hear the vocal line proceeding in a measured 3/2 against the skittish piano part—the singer maintaining the stately declamation of her previous song over the fresh double-time rhythms.[62]

The mixed message is useful in capturing both Eve's breathless pleasure and the sensory overload of the poem itself, with its irregular, short-breathed

EXAMPLE 1.6 Fauré, *La Chanson d'Eve*, "Roses ardentes," mm. 1–10

lines. The texture seems to hark back to the offbeat passion of the Verlaine-inspired "C'est l'extase l'amoureuse," from the *Cinq Mélodies de Venise* of 1891. But here the sheer awkwardness of the expression begins to suggest something about the consequences of Eve's heightened awareness of Paradise. In addressing the "impassioned roses" of the night, the "supreme force" of the sun, she begins, in effect, to define herself, observing her own relationship to the objects she has just named, through the very language she has used to name them. And it is this shift of perspective that seems to throw her song out of whack, as if Eve were disrupting the delicate balance of Eden—with all its moody silence—simply by thinking.

The mood becomes only more pensive, however, in the next song, as Eve turns her gaze away from the sun to look inward, contemplating not creation but the creator. "How God shines today," she muses in the first line, "how he exults and blossoms among these roses and fruits!" (*Comme Dieu rayonne aujourd'hui, / Comme il exulte, comme il fleurit / Parmi ces roses et ces fruits!*). The first, rising theme of Paradise sounds in the piano, reminding us of our whereabouts, but the effect this time is completely different: the once static motif is no longer so inert. It has become, in fact, the subject of a "learned" counterpoint, moving resolutely beneath Eve's words as if newly motivated by her act of reflection. Then it is lost altogether as the counterpoint twists itself into a thicket of chromaticism (Musical Example 1.7).

The idea of God also winds in a new direction as Eve begins to hear his voice in birdsong, feel his breath on the fragrant spring air (*Ah! comme il chante en ces oiseaux / Quelle est suave son haleine / Dans l'odorant printemps nouveau*). The exaggerated leaps of the vocal line call attention to the change, while subtly linking the image of the creator's *suave haleine* to the singer's own breath—and thus the *souffle nouveau* that brought forth her first song in Paradise. Fauré makes the link even stronger by reassembling the musical ingredients of that original *souffle*, as the Eden theme returns against a descending whole-tone bass (see again Musical Example 1.2). And as before, this sound will usher in the more haunting image of Eve's breath, her sweet cantabile melody, which we hear once again in its original register and key (Musical Example 1.8). The melody's fulsome, rocking accompaniment, with its slippery modulation, transforms the texture, erasing all memory of the antique style of the opening, just as the God of the song's first phrase (*Dieu* with a capital *D*) is transformed into a mere god (lowercase *d*) through the excitement.

In twenty-five short measures, Fauré has made this *mélodie* traverse more ground than the epic "Paradis," taking us not only from stillness to sensual agitation but also, significantly, from a somewhat dry lesson in counterpoint to a full-blown aria. The song's breathtaking sweep would seem to uphold

EXAMPLE 1.7 Fauré, *La Chanson d'Eve*, "Comme Dieu rayonne," mm. 1–14

EXAMPLE 1.7 (Continued)

the praise of Robert Brussel, who declared that Fauré knew how to write "more *real* music in a simple lied than one usually hears in a whole opera."[63] In terms of the purely musical plot of *La Chanson d'Eve*, however, the over-loaded form is more revealing. The extreme shift in style creates, once again,

EXAMPLE 1.8 Fauré, *La Chanson d'Eve*, "Comme Dieu rayonne," mm. 15–19

a sense of difference or an imbalance that suggests the innocent Eve—and her *mélodie*—have now begun to sing a bit too much.

The shimmering conclusion of "Comme Dieu rayonne" will nevertheless reverberate into the next *mélodie*, "L'Aube blanche," where we will find Eve, now in the middle of the cycle, fully awakening to her youthful sensuality. Eve is, in fact, all over this song, permeating the text whose regular lines conspicuously whisper her name, quite audibly in its principal verb, *éveiller*. The opening strophe offers us three different permutations of the musical word:

L'aube blanche dit à mon *rêve*:
*Eve*ille-toi, le soleil luit.
Mon âme écoute et je soul*ève*
Un peu mes paupières vers lui.

(The white dawn says to my dream: / Wake up, the sun is shining. / My
soul is listening, and so I lift / My eyelids to light.)[64]

The vibrations extend into the next two stanzas, as Eve recounts the fire in her
mouth (*une flamme éveille ma bouche*), the breeze in her hair (*un souffle éveille mes
cheveux*), the beauty in her soul (*mon âme . . . s'éveille à la beauté des choses*).

Fauré's setting is fully attentive to the reverberation. For one thing, the
piano accompaniment subtly calls Eve to mind by featuring the same kind of
figuration that earlier animated her cantabile theme—the palpitating, offbeat arpeggios still in our ear, of course, from the end of the last song
(Musical Example 1.8). What is novel is that now the singer plays the
leading role, her vocal line replacing the theme and thus reclaiming the
downbeats that had earlier been filled by its more restricted melody (Musical
Example 1.9). In this new arrangement, we can hear a kind of convergence
between the singing Eve and the previously *unsung* melody that we can now
identify—perhaps more clearly—as "Eve's song." In "L'Aube blanche," Eve
the singer begins to take control of the music that had once roused Paradise
without her knowing, as if the siren in the garden were suddenly becoming
aware of her seductive powers.

This impression is reinforced in the second half of the song, where the
echoes of her presence in Paradise become even stronger. It is significant that
the meter of "L'Aube blanche" has returned to the more animated triple time
of the cycle's opening tableau. But also returning is a distinctive savor in the
harmony, a sound largely absent from the intervening chansons: it is the
delightful buzz of the major seventh, which had first accented Eve's song in
the garden. As she sings of the "ray of light touching her blue eyes" (*un rayon
de lumière touche la pale fleur de mes yeux bleus*), she maneuvers a striking whole-
tone descent, not unlike the one in the bass line of the first song, when Fauré
announced Eve's arrival (see again Musical Examples 1.2 and 1.7). In "L'Aube
blanche," the whole-tone melody, now in the treble voice, broadcasts Eve's
presence more loudly still, by injecting her characteristic major seventh at
every turn. But this time, it is Eve herself who produces the buzz, so to speak,
her vocal line forming the series of pleasurable dissonances with the bass
(Musical Example 1.10a). And when the phrase continues, sequentially
expanding to accommodate the new "flame awakening her mouth," she

EXAMPLE 1.9 Fauré, *La Chanson d'Eve*, "L'Aube blanche," mm. 1–6

will even reproduce, at the original pitch, a fragment of that familiar motif. We can make out the first four notes of her theme, at least, shuttling between voice and piano and returning us once more to the radiant key of E major (Musical Example 1.10b).

The singer's conscious appropriation of her own "song" at this moment— the exact midpoint of the cycle—may help us finally grasp the poem's compelling image of her mouth afire: if language is power, then Eve seems to be thrilled with her first taste of it. And this, as we all know, will be her

EXAMPLE 1.10A Fauré, *La Chanson d'Eve*, "L'Aube blanche," mm. 11–15

EXAMPLE 1.10B Fauré, *La Chanson d'Eve*, "L'Aube blanche," mm. 16–19

undoing. Fauré seemed to think so. That he saw the moment as a significant turning point in Eve's story can be inferred from a telling slip in his setting of the next phrase. Van Lerberghe's text reads: *Et mon âme, comme une rose / Tremblante*... ("And my soul, like a trembling rose..."). The composer, however, seems to have erred in transcribing the verse, writing *troublante* for *tremblante*, as if he could already sense the turmoil (*le trouble*) that lay in store for his still unsuspecting protagonist.

Melos and Mimesis (Songs 6–8)

The fall from grace is yet to come, but the next three songs, completed between 1909 and 1910, expose the path that will eventually lead us there. It is noteworthy, of course, that Fauré chose only one poem from the chapter Van Lerberghe called "La Tentation" and none at all from "La Faute," although this fact, I think, has often led critics astray, encouraging them to see in Fauré's choices a willful attempt to rewrite Genesis, to maintain Eve's purity right to the end. Mockel offers us a more likely scenario when he calls the poems from Van Lerberghe's second part regrettably "long-winded." This condition alone would have warned off a *mélodiste* like Fauré, who tended to prefer his verses shorter if not sweeter.

Yet in looking at the texts Fauré did choose from *La Chanson d'Eve*— and the unique way he interpreted them through music—we can find evidence that he had nonetheless absorbed the poet's view of Eve's original temptation. Indeed, the development of his own musical narrative corresponds remarkably with the way the critics interpreted Van Lerberghe's story. Here, once again, is Mockel:

> Up to now, Eve has looked at the world without seeing it, completely absorbed by a vague, childlike dream.... But the obscure forces of adolescence begin to stir in her. A slight agitation [*trouble*] pervades, which is not yet love, only its dim suggestion. But the suggestion soon becomes more definite, to the point that Eve has the illusion of seeing, of loving and being loved. And the world immediately appears in a new light. The primitive forms of nature rise up around her, now dressed as living forms.[65]

As I have been arguing, Fauré seems to read the same kind of trouble into the verses of "L'Aube blanche" (Mockel, we see, uses the same word), even though the poem comes from the supposedly innocent first chapter of Van Lerberghe's book. How else should we interpret the song's last phrase, when Eve proclaims the new pleasures awakening in her heart, than as an intimation that she has already attained the condition Mockel suggests, the illusion of "loving and being loved"?

And just after the end of "L'Aube blanche," whose poignant D♭ cadence awakens us to the startling beauty of things, something extraordinary happens. As the singer begins the sixth chanson, which Fauré would specially title "Eau Vivante," Eve's world, her *mélodie*, is suddenly transformed.[66] Now washed clean of its multiple flats, the song appears to us, as Mockel would say, in an entirely different light. Fauré, moreover, introduces an effect he has not yet employed. The poetic theme appears "dressed as a living form" (a "living water," as the title says), in which the notes themselves conspire to speak. Yes, the running scales of the piano accompaniment, for the first time in the cycle, present an unmistakable aural illusion of the song's title image: the sound of running water (Musical Example 1.11).

Fauré had isolated the title from the poem's notably terse second line.

Que tu es simple et claire,
Eau vivante,
Qui du sein de la terre,
Jaillis en ces bassins et chantes!

(How simple and clear you are, / living water, / you who spring and sing / from the bosom of the earth!)

The apparently simple imagery conceals, however, a deeper message. Here we see Eve, again for the first time in Fauré's cycle, addressing the water intimately, employing the familiar second person (*tu es simple et claire*) by contrast to the more distant third person of "Prima Verba" (*Comme elle chante dans ma voix*) or the formal *you* of "Roses ardentes" (*C'est en vous que je chante*). The shift in perspective suggests a kind of projection. The water appears now like the singing Eve, the song surging in her own breast transferred onto this natural element flowing toward its ultimate source (*vers l'océan originel*), that is, toward the place Eve herself has come from.

This reflexive inversion of subject and object is even signaled, in an oblique way, by the two words of Fauré's title, whose beginning and ending letters silently project back an image of Eve's name: "*E*au *v*ivante." The image of living water functions, then, as a kind of code, exposing Eve's new

EXAMPLE I.II Fauré, *La Chanson d'Eve*, "Eau vivante," mm. I–8

relationship to the objects of Paradise she had earlier sung. The puzzle of the title, with her name snaking through the letters, could be said to symbolize the very circumstance that has traditionally defined Eve's temptation in the garden, and her desire to claim creation for herself.

But Fauré's song embodies distinct temptations of its own. One can hardly imagine, in fact, a more powerful enticement for a composer of lieder than the seduction of word painting. In a song whose text recalls the Romantic topos of the drifter communing with a river, how could Fauré resist the patently Schubertian effect of making the river talk back? What could be more "clear and simple" than the musical portrayal of a babbling brook? It is a temptation that implicates the listener as much as the composer. What a relief, we think, finally to recognize something, after five songs whose main poetic images—of roses, or god, or the white light of dawn—could hardly be represented in music. It is no wonder that critics have typically registered some delight, even excitement, in pointing out the little pianistic detail. "Don't you just feel in these agile, feverish, even nervous lines," asks Jankélévitch, "a kind of fluid electricity?"[67] Yet the pleasure has also promoted critical blindness. I find it striking, at least, that although the novelty of Fauré's piano part has been pointed out (Barbara Meister commented years ago that "Eau vivante" was one of the rare songs by Fauré with an "onomatopoeic accompaniment"),[68] the rarity has not been cause for further comment. What, after all, is this sound effect doing in a song from 1909? Surely we are not meant to take Fauré's unusual turn toward "onomatopoeia," the most direct sort of musical mimesis, at face value.

That much is suggested by a writer much closer to the time of *La Chanson d'Eve*—Fauré's former student Koechlin—in a passing remark from his aforementioned essay on *mélodie*. Setting the historical stage, he begins by explaining what modern French song was not, observing that "for a long time in the past [our music] was satisfied with mere description." The phenomenon could be seen, he says, in songs such as "Le Réveil des oiseaux" of Clément Jannequin, or the keyboard pieces of Couperin, Daquin or Rameau,[69] but this tendency had essentially disappeared in modern music, as composers began avoiding descriptive mimesis in favor of far less palpable effects. Echoing the more famous dictum of Mallarmé, who had enjoined modern poets to "suggest" rather than describe, Koechlin idealized modern French song as a precious and indescribable art of "evocation."[70]

This was an art, as he would say elsewhere, of "impeccable breeding" (*d'une impeccable tenue*),[71] and "one of the most 'aristocratic' forms of musical expression."[72] The collection of judgments begins to shed light on the apparent lapse of taste that had led Fauré, in "Eau vivante," down the garden path, so to speak, to succumb to a form of musical representation that Koechlin, at least, saw as far too easy, too common for the ennobled art of French song. Indeed, they point us to the more evocative implications of Fauré's lapse. Not only is the familiar mimetic figuration consistent, for example, with the familiar "tu" of the opening line, Eve's more common mode of address, but Fauré's sheer indulgence in the water topos (it runs, after all, for the entire length of the song) also obliterates much of her music's earlier mystery. It is as if by overtly compromising the "aristocratic" art of the *mélodie*, he reveals the threat to Eve's own ennobled status as Queen of song, the figure who was once the most evocative voice of Paradise.

But the order of the song in the cycle's narrative gives this compromise another, more significant import, a moral weight that shows mimesis itself, and the clarity it promises, as a kind of lie. The subject of "Eau vivante" is ultimately not the flowing waters of Eden but, as Laurence Porter would say in very different context, "the structures of illusion we create for ourselves and the irrepressible hope . . . that they might be true."[73] It is certainly striking that the water topos, one such structure of illusion, arises on top of a familiar foundation, that of the Eden theme itself, in its original key (see again Music Example 1.11). It is more striking still that the ear can no longer perceive that underpinning theme, the noise of the rushing scales serving to mask—indeed, to drown out— the figure that once stood for the silence and truth of Paradise. But this masking is precisely the point. We, like Eve, enticed into the garden of knowledge, may be certain we can hear water in the piano's streaming figures, but the tempting musical insight turns out to be our ultimate deception: the babbling brook is, in the end, merely babble.

The sense of delusion will persist well into the seventh song, "Veilles-tu, ma senteur de soleil . . . ," as agitated running scales are exchanged for even more nervous tremolo chords, and Eve turns her attention from flowing things to floating things—from moving waters to the invisible aromas of her intimate world (Musical Example 1.12).[74] The tremolo piano seems to be squarely aimed at the "blond bees" of the poem's first line: *Veilles-tu, ma senteur de soleil, / Mon arôme d'abeilles blondes, / Flottes-tu sur le monde, / Mon doux parfum de miel?* ("Are you keeping watch, my scent of sunshine, / My blond-bee aroma, / Are you adrift above the world, / My sweet honey perfume?"). But this apparently innocent, even pastoral, piano figuration atremble in D major simply piles deception on deception, concealing the true subject of the poem, which has less to do with bees than with "the birds and the bees," one might say—the earthy, erotic stream of images creating their own sort of buzz around Eve's exhilarating sexual scent.

EXAMPLE 1.12 Fauré, *La Chanson d'Eve*, "Veilles-tu," mm. 1–11

Eve addresses her own bodily essence as an *intime*, in fact, asking in the second stanza (and, once more, in the intimate second person), "O scent of my lilacs and my hot roses, do you now proclaim me?" as if transforming the flowers of Paradise, which were once words blooming on her lips, into servile subjects that do her bidding. In the next stanza, she continues coyly, "Am I not like a bunch of fruits, hidden in the foliage, that you can't see but that you just love to smell at night (*mais qu'on odore dans la nuit*)?" The sense that Eve, in this new guise, has in effect become drunk with her own perfume is suggested by the neologism enclosed within the question: she coins the fanciful verb *odorer* by combining *adorer* (to adore) with *odorant* (perfumed), sealing her fantasy with the mot juste.[75]

The drunken vision intensifies as she next imagines her long tresses breathing, and then begins to wonder, in the final stanza, whether "he," the god she once adored, now adores her: "Can he feel (sense, smell) that I'm reaching out my arms, and that my voice, which he cannot hear, is embalmed with the lilies of my valleys?" The poem's radical shift in perspective is here most obvious, for we see how the very idea of Eve's voice, which had once formed her identity in Paradise, has been forgotten in favor of the headier experience of other orifices—the intoxication of her own animal odor—as the poem's image repertoire replaces song with scent, exhaling with inhaling, *chanter* with *sentir*.

That this revised worldview has upset the stability of Eden is projected by Fauré through that trembling piano accompaniment, which, on closer inspection, begins to suggest something a bit different from the buzzing of blond bees. With its steady harmonic rhythm, changing on each beat of the 2/4 measure, the song almost recalls the style of the chordally accompanied hymn featured at the beginning of the cycle in "Prima Verba." The opening phrase even makes a vague gesture to that earlier *mélodie* in the shape of its initial vocal line, which rises a sixth just as the opening phrase of "Prima Verba" had fallen one (see again Musical Examples 1.4 and 1.12). But the formerly slow and noble piano accompaniment is now not just fast but frenetic, as if Fauré were representing the intense heat of "Veilles-tu" in performative terms: the progression is tangibly undone as the song becomes, physically speaking, too hot to handle.

The real undoing will not occur, however, until the very end, when the singer's melody, normally a modest vehicle for the text, surges upward to claim a high F, announcing itself loudly *as* voice (tellingly, on the words *ma voix*), only to acknowledge, in the same breath, that the effort is worthless (Musical Example 1.13). "He" no longer hears it (*il n'entend pas*). The personified scents of the first line are emanating, it seems, from a corpse,

EXAMPLE 1.13 Fauré, *La Chanson d'Eve*, "Veilles-tu," mm. 53–63

the verb *veiller* also meaning to "stand watch over the dead." Now defunct, the voice lies preserved—"embalmed," as the poem says—in the heady aroma of Eve's earthly scents.

When we next encounter Eve, at the beginning of the eighth song, we have moved right into the middle of this funereal perfume ("into a perfume of white roses"), and the voice is, in fact, already buried. It is hiding in the little

EXAMPLE 1.13 (Continued)

cantando melody that we have been calling "Eve's song," unheard since the fourth melody of the cycle. But the familiar has become strange: deflated, the siren song lies at the bottom of a skeletal counterpoint, emptied of its former enchantment. Indeed, we almost see the voice more than we hear it in this awkward mesh of lines, for its aimless contour serves as an unlikely bass line, suggesting no real harmonic direction as it sequentially repeats in an inexorable downward spiral (Musical Example 1.14).

The point of view of the poem has shifted as abruptly as the musical texture, the "I" apparently having vanished with the voice itself, replaced by a musing, third-person speaker. This is not a return to the omniscient narrator of "Paradis," but a reflection of Eve's own changed condition, as a split personality that now looks down on herself—"Eve"—with a detachment that reveals her principal offense. There is no apple, of course, only the idea of divine knowledge implied by that forbidden fruit, but the consequences are the same. In desiring to know herself apart from her God, Eve unwittingly forsakes the innocence of Eden and experiences as an effect, if not a sin, a new reality: what we might call the burden of her own self-consciousness. Addressing herself in the third person, Eve's voice-once-removed is tellingly signaled in the poem's typography, her words rendered in distancing italics:[76]

Dans un parfum de roses blanches
Elle est assise et songe;

EXAMPLE 1.14 Fauré, *La Chanson d'Eve*, "Dans un parfum," mm. 1–11

Et l'ombre est belle comme s'il s'y mirait un ange.

(*In a perfume of white roses / She sits and dreams; / And the shade is beautiful, as if an / angel were reflected in it.*)

Certainly, the estranged third-person perspective fits neatly with the purposeful inversion of the musical setting, where top has become bottom—as if Fauré were representing in the dissonant, not-so-invertible counterpoint the painful reversal of fortune that visits the inhabitants of Paradise after the Fall. Listening to the strained texture, I find it impossible to hear the song's words as the complete "pantheistic celebration of nature" that certain writers have perceived.[77] There is something darker here, a tone that can be sensed already in the third line, whose shadow (*l'ombre*) is clearly double-edged: no longer the peaceful shade of a pastoral grove, it represents something closer to the "shade" of the underworld, I think, where "she"—the voice of the first line—appears in her detachment as a shadow of her former self, a kind of ghostly reflection.

The next stanza shows us how far from Eden's glade we have finally strayed, as darkness falls and the poem envisions another, "golden" Paradise built on top of the blue garden, like some primeval Vanity Fair (*Sur le paradis bleu s'ouvre un paradis d'or*). More pointedly, the song that had once resonated throughout that magical place has been virtually silenced. The third person tells us, with mild disorientation, "A voice that was singing just a moment ago is now murmuring"; she hears the murmur going out "in one long breath, then extinguished" (*Une voix qui chantait tout à l'heure murmure. / Un murmure s'exhale en haleine, et s'éteint*). It is as if the third-person speaker can hear that forlorn bass line but can no longer recognize who is singing. What has happened to "her"? She doesn't even know.

It is interesting that Fauré's setting becomes noticeably less tortured at this image of the final sigh, the imagined death of the voice somehow signaling a much longed-for tranquility. The image certainly points to the cycle's ultimate resting place in the tenth and final song, where the idea of the extinguished breath will return once again (Eve will actually say in the second stanza, *je veux . . . m'éteindre*, "I want to be extinguished"). But in that song, the wish will be completely fulfilled, as Eve finally goes back into the water—the sea—whence she came. Fauré, however, seems to anticipate this eventual return, and thus the end of his story, in the becalmed conclusion to "Dans un parfum," when he brings back a motif we have not yet had occasion to mention, a brief musical gesture based loosely around the sonority of "Eve's song."

EXAMPLE 1.15A Fauré, *La Chanson d'Eve*, "Roses ardentes," mm. 18–20

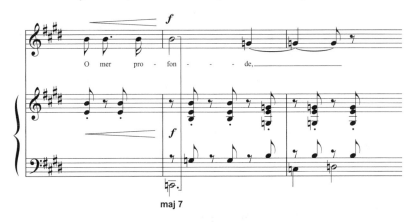

EXAMPLE 1.15B Fauré, *La Chanson d'Eve*, "Eau vivante," mm. 21–22

It is a little figure that first made its appearance in "Roses ardentes," when Eve, at the song's end, salutes the awesome power of the sea, the blond wave in which she will experience her rebirth (*O mer profonde, c'est en toi que mon sang renaît* [Musical Example 1.15a]). A very similar motif can be heard—at the same pitch and register—floating through the sixth song, "Eau vivante," when Eve envisions the personified river flowing back into the ocean (*vers l'océan originel* [Musical Example 1.15b]). And now we hear it once again, in the piano accompaniment of the eighth song, after the last sigh has been breathed, after the murmuring voice has been snuffed out (Musical Example 1.15c). It is as if the piano now points the way to the quiescence of the song's final phrase: "In the silence," Eve will cryptically conclude, "petals are falling" (*Dans le silence il tombe des pétales*). If the song's last cadence still sounds somewhat inconclusive, this tiny musical detail recalling the beckoning waves nonetheless hints that we have reached the beginning of the end.

EXAMPLE 1.15C Fauré, *La Chanson d'Eve*, "Dans un parfum," mm. 29–34

Mortal Melody (Songs 9–10)

And so we have. At a turn of the page, Fauré's cycle turns one last corner, offering two concluding pieces drawn exclusively from the last chapter of Van Lerberghe's *La Chanson d'Eve*, the chapter the poet called "Crépuscule." Fauré, in fact, borrows Van Lerberghe's title to mark the final structural division of his own cycle, just as he had marked the previous stages of his narrative with specially conceived titles suggesting separate chapters: "Paradis," "Prima Verba," "Eau vivante," "Crépuscule." Figure 1.1 outlines the complete narrative trajectory we have now covered, starting with the long introductory song, "Paradis," that stands slightly outside Eve's story, forming a self-contained unit that writes the beginning of history. Only after this does Fauré begin the narrative proper, whose telescoping form is broken into the standard three parts: we encounter Eve first awakening to her blissful surroundings in the four songs of "Prima Verba," later straying into

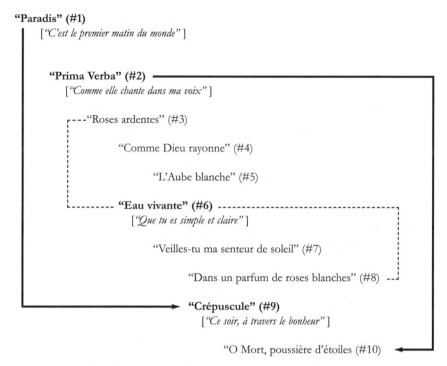

"Paradis" (#1)

[*"C'est le premier matin du monde"*]

"Prima Verba" (#2)

[*"Comme elle chante dans ma voix"*]

"Roses ardentes" (#3)

"Comme Dieu rayonne" (#4)

"L'Aube blanche" (#5)

"Eau vivante" (#6)

[*"Que tu es simple et claire"*]

"Veilles-tu ma senteur de soleil" (#7)

"Dans un parfum de roses blanches" (#8)

"Crépuscule" (#9)

[*"Ce soir, à travers le bonheur"*]

"O Mort, poussière d'étoiles (#10)

FIGURE 1.1 Fauré, *La Chanson d'Eve*. Diagram of the cycle's telescoping form

temptation in the three of "Eau vivante," and finally accepting pain and mortality in the two concluding songs of "Crépuscule."

The "silence" that reigned at the end of "Dans un parfum" extends into the beginning of "Crépuscule," a silence that is projected through the most striking aspect of the setting: the return of the long-forgotten motif, with its slow 3/2 meter, that marked the extreme serenity of "Paradis" (Musical Example 1.16). The thematic reminiscence, which fills almost every bar, is all the more significant when we realize that "Crépuscule" was the very first song Fauré completed, in 1906, before he had ever conceived a note of "Paradis." The Eden theme that haunts the first measures of *La Chanson d'Eve* was born, in other words, in the darkness of "Crépuscule."

But that song had itself been built atop another piece, a previously unpublished setting composed, but never performed, as part of Fauré's incidental music for *Pelléas*—a piece called "Melisande's Song," whose cryptic text recounts a weird nocturnal vigil and turns on a series of unanswerable questions.[78] Perhaps it was the nocturnal gloom that suggested a connection with the end of *La Chanson d'Eve*, perhaps the tone of persistent doubt. In any case, Van Lerberghe's dark poem, also containing a string of unresolved questions, was adapted to the discarded music for Mélisande, with its antique

patina, its tone of muted stillness, and that music came to represent another kind of mystery, in the primordial silence of Eden.

Yet the first stanza of "Crépuscule" will break this silence as soon as the speaking subject begins its agonized interrogation. "Who is it that sighs tonight?" asks the voice over the obstinate rising line in the piano, keening on a high F as it continues, with a tiny trace of the hysteria that marked the "voix" at the end of "Veilles-tu": "what weeps?" (*Qui donc soupire, qu'est-ce qui pleure?*). And in the second stanza, "Is this some voice from the future, or a voice from the past?" (*Est-ce une voix future, / Une voix du passé?*) Posed as if from some distant observer, the questions belong to Eve herself, who sounds even more isolated, more disoriented, than she was in "Dans un parfum." The "she" who looked down, with third-person detachment, on the shade of herself, has now become an "I" looking directly into the mirror of her unconscious, and so she fails to perceive that it is, in fact, *her* song that pierces the darkness. "I listen until it hurts," she confesses, and the "Eve" of this dark night shouts through the glass to that more innocent Eve of "Paradis," trying to reach her former self and the garden she has forsaken: "Isle of forgetting, O Paradise!" Yet, from her own lost perspective, it is Paradise itself that seems to weep: the timeless "Eden theme" falls to pieces, as the rising triad loses composure on a falling diminished seventh. "What nocturnal cry rends your cradling voice?" she asks over the noise, once more unable to grasp that it is she herself who is crying (Musical Example 1.17).

In the final musical period—with its lone question—the cycle of pain is broken, as the focus of attention shifts from the beginning to the end of the tercet, from the piercing cry to the image of Eden's flowers, which were once Eve's flowers: "What cry blows through your sash of flowers, your lovely, elated sail of happiness?" (*Quel cri traverse / Ta ceinture de fleurs / Et ton beau voile d'allégresse?*) It is Fauré himself who leads us out of the misery, replacing the relentless and haunting ostinato with a rising sequence that later modulates into an airborne scale, as if to draw out the glimmer of hope suggested by the question's ever rising inflection, and finally to dry Eve's tears by recapturing a sense of the lightness of being (*allégresse*) that she had once known (Musical Example 1.18).

The unexpected lightness that visits the end of "Crépuscule" recalls, in many ways, the paradoxical conclusion of "Prima Verba," with its image of "lightened" souls (*âmes allégées*). The composer seems to stand in for Eve, performing the same sort of generous act that she proclaimed there: he lightens the expressive burden of her anguished *mélodie*, extracting "a deep and contented

EXAMPLE 1.17 Fauré, *La Chanson d'Eve*, "Crépuscule," mm. 25–28

EXAMPLE I.18 Fauré, *La Chanson d'Eve*, "Crépuscule," mm. 32–41

silence" from it, just as she, fulfilling God's command, unburdened the word through her song and turned expression into silence. By easing the pain of "Crépuscule" in this way, Fauré produces a sense of the same muted ecstasy that would define Eve's original, *un*heard song in his setting of "Paradis," an ecstasy, as Mockel saw it, that must always be *sans voix*.

———

And with this benevolent act of silencing, we reach the final number of the cycle, Eve's uncommonly tranquil chant to death, "O mort, poussière d'étoiles." Death is always an easy sort of conclusion, but the demise of Eve offers us another, quite different sense of the cycle's end, illuminating the goal toward which Fauré's story had been striving all along. It is only here that we begin finally to understand the role played by Fauré's main character within the garden of his *mélodie*: to grasp how, in effect, he has used Van Lerberghe's poetic image of Eve, as a figure of *melos* in Paradise, to represent the truth of *la mélodie française*.

In the beginning, there was song, though Eve knew not how nor why. She did not think, she merely sang, thus producing a song with no intention—a song that expressed nothing more than the sound of her newly acquired language. Then came the temptation, the desire for melodious self-expression, that disturbed the natural order of things and separated Eve from her earlier, blissful state of unknowing. What is left for her to do? How can this supreme figure of melody right the wrong and restore the Edenic order? There is only one way. She demands to be put to death. And thus the final song of Fauré's *La Chanson d'Eve* enacts the ultimate origin myth of modern French song. From this allegorical death, the primordial passing away of *melos*, is born a new and very different form of expression: a *mélodie* without melody.

"O Death, starry dust, rise up under my feet," Eve sings in the first stanza, "Come, sweet wave . . . carry me off into your void." Later she will divulge, "it is in you that I want to be extinguished [in a] death to which my soul aspires!" Van Lerberghe's verb *aspire*—which comes at the middle of the song, and which can also mean to inhale, to suck in (liquid), or to aspirate (consonants)—is, of course, loaded with resonance for the situation of his orphic first person. It was also, incidentally, a word that resonated within his oeuvre as a whole and that leaps out of one of his rare short stories, written close to the time of *La Chanson d'Eve*. It was a little parable about poetry, with a plot strikingly pertinent to the present discussion. Here is how Mockel summarized the tale in 1904:

> The prince of Cynthia travels across a lunar sea in a ship filled with heavy cargo: it contains all the words of the universe! The weight of this cargo works against the power of the sails, the ship must be

lightened; and so one by one the massive adverbs, the dense pronouns, the leaden substantives, adjectives, verbs, even articles, are all thrown overboard. The frothy waves then bear the ship aloft; but there is only one word remaining: *j'aspire*.[79]

By means of this "curious allegory," as Mockel concludes, Van Lerberghe would reveal something about his own values as a "poet of the ineffable." But the image of the ship of language born aloft on waves of purified sound must also be seen, I think, as an equally powerful musical ambition. For just as Van Lerberghe aspired to a vocabulary that was (in Mockel's words) "fluid, airy, and incredibly reduced,"[80] so, too, did Fauré seek to lighten the expression of his own melody in *La Chanson d'Eve*—to the point of leaving hardly any trace of "melody" at all.

Nowhere is this tendency clearer than in his setting of "O Mort, poussière d'étoiles." The character of the music returns to what Johnson called the chordally accompanied hymn, that utterly reserved style pointing to the heart of French music (or, at least, to "whatever distinguishes French music from that of the rest of the world"). Indeed, in this final song of *La Chanson d'Eve*, the music is even more reduced than it was in "Prima Verba," the singer mustering barely enough energy to utter her series of strangely dispassionate commands. In the song's first phrase, for example, she will no longer enjoy the easy fall of a sixth that had marked the opening of "Prima Verba." Here the voice chants—"psalmodizes," as Jankélévitch says—on a single pitch, before inching its way, in an uncertain chromatic demise, to the tonic D♭ (Musical Example 1.19).

The melody's tentative downward slide is further confused by the harmony. If the chords of the opening measures seem at first to provide a stable "ground" for the recitation (again, as they had in "Prima Verba"), they later shift so easily that, in the space of a few measures, the ground seems to vanish—as if the bass line were responding directly to Eve's command: "rise up under my feet." When we finally reach the D♭ cadence, in fact, by way of a too rapid cycle-of-fifths progression, the chord itself will have lost much of its meaning, becoming a symbol, perhaps, of the very void into which Eve seeks to be carried.

Mockel would critique the ultraspare style of Van Lerberghe's poetry when he observed that "a certain verbal monotony might ensue if [the poet] did not know how to renew the nuances through lively and varied arrangements."[81] The observation could also stand as a commentary on Fauré's own working methods, especially in "O mort," whose second stanza shows us exactly this sort of highly nuanced variation. When the first phrase

comes to its curiously unstable end, the song simply begins again, pulling itself from the cadence by resuming the same chord progression and melodic recitation it had started with. But this time we will be taken somewhere different. Aimlessly, and apparently without will, the melodic line peaks and breaks, feigning to lift itself higher with the crescendo. Yet it falls only more decisively to Db with the appearance of its principal (and pointless) poetic image, the "drunken flame," set aflutter by death's dark sigh (Musical Example 1.20).

The pointless flame, indeed, cries out to be extinguished, just as Eve, the woman born of the sea, begs to be returned to its airy froth: "Come, break me apart like the foam glinting on the crest of the waves!" she pleads in a more elaborate command, and the setting becomes at once more purposeful. Falling down a whole-tone scale from high Eb, the melody checks the slight upward momentum of the previous phrase, pulling us in the flat direction as if in a tiny harmonic undertow (Musical Example 1.21). The line constitutes the most dramatic and, in many ways, the most "expressive" gesture of the whole song—the singer's free fall resembling, as Carlo Caballero has pointed out, a very similar descent in the only other Db song of *La Chanson d'Eve*: Eve's sensual and self-aware exclamation at the middle of "L'Aube blanche" (see again Musical Example 1.10b).[82]

Caballero's interest in the long-distance rhyme is focused on demonstrating the "formal symmetries" of the cycle and the intelligence of Fauré's large-scale tonal design. But the melodic reminiscence is also remarkable for the poetic reversal it enacts: the earlier melody, which had originally expressed Eve's first, thrilling taste of language—the "flame awakening her mouth"—is here turned on its head. The flame now wants to be extinguished. If Eve's first heady experience of self-awareness had carried with it a delicious sense of power, it has now left a bitter aftertaste, one that she wants to replace, it seems, with the engulfing sea.

And it is at the cresting of her own melodic line that she gets her wish, her command swallowed by the piano accompaniment, which responds at once by outlining her form in the sea of its own melody, in that version we have come to know so well. Yes, we hear for the last time a portion of her signature motif, the phrase that had accompanied both her awakening to Paradise and her temptation in the garden, a motif that I have called "Eve's song." This time the abbreviated motive has a clear destination: it now belongs to the sea, the voice a liquor "poured into the abyss," as the poem tells us. The fragment of song rides the wave in a long, rocking chromatic descent by minor thirds, a descent that spans the full distance of an octave (Musical Example 1.22).

At this point, I suppose, the sequence could start all over again, but that is evidently not what Fauré had in mind. The voice, and the shadowing right hand of the piano, simply stop on middle C, while the left hand goes on to make one more move. At the word *abîme*, the bass breaks the sequence, slipping down a whole step to reclaim a Db harmony essentially unheard since the cadence of the first period. While the piano's right hand does not

continue, another inner voice sounds a fragment from the *end* of "Eve's song," as if to demonstrate a further descent into the depths (Musical Example 1.23). The stationary right hand does contain a hint of her voice at the point it merges with the left, when it once again becomes a dissonance—in fact, a major seventh—with the bass. And at this moment, it becomes clearer than ever that Eve's voice was simply *about* this sonority, the sound of the major seventh. The bittersweet interval lingering on the surface of the song's concluding phrase is her dying gasp.

   This time around, though, the function and the direction of this charac-teristic sound has changed. On that first morning of the world, the buzz of the major seventh did little more than color the opening of Eve's little song, appearing unresolved—and requiring no resolution—as a value that simply affirmed the pleasure of her voice, the utter harmoniousness of her singing within the greater cosmic harmony of Eden. In the last phrase of the cycle, the seventh no longer sits so easily; when the bass moves to its D♭, the dissonant C is now heard as a disturbance, an appoggiatura reaching upward

EXAMPLE 1.22 Fauré, *La Chanson d'Eve*, "O mort, poussière d'étoiles," mm. 18–21

toward resolution. And so it is that a sound that once represented the gentle felicitousness of the first woman in Paradise comes to be undone. Eve is symbolically pulled into the void, as the ebbing seventh, the last sign of her voice, resolves and dissolves into the emptiness of an octave.

Perfect Prosody, Androgynous Melody

With her last wish fulfilled, Eve's song thus becomes linked to the breath of the dead, the *souffle nouveau* that announced her voice in Paradise in 1906 modulating into the *souffle des morts* by the time Fauré finished his cycle in 1910. This key image of expression now extinguished—which I take to be central to the aesthetics of French melody—is brought out by Fauré in another way in the *Chanson d'Eve*, by means of a compositional feature that we have not yet closely examined: the musical prosody. I will be considering

the subject more fully in later chapters; here, I want to examine a single piece of evidence, in Fauré's autograph manuscript of the final song.[83]

In looking at the autograph, we can sense the considerable effort Fauré expended—as late as in 1910, when he was already a highly experienced composer of "lieder"—to achieve the apparently natural prosody of this musical setting. Despite the otherwise tidy penmanship, the manuscript reveals a good deal of rewriting in the vocal line, especially in the song's final measures, starting at the words "Et comme d'une amphore d'or." Musical Example 1.24 shows the (erased) first version of the melody still legible beneath the later inked-in revision, a revision that was written directly on top of the original pitches and that essentially matched the melody in the published score. Fauré evidently rethought the vocal line while he was making the fair copy of the manuscript for the printer, revising the declamation on the fly, while keeping the piano part the same.

Most revealing in the present context is his work on the final five measures (Musical Example 1.25). In both versions, we can make out the composer's

EXAMPLE 1.24 Fauré, *La Chanson d'Eve*, "O mort, poussière d'étoiles," mm. 18–21. Original, unrevised prosody from autograph

EXAMPLE 1.25 Fauré, *La Chanson d'Eve*, "O mort, poussière d'étoiles," mm. 22–23. Original, unrevised prosody

sensitivity to the verbal assonance in two phrases that did not, strictly speaking, constitute a rhyme:

> Et comme d'une amphore d'or,
> Un vin de flamme et d'arome divin,
> Epanche mon âme
> En ton abîme, **pour qu'elle embaume**
> **La terre sombre** et le souffle des morts.

Fauré observes the sonic resemblance in both versions of his melody, although he hears the phrases differently each time: what changes is the general shape of the line and, more important, the emphasis. Whereas in the first version he rhythmically "rhymed" *pour quelle* and *la ter-re*, in the published melody he decided to shift the weight of the phrase from the beginning to the end, not only relieving the somewhat awkward downbeat emphasis of *pour* and *la* but also bringing out the tonal similarity of *em-baum-e* and *som-bre*.

I do not want to make too much of the revision, but it does seem useful to ponder the hidden fussiness in this deliberately simple, even artless, verbal setting. The revised declamation, with its parallel rhythms, its gentle rocking between F and C, not only makes for a more balanced melody, it also creates an overall darker impression: the rhythmic deceleration on the long syllabes of *embaume* and *sombre*, which causes the phrase to linger on middle C, underlines the obscurity of the words themselves. By contrast to the relatively pale *e* of *quelle* and *terre* declaimed on the F, the gentle fall to C serves to bring out the somber quality of the *o* vowels—a quality that will shade into the song's final word, *morts*. In a similar way, the revised declamation extends the long exhalation on the final mute *e*'s of the phrase. It was as if the composer wanted to "express," through his painstaking prosody, not the literal meaning but the evocative impression of these final words and thus to capture the openness—even the intentionlessness—of Eve's expiring sigh.

———

Fauré's revisions may not lead us to reinterpret the end of *La Chanson d'Eve*. But they do help to reveal, in a more tangible way, something about the ideal of "melody" as it was understood by French composers and writers at the turn of the twentieth century. In his history of the *mélodie*, we can again find Frits Noske complaining that, even as late as 1902, the music critic René Brancour seemed oblivious to the existence of this important vocal genre.[84] Noske was referring to Brancour's article on *"mélodie"* for *La Grande Encyclopédie*, an essay that dealt at length with the term's connotations, beginning with the more abstract musical concept and then taking up practical applications. Yet if the latter half of Brancour's essay failed to indicate much about *la mélodie française* as we now know it, it did offer an elaborate formulation about the more evocative nature of song, one that sheds important light on how a composer like Fauré might have conceived of his art. As Brancour saw it, when "destined to be joined with words," the role of *mélodie*:

> consists in evoking the very soul of the poem, making thought spring
> forth from the envelope of words, making the intimate splendor and
> the mysterious beauty of the idea perceptible through the intermediary
> of sound and rhythm. And from this magical association of music and
> word a new aesthetic being is born, created by their reciprocal

penetration, participating in their double nature, but realizing [this doubleness] in a new and vibrant unity.[85]

The most important effect of this melody had little to do, Brancour goes on to say, with the literal expression of the text through music. Rather, it had to do with the third term it created, what he saw as a new aesthetic being (*un être esthétique*) that was neither word nor tone but proceeded uniquely from both.

The magical reunion of word and tone is, of course, a familiar trope in the history of music, harking back to monody and the neoclassical origins of opera. But Brancour's sexualized image of a form created from the "reciprocal penetration" of two otherwise separate unities puts a slightly different spin on this history, in part through the more conspicuous classical allusion it makes. I am thinking of the mythical androgyne. Aristophanes introduced this figure in Plato's *Symposium* to exemplify the original union of the sexes, a union whose destruction had led humankind on a quest to re-create, through coupling, its lost wholeness. Brancour's image of the "reciprocal penetration" of word and music might be more fruitfully compared, then, to the kind of dramatic recoupling Wagner conceived as the basis for the true artwork of the future. Jean-Jacques Nattiez has traced what he calls the "fundamental androgyny" of Wagner's merger of poet and musician in *Opera and Drama*: "they are as one; each of them knows and feels what the other knows and feels. The poet has become a musician, the musician a poet: *both* are now a consummate artist and human being."[86] For Brancour, however, the merger yielded no new musical species. The result was a more modest ideal, defined simply as a quality of "melody."

It should by now be clear that the almost indescribably neutral melody through which Fauré chose to present both Eve's first words and her last words—the form Johnson called the "chordally accompanied hymn"—offered something like the ideal of that ideal. Within the whole of the composer's oeuvre, this kind of melody stands out as a special case; in *La Chanson d'Eve*, it represents the ultimate goal. Fauré's final song creates the impression of a music that has given up its musicality to become more verbal and of a poem that has resisted the poetic to become more musical. If the image of word and music disappearing into each other recalls Brancour's suggestive definition of melody, it also reinforces Van Lerberghe's vision of the origins of poetry. His Eve, after all, was herself a sexually neutral figure in Paradise, an androgynous woman-child unaware of her separateness at the beginning of time. The world and the word were literally and figuratively in her, and she in them, like her dream—making her arousal a veritable pun of reciprocal penetration: *Eve / éveillée*. Awake or dreaming, Eve sang without thinking, and so her song was essentially nothing to her. Later, she would long to return to this nothingness, her original state of unknowing, calling out to Paradise as a blissful "isle of forgetting" (*île d'oubli*). Her willful act of self-emptying at the end of the cycle can be read as a wish to reclaim the wholeness that defined her original poetic condition. But it was also, as should be obvious, a powerful musical goal. And Fauré's impassive *mélodie*—a melody that strove to be nothing—became its ultimate fulfillment.

Selfless Singers

The blankness of Van Lerberghe's and Fauré's Eve reappears in one final form that we should consider before ending our story of *La Chanson d'Eve*, one that will bring us back to the concerns of Fauré at the Conservatoire: I am speaking of vocal performance. Performance is, of course, a crucial element in any act of interpretation, the alpha and omega that precedes and defends analysis. And so it is fitting that my reading of *La Chanson d'Eve* should end with a few closing thoughts on the modern and very French art of singing that informed Fauré's own view of *mélodie*.

The nuances of this art are in many ways lost to us today, despite the numbers of increasingly available historical recordings. As every historian knows, we hear what we want to hear in voices from the past, and what is perhaps most difficult to perceive through the patina of those rare recordings made in the 1920s—by singers who had been active during Fauré's lifetime—is that quality of voice in which French words found such a strangely felicitous union with French music. In the mouths of Claire Croiza, Jane Bathori, or Charles Panzéra, or even Maggie Teyte or Reynaldo Hahn, French melody achieved a most uncommon expressive condition, sounding, as in the paradoxical case of Eve's own song, like nothing you've ever heard and, in another sense, like you've heard nothing at all. It is the exceptional musician in the new millennium who wants to listen to, let alone reproduce, this nothing, the reserve we hear in these voices, with their deliberately dispassionate singing. It is the extraordinary singer indeed who can forsake "expression."

But that is exactly what must happen if we are ever to understand this repertory. It was precisely this quality of reserve that Roland Barthes admired, and believed he could hear, when listening to the old 78s of his beloved teacher Panzéra. Barthes was no musician, just a passionate *amateur* who as a student during the occupation wrote a fan letter to Panzéra, asking for voice lessons. The great singer took him on free of charge. Thirty years later, in his essay "The Grain of the Voice," he honored his once-famous teacher.[87] The essay tried to make sense of a music that no longer mattered to intellectuals after May 1968 and of a singing voice that seemed to have nothing to say, a voice Barthes would famously contrast with that of Fischer-Dieskau. The effort drew him to another curiously affecting figure of *melos* in the history of French music, the character of Mélisande in Debussy's *Pelléas*. Like Eve, Mélisande also suffers a strange but inevitable death: she dies, as Barthes puts it, "without any noise," a demise that seems, at least by comparison to other, more histrionic operatic endings, peculiarly French. Behind it lies a condition that Barthes would ascribe to all French *mélodie*: the "production of a music-language whose function is to prevent the singer from being expressive."[88]

The description may strike us as somewhat cold, even punitive, but its general sentiment has been echoed by others. Consider, for example, this revealing comment by Graham Johnson, discussing the late songs of Fauré:

> the music encourages a selflessness which frees [performers] from the need for the normal interpretive apparatus of moulding and "mean-ingful" presentation. . . . When the performer is able to "tune in" to Fauré in this way, observing the tempo and dynamic markings, and avoiding the gratuitous rubato and histrionics, the surrender . . . brings its own best reward: the elation born of restraint.[89]

The talk of selflessness and surrender seems to recall the demands made by Eve herself in the last song of *La Chanson d'Eve*. Yet the restraint that brings its own rewards is perhaps more difficult to appreciate than Johnson lets on, or, at least, he idealizes a condition that others have acknowledged with more regret. Even a well-known Fauré scholar like Beltrando, for example, would describe the challenges of the composer's late songs in less rosy terms. For her, the *melodies* from the period of *La Chanson d'Eve* and after represent a "lack" that is no longer entirely positive. "The melodic phrase has lost its sinuous character in favor of a more graduated, disjunct line," a quality that turns out to be, she says, "much less natural for the singer."[90] She goes on to attribute much of the current "disdain" for Fauré's melodies to this fact: "the genre of the *mélodie*, no longer cultivated by modern composers, has become anachro-nistic; and without models to identify with, young singers no longer know how to approach it."[91]

Barthes himself would confront such anachronism in belatedly trying to understand the art of French song and the important role Panzéra played in it, for it was true: the *mélodie* no longer meant much in the culture of late-twentieth-century France. Its disappearance in the postwar era could be attributed, as Barthes supposed, to many things: to the rise of mass culture, to the long-playing record, or to the triumph of easy-listening Baroque. But the most important phenomenon had little or nothing to do, in his view, "with the history of music or with that of musical taste." Thinking about a very different kind of loss, he makes a remark more in line with his own vocation, not as a music lover, but as a writer and critic: "the French," he claimed, "are abandoning their language."[92] It was not the "noble value" of French clarity he longed for, but another French altogether, a zone of free speech, as it were, that represented his own values as a French intellectual in the 1970s: in his words, "a space of pleasure, of enjoyment, a site where the language works on *itself for nothing*."[93]

Barthes's desire seemed to point, then, to another, very different kind of performance practice, a form of free play that stood outside the history of music, as well as the larger institution of the French language. Yet I want to argue, somewhat contrary to his view, that this tantalizing question of the French language and its evident gratifications had *everything* to do with the history of music and especially with modern French music. We have already seen the extent to which a modern composer like Fauré and a modern poet like Van Lerberghe were prepared to play with French—with its muted timbres, its rhythmic nuances—in order to create an ideal music-language. In their respective chansons, they invented what Mauclair saw as a rich, polyrhythmic form that ultimately led to another kind of free speech, a music whose garden of sounds flourished "for nothing," that is, with the aim of turning expression into silence.

But this site of freedom that Barthes envisioned again in 1972, a space that he saw vanishing (together with the collective memory of Panzéra's voice), was not as free of institutional history as his remarks might suggest. The modern act of speaking French had its own history, in other words, a history that involved a number of different, though related, French institutions, as the next chapters will try to show. The deepest origins of this history can be traced to the years around 1870, which marked the beginning of the long political era known as the "IIIᵉ République"—the very age that produced, as it happens, the cultivated, modern voices of singers such as Bathori, Croiza, and Barthes's beloved Panzéra.[94] It was the larger political stakes of this era, with its entwined histories of speaking and singing, that both formed and *in*formed the modern history of *mélodie*.

And some of the most compelling evidence can be found right in the pages of *La Chanson d'Eve*. Much of the enjoyment that Eve experiences in Paradise translates easily into performative terms, especially when seen in relation to the singer and the delight she experiences in the sounds of her own language. Fauré dedicated the cycle to the French mezzo Jeanne Raunay, who gave the first performance, and who is mentioned on the first page of Brussel's essay on Fauré as one of the composer's "best interpreters." Her unmistakable visage, with piled coiffure and bare shoulders, would eventually appear on the cover of the published score, depicting a stylized—and very modern—*Eve décolletée* (Figures 1.2a and 1.2b). Through Raunay's Eve, we are treated, in fact, to a veritable oral education, showing us what singers do best: she learns to "read" creation through her mouth, savoring the ripeness of the words that God has commanded her to speak. This lesson constituted, we could say, an even more potent origin myth informing the history of French song, presenting us with God's very first lesson in the pleasures of the text: in the beginning was the word and, well, it tasted very good.

These first, delicious words spoken by the young Eve are as free as the girl who thoughtlessly utters them. Van Lerberghe describes her *parole* in "Paradis" as a *chose qui fuit*—a fugitive thing. The image is striking in more than one way, for it recalls a telling comment made by the linguist Arsène Darmesteter in 1887, a remark in which he defined the power of the spoken word in precisely these terms: by contrast to written language, the *parole* was, as he put it, a *chose fugitive, instable, insaisissable* ("something fugitive,

LA CHANSON D'ÈVE

CHANT ET PIANO

Poésies de

CHARLES VAN LERBERGHE

FIGURE 1.2A Drawing of Jeanne Raunay on cover of published score of Fauré, *La Chanson d'Ève* (Paris: Heugel, 1910)

Mlle JEANNE RAUNAY
une des meilleures interprètes de Fauré.

FIGURE 1.2B Photograph of Jeanne Raunay, circa 1907. Courtesy of the
University of North Texas Libraries

unstable, ungraspable").[95] The larger context for that comment, which I will
explore more fully in chapter 2, brings us into contact with a whole new
science of language that emerged after 1880—in distinction to the words
governed by the French Academy and its famous dictionary—concerned
exclusively with the material complexities of spoken French.

Such linguistic awareness played directly, as we shall see in chapter 3, into
the ideas and the evident freedoms that motivated young poets like Van
Lerberghe in the next decades, especially in their more radical and "sincere"

practice of free verse. It also played, as I will show in the final chapters, into the ideology governing another pleasurable manifestation of the French language at century's end, informing those singers and actors trained in the distinctly French performance practice known as *l'art de dire*. Fauré's *Song of Eve* forms, then, an apt introduction to this larger history of language performance as it flourished in the years around 1900. As should now be evident, the cycle's own densely layered portrait of Eve situates us squarely within the culture of this modern, musical tongue: a tongue whose rare nuances would make modern France, as Mauclair was moved to decree in 1908, the new "Queen of Song."

_____

But the reign of France would be short-lived. As we learn from the memoirs of the colorful Reynaldo Hahn, whom we will meet again in chapter 4, the rich culture of performance that sustained the modern art of song had essentially fallen on hard times by the 1930s, replaced no doubt by other, more relevant sorts of musical pleasures.[96] The disappearance suggests that the fate of French song was sealed long before those heady days of the 1970s when Barthes was moved to memorialize it. Rather, we should probably trace the final demise of the *mélodie* to a much more remote historical moment, the moment when that small group of French performers, who had made French melody what it was, performed a different kind of selfless act, when those sincere artists whom Mauclair had praised in 1908 for having invented a whole new art of diction (some of them now aging singers, no longer in their prime) undertook —in the late 1920s, just after Fauré's death—to put the music they loved on record. Such an act of preservation was in many ways the sign that the social milieu in which the songs had flourished was already a thing of the past.

Even Koechlin would admit, between the lines of his long encomium to French melody, that the "young composers" of 1925, smitten by other, more mechanical forms of expression, no longer showed much feeling for the nuances of the older song forms. At the conclusion of his essay, he nonetheless expressed a kind of defensive hope that this generation, with their neoclassical tendencies, might find something to inspire them:

> For, truly, the majority of melodies of Fauré and Debussy ... reveal the best classical qualities. In France, as abroad, no doubt, today's composers knock against a certain disdain for modern music—and particularly of "melodies." We will grant that this music is sometimes "charming," but because of this charm it is often taken to be superficial . . . as if austerity were a necessary virtue! And then one has become so accustomed to . . . an art that underlines everything, as in books for

beginners (which many listeners in fact are!), that certain audiences would believe it beneath them to thrill over such and such a melody. However, an elite has formed here at home that knows how to understand the splendor of this art.[97]

Koechlin's evidence for this new, more highly educated audience was a recent performance at the Société nationale de musique—a memorial concert for the late Fauré. Commenting on the "shining triumph" of a performance of Fauré's 1894 song cycle, *La Bonne chanson*, Koechlin concludes: "The people *knew* they were in the presence of an elevated and profound music."[98] In other words, it was only after the passing of its greatest master that the art of French song began to acquire the understanding it truly deserved.

This brings me to a final point and to a final irony. It was also at this juncture, the point of its demise, we could say, that a melodic practice built on the infinite nuances of the French language came to be recognized as something more. Indeed, French melody would finally rise to the status that music historians have wanted to claim for it ever since—changing from a nuance, an accent, an elusive quality of voice into something far more concrete: the form of a whole repertory. It became, in a word, a genre. The following chapters are dedicated to unearthing not just the pleasure but the very specific culture that gave birth to this genre, in the hope of locating the substance of a music that, as Charles Koechlin loudly insisted in 1925, we now must call (without quotations marks and without really knowing why) *la mélodie française*.

| The Mother Tongue

Exercez d'abord les enfants à parler clairement, distinctement, avec attention, de manière à leur faire distinguer chaque son, chaque articulation.

—*Méthode de Lecture, 1878*

T HE SECOND HALF OF Sartre's errant autobiography, *Les Mots*, initiates a long reflection on the vocation of writing with this reminiscence of the author's Alsatian grandfather:

> Charles Schweitzer had never taken himself for a writer, but the French language still filled him with wonder at the age of seventy because he had had a hard time learning it and it did not quite belong to him. He played with it, took pleasure in the words, loved to pronounce them, and his relentless diction did not spare a single syllable. When he had the time, his pen would arrange them in bouquets. He was only too ready to shed luster on family and academic events by works written for the occasion: New Year wishes, birthday greetings, congratulations for wedding parties, speeches in verse for Saint Charlemagne's day, sketches, charades, verses in set rhymes, amiable trivialities; at conventions, he improvised quatrains in German and French.[1]

Schweitzer's penchant for making rhymes inspires the boy to begin writing his own verses and then to try his hand, precociously, at a notebook-sized novel. The youthful endeavor turns out to be a revelation. A teacher by profession, the colorful older relative has unknowingly opened the door, as Sartre puts it, to "a new imposture that changed my life."[2] Through the boyish "scratchings of a steel nib," he enters a new world that will be his salvation, an alternative reality embodied in signs.[3] Yet this cunning imposture of the written word merely repeats a prior masquerade—that of the grandfather uttering an official language "that did not quite belong to him." The first lesson about the power of words comes not from the pen but straight from the mouth of one who never ceased to be a child: from the Alsatian schoolmaster who endlessly played with words, taking enormous pleasure in the act of speaking French.

This tale of a boy's sidelong entry into the symbolic order finds a curious echo in the memoirs of another writer of Sartre's generation, the sometime poet and ethnologist Michel Leiris. The 1948 essay "Alphabet," from a collection Leiris whimsically called "scribblings" (*Biffures*), shows the former surrealist looking back to the moment when he, too, first learned to read and write. We soon learn that this effort of remembering was part of a larger psychological project. Leiris hoped to determine the "rules of his own game" (he called his trilogy *La Règle du jeu*) by exploring the peculiar sensibility that had governed not just his early efforts in poetry but also his lifelong relationship to words.[4]

The ABCs of that game might well have started with the word *alphabet*. In childhood, the word suggested to Leiris both a pun (by way of a silly *correspondance*, the sandy, buttery texture of a biscuit manufactured by "Olibet") and an object (the book of ABCs he read in school). But the set of letters also opened an unexpected reservoir of sensation:

> *alphabet* is, in short, something you hold in your mouth when you actually pronounce it, either aloud or silently; it is what we call a concrete word (*un mot concret*), that fills the cavity contained between the throat, tongue, teeth, and palate with a perceptible content. *Alphabet* is, then, a thing having opacity and consistency. . . . I pronounce it, and I penetrate its savor.[5]

Born in 1901, Leiris could probably date this physical memory to right around 1905, the same era when both Van Lerberghe and Fauré were chronicling Eve's initiation to language in *La Chanson d'Eve*.[6] Certainly, the image of savory letters reminds us of what Eve herself tasted as she recited the ABCs of God's creation. But in that ripe image lingers a larger set of questions. The shared impression of the sensuousness of French—the oral pleasure Leiris would trace back to a cookie and Van Lerberghe to the mother of us all—casts an unexpected light on the idea of the mother tongue itself, making us rethink the feelings it aroused not only for writers like Van Lerberghe but also for the more linguistically aware generation of Sartre and Leiris. To what, in fact, should we ascribe this linguistic self-consciousness, revealed in the childhood reminiscences of two twentieth-century authors? What circumstances might have caused the new generation, born in the years around 1900, to begin imagining words as material things?

To answer, we must take an unlikely but necessary detour in our story of French *mélodie*—necessary, because the history of modern French song cannot be written, as I suggested at the end of the last chapter, in terms of music alone. Evaluating the significance of this repertory has always meant delving into the rich culture of language that sustained it. And yet, beyond references to poets or changing concepts of prosody, musicologists have hardly known where to begin. In this chapter, I hope to begin a good deal closer to the beginning—with the ABCs of French itself—by taking up one of the most contentious issues surrounding the French language at the turn of the twentieth century: the question of learning the *langue maternelle*.

This means, of course, expanding our field of vision. From the close examination of one song cycle, I propose to take not one but two careful steps back, shifting our focus from song to speech, and from speech to the school. That is where we find the clearest ideology of the mother tongue on the eve of the twentieth century. As the example of Sartre's grandfather suggests, the most significant ideas about language usually came to children by way of schoolmasters. But boys like Sartre and Leiris absorbed an even more potent set of beliefs, for they learned their ABCs in a truly idealistic moment: during the heyday of the new republican school. And so that is where we shall begin, with the curricular reforms of France's Third Republic. Gazing into the modern classroom, we will see how a nation not only relearned the French alphabet but also, in the process, reformed the state of its own tongue.

Teaching the Modern ABCs

The nineteenth century was the great era of French literacy, the period that sought to achieve what François Furet and Jacques Ozouf have called the *alphabétisation* of the French people.[7] For decades, zealous republicans had been debating "one of the fundamental legacies of the Revolution: namely, the emancipation of the people through education."[8] After 1870, the issue became all the more intense. France's defeat by Prussia caused French officials to take a hard look at their own conscripts and to face the humiliating fact that—by contrast to the enemy soldiers—most could not read.

"History has shown us," wrote Michel Bréal in 1872, "that after great wars, and above all after unsuccessful ones, the public's attention turns toward education."[9] Bréal was a young but already influential professor of comparative grammar at the Collège de France who had come to Paris in 1864 after completing philological studies with Bopp and Weber in Berlin.[10] Many years later, he would become known for his path-breaking investigation of linguistic meaning, *Essai de sémantique* (1897). But in 1872, his career just beginning, he was evidently following history's lead by turning his thoughts "toward education" in a pithy, postwar study on public instruction. Indeed, as a linguist born in Bavaria to French parents, Bréal was perhaps uniquely qualified to carry out the work, which amounted to a comparative analysis of German and French schools.

Bréal insisted that "the events of 1870" had not provoked the study, but the Prussian victory no doubt spurred him to finish. He now held up that victory as a warning. Some sixty years earlier, he explained, after Napoleon's defeat of the Prussian army, King Friedrich-Wilhelm had commanded his diminished empire to "regain in intellectual force what it [had] lost in physical force."[11] And with the help of powerful ministers such as Humboldt (who reformed the university system), he had got his wish. The Prussian state had effectively reorganized its entire system of education in less than a decade. Bréal soberly advised his readers to take heed. "The story is an example for us all," he said, "however different the task in France might be."[12]

The task in France was indeed more complex, for it was not just a matter of teaching the soldiers to read but of teaching them to read French. The peasant conscripts spoke other idioms, of course, "a wealth of tongues," in the apt phrase of Eugen Weber, referring to the dialects and local patois that prevailed in the largely agricultural regions they called home. As late as 1863, at least a quarter of the population was said to know no French at all.[13] The nation's language was, in Weber's words, "a foreign language for a substantial number of Frenchmen, including almost half of the children who would reach adulthood in the last quarter of the century."[14] One of the daunting tasks facing officials after 1870 was to reverse the trend, both practically and ideologically. The next generation of republican instructors would be expected not just to teach French but to make the *patoisant* population of France embrace this "other" language—*la langue française*— as heartily as Sartre's grandfather had. Modern peasant children would become more than merely literate. They would learn how to speak, and to think of, unfamiliar French as their mother tongue.

For this, schoolteachers had to change their ways, and Bréal had more than a few suggestions. He criticized, for example, the tendency among professors to treat French "as if it were a dead language," presenting it to young pupils as a cumbersome set of grammatical rules. Equally harmful was the habit of reducing the classroom to silence and allowing written exercises to inhibit classroom exchange.[15] In the home, children learned to speak by means of wholly oral instruction: listening to and imitating their parents. Was this not a sign of the most effective teaching methods? "One must learn grammar through language," Bréal countered, paraphrasing Herder, "and not language by means of grammar," and he went on to enjoin instructors, even more insistently, to keep their students "talking, talking, always talking":

> Have French books at your disposal from which to read aloud. Choose interesting stories, so that the child will delight in listening, and will thus acquire a taste for reading. After having read a portion in class . . . make someone repeat it from memory . . . [letting] other students come to his aid [as questions arise]. . . . The class will learn more French from this exercise than from all the grammar treatises combined.[16]

Bréal implied that the emphasis on oral lessons—keeping French continually in the mouths of students—would bring its own rewards. With a newly developed awareness of the word, schoolchildren would soon acquire the most important sensation of all: a singular "taste for reading," as he put it.[17]

This very palpable reward looked forward, perhaps, to the oral pleasure that the young Leiris would experience some years later, happily savoring his first recitations of the French alphabet. But the idea of taste (or "goût") was also to be understood more broadly, as we see in a curious story Bréal draws from the annals of France's recent war. He relates the shock registered by German soldiers who had observed French prisoners sitting idly behind bars without so much as touching a book.[18] If, as it was believed, the conscripts' collective lack of education had been responsible for France's defeat, this story presented something even more embarrassing to contemplate: an idle soldier who was not just illiterate but ill bred; in short, a Frenchman who appeared to have no taste at all.

To ensure the future good breeding of the unlettered classes—the non-French-speaking population that made up what Bréal called "the people"—a truly national system of education would have to appeal to the popular spirit. And this goal would be met most efficiently, he claimed, by teaching poetry. "It is above all through poetry that the child becomes master of his language," he wrote, summarizing the view of the great Romantic philologist Friedrich August Wolf, who believed that in all classes of society "verse served [the child] better than anything else." Poetry not only "imprinted itself more easily in the memory," it also "engaged the mind more vividly."[19] The crucial task was to find appropriate verses, poems whose sentiments reflected what the child himself had experienced. "Let us speak to [the child's] imagination," Bréal urged. "Let us make him understand the charms of the popular life, whether in the field or in the shop."[20]

The unmistakable paternalism suggested there was more to be absorbed from such "imaginative" lessons than improved grammar or an enriched vocabulary. Through proper education, diligent children of the people would also learn to rethink their own existence. The rough edges of country life—with its harsh and often unforgiving seasons, its evident deprivations—would be smoothed into a more acceptable bourgeois vision: a pastoral idyll "of field or shop." Most important, such a revised worldview would come only by means of another tongue, not the rude patois of the countryside, but the infinitely refined forms of modern French.

We can see this refining process at work in one of Bréal's suggested grammar lessons. The goal: to learn the proper handling of the conjunction *quoique* ("although"), with its corresponding subjunctive. True to form, he recommended that teachers first introduce relevant phrases aloud, repeating and exaggerating the enunciation in order to suggest, solely by ear, the inflection of the unfamiliar verb: *Quoique tu fasses.* Only then were they to explain the grammatical function of the subjunctive mood, and its capacity to express doubt or uncertainty. Bréal's final recommendation was even more revealing. He proposed that students eventually furnish their own examples of the verb in action, drawn from real life, and offered the following sentence by way of illustration: *Quoique tu sois pauvre, n'envie point le sort d'autrui* ("Though you may be poor, do not envy another's fortune").[21]

One can almost hear the singsong slogan repeated earnestly by a choir of unsuspecting little voices. Indeed, the apparently innocent turn of phrase exposed the moral content of this oral "education," its larger socializing mission. As the little peasant learned some advanced syntax, he also learned to know his place. Recasting poverty as a subjunctive proposition (*quoique tu sois pauvre*), the grammatical construction also hinted at a more dubious conclusion. It offered pupils a fleeting "taste" of a different sort of life and encouraged them to appreciate, even to accept, the "fortune of others," not least the upward mobility of the bourgeoisie.

Nor was it surprising that such a message should come by way of a language lesson, for the social hierarchies it implied only replicated those within linguistic families. From the apparently liberal perspective of Bréal's own field—comparative grammar—cultivated French was the ideal toward which all lesser (French) idioms strove, the final link on an upwardly mobile language chain. Even the simple chanson of the countryside, however impoverished as literature (*qoiqu'il soit pauvre*), had managed to climb the social ladder. Had not great poets of the past perfected its "naïve and touching character" through "the clarity of [their own] learned poetry"?[22] As Bréal went on to suggest, the judicious use of such enhanced poems could have a salutary effect in the modern classroom. Instructors were thus advised to enliven their daily lessons by following the example of a Goethe or a Burns, recomposing traditional chansons into acceptable modern French. "With careful triage," he reasoned, the humblest rounds of the countryside could eventually "make their way into the school, so that our little peasants might recognize the songs of their own village under a more cultivated form."[23]

Such ennobling logic extended to the children's speech habits, the various forms of patois they were expected to leave at the schoolroom door. In his zeal to teach French as a living language, Bréal dismissed the typical view of the patois as a bastard form to be banned from the classroom, presenting it instead as a "useful auxiliary" to the child's acquisition of the mother tongue. Studies in comparative grammar had certainly shown how much clearer a language could be when approached, as he put it, "by another of the same origin." Yet, here again, the liberal perspective carried a mixed message. Through the comparison, the child would always see the secondary status of the popular tongue, the French language remaining, in Bréal's words, "its corrective and ideal." Injected into the rural classroom, the patois would function, then, more like a homeopathic cure. Its presence strengthened the immunity of the mother tongue, ensuring that, in the midst of democratic reforms, French itself—this other language of polite society—would emerge more or less unscathed.

If I have lingered over Bréal's dream of popular education, it is largely for what his lessons can show us about the political climate in France of the 1870s. The unique brand of liberalism he brought to bear on the classroom reflected a new spirit of conformist democracy. This was a conservative sort of progressivism (or progressive conservatism) that emerged from what historian Sanford Elwitt has called a second "republican revolution," which managed to produce a stable Third Republic "from the ruins of the Empire."[24] The term *revolution* is used with some irony, it seems, for this republic suffered no radical factions. The violence that marked its beginning, with the massacre of the Communards in 1871, represented nothing less than a bloody suppression of the revolutionary element, silencing the workers and all their mutinous idealism.

Despite, or perhaps because of, this terrible history, France's Third Republic would be known as a resourceful era, one that finally succeeded in fulfilling the mandate of that first, more celebrated revolution, without any of the terror. Controlled not by anarchists but by industrialists, its liberal policies enshrined a very particular idea of freedom, committed both to attaining universal suffrage and, at the same time, to maintaining a stable, bourgeois social order. "Society cannot function," Émile Durkheim once commented, "unless there exists among its members a unity of purpose and outlook."[25] The new republican elites after 1870 were committed to achieving, if somewhat opportunistically, just this sort of unified vision.

It is easy to see how Bréal's suggestions for a reformed public school spoke to their concerns. The teaching of French to peasant children was believed to foster not just national unity but also something like social harmony, which meant increased respect for "the fortune of others." The republican leader Léon Gambetta shared this view. He argued in 1878 that the expansion of public instruction—in this case, technical training schools for the poor—could be "the solution to the social problems that weigh heavily on our conscience."[26] Yet it would require several more years, and another change of administration, for such solutions to be put fully into practice. By then, many more voices had joined the chorus for national reform. Indeed, universal, secular education would soon be trumpeted as the surest means of attaining not only human liberty but also national prosperity. I want to linger over this historic moment, and to listen to a few of the voices that counted most.

———

One of the loudest belonged to an idealistic civil servant, Ferdinand Buisson. He was an outspoken Protestant "free thinker," who made a reputation at an early age as a zealous promoter of republican values, a political commitment he would maintain throughout his long life. He may be best remembered for his role in establishing the Ligue des droits de l'homme during the Dreyfus Affair, an achievement that eventually helped him win the Nobel Peace Prize, five years before his death in 1927. Yet even at the beginning of the Republic, we can see him embarking on his life's path. By 1871, when he was barely thirty years old, he had thrown himself into the cause of progressive education in his work as an inspector, later inspector general, of primary schools. One of the more visible traces of these years was a major study of pedagogical history and method: a huge, multiauthored reference work he titled the *Dictionnaire de pédagogie et d'instruction primaire*. The four hefty volumes appeared between 1882 and 1887.[27]

Buisson had, in fact, begun the research for this project on more distant shores. As early as 1876, he secured funds from Minister of Public

Instruction Jules Simon to send a group of delegates across the ocean to attend the Philadelphia World's Fair. Their goal: to evaluate the free school system of the United States.[28] The delegates intended, in other words, to carry out in public the kind of comparative task Bréal had undertaken privately, but they would do even better. By traveling to America, they expected to discover more relevant, and more modern, pedagogical methods, methods that reflected the ideals of what was by then a fully functioning and secular democracy.

The committee's extensive report, published in 1878, certainly repays closer reading, if only for the tantalizing glimpse it offers of a nineteenth-century America seen through the eyes of idealistic foreigners. "If ever there were a people mindful of the power of education," the text began, "[a people] that has united its national destiny to the development of its schools, that has made public instruction the supreme guarantor of its liberties, the condition of its prosperity, the safeguard of its institutions, it is surely the people of the United States."[29] The 600-page document went on to describe the bureaucratic foundation of this American dream. It began, admiringly, with the organization and classification of administrators, districts, governing boards, and schools in both cities and countryside (with a separate chapter devoted to the South) and then covered the standard types of buildings and the furnishings used in the American classroom. Finally, it broached the scholastic subjects themselves, starting with the first of the three Rs, the child's instruction in reading.[30]

Interestingly, the committee's findings on this important subject turned on a number of points we have already encountered. Like Bréal, the French instructors were quick to praise the emphasis on oral instruction. The old-fashioned spelling method, still prevalent in France, forced the child to memorize the names and shapes of each letter before learning a single word. Such pedagogy had all but vanished in the States. In its place were various phonetic methods, imported from Germany (though "ingeniously modified," the report insisted). These techniques obviously emphasized sounds over signs, although one aspect came as a complete surprise. In America, a good portion of class time was also spent on imitative elocution:

Nothing is overlooked in obtaining from the students correct pronunciation, not only in the elementary classes, but also in the most advanced. In such classes, the teacher reads a passage from the designated Reader, in a loud and intelligible voice. The children then reread it in the same tone, and with the same vocal inflections. It is one of the liveliest and most curious exercises of the American school, which we have witnessed many times with keen interest.[31]

If the tone of the description recalled Bréal's insistence on classroom discussion ("talking, talking, always talking"), the conclusions were notably different. The welcome consequence of the American reading method was not simply the active learning it encouraged but the effect such learning had on the national tongue. The visitors announced with some astonishment that the imitative routine promoted "an identical pronunciation...across an immense territory stretching from one ocean to another." And they could hardly contain their excitement when pointing out the larger implications, the most "marvelous" fact of all. "The great quantity of immigrants of every nationality that has flooded into the United States," the report claimed, "*has not noticeably modified the common language.*"[32] Learning to read aloud was more than efficacious. It represented one of "the greatest instruments of intellectual and moral culture."[33]

Never mind whether these Parisian inspectors, armed with their high school English, could really pick out the accent of a little German or Polish or Irish immigrant as they recited from their American readers. Never mind that they had visited only Philadelphia. It was the very idea of a nation unified by speech that fired the imagination. Not only did the vision appear to fulfill, almost a century after the fact, a prominent Revolutionary ideal.[34] It also addressed another, unspoken problem implied by its fulfillment. Even as one imagined the French language spreading among the people, creating solidarity among rich and poor (and, by 1870, colonizer and colonized), one could foresee "the people" spreading into the language. Those non-French-speaking populations, with their flood of rude accents, posed a palpable threat to this common tongue. What would become of *la langue maternelle* when it issued from this collective mouth? How would it be possible to stem the tide of corruption, indeed, to preserve what was beautiful—and truly French—about French speech? Encouraged by the "identical pronunciation" of the United States, Buisson's commission placed its bets on a more active, modern pedagogy. The report's concluding statements thus urged the minister of public instruction to follow the American example, by requiring primary school teachers to "give more attention to pronunciation, to delivery, to accent, to reading with expression."[35]

The ministry took the advice to heart. Within the year, an esteemed member of the Académie, the seventy-year-old author and playwright Ernest Legouvé,[36] had responded with a book of instructional essays intended for students at the Ecole normale supérieur—that is, for future civil servants. The book was called *L'Art de la lecture (The Art of Reading)*.[37] Reissued in three editions between 1877 and 1879 (and translated into English), it eventually was adopted as a standard text for all levels of the French school system, extending its reach more broadly than Buisson's *Dictionnaire*. It even came to play a role at the national Conservatoire, as we shall later see. And so it is worth looking at this little book more closely, to see how Legouvé imagined the task of teaching France's children.

"In the great Republic of North America reading aloud is justly considered to be one of the very first elements of a child's education," Legouvé began, predicting that it would soon be "one of the most indispensable items of the curriculum" in France as well.[38] His chatty exposition offered a series of stories about professional actors and academics, the vicissitudes of the voice, and the ample rewards that came from using it properly. The educational publisher Joseph Hetzel made these life lessons even more indispensable by quickly issuing two slightly abridged primers: the *Petit Traité de lecture à haute voix* (1878), intended for primary school children, and *La Lecture en action* (1881), for school and home.[39] Bréal would certainly have approved of this sudden explosion in oral training manuals, which were bound to develop the child's most discriminating sense, a taste for reading.

A more thoroughly tasteful activity would probably be hard to imagine. Indeed, it may strike a pragmatic American sensibility as more than a little strange that the French Ministry of Education chose to invite a celebrated playwright to introduce this "art" of reading aloud into the French curriculum. The task obviously exceeded the American example. Far more than utilitarian skill, *la lecture à haute voix* represented the ultimate mark of deportment in the leisured classes. Legouvé was well aware of the potential absurdity of making such training "democratic," teaching its secrets to children who were likely to remain artisans or laborers all their adult lives. "Yes, certainly, the art of reading is a pleasant pastime," he admitted. "Yes, it has its notable place in the elegant education of the wealthy [*les classes riches*]." But he dismissed the implied objections out of hand. He would teach this art to "the general populace [*les classes populaires*] . . . in the same manner as geography or grammar," for its techniques were "not merely the privilege of a few, but a necessity for all."[40]

Admittedly, almost every activity in the child's education depended on the speaking voice. Teachers taught their lessons, issued assignments, and corrected mistakes, all by means of the voice. Was it not crucial that such lessons be delivered clearly and with an exact pronunciation? The evidence was "incontestable," he said, hastening to add that a lesson involved more than ideas. There was also "the music of the words," as he put it, "the accent of the words," which contributed to a concept's overall impression. "They are to speech," Legouvé suggested, "what feathers are to the arrow: they carry the word farther and point it forward."[41] His method would teach students and their instructors to hit the mark more consistently, to make the aim of their words truer and more sincere, by attuning them to language's corrective music.

The little treatise thus continued with a brief lesson on the voice as not merely an organ of speech but as an expressive "instrument," with a wide range of colors, dynamics, and registers. This led to the more technical aspects of controlling the instrument, to notions of breathing and proper articulation (including a description of common speech impediments and their cures). The final chapters moved from technique to interpretation, closing with an ingenious argument about declamation as a form of critical reading. "A skilful reader is a skilful critic," Legouvé said, quoting Saint-Beuve. He then developed the point with an account of the most difficult interpretive art: that of reading poetry.

If the progression of topics appeared to lead the child toward greater and greater heights of aesthetic refinement, Legouvé's concluding words brought the discussion quickly back to basics. He reminded his young readers that learning to speak well and to read well would serve all men in all walks of life, especially a life that had become "increasingly oriented toward public discourse." Now that farmers had their agricultural exchanges and workers their collectives, the art of reading must be seen not as a tasteful activity but instead as a thoroughly *useful* activity, for it addressed the aims of the Republic itself. This art was now a skill that would help men "better fulfill their duties, and better exercise their rights, as citizens."[42]

―――

With its strange blend of bourgeois sensibility and republican rhetoric, of refinement mixed with practicality, Legouvé's novel pedagogy offered further evidence of the complex socializing mission of France's Third Republic, especially as it rounded the corner of its first decade. It would not be long, in fact, before all these modern pedagogues—Legouvé and Buisson and Bréal—saw their dreams realized. The same year Buisson issued the first volume of his ambitious *Dictionnaire*, the Chamber would pass the last and most important of a series of bills devoted to the reform of primary education. The new legislation, which insisted on the secularization of modern education, has often been linked to the fiercely anticlerical Minister of Public Instruction Jules Ferry.[43] He was the one who pushed the bills through the Senate in March 1882. His name still adorns the entrances of countless public schools across France. But the new laws, it should be clear, were actually the culmination of an era. Ferry put the crowning touch on a reform that had been underway for decades. And when he did, France acquired something that radicals of another century had only imagined: a free, compulsory, and completely secular school system.

The laws were as thorough as they were idealistic, accounting for nearly every scholastic need. A much expanded, tuition-free educational track, the so-called primary school, now proudly took its place alongside the traditional secondary school. Incidentally, the notion of "primary" and "secondary" schooling meant something quite different in France, where they referred to parallel tracks, not contiguous segments of a child's education. The system Ferry put into place involved, then, two schools in one: the *école primaire*, designed for students who would probably return to work at a young age, and the *école sécondaire* (or *lycée*, what we call high school), for those who were university bound. Students in the first track were required to attend to at least thirteen years of age. Beyond that, they could continue (for a maximum of two years) in what was called an *école primaire supérieure*, all of which was tuition-free. Students in the second not only paid tuition but also pursued more rigorous studies in literature, language, science, and mathematics through to the *baccalauréat*, which made them eligible for advanced degrees and bureaucratic posts.

Once a course of study had begun, however, those in the *primaire* rarely became *sécondaire*.[44] For that reason, the new primary school boasted an enlightened modern curriculum that supplemented the conventional sub- jects with moral (as opposed to religious) education, as well as loftier pursuits such as drawing, music, and Legouvé's beloved art of elocution.[45] But Ferry's laws foresaw other, more material needs. The ministry had, in fact, estab- lished a special treasury to fund the building of new republican schools that would be needed to house the influx of students, as well as teachers' training colleges (*écoles normales primaires*) to turn out qualified instructors. It had also prepared more rigorous state examinations to certify the new *maîtres* in all subjects. Through its standardized classrooms, its uniform curriculum, and its government-trained teachers, the state thus did more than normalize its forms of instruction. It believed it had forcibly extended its reach to all classes of society, no longer leaving the least fortunate at the mercy of underpaid itinerant teachers or the clergy. "On this point," wrote one informed observer, "we could say that the French Revolution has indeed been accomplished."[46]

It was with evident pride that the republican press in 1882 reported the most recent political victory. In an article printed just two days after the historic vote, the *République française* proclaimed the new education system "the most liberal in the civilized world," calling it not only "the most modern" but also "the most true to the desires and needs of a nation newly emancipated from the yoke of theology."[47] The liberated nations that came to mind—Switzerland, Holland, America—had admirable educational policies of their own, of course, but none that could compare with what France had now put in place, the French having realized, one more time, their destiny as leaders of civilized culture. As the text concluded: "In a single leap, France, who was behind, has taken its place at the head of all peoples."

In terms of language instruction, few could argue. In fact, it would take less than a generation for the success of the new French methods to be proclaimed from afar. In 1912, an American professor of college rhetoric traveled to Paris on a mission strikingly similar to Buisson's Philadelphia voyage—hoping to "observe how pupils learn to write in another country."[48] His published account described, enviously, the liveliness of the Parisian classroom, where teachers and students enjoyed vigorous debates about French literature. Legouvé's influence was especially evident at that sacred moment when a student, "exceedingly accurate and distinct in his pronunciation,"[49] would read the text aloud—with feeling—before the class. "It seems not to be thought unworthy of a young gentleman," observed the author, "to read pathos, simple narrative, humor, tragedy, or exalted poetry, as if he felt what he read."[50] Moreover, the effects of this modern schooling were to be observed well beyond the classroom. It was just as common to hear "barbers, cobblers, messenger boys, autobus conductors, grocers, and waitresses" speaking with clarity and distinction, even expounding on "questions of grammatical and rhetorical usage." The American observer was forced to conclude that a superior education had imbued the French populace with a new linguistic "conscience," one that placed significant moral weight on "accurate speech and writing."[51]

The People's Mouth

The professor's judgments make it all too clear that, in assessing the modern French school, we cannot judge the efficacy of the reforms by literacy statistics alone. The country's modern curriculum had obviously spread certain ideas about French as democratically as it had the language itself. The American observer spoke of "accuracy," "distinctness"—in a word, *clarté*. The idea harked back to the Enlightenment philosophers and the celebrated dictum of Rivarol: "that which is not clear is not French."[52] Yet by the time Ferry's laws had gone into effect, such notions had taken on greater meaning, suggesting new directions for French education. If in the eighteenth century this notion evoked the transparency of French thought, by the end of the nineteenth, it pointed to the lucidity of French sound. The grand republican project of putting French "into the mouths of the people" imbued the idea of language with a new particularity. Speech had turned into a matter of national interest, the spoken word had come into clearer focus, and so *clarté* now became linked to the actual instrument of French, the voice.

That, at least, is how a certain group of modern French linguists began to see it in the 1880s, as they ventured into the deeper recesses of this mostly uncharted oral territory. To the extent that the work of these reformers forged a link with the new French school, it is pertinent to consider them alongside our brief history of French education—and to follow them into what was obviously a brand new field. Their efforts did, in fact, make a difference to the modern classroom, significantly altering the meaning of the ABCs. Shining light on the site of language's production, they made the French alphabet itself appear with a new *clarté*. What is more, their linguistic teaching helps to bring the two sides of our argument into clearer focus. We witness the French language merging with the idea of music in an unusual linguistic trope: a curious vision of the well-tuned mouth. Fount of oral purity and discipline, the mouth soon came to be seen, alongside the school, as a powerful instrument of national culture and one of France's most civilizing natural resources.

Cultivating this resource, however, added a whole new level of complexity to questions of national literacy. The state may have made it mandatory for all citizens to adopt French as their mother tongue, but from a linguistic perspective the French tongue was still an open question. Which pronunciation actually represented the right way of speaking French? Which accent *le parler juste*? The Académie française, traditional arbiter in matters of usage, offered little help. Its authority had always fallen to the side of written language, the comforts of a dictionary. But the dictionary's spellings could hardly address the well-known regional differences in French pronunciation. Nor could they justify the ways the mother tongue itself had changed—and would continue to change—over time, its textures both toughened and eroded through rocky histories. The Academy's regular written edicts had done almost nothing to prevent such decline. Far from purifying the language, the unyielding dictionary, with its absolute spellings, was even seen as part of the problem.

Saussure called it *la tyrannie de la lettre*. The traces of a sonic history always lingered in the written word, in letters now gone mute. But silent letters were unstable. Over time, they tripped the tongues of unsuspecting generations, bringing on inevitable (Saussure would say, "pathological") errors in pronunciation.[53] In his courses, he noted, for instance, how Parisians were now articulating the silent *t* in *sept* (residue from the Latin *septem*), something they had not done decades earlier, and he added that his former student

Arsène Darmesteter[54] even foresaw the day "when we will pronounce the two final letters of *vingt*—a veritable orthographic monstrosity."[55] Darmesteter had put the matter more globally (and pessimistically) in an article for the *République française* in 1887. As he saw it, the written word was so dominant that the future of spoken French could only be grim: "the twentieth century will *really* have a beautiful language," he observed, derisively, "if all the words are pronounced as they are written today."[56]

The pessimistic vision revealed a crucial shift in linguistic thinking, one that embraced the totality of oral expression and announced the beginnings of a modern field. Saussure had insisted that the science properly known as linguistics, by contrast to comparative philology, concerned only the living speech (*parole*) of human communities. But that object was, of course, elusive. As "the sum total of things [particular] people had spoken,"[57] speech always escaped the generalization implied by a collective instrument, the *langue* that was common to all. Saussure accepted this distinction as a basic if paradoxical premise of the new science. And yet the same distinction caused anxiety for those who would make science conform to real life. What about good republicans like Darmesteter, who desired to see the nation unified through speech? If speech was always individual, how could the collective be ensured? How, in other words, could speaking be made uniform?

French national unity was not, of course, a big concern for the Swiss Saussure. But such republican values did fuel the fires of another, more pragmatic class of language scholars in the 1880s. These were men who came of age just after the ratification of Ferry's laws and were prepared to use their position to aid the national cause: to change the way "the people" learned to read and write. I want to turn now to a few of these scholars, working both in and outside the system of higher education during the three decades before the Great War. We will begin with one of the period's most fascinating and influential figures, an idealistic instructor of modern languages named Paul Passy.

Passy was almost an exact contemporary of Saussure, and in many ways, he was equally precocious.[58] In 1886, at the age of twenty-seven, he helped form the small collective of progressive language teachers that would eventually call themselves the International Phonetic Association.[59] As the name implied, their concerns rested not just with "the living speech of human communities" but, more specifically, with the *sounds* of the living language (what Saussure called *phonologie*) and the related problem of how to represent them. Passy soon became an outspoken advocate for orthographic reform in France, dreaming of a purer, more precise, and ultimately more populist "dictionary" based on the speaking voice. The dream led him to develop, with some like-minded English colleagues, the prototype for a utopian writing system—the now widely accepted method of phonetic transcription known as the IPA, the international phonetic alphabet.[60] We can see the ideology of this alphabet most clearly in the book that first announced it to the public. It was a modest treatise from 1887 that Passy called, simply, *Les Sons du français.*[61]

————

The first edition was dedicated to Passy's colleagues at the Parisian Society for Orthographic Reform. Because few were linguists, Passy tried to make his subject as accessible as possible, translating science into lay terms. The populism shouts from every page. Passy had the text printed in a modified alphabet—not quite phonetic, but reduced enough to make his book *un travail de vulgarizacion* ("a popularizing work," as he spelled it) in more ways than one.[62] Teaching the principles of phonetics in both word and deed, he intended to rally support for a new and simplified French orthography. In the end, the hoped-for reform never came,[63] but the failure did not mar the importance of Passy's little book, which was coming out in revised editions long after 1900. Even without its progressive political agenda, the popular manual continued to enjoy, as he predicted, "many other applications."

The most important, of course, was to make people hear—and see—the sounds of French in a whole new way. And so the book began with some basic science, introducing the principles of acoustics. Passy explained the quality of vibration that distinguished a "musical" tone from noise, and the quantities that determined pitch. He taught the series of overtones that together formed the color of an instrument, the unique aural "stamp" of a trumpet or a flute, known, in French, as its *timbre*. The analogy brought him closer to his actual object of study, the so-called organ of speech (*l'appareil de la parole*). In Passy's view, this, too, was an instrument, "a musical instrument of incomparable perfection," as he put it,[64] made of an intricate assembly of parts: lungs, diaphragm, larynx, nose, and mouth. Their complex inner working produced the astonishingly nuanced range of tones—both musical sounds and noises—that made up a language.

Passy was concerned, of course, with French. To represent its unique gamut, he made use of a telling graphic conceit. He attempted to depict the acoustic reality of French by lining up its most musical tones—the vowels—on a musical staff. Like the instruments of the orchestra, vowels were also stamped with a distinctive *timbre*. The German physiologist Hermann Helmholtz had made the point early in the 1860s, revolutionizing the field of phonetics.[65] With a series of electromagnetic tuning forks, he had discovered what he thought to be the unique "pitch" of each vowel, the main

FIGURE 2.1 Diagram of vowel scale, from Passy, *Les Sons du français*, 1899 ed.

sound governing what we would today call their formants, or frequency ranges.[66] The importance of Helmholtz's discovery can be judged from the fact that Passy, although addressing nonspecialists, took pains to reproduce a version of the vowel scale in his little treatise. He advised readers to test it out by whispering the sequence, while striking the corresponding note on the piano (Figure 2.1).

The idea was suggestive. By following Passy's instructions and performing the little experiment, we reimagine our own mouth as a resonating chamber and thus begin to experience the vowel scale as a purely physical phenomenon. An acoustic principle becomes organic reality. And that experience has the potential to reveal something even more vital about the nature of language. Indeed, we seem to revisit the site of Eve's first words. The audible scale offers a perfect illustration of the origins of language in musical sound—in the pure vibrations of the overtone series.[67] Such evidence had already encouraged Passy's colleague Otto Jesperson to conclude, "In the beginning, speech and song were one and the same thing,"[68] turning neoclassical dream into positivist reality. This conclusion would eventually have a profound effect on both the future of French verse and the modern art of *mélodie*.

But the musical truths of phonetics dug deeper. Its organic aspect, grounded in the physical reality of the mouth, could also speak to the nationalist concerns of French education. Passy had pointed out at the beginning of his book that as a subfield of historical linguistics, phonetics played a role analogous to that of "geography in relation to history."[69] Geography, of course, implied an idea of physical terrain, as well as its borders, fusing the facts of geology with those of politics. In a similar way, Passy's *Les Sons du français* charted a dual course through language. Introducing the mouth as the site of French, it also defined border conditions, the sounds that were "not French." Like a national terrain, the mouth became a rich natural resource, giving rise to the more complex political reality known as a language community.

As before, an extended description of French vowels spoke to this geopolitical dimension of phonetics, and again, a picture did most of the talking. Opposite the Helmholtz scale on a facing page, Passy included another, more

	d'avant		d'arrière
Fermées	i		u
Mifermées	e		o
Miouvertes		ε	ɔ
Ouvertes		a	ɑ

FIGURE 2.2 Triangulated diagram of "normal vowels" from Passy, *Les Sons du français*, 1899 ed.

schematic diagram of the French vowels. This time, however, the viewpoint emphasized production rather than perception. The timbres were positioned along two axes, forming what is now a familiar linguistic model, a triangle of vowels. The coordinates, in fact, outlined the basic landscape of the mouth: open to closed, back to front (Figure 2.2).

This was in itself a cartographic conceit, but the map would become clearer only with additional markers. As it happened, French included a much larger range of intermediate vowels, owing to the subtle movements of its hard-working *langue*. Hence, the timbre Passy indicated with the symbol (y), "as in the French word *nu*." To produce this hybrid sound (a sound Barthes would later dub "the most French vowel of all"),[70] the lips and the tongue worked against each other, Passy explained, "the tongue raised in the forward position as for (i), making the timbre bright, while the lips remained rounded as for (u), thus darkening it."[71] The same kind of mixed lingual message gave rise to the other, so-called abnormal vowels: the (œ) of *seul*, lying between (ε) and (ɔ); the (Ø) of *peu*, between (e) and (o), not to mention the commonly nasalized ones, the (ɛ̃) of *bain*, (ã) *banc*, (õ) *bon*, and (œ̃) *un*, enriched timbres produced by lowering the soft palate.

The list of distinctions concluded, however, with a final category. Here the tongue was "less taut," the sound "less distinct." Passy called this group *voyelles faibles*. It was, by the way, the same category the young Freud singled out for comment after his arrival in Paris in 1885; he complained bitterly to a friend about the difficulty of learning French, with all its "poor vowels."[72] Where Freud saw weakness, though, Passy saw virtue. He even saved the best of these vowels for last, giving the feeblest, most delicate, and—in his view—the most French timbre pride of place. This was a pale, receding vowel, uttered with relaxed tongue and "lightly rounded lips," a vowel he indicated, simply, by the schwa symbol (ə).

In referring to this interior ə, Passy avoided the colloquial and somewhat paradoxical term "mute" (which I used in chapter 1). He was quick to note, however, its unique capacity to disappear within a spoken phrase, as when, for example, the sentence *je leur dis* became *zhloerdi*.[73] The ease with which it came and went suggested that alone among the vowels, the ə was the easiest to pronounce, and therefore, as Passy put it, "the most natural to French people." It was the sound toward which all other "weak vowels" tended, the sound that naturally lubricated the space after certain consonants "to make them more distinct," and the sound that could leak out when one's thoughts were not fully formed, when one "opened one's mouth without a clear intention," as Passy put it. The ə represented, then, something like the Ur-phoneme. It was a completely *neutral vowel*, as Passy emphasized, whose willfully indistinct timbre defined the distinctness of French as a European language.[74] The most natural linguistic resource of the French people lay, it seemed, in their most interior and impartial vowel, one with a sound so recessive and pale it could easily disappear.

We will mine this rare natural resource for its deeper musical meanings in chapter 4. For now, I need only point out how this sort of phonetic enter-prise—locating the basic, organic material of language—could modulate into more global concerns. Passy was quick to remark, for example, "in considering the system of French vowels in general, . . . that French tends to rest in the middle between the very simple systems of Spanish and Italian, and the more complicated German languages."[75] This geographical vision of a centrist *langue*, poised between south and north, certainly drew out the political implications of its centrally neutral phoneme ə. But it also rein-forced the classic view of the centrality of France itself. The observation seemed to offer, in other words, a purely phonetic rationale as to why "neutral" French had remained, for so many centuries, a superior language of diplomacy.

Still, middling did not mean wishy-washy. The French vowels, Passy insisted, were "formed from very definite positions, not average positions," each occupying a clear "harmonic distance from the other." Such precision set French mouths apart from neighboring ones, putting a new slant on the whole idea of "expression." The facial muscles, he said, were always "very taut, not lax as in . . . English or German."[76] This obviously chauvinistic claim found support from Henry Sweet, one of Passy's English colleagues in the Phonetic Association. Explaining what he called the "organic basis" of articulation, Sweet admitted that English pronunciation, by comparison to French, tended to a certain lassitude. His description is worth quoting in full:

The tendency of the present English is to flatten and lower the tongue and draw it back from the teeth, while the lips are kept as much as possible in a neutral position. The flattening of the tongue makes our vowels wide and favours the development of mixed vowels, and gives the dull quality which is especially noticeable in our (l); and its retraction is unfavourable to the development of teeth sounds; while the neutrality of the lips eliminates frontround vowels. In such a language as French everything is reversed. The tongue is arched, and raised, and advanced, and the lips articulate with energy. Hence French sounds tend to narrowness, dentality and distinct rounding.[77]

Passy himself would put the matter more succinctly: "All this manages to give our language a remarkably clear character."[78] The sum total of phonetic distinctions seemed to form, once again, a grand apologia for that most cherished of French values, the idea of *clarté*.

————

Not surprisingly, the same sorts of values accrued to the graphic side of Passy's project: the attempt to represent speech sounds in writing. The final section of *Les Sons du français* took up this concern with unmistakable reformist zeal. Passy proposed a new "international" phonetic alphabet as the only viable method for capturing the language, far clearer than the modified French orthography used elsewhere in his text. Originally created for *Le Maître Phonétique*, the official organ of the International Phonetic Association, this new writing embodied the same sort of universalizing, diplomatic tendencies that informed the classic view of French itself. A graphic system adapted specifically "to the needs of the French language," as Sweet put it, was to serve as "a general notation for all languages."[79]

Passy's foreign colleagues remained dubious, arguing that the abnormalities of French compromised the notation's wider application. "Although well suited for French," Sweet went on, "this [international] alphabet must . . . be regarded as a failure." The judgment did not deter its French advocates. Far from it: the final section of Passy's treatise ultimately exposed the republican utility of phonetic writing. Moving from scientific description to practical application, Passy showed his alternative alphabet for what it really was: a great leveler of French civil society.

Such a tool proved useful, of course, for the elevating mission of universal education. The need for teaching good reading habits and correct pronunciation had been echoed again and again by school officials. Phonetic instruction now promised to lead directly toward that goal. It alone could "deal effectively with vulgarisms and provincialisms" and help to promote "uniform speech."[80] Passy showed exactly how through a series of oral exercises he included in the appendix of *Les Sons du français*: a little manual for reading aloud. But this appendix was no ordinary reader. It had a secret weapon. All the French appeared in phonetic notation.

If these readings were designed to encourage a more accurate and informed pronunciation, the subject matter sought to educate in other ways. Like Bréal's curricular reforms, the selections were pitched to a provincial audience, chosen to enrich and expand the popular imagination. And so, alongside passages from the Bible or ditties about factory workers and peasants, we find poems by Hugo, Musset, and Gautier; various instructional essays; and even, in the 1899 edition, Jean Jaurès's political sermon, recently published in the *Petite République*, bearing the title *burzhwa:zi e sosjalism*.

By then, Passy had actually parlayed his phonetic transcription business into a cottage industry, producing what he called "popular editions" of the Gospels, as well as short stories and popular songs, all at cheap prices. In 1897, he even brought out, with Hermann Michaelis, the most impressive (not to say bizarre) piece of this new oral literature: what he called a "phonetic dictionary." This fulfilled his dream of an alternative to the official *Dictionnaire*, proving "the legitimate existence of the spoken tongue, apart from the written," as he wrote in the preface.[81] The proof was indeed striking, for in this novel dictionary, the words, printed in his prototype IPA, no longer appeared in alphabetical order. They were listed in the order of their pronunciation.

The elevating purpose of such texts is easy enough to understand. Less obvious, perhaps, was the effect they would have on the already educated public. The notation proved more democratic than it might first appear. As a social leveler, it went both ways. The act of reading became as deliberate (and laborious) for the literate as it was for the illiterate—which was, presumably, the point. "In reading our texts," Passy warned, "one is obliged to go slowly."[82] Exchanging conventional letters for a broader range of sound-symbols, the new, "clarifying" notation actually obscured the conventional sign and the meaning normally housed within it, forcing even veterans of the French language to experience the mother tongue anew. By a perverse sort of logic, the unfamiliar writing returned readers—and by extension the French language—to a condition of primary orality.

A single example from the 1887 edition of Passy's treatise will illustrate the point (Figure 2.3). It was a poem by Victor Hugo, and from a quick perusal, we can see that the phonetic notation was still at an early stage, less elegant than the alphabet he would use a decade later (see again Figure 2.2). Here, for example, he writes (y) for the liquid (i) of *rouille*, an upside-down (m) (or a rounded *w*, depending on your perspective) for the *u* in *nu*, (ae) for the open (e) of *fait*, (oe) for the hybrid vowel in *peur*, small capital (N) for nasalization, and a period (.) to show vowel lengthening.

Dyœ, ki-surit e-ki-dɔn,
  e-ki-vyæN vær-ki-l-atAN,
  purvɯ k-vu-swaye-bon
    sra-kɔNtAN.

Lə-mɔN.d, u-tut etæNsæl
  mæz-u-ryæN n-æt-ANflame,
  purvɯ k-vu-swaye-bæl
    sra-carme.

MɔN-kœ.r, dAN-l-ɔN.br amurœ.z
  u-l-ANni.vrə dœ-boz-yœ,
  purvɯ k-tɯ-swaz-ərœ.z
    sra-jwayœ.

Victor Hugo.

FIGURE 2.3 Hugo, "Chanson," transcribed into phonetic notation, from Passy, *Les Sons du français*, first ed., 1887

The particular symbols are less significant, however, than their overall effect. As readers, we discover the meaning of the text in two stages: first positioning tongue and lips to interpret the signs—sounding, rather than "saying" the words—and then, like a silent partner in our own dialogue, stopping to listen to what we have just uttered. A quatrain slowly emerges: *Dieu, qui sourit et qui donne, / et qui vient vers qui l'attend, / pourvu que vous soyez bonne, / sera content* (God, all smile and gift / who comes to those who wait for him, / if ye be good, / will be content). Like the good Lord himself, the example seems to say, the meaning of the phonetic lines will "come to those who wait." But more important than meaning is the primitive condition to which the text is returned, a condition signaled perfectly by Hugo's title: "Chanson." Through an alienated act of sight-reading, performed on "a musical instrument of incomparable perfection," the poem becomes, in effect, an exquisite monotone. The reader, lost like a naive singer in the oral landscape, hears the poem as sound, and words made strange, in a flow of expressionless "melody."

The unusual example shows us, through deed more than word, the decisive transformation in linguistic thinking through which a modern language education would embrace French as music and thus merge the spoken word, obliquely, with the idea of song. Nonetheless, despite considerable promise, Passy's new writing method failed. It failed to be adopted by a broader public, just as it failed to fulfill the nationalist agenda of representing French with absolute "clarity"—or, at least, with enough clarity to promote uniform diction across the Republic. No alphabet could do that. As a prescriptive tool designed to *evoke* the voice, writing always required individual speakers to interpret its signs. Phonetic notation thus remained open to the very problem it was trying to solve, the audible differences in styles of pronunciation.

By 1899, the orthographic reform movement had become a distant vision, and Passy himself had moved on, now promoting his IPA—more realistically, perhaps—as a tool for scientific analysis. He eventually put it to the test with a formidable project, one he included as the appendix to a later edition of *Les Sons du français*. It was a huge, comparative transcription of a single verse from the Gospel of John (3:16, "For God so loved the world . . . ") in 170 different languages. As it happened, though, fifty of those "languages" were French. He had included in his roster, in other words, not just Parisian French but all the regional accents and patois of the countryside. Hoping to demonstrate the utility of the IPA for comparative phonology, Passy ended up revealing (unwittingly, I think) the basic instability of French pronunciation.[83] In light of the evidence, one could only ask: what *was* the "sound of French"? Was there such a thing as a true French accent?

Or to put the question still another way, as Eduard Koschwitz did in 1891: where could one find that elusive quality known as *le bon usage*? Koschwitz was not a Frenchman, nor did he live in France. But as a professor at the University of Greifswald, he enjoyed a reputation as one of the leading scholars of Romance languages, largely for his 1879 edition of the *Cantilène de Sainte Eulalie*, the oldest known poem in the French language. Ever since the twelfth century, he said, inhabitants of the Île de France had been laying claim to that prized possession of beautiful speech. Yet over time, it had become increasingly difficult to define what that prize was and who, in fact, possessed it. Koschwitz was prepared to settle the matter himself. In 1890, he traveled to Paris to pursue formal research, publishing his results the next year as *Les Parlers parisiens*: Parisian ways of talking.[84] The plurals of his title hinted at the book's somewhat skeptical conclusion. The ideal of a single, correct pronunciation—in short, *le bon usage*—could be little more than wishful thinking, for even in Paris, one could find many ways of speaking beautiful French.

The claim challenged the views of a phonetician like Passy, who never once questioned the existence of a single speech ideal. In the preface to his pronouncing dictionary, Passy in fact admitted, without apparent shame, that the "usage" he recommended reflected the linguistic habits of his immediate family.[85] Koschwitz cast his net a good deal wider. In the end, he produced a more extended survey, a "phonetic anthology," as he called it, of a whole range of talking Parisians. That his study was rigorously comparative—more descriptive than prescriptive—became evident from the layout. Rather than leaving the reader stranded with the strange phonetic notation, Koschwitz preferred to include the "original" French texts on facing pages. He also provided biographical notes on the speakers, describing their native origin and overall speaking habits ("Monsieur Edouard Rod, born in Nyon in 1857, living in Paris since 1892, provides a good example of the Parisianized provincial pronunciation . . . [he] does not pronounce the *r* in the manner particular to Parisians").[86] In this way, he sought to represent a broad constituency, exposing the "men of letters, the scholars, the politicians and priests, the actors, professors, and theorists of language who today embody the [linguistic] authority formerly held by the royal courts."[87] The book represented them, in effect, through pages of impeccable transcriptions. It offered poems, plays, and scholarly addresses declaimed by more than a dozen Parisian notables, among them, Émile Zola, Gaston Paris, Ernest Renan, the great actors Ferdinand Got and Julia Bartet of the Comédie française, and official poets such as Sully-Prudhomme, Leconte de Lisle, and Coppée.[88] The list of stars made two things exceedingly clear. "Good usage," even with all its minor variations, was a bourgeois affair. And the focus of this affair remained, as always, squarely trained on Paris.

For historical linguists, as well as for singers, actors, or anyone else interested in performance practices of the past, the book is a veritable bonanza, offering evidence of how a certain class of Parisian spoke French in the last years of the nineteenth century. Yet Koschwitz's endeavor is perhaps more interesting for the history it could not tell. The tools of his trade prevented him from settling some of the most important questions of pronunciation. "There are almost as many systems of phonetic transcription as there are phoneticians," he complained. "But even the most scrupulous phonetic transcription cannot exactly render the intended pronunciation; for such writing removes all individuality, fails to render not only the personal timbre of the voice, but neglects most of the transitional sounds and intonations as well."[89] To remedy such omissions, one needed a supplemental notation, a "musical notation," as Koschwitz put it, that would allow the listener to indicate the "andantes, the crescendos and decrescendos, in a word, the linguistic or acoustic expression of the movements of the soul" (*l'expression linguale ou acoustique des mouvements de l'âme*).

Searching for the beautiful element of French speech—for *le bel* in *le bon usage*—Koschwitz thus raised the bar. If Passy had revealed the "music" of

French as a purely phonetic phenomenon, a function of vowels and their timbres, Koschwitz here invoked the liquid continuity of a whole phrase. Elegant speech involved not just good pronunciation but a more elusive quality of voice, a cadence or intonation: the same musical resources that governed poetry, song, *mélodie*. Koschwitz realized that his transcriptions, however meticulous, had failed to capture this other side of the French "accent," the immaterial *mouvements* that gave speech its charm. And it was this omission he regretted most.

The regret was no doubt tinged with envy, for during the course of his research, Koschwitz had seen that it could be done. On his arrival in Paris in 1890, he had found his way into the classes of the Abbé Pierre-Jean Rousselot, an unusual scholar of modern languages who had established a small laboratory for phonetic research at the Institut Catholique.[90] Half humanist, half scientist, Rousselot had completed studies in the 1880s with the famous scholar of romance languages Gaston Paris and the equally famous physiologist Etienne-Jules Marey, and he had soon begun to perform experiments on the speaking voice, using a remarkable range of new phonetic tools, mostly of his own design. At the Institut Catholique, he had ventured to look more deeply into the landscape of the mouth; he had heard the multiple timbres of a single vowel; he had learned to stop a sentence dead in its tracks. Most inspiring to Koschwitz, he had begun to evoke that evanescent "music" of the spoken word and to put it all in a form of writing that made the French tongue appear in a whole new light.

Figures of Speech

Koschwitz may have placed the Abbé a cut above his peers, but in some respects Rousselot's phonetic research followed in the same path. Like Passy, he, too, would explore sound reception and sound production, the acoustic and organic aspects of French speech, and the mouth's complex geography. He, too, would see the practical advantages of phonetics for a modern language education. And like many linguists in post-1870 France, he, too, would worry over the state of regional accents and the disappearing patois. The same year that Passy brought out the first edition of *Les Sons du français*, Rousselot established, with Jules Gillérion, a new journal on the regional languages, the *Revue des patois gallo-romains*.[91] Indeed, Rousselot's research at the time had centered on a very special patois, that of his home village of Cellefrouin, in Charente. In other words, he, too, staked his career, like Passy, on phonetic knowledge drawn from the bosom of his family.

What set Rousselot apart, then, had less to do with content than with method. Simply put, he wanted to bring greater precision to phonetic studies. The need became evident with his first scholarly project. After noting an audible difference between his mother's speech and his own, he decided to research generational shifts in pronunciation, only to discover how fickle the ear could be. It was nearly impossible to grasp, solely by ear, something as fleeting as an accent. *La parole est un mouvement*, Rousselot was fond of saying. Speaking was movement, in at least two senses. Not only did it represent an acoustic movement, the travel of evanescent sound through time, but also speech resulted from *physical* movements, the infinitely subtle activity of countless muscle groups. In 1885, hoping to seize this moving object once and for all, Rousselot took a crucial step. He went to visit the laboratories of Etienne Marey. As the first French physiologist to analyze the full range of human and animal locomotion, Marey had garnered considerable fame in the 1870s by perfecting several writing machines that made it possible to transcribe the physiological impulses of human movement.[92] Rousselot turned to Marey in the hopes that he, too, might discover what made speech tick.

At least one other scientist in Marey's laboratory had begun to conduct experiments on speech functions by 1885. In the next few years, Rousselot worked alongside, developing the analytical instruments that would allow him to carry out his own research. Then he returned to Cellefrouin, armed and ready to measure the precise timbral differences between three generations of Rousselots speaking the Charentois dialect. The results appeared in 1891 as *Les Modifications phonétiques du langage étudiées dans le patois d'une famille*. Pinning down the tongue of his own mother, the Abbé created a whole new field. He called it experimental phonetics. Whereas Passy had been content to declare the mouth a beautiful machine (*l'appareil de la parole*), capable of infinite nuances, Rousselot now measured the precise content of those nuances, putting machines directly in the mouth.

The tools were illustrated in what would become the official reference work of the new field: Rousselot's *Principes de phonétique expérimentale* (1897). By the time this book was published, the new science had achieved enough of a following that the Abbé moved his base of operations from the Institut Catholique to the Collège de France, where Michel Bréal had established a new chair—and a new laboratory—for him to continue his research. Among the various resonators, tuning forks, and other Helmholtzian instruments stocking the laboratory's shelves, Rousselot prized a small collection of writing machines (*appareils inscripteurs*) for their capacity to provide "a material, visible and palpable image" of the fleeting content of speech.

As Marey had put it before him, "When the eye has ceased to see, the ear to hear, the hand to feel, or especially when our senses have tricked us, these writing tools are like a new sense [organ], endowed with astonishing precision."[93] Rousselot devoted an early chapter of his *Principes* to such "artificial means of experimentation," giving pride of place to the most unmediated writing, methods of "direct inscription." He began with a little device called the artificial palate.

Rousselot had created this appliance to track one of the least perceptible components of speech: the movements of the tongue across the mouth's ridges and valleys. It was relatively simple in conception, a thin piece of flexible material molded in the shape of the hard palate. The *phonologiste* need only powder the underside with talc before inserting it into the mouth of his experimental subject. As the subject began to utter a sound, a trace of articulation was left in the dust. The "writing" issued, then, from the act of speaking. The palate was quickly removed, the results transcribed, and the emerging patterns analyzed and categorized.

This was, needless to say, a completely literal approach to the French "tongue." And its direct method, in turn, put a new spin on what we have been calling linguistic geography. Certainly, the artificial palate made it possible for the phonetician to track the subtle migrations of the tongue for any given sound, vowels and consonants alike—something that speakers alone could hardly perceive. But the cumulative trail left by this agile muscle produced another impression. It exposed what had previously been an obscure, interior terrain. In 1899, the Abbé charted that ground more systematically in his first full-length study of Parisian speech, *Les Articulations parisiennes étudiées à l'aide du palais artificiel*.[94] If Passy's vowel triangle, with its twin axes of open-closed, back-front, offered nothing more than a vague, directional compass (north-south-east-west), Rousselot's tongue prints replaced this abstract geometry with a far more concrete topography. His research now revealed the crater-like surface of the mouth as a marvelous landscape, one that seemed to resemble, oddly enough, the map of France (Figure 2.4).

The measurements eventually added up. Not only did the experimental data confirm the sites of linguistic difference, those border conditions that produced the so-called *nationalismes* of a citizen's accent ("The letter *l* in French," Rousselot asserted, "is never voiced as it is in English"), but also Rousselot exposed a more nuanced phonetic landscape. Most significantly, he now asserted the existence of three distinct timbres for any given vowel: what he called the *moyen* (medium), the *grave* (low, or "open"), and the *aigu* (high, or "closed"). Here is how he described, for example, the performance of the vowel *a*:

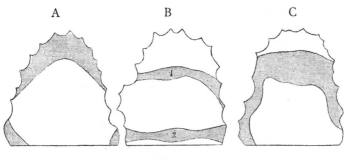

Fig. 46.
Articulation de *l*.
(Palais artificiel).

A. — *l* parisienne.
B. — 1. *l* alsacienne (vallée de Munster).
　　2. Imitation par un Alsacien de *l* anglaise.
C. — *l* anglaise.

FIGURE 2.4 Tongue prints made with artificial palate: Articulation of the letter *l*, as pronounced by a Parisian, an Alsatian, and an Englishman and illustrated in Rousselot and Laclotte, *Précis de prononciation française* (1902)

The medium *a* is pronounced effortlessly, with open mouth and lips in a neutral position, neither rounded, nor pulled back at the corners, the tongue extended almost to the teeth, and just barely lifted toward the middle. The open *à* requires a larger opening of the mouth; the tongue pulls back, about 17 millimeters from the lower teeth, while the corners of the mouth come together in such a way as to diminish the aperture in the rounding of the lips. The closed *á* is emitted with a smaller resonator than for the medium *a*: the tongue is slightly raised and carries its point of articulation forward, around 5 millimeters; the corners pull back on each side.[95]

It was a whole new order of performative precision. And yet even this exhaustive description remained incomplete, for the basic trio allowed further subtle variations. One could find, for example, an open and closed *a* that were both more open and more closed (as when Parisians pronounced *gare* as if it were *gore* or *Montparnasse* as *Montpérnasse*) and less open and less closed. That made a total, by Rousselot's count, of "seven *a*'s that a well trained ear can easily distinguish." How these sounds were deployed throughout France was another matter. Different regions had their own curious habits, leading Rousselot to advance a most unexpected conclusion. The basic vowel *a*—in many respects, the most open of all French timbres—could be "extremely difficult to teach," he said, "even to French people."[96]

The multiplication of distinctions may have caused alarm, but the proof, once again, lay in the writing. Passy's IPA had gone some way to representing the sounds of French, but Rousselot's *appareils inscripteurs* took them to a whole new level. His machines represented speech in the making, "the living reality itself" *(la réalité vivante elle-même)*, as Rousselot put it. Tongue-writing led to voice-writing and a new kind of indirect inscription. This was what had most impressed the young Koschwitz. Going beyond isolated sounds, Rousselot adapted Marey's graphic methods to capture speech as it unfolded in time. That required another, more complex instrument. He called it the *inscripteur électrique de la parole* (Figure 2.5).

Marey had conceived the basic mechanism by 1878,[97] but the rapid, commercial development of recording technology by 1890 made the new tool even more viable. After Edison etched "Mary Had a Little Lamb" onto tinfoil in 1877, it was only a matter of time before recordings would be developed for more general use. The "graphophone" of Chichester Bell and Charles Sumner Tainter, patented in 1887, was the first to capture sound by chiseling grooves

FIGURE 2.5 Inscription de la parole, from Rousselot and Laclotte, *Précis de prononciation française* (1902)

onto a replaceable cardboard cylinder. Not long after, Edison issued his "improved" phonograph, making use of the same process, now with solid wax cylinders that could be used more than once. From Figure 2.5, we can see that Rousselot's rotating cylinder ran on similar principles, although here the recording surface was a roll of blackened paper, and the "groove" a line scratched into its surface. The resonances of mouth, nose, and throat were directed into a trio of separate embouchures, each with its own stylus. In the face of this more sophisticated writing machine, Passy's IPA must have seemed miserably second-rate. For Rousselot, moving script would always trump inert symbols, as electric impulses turned transcription into a remarkable new phonography.[98]

The more advanced writing captured precisely what ordinary phonetic transcriptions missed: the intonation, the andantes, crescendos, and decrescendos, in a word, the subtle *mélodie* of French speech. It was, then, no surprise that Rousselot decided to include a self-consciously musical item among the pages of his treatise. Into his inscription machine. he had recorded a solemn reading of one of the oldest poems in the history of French literature: *La Chanson de Roland* (Figure 2.6). With its undulating, monotone lines, this transcription revealed the "living reality" of the ancient chanson in more ways than one. We can perceive in the trembling script not only the

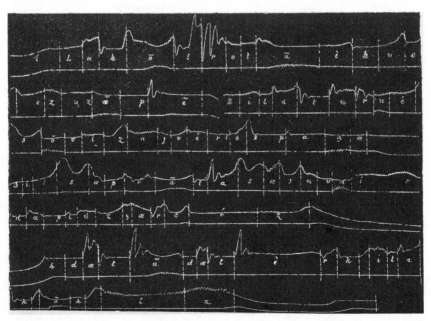

FIGURE 2.6 "La Mort de Roland," from *La Chanson de Roland*. Graphic "readings" taken by the *inscripteur électrique de la parole*. Rousselot, *Principes de phonétique expérimentale* (1897)

rhythm and volume of the words but also their pitch, what Rousselot called the *hauteur musicale* of the spoken phrase.

The readings in Example 2.6 show output from only two of the three needles, the vibrations coming from mouth and nose, leaving aside those fluctuations from the throat that Rousselot called *intensité*. Viewed with the naked eye, the wiggling outlines offered only a general idea of the poem's "music." Noisy consonants make the top line jump; clear vowels set it atremble; nasals make the lower line purr. To see anything more, one needed a microscope. Rousselot segmented the readings after the fact, adding vertical slashes (as we can see) to mark off different phonemes and phonetic characters to identify them. But with a microscope, he could also measure more precise values. Each lurch of the top line became, then, a numerical height (a pitch), each segment a numerical length (a rhythm). After gathering the data (Figure 2.7a), he could then create a more legible picture by transferring those measurements onto ordinary graph paper (Figure 2.7b).

The graph (Figure 2.7b) turns up the volume on the chanson's subtle music. The solfège syllables alone, climbing the y axis, signal a song hidden deep within the folds of speech. But just as striking is the graph's overall impression. A single *décasyllabe* (*Le comte Roland est couché sous un pin*) explodes in a veritable symphony of data. In deciphering it, we may experience some of the mild alienation we observed in reading Passy's phonetic transcription of Hugo, for here, too, we are obliged to "go slowly." Yet it should by now be clear that Rousselot's transcribed *Chanson* does not merely suggest the idea of music. It puts the performative evidence right before our eyes. Making the poem even more visibly strange, the meticulously graphed measurements turn a single line of verse into an overwhelming polyphony of time and tone: a complex visual score of language in motion.

––––––

In shifting his attention from individual sounds to *mouvement*, from the letter to the spirit of the spoken phrase ("the acoustic expression of the movements of the soul," as Koschwitz put it), Rousselot's phonography outclassed Passy's phonetic alphabet by a significant margin. And yet the hypertranscriptions

H.M. 6	7	7,7	7	7,3	7	7,7	6,5	7,5	8	8	7	8	8.9.10.11
I. L	œ	k õ t	r	o	l	ã	é	k u ε é	s u χ	ã		p ɛ̃	♯
D. 10	5	9 18 9	9,5	5,5	10	17	12	9 10 9	9	8 5	9	10	10 19
I 35		42		26	30	10		18 27	31	30			29.10.9.0

FIGURE 2.7A First line of "La mort de Roland," measuring pitch height (H.M.), duration (D.), and volume (I.) in millimeters. Rousselot and Laclotte, *Précis de prononciation française* (1902)

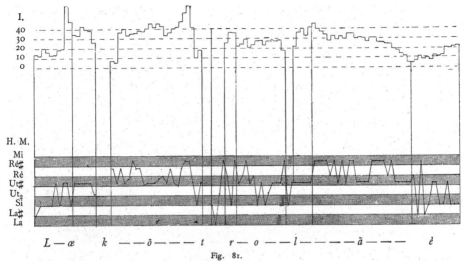

I.
40
30
20
10
0

H. M.
Mi
Ré♯
Ré
Ut♯
Ut₂
Si
La♯
La

L — œ   k — ō — — t   r — o — — l — — — — ã — — —   è

Fig. 81.

Chaque degré de la ligne I (intensité) et chaque point de la ligne H. M. (hauteur musicale) correspondent à une vibration.
Il suffit de mener une perpendiculaire de l'un à l'autre pour établir la concordance. L'intensité est marquée en millimètres.
Les consonnes sourdes et l'explosion de l'*l* de Roland sont supprimées.

FIGURE 2.7B Same data as in 2.7a, transferred to a double graph

were more than scientific curiosity. At the end of his *Principes de phonétique expérimentale*, the Abbé acknowledged that all such work pointed to a practical goal—to the same sort of goal, in fact, that had motivated Passy's phonetic research. His studies, he claimed, would help people speak more perfect French.

Even a meticulous laboratory scientist could defend his data, it seems, in terms of the broader educational mission of the Republic. Rousselot would express the point most clearly in 1902, in the opening pages of another, more practical text, a manual he called the *Précis de prononciation française*. "This is a teaching manual," he began. "It is addressed both to foreigners who want to acquire a more correct pronunciation of our language, and to natives of the provinces who are not sure they speak the best French, and wish to rid themselves of their regional 'accents.'"[99]

Experimental science proudly upheld the banner of a purified national language. And by 1902, Rousselot knew exactly how civilizing such experiments could be. In 1899, he had developed a popular course for the relatively young Alliance française,[100] bringing the principles of experimental phonetics to a wider audience. With a few portable tools, he began tuning the ears and mouths of native and foreign students, making them more sensitive to the true French "accent." What was this elusive music? Rousselot's evocative response formed a lesson in itself. Here is the long answer he gave in the introduction to the 1902 *Précis*:

> A large number of cities in France pretend to possess the best pronunciation. They all come from the central regions, some distance from the provinces still governed by their distinctive French *patois*. . . . Still, on this point one should have no doubt. If one wants to find the foundation of French pronunciation, one must look for it in Paris.
>
> What, in fact, is French? An artificial language, such as Italian or German, imposed on the people through significant works of literature? No, it is the language of the king carried by his court into the provinces. Literature did not come until sometime later. Hence French is originally the tongue of Paris. Even so, because its principal means of expansion was writing—a vague alphabet in which each person, at least in his vowels, could read the sounds proper to his own dialect—it was inevitably penetrated by all the patois it was meant to replace. From this situation we have all the regional varieties of French that we designate by the term "accent."
>
> . . . Even in Paris the language is not always the same . . . varying according to neighborhoods, and to the social condition and intention of the speaker. An upper class Parisian will not speak like a man of the people. . . . Indeed, there are certain vulgarities never to be found among the old bourgeois families of Paris.[101]

Such observations left no doubt about which language one should prefer. Rousselot nonetheless spelled it out, in effect closing the door on a matter that Koschwitz had left open. "The French we recommend to all," he said, "is that of the *best Parisian society.*"

One could hardly imagine a clearer statement of the *mission civilisatrice* of the IIIe République. Yet Rousselot's conviction became only stronger as he continued, posing the question that burned on every reformer's lips: "Where can one find this pure, unmixed society?" (he uses the expression *sans mélange*, as if referring to a genetic breed). "Does it in fact exist?" There were still good Parisian families going back a few generations. But as a non-Parisian transplanted from the provinces, Rousselot preferred to look to the future, to the society of *les enfants*. "Children born in Paris are Parisian," he said, "and even those who move to the city will become so very quickly." Why? It was a foregone conclusion: "Because they are attending public school."[102]

The illustrations in his teaching materials seemed to reinforce this faith in state education. Gazing out from the graphs, the numbers, the prints and diagrams, one could occasionally see the faces of children—a boy and a girl—caught in the act of perfecting their speech. By their youth alone, they conveyed a sense of the purity of the phonetic enterprise. But they also served to remind readers of the nation's larger educational objective. Their presence verified that the real future of French society lay here, in the training of innocent little mouths.

The child in Figure 2.8 appears in the lead article of the *Revue de phonétique*, a journal Rousselot created in 1911 to promote his now twenty-year-old discipline of experimental phonetics. Clad in a crisp, beribboned *tunique d'école*, this little boy illustrated an essay on French vowels (what else?) and seemed to be engaged in a curious form of linguistic hygiene. He holds before his lips an ingenious device, a tunable tuning fork that Rousselot had developed for his pronunciation classes at the Alliance française. The fork was designed to produce the vowel's principal frequencies with ease, by means of a movable bridge. The student located the appropriate pitch, then brought it close to the mouth as he prepared to articulate a given vowel (*a, e, i, o, u*). When the oral cavity took the correct position, the vibrating fork pinged more loudly, in sympathetic resonance. Repeated practice ensured that even from the mouths of babes these most musical of timbres would ring true.

Engaged in this act of tuning his French, the boy brings to mind something of the childhood education of Michel Leiris, acquiring his first "taste" of the alphabet. Yet Rousselot had fully anticipated this oral training in his 1902 *Précis de prononciation*, where he featured the image of another child. Photographs of a Parisian girl recur throughout, offering a somewhat different perspective on the idea of French taste (Figure 2.9). She is, for one thing, more stylishly dressed. Her white lace collar, crucifix, and unassuming coiffure are clear signs—far more than the boy's simple school costume—of her bourgeois credentials and of her promising future in *la bonne société*

FIGURE 2.8 Boy tuning his vowels, from *Revue de phonétique* 1, no. 1 (1911)

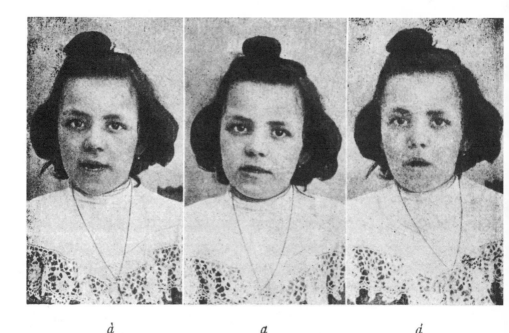

à   *a*   *á*

FIGURE 2.9 Girl pronouncing the Parisian *a*, from Rousselot and Laclotte, *Précis de prononciation française* (1902)

parisienne. As if to reinforce this status, the photographs capture the little *bourgeoise* demonstrating the very thing her society was thought to do best. She pronounces not one, not two, but three forms of the Parisian phoneme *a*—open, medium, and closed—as purely as she possibly can.

These photographs leave another impression as well, something like an aural illusion. Look more closely, for example, at the girl on the right. You can sense her concentration. With her jaw dropped, she looks like a voice student caught in the middle of an arpeggio or an extended *vocalise.* Now look at the girl on the left. She, too, is concentrating, but the image projects a different sound, brighter, somehow sweeter. We know she's just saying "ah," but because the camera freezes her face in time, her utterance seems to go on forever: ahhhhhhhhhh. What did that sweet vowel sound like? We might almost begin to hear it if we stare long enough, for this was the sharpest of the vowels Rousselot had endeavored to capture, the sound that accounted for the uniquely "clear" timbre of spoken French. Rousselot called it the *a chantant*: the *a* that sings.

———

With this uncanny image of a singing voice lurking in the shadows of a photograph, I want to pause to reflect on our discussion of French phonetics.

Two tendencies have emerged, one material and the other musical. Together, they suggest an unlikely connection between the objects of our history so far, the French school and French song. In a sense, the science of phonetics at century's end had been created both by and for the school. And yet its attempts to capture the "living reality" of French, to pin down all its subtle nuances, became a self-perpetuating activity for those who pursued it, with an ever-receding statistical threshold. In order to prove "the legitimate existence of the spoken tongue *apart* from the written," as Passy put it, one needed, ironically enough, more and more kinds of writing. The phonetic alphabet was supplemented by ideographs (the tongue print); the ideograph by phonographs (electric inscription). The result was an ever-growing stream of graphic material, figures whose uniqueness, variety, and sheer quantity would serve to represent the infinite nuances of French speech.

Saussure had kept his distance from such studies for a good reason. "The phonation[of even the smallest word represente[d] an infinite number of muscular movements," he said, so many that it would be impossible to "recognize and figure them all."[103] And yet it was precisely this impossibility that the new experimental phonetics had embraced. The particularity of the data may have inhibited generalization, but the excess nonetheless served a purpose. Decades of phonetic research, disseminated through laboratories, journals, and popular courses, raised the nation's consciousness about its habits of speech. Modern methods of language education developed under this awareness, and so did the notion of literacy. Under the broad influence of phonetics, the pedagogy of reading itself was subtly transformed. Primary school readers ("Méthodes de Lecture") now put phonemes before letters, sound before meaning. Students learned first to form isolated syllables (*ba, bé, bi, bo, bu*), which later were strung into puns and phrases. The most typical exercises seemed to favor imaginative combination over wrote memorization, resulting in playful, almost Dada-esque sequences across the page (Figure 2.10).

Even a work as serious as Rousselot and Laclotte's *Précis de prononciation* would include several pages of similarly nonsensical exercises, forms of verbal calisthenics that privileged pronunciation over meaning, diction over denotation. Consider, for example, this long sequence for the letter *D*:

dada, dédaigner, dédain, dédale, dedans, dédier, dédit, dédommager, déduction, démodé, désiderata, dédire, descendant, diadème, didactique, Diderot, Didon, dindon, dissuader, dodeliner, dodu, bidon, baudet, Daudet, Diderot, désirer, Rodez, dinde, craindre, plaindre,

FIGURE 2.10 Lesson from *Méthode de Lecture* circa 1900. Note how the simple phrase *Papa, ta pipe* ("Daddy, your pipe!") morphs, by a slow mutation of *p*, *t*, *a*, and *e*, into *Papa a été petit* ("Daddy was once little")

feindre, rôder, démontrer, discuter, rude, prude, druide, peindre, plaider, pendre, rendre, etc.—"Didot dina, dit-on, du dos d'un dodu dindon [Dido dined, they say, on the back of a fat capon]."[104]

Such instructional exercises may have hinted at the playful worldview of surrealist poets of the next generation. But that was only because the pedagogy had worked. It seems quite clear that, by 1900, the alphabet was no longer just something one learned to read and write in France. It had become, as Leiris himself remembered, a sonorous material object, a concrete thing "having opacity and consistency." It had become something one learned to hold—and to exercise—carefully in one's mouth.

This kind of material awareness has, of course, suggestive implications for a history of *mélodie*, for to speak of letters as material objects was also to evoke, quite physically, the oral experience of words in a song. Like linguists, singers usually refer to this feeling as "phonation." By focusing on the production of linguistic sound, the new science of phonetics served in a singular way to remind speakers of this musical resonance of language. Indeed, all the evidence seemed to point to the same conclusion. The French language did not merely aspire towards the condition of music, to paraphrase Walter Pater. From the perspective of phonetics, it *was* music. If Legouvé saw the speaking body as a kind of instrument, Passy and Rousselot showed exactly how resonant that body was. The acoustic truths that formed the basis of their work—and of all phonetic science—refashioned the mouth as a finely tuned lyre, and *parole* its ineffable music. By the time Rousselot brought out his *Précis de prononciation*, it was a well-known fact: the French word was not spelled but composed, not a collection of vowels and consonants but a *"composition of musical sounds and noises."*[105]

Of course, the tendency went both ways. After the phoneticians closed in on music, musicians began to learn phonetics. Claire Croiza, one of the premier interpreters of French song in the 1920s (whom we will meet again), occasionally quoted this definition of Rousselot's in the public master classes she gave at the height of her singing career.[106] More tellingly, a copy of Rousselot's *Principes de phonétique expérimentale* made its way into the library of the national conservatory. And it made a certain sense. The Conservatoire national de musique et de déclamation was, after all, the principal training ground for both singers and actors—for those, in other words, trained to use their native language in public, especially in the state-funded theaters, the Comédie- française or the Opéra-comique. It should not be surprising, then, to witness even a conservative establishment like the Conservatoire opening itself to the progressive lure of phonetic science, with its promise of linguistic purity. But this was because the science had learned to speak more directly to artists. Between 1904 and 1911, a curious figure who signed himself simply "Docteur Marage" began offering a series of public lectures at the Sorbonne—an open course in physical biology—on the subject of phonation and hearing. He later compressed the lectures into a small volume, *Petit Manuel de Physiologie de la Voix*.[107] What did Marage have to say to artists? We know that at least one prominent singer from the Conservatoire, the bass Jacques Isnardon, counted himself among Marage's disciples.[108] I want to sit in on a few lectures to learn more and to bring our discussion of French education full circle.

The Sorbonne turns out to be a fruitful place to end our discussion for another reason. There we will meet one last scholar, a figure who contributed far more to modern language studies than the experiments of Marage, or even Rousselot and Passy. I refer to the great historian of the French language, Ferdinand Brunot. In the course of compiling his own monumental history of the French language, Brunot launched an unusual educational project, which I want to consider as the final example in our survey. Indeed, looking at Marage and Brunot side by side affords us another, more pointed view of the whole phonetic enterprise. We witness scholars striving not merely to record but to *reproduce* the sounds of their own language. And that twist, in turn, will force us to reconsider the question of literacy from a whole new angle as we explore the larger consequences—historical, emotional, and one might say, ethical—of inscribing French voices for posterity.

Talking Machines

Like Passy before him, Marage was a popularizer. He had no trouble simplifying the technical aspects of his subject to reach his audience of nonscientists. Tailoring the science to meet their needs, he summarized the scope of his project in the following proposition: "an artist who speaks or sings in a hall can become more or less tired when performing in front of an audience who has come to listen to either operas or tragedies." It was an unwieldy sentence, to be sure, but it apparently contained the whole program for the original twelve-week course. The table of contents of Marage's *Petit Manuel* made this clear, breaking down the sentence into its separate components (marked in boldface) and filling in the relevant content and chapter headings.[109] Thus, we read:

An artist is a talking machine composed

of *Lungs*	Chapter	I
of a *Larynx*	—	II
and of *Resonators*	—	III
that transform the sound:		
Principles of acoustics	—	IV
speaks or sings		
Vowels and Consonants	—	V
in a hall		
Acoustics of performance halls	—	VI
becoming more or less tired		
Exercises for vocal projection	—	VII
in front of an audience who is listening		
Theory of hearing	—	VIII
to either operas		
The singing voice (voix chantée)	—	IX
or tragedies		
The speaking voice (voix parlée)	—	X

One thing immediately stands out. Although Marage addressed his course to both "singers and orators," the latter group seems to come out on top, with speech (*voix parlée*) rather than song (*voix chantée*) forming the culmination of the study. The importance of the speaking voice would become more evident, in fact, in the second half of the book, where Marage turned from the physiological study of larynx and lungs to the "scientific bases for the teaching of singing." That subject brought him to the all-important (and by now familiar) question of how to form one's vowels.

The theory, which rehearsed the findings of German physiologists from Helmholtz to Hermann, had been told before, of course, but the application was unique. Whereas Marage, like Rousselot, would experiment with numerous artificial methods of inscription, he also took the image of the artist as "talking machine" more literally. He sought not just to record but to re-create the sounds such a speaker would make, those subtle timbres exposed by experimental phonetics. "If our written evidence is sound, we should be able to *reproduce* the vowel,"[110] he claimed. The terms were those of the recently deceased Marey, whose own studies had involved not only analysis but also what should properly be called resynthesis of physiological activity. In other words, Marey had worked to reconstruct, by mechanical means, almost all the movements analyzed with his various graphic methods. The same ideal drove Marage in his own early efforts at speech resynthesis, and it resulted in a most astonishing invention. He called it the *sirène à voyelles* (Figure 2.11).

This almost surrealistic appliance produced three kinds of vowel, replicating the effect of singing, whispering, or speaking. The simplest of these, Marage tells us, was singing. He conjectured that the phonation of a vowel by the singing voice required only the operation of the larynx, which worked, in essence, on the principle of a siren. The act of driving compressed air against a resisting force (the vocal folds or, in the case of a siren, a rotating wheel) produced a continuous noise, like the siren's wail. The particular resonance of the noise depended on the nature of resistance. Marage cut the wheels to produce the resonance of five different vowels, with perforations that approximated the formant pattern for each. The shape of the cut, either wedged or straight, re-created, he said, the form of the vocal cords during pronunciation.

Set spinning, the disk broke up the flow of air according to its perforated patterns, emitting a clear and decipherable timbre—in effect, an artificial vowel. Marage confirmed its accuracy through further analysis, using the same type of inscription machines employed by Rousselot. "Experiments verify that if we take traces of these artificial vowels we will get the same

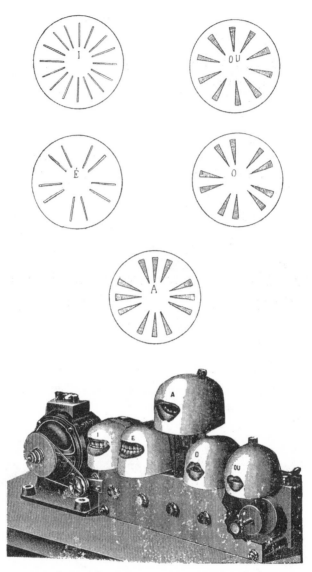

FIGURE 2.11 Vowel siren, from Marage, *Petit Manuel de physiologie de la voix*, circa 1911

curves as in natural vowels."[111] But the machine also verified something more basic—showing, in the end, that pure singing was more primitive than speech.

To make the siren song articulate, one needed to append a rubber mouth. So that is what Marage would do. He made a set of eerily lifelike examples, modeled on human subjects, that showed lips, teeth, and tongue in phonation. And they worked. When air alone passed through the forms, one could hear a whispered vowel, as in the exercise Passy recommended to readers of *Les Sons du français*. But when the siren whined through a pair of matching lips, the machine produced, he claimed, a faithful likeness of speech. The additional resonance from the rubber cavity reinforced the basic timbre of the siren just as the mouth's resonance reinforced that of the larynx. The superiority of these more complex *voyelles parlées* could then be verified, once again, through graphic analysis.

Yet, by pairing a given disk with the *wrong* corresponding cavity (an *a* siren with an *é* mouth, for example), Marage went on to show how the *voyelle parlée* could quickly lose its clarity. The effect, he said, was not unlike that of bad singing. The artificial data led him to conclude, strongly: "We can see why it is so rare to encounter singers with good diction; a beautiful voice depends uniquely on the larynx and the ear, that is, on anatomical conditions; but good diction requires a series of long and difficult studies, which few singers have the courage to undertake."[112] The machine thus presented the performer (that other "talking machine") with an unmistakable challenge. To become intelligent artists, singers would have to rethink the limits of their instrument and learn to embrace not empty tone but colorful articulation. They would learn to reinforce their song with the articulate timbres of the speaking voice. That meant, in short, that smart singers would begin to resemble Marage's other ideal: the *voix parlée* of the public speaker. We shall see how French artists met the challenge of intelligent diction in chapter 4. But the example of Marage shows to what extent these questions had come to occupy the concerns of scientists and, indeed, how science began to inform vocal pedagogy.

Marage turned exclusively to the *voix parlée* in the last chapter of his book, where he made use of a different set of talking heads. A neat cinematographic process revealed the speech act in motion, on continuous columns of film (Figure 2.12). The featured actor had been photographed in Marey's laboratory at the Collège de France sometime in 1902.[113] He uttered a sibilant tongue twister (*Cinq ou six officiers Gascons . . .*), speaking slowly and articulately, so the camera could catch all the relevant movements. As Marage observed, the speech was so clearly represented that "a deaf-mute could easily read these words on the lips of the artist."[114]

The cinematic exercise actually recalled a pedagogical technique once used by the great actor Régnier. As reported by Legouvé, he liked to make his students articulate with lips alone, as if speaking to the deaf, or relating a secret with no sound.[115] In this sense, Marage's novel pictures represented the inverse of the noisy *sirène à voyelles*, replacing stationary lips with the multiple movements of an entire, animated face. This time, of course, the animation was voiceless. However real this photographed speaker might

FIGURE 2.12 Cinematograph of man pronouncing sibilant tongue twister, *Cinq ou six officiers gascons....*From Marage, *Petit Manuel de physiologie,* circa 1911

seem, with his quaintly crooked bowtie, his voice would always remain silent. In order to appreciate the subtle accents of his *voix parlée*—to examine not the speaker but the speaking—one needed a very different kind of apparatus. One needed a phonograph: the only machine in history that could "transmit speech in its absolute integrity."

———

That was exactly how Ferdinand Brunot put it on the third of June, 1911, during an address inaugurating a brand new repository for the spoken word, the Archives de la Parole. It was an auspicious occasion. Brunot had established the archive at the Sorbonne through the generosity of Pathé, the French company that had been successfully marketing modern talking machines since 1894. By then, recording technology had improved in quantum leaps, records having become cheaper, and the reproductions more reliable. Mass-produced flat disks had replaced the old-fashioned wax cylinders, and the change had led to the domestication of records, as new gramophone machines entered the bourgeois home. All this made a library of aural documents imaginable in a way it could not have been a decade earlier. And so Brunot had imagined it. He now stood at the helm of the first national archive dedicated to speech records. His mission: to found an aural heritage of the French people, a *patrimoine sonore* destined for future researchers of the French language.

For this reason alone, the event forms a fitting conclusion to my history of French education and phonetics. Not only does the future that Brunot imagined in 1911 belong now to our present tense, in a new millennium, but some of the voices he saw fit to preserve have also played an important role in my research. His talking archive forms the oldest layer of the extensive collection of audio materials—the so-called Audiothèque—currently housed in France's Bibliothèque nationale. But in 1911, newly fitted out in the Sorbonne's examination rooms on the rue St-Jacques, the archive was obviously the very latest thing. Indeed, it represented the logical extension of the work done by Marage, Marey, and Rousselot in capturing French speech, for it provided "records" of a very different sort, with the potential to revolutionize, in more than one sense, the course of linguistic history.

As a historian himself, Brunot perhaps felt the need for such an archive more acutely than most. A decade earlier, in 1900, he had been appointed to the newly established Chair of the History of the French Language, and by 1911, when Pathé contacted him, he was hard at work on his magnum opus of the same name: *L'Histoire de la langue française*. The first volume of that enormous reference work—what would eventually become a twenty-volume monument to the French language—had appeared in 1904. The last would not appear until after his death, completed by his protégé, Charles Bruneau. But it was surely the engrossing labor of this linguistic history that made Brunot aware of the faults of the traditional archive, of what the written record could never say. Even the most intimate document could not, after all, bring back the voices of the dead. Such knowledge seemed to affect the tone of his inaugural remarks as he stood at the threshold of the future archive. For the occasion, his words were more grave than festive, suffused with a palpable sense of melancholy.

I want to listen to his historic address as a way of framing—and thus concluding—the larger argument outlined in this chapter, a modern history of French speech that unexpectedly converges, as we have seen, with a modern history of music. Here we will see those histories converging one last time. Brunot's views on the history of language, in fact, anticipate many issues that would eventually inform the future history of musicology itself and serve, almost uncannily, to predict the historical performance movement of the later twentieth century. Still, those predictions were not always bright, precisely because of what Brunot knew *about* history. As he put it, "the study of the past can fill those who love literature and art with distinct regrets." His remarks are worth quoting at length:

> Penetrating [literature] with all our analytical powers, ... we some-
> times bring to the stories and poems of the past rhythms and harmo-
> nies that we can enjoy. But all too soon we become frustrated in this
> aesthetic pursuit, first by the feeling, then by the certainty, that our
> pleasure has been partly a lie, for we have made it our personal
> creation—remaking for our own purposes a text that was never pro-
> nounced, never delivered, in the way we now deliver it. Whatever
> progress has been made in the history of the pronunciation of our
> language, whatever our instinct may add to this positive knowledge, it
> is still impossible for us to restore an authentic line of Racine. The
> psychological truths may still be there, the expressive beauty in some
> way accessible. But we will have only a dimly approximate knowledge
> of the sonorities and the rhythms that created their original charm.
> A part of their beauty has been erased and abolished forever.[116]

Brunot's regrets did not cease, however, with the poets of the remote past. He also lamented the fading of more recent voices, those of performers like the celebrated actress Rachel, who had performed Racine's *Phèdre* in 1843 to great acclaim. Her thrilling accents, though immortalized by the critics, would never be heard again. "One by one," he said, these performers "have also joined the poet in silence." Without the aural testimony of such actors and actresses, certain crucial developments—modern stage practices—remained forever a matter of conjecture. "We do not know when performers ceased observing the division of hemistichs [in the alexandrines of classical theater], or ceased pronouncing the final long syllables of plural words." He went on to conclude: "No phonetic writing, however charged with diacritical marks, will be able to give back the accents, the intonations of what we have never heard."[117]

Of course, the same could be (and has been) said about a musical score. Koschwitz may have longed for music notation while attempting to transcribe selected Parisian accents, but his envy was largely misplaced. As we all know, the most detailed music notation can never capture the particular quality of voice that makes up a thrilling performance. Mary Garden's Mélisande remains, in this respect, just as out of reach to the twenty-first-century operagoer as Rachel's Phèdre was to Brunot.[118] Nor is a musical score helpful in preserving a performance practice, once the style has been forgotten. Modern Mélisandes have continued to make do at the Opéra, just as modern Phèdres at the Comédie française have managed, hardly worrying about "what they have never heard" and delivering the words the only way they know how: by following their instincts. Yet this was precisely what Brunot lamented. The psychology may be there, he said, but not "the sonorities and the rhythms that created their original charm."

In that respect, Brunot's argument serves as a kind of defense for the work I pursue later in this book. Listening to old recordings and a few dimly remembered performers, I try in my own way to recapture, if not the "original charm," then something of the original meaning that surrounded a repertory of song from the past, a past that has thankfully been supplemented with such aural documents. Poring over this testimony may be our only means to rescue that part of a repertory that has already slipped into a kind of oblivion. This was, we recall, what Barthes suggested when describing the fate of the French *mélodie*. He even echoed Brunot's misgivings more than a half century after the fact, when he told us, solemnly, that "the *mélodie française* has disappeared; one might even say it sank like a stone."[119] Among the many causes he adduced for its demise was, of course, the disappearance of certain French performers, along with their recordings.

The judgment should give us pause, not so much for the way it ratifies Brunot's sense of history as for its tone. Barthes's peculiar nostalgia for this lost music, and for a beloved singer, strikes much the *same* tenor as the words of the older historian. And for this reason, I find myself returning to his oddly compelling essay on *mélodie* (as I do at least once more before the book is finished), not to harp on its authority, but to understand, finally, its place in history. We may now begin to sense how his remarks belong to a much longer history of regret, one that stretches back at least to the beginning of the twentieth century. This was, it seems, a very French history, rooted in a modern image of the French language. One might even say that such history could not emerge until the moment when the fleeting accents of the French tongue had become the subject of intense scrutiny and desire, until the moment when, demanded by a newly democratic education and exposed by linguistic science, the spoken word, and its inevitable disappearance, became palpable and real for the first time. As a Frenchman schooled in the early decades of the twentieth century, Barthes had no doubt tasted this reality as palpably as Sartre and Leiris.

The phonograph itself was instrumental in shaping this modern sensibility, this modern sense of loss. Brunot would soon become famous for his phonographic excursions to the French countryside where, like Bartók in Hungary, he labored to collect the living voices of "the people" (Figure 2.13). Yet such collecting was simply evidence of the condition it was trying to forestall. The trips would not have been necessary without the forward march of democratic education—the very spread of the French language that had made an American professor rightfully jealous on his own trip to the country in 1912. In asserting French as the nation's mother tongue, the state had all but seen to it that the distinctive patois of these regions would fade into oblivion. Falling out of the mouths of the people, they now needed artificial resuscitation, which is precisely what Brunot's archive provided. His records safeguarded the memory of other voices as well, those of more famous public figures such as Apollinaire, Colette, and Sarah Bernhardt. All these accents, it seems, were preserved as if in fulfillment of a historical imperative commanded by the phonograph itself, filling the present, and the future, with records of "what we (otherwise) might never have heard."

In one way, such records could be said to perform a function quite similar to Passy's phonetic alphabet or Rousselot's more elaborate graphic scores. They marked the next logical step—indeed, the culmination—of an increasingly literal phonography of the French language. And yet they could also be described as an extreme form of melancholic writing. Driven by the very idea of future loss, the script attempted to capture, and to fix in place, the spoken word as a Frenchman actually heard it in the present. Now, of course, the sounds were inscribed in shellac rather than ink, in sensitive, illegible grooves that one would not so much read as *replay* in some distant future. The responsibility of correct speech could finally be lifted from fallible readers (who would always bring to it their own rhythms and accents) and left on a talking machine.

Only this vision of mechanical perfection could bring a glimmer of hope to Brunot's inaugural remarks on June 3, 1911, as the new archivist contemplated the beginning of a not-so-silent future. "We live in the century of marvels," he declared, reflecting more brightly on what science had finally

FIGURE 2.13 Ferdinand Brunot (center), his wife, and Charles Bruneau collecting in the Ardennes. Courtesy of *Bibliothèque nationale de France*

overturned. It was now possible to forget, for example "those commonplaces about the winged word, or the earthbound man" that "people had been repeating since antiquity." For the first time in history, such commonplaces had become uncommon. Through the veracity of the machine, the fate of people and their speech would be reversed. Brunot drove home the point in his conclusion, linking the airplane and the phonograph in a marvelous futuristic vision: "Just as man has begun to make his way toward the sky," he said, the word had returned to earth. Speech had at last become tangible, physical, and material, in a way never before imagined. In Brunot's words, it was now "engraved in matter for all time."[120]

Indelible Accents

Burying words in black grooves, the gramophone would settle the problem of the French accent by arresting the "fugitive thing" that had so worried Arsène Darmesteter in the early years of the Republic. And with this modern record, our own story of the mother tongue winds down. Circling back to the questions we started with, we can reflect, once more, on the broader legacy of French literacy. When Brunot commended the machine for eternally "engraving" the airborne word, he was also, of course, addressing a long-standing ideal of literate culture. The great contemporary analysts of French literacy, Furet and Ozouf (whom we met at the beginning of this chapter), put it most clearly. It was the French Revolution, they argued, that "most intransigently insisted on the benefits of written culture as opposed to the pernicious influence of oral tradition." For revolutionary Republicans, the dichotomy between the oral and the written "was coterminous with the temporal opposition between old and new, barbarity and enlightenment, bad and good. . . . Whether transmitted through the school or through the family, writing was both a vehicle for and a symbol of the advent of civic and private virtue, and at the same time an instrument of republican surveillance."[121]

Such thinking persisted among the republican reformers of the nine-teenth century, spawning the tools they employed to ensure their success. The gramophone was the most powerful of these tools, a modern "instrument of republican surveillance," for it, too, had the ability to contain and regulate behavior, although through a very different kind of revolution, the repetition of its rotating disks. In this respect, it is certainly worth noting that in 1911—the same year Brunot inaugurated his new speech archive—Rousselot introduced a revolutionary educational feature in his own journal, *La Revue de phonétique*: a form of distance learning he called the *Cours de gramophonie*.[122] The monthly feature offered phonetic transcriptions of the speech of famous actors and poets—in some cases, the same actors housed in Brunot's ar-chive—recorded onto gramophone disks. Readers were to practice their diction by following the printed transcriptions in the magazine while they replayed the relevant disks at home, on their own talking machines.

This application of the technology can easily be read in terms of the dichotomy proposed by Furet and Ozouf. The republican logic linking writing to democratic progress and orality to the failures of the ancien régime in fact encourages us to see such novel uses of the gramophone, as well as the whole, positivist study of French, in a new light. Rather than displacing conventional writing, overturning what Saussure had called the "tyranny of the letter," the new phonography of French simply reinvented writing, investing it with untold power. The thirty-year history that we have traced in this chapter—from Legouvé's *Art de la lecture* to Brunot's *Archives de la parole*—could thus be seen as a brilliant completion of the revolutionary project.

That historical development, of course, carries intriguing implications for the oral art that is the subject of this book, the art of song. If, as we have seen, an increasingly precise phonography was instrumental in evoking the music of the French alphabet, that same act of inscription also helped define the very idea—or, one might say, the modernity—of the French *mélodie*. Once again, it is to Koechlin that we must turn to understand the distinction; once again, it is he who makes the most cryptic claims. He was the first, for example, to presume the quasi-aristocratic status of the *mélodie*: "The people," he insisted, "are far removed . . . from the *mélodies* of Claude Debussy, of Henri Duparc, of G[abriel] Fauré."[123] Apart from elevating French song over its poor German cousin, Koechlin seems to suggest that France's *mission civilisatrice* had actually fostered a more civilized form of vocal music. The one genre most strongly associated with oral tradition—namely, song—had forsaken all ties with such tradition. The modern French *mélodie* became a shining example of modern French civility, a song that was, so to speak, completely "literate."

Musicologists since Koechlin's time have echoed the point, usually by linking the art of *mélodie* to the extreme literary sophistication of contemporary French poets. I have tried not so much to echo as to explain this idea, reframing its triumphalist logic in a more palpable linguistic history, where we might glimpse the cultural and institutional values lying beneath it. In this new frame, the retrospective view of the *mélodie* offered by Koechlin (who was also, as it happens, a well-known socialist) is not so different from Michel Bréal's progressive vision of a cultivated countryside, where peasant children, inspired by their new democratic education, learned to translate their village ditties into perfect French.[124] The songs of Fauré and Debussy, in other words, become more than just an example of French refinement. They represent the ultimate musical realization of French literacy: the *alphabétisation* of the very idea of song.

And yet there is one more implication written into these ABCs of the French *mélodie*, an implication that recalls Brunot's more melancholy history. In 1899, Brunot announced that "the forward march of democracy ha[d] brought about an undeniable change in the French language," noting with a kind of youthful glee how the speech of the popular classes had invaded the older bourgeois forms. By 1911, his enthusiasm would be muted, his view of progress tinged with regret. If the *alphabétisation* of France had served to bring the singing voices of "the people" into the bourgeois public sphere, it did so, one could say, by making them disappear. The patois, the chanson would be exposed as objects of desire and regret precisely at the point when the mother tongue was poised to devour them.

Such food, once tasted, would leave a sharp sensation on the tongue. The modern notion of the French alphabet ultimately retained an impression of this oral stuff, taking, as Leiris suggested, a more "concrete" form, like a lingering taste inside the mouth. It is this paradoxical taste of progress that I have tried to illuminate in the present chapter, by exposing the confusion of reading and writing, of orality and literacy, that defined the modern republican project. The most pointed result, or aftertaste, can be found in the unique material residue of this history. It was a physical concept whose name represented both something written (a diacritical mark) and something that could hardly be written at all (a voice), a concept that represented the necessary doubleness of phonography, or of music notation. I refer, of course, to that complex, modern idea known as the French "accent." This was one of the most contested ideas to emerge from the modern history of French literacy, one whose repercussions were to be felt far beyond the classroom or laboratory.

In the next chapter, we shall hear how such an idea, as both sound and symbol, comes to affect a different kind of population in the 1890s. Turning again to French poets and composers, we begin to see how the republican values that supported the new French school came to reshape, as well, the modern idea of lyric. A fresh generation of writers, tuned to the voice of the people, began to hear poetry in a new key, and the special timbre of their verse would leave its unique stamp on the *mélodie*. We shall cock an ear, then, to this new verse, to catch its harmonious accent.

Free Speech, Free Verse, and "Music before All Things"

E coi vréman, bon Duvignô,
Vou zôci dou ke lé zagnô
É meïeur ke le pin con manj,

Vous metr' an ce courou zétranj
Contr(e) ce tâ de brav(e) jan
O fon plus bête ke méchan
Drapan leur linguistic étic
Dan l'ortograf(e) fonétic?

Kel ir(e) donc vou zambala?
Vizavi de cé zoizola
Sufi d'une parol(e) verde.

Et pour leur prouvé sans déba
Kil é dé mo ke n'atin pa
Leur sistem(e), dizon-leur: . . .

(And what, really, my good Duvigneaux / You who are as sweet as a lamb, / Better than sliced bread, / What puts you in this strange wrath / Against a heap of good men, / Basically more stupid than evil, / Covering their linguistic ethics / In phonetic spelling? / What anger has you all balled up / Regarding these birds / Satisfied with a tart word? / To prove to them / That we have words that won't work / In their system, let's just say to them: . . . [expletive deleted].)[1]

So wrote, of all people, the poet Paul Verlaine. The sonnet is a period piece, a bit of occasional verse—so occasional that its original circumstance has been all but forgotten. When it first appeared in 1891 in the humorist rag *Le Chat noir*,[2] it bore a dedication to one "A. Duvigneaux, passionate opponent of phonetic spelling," although all details about this figure, like those of the motivating occasion, have by now gone missing. At least one modern critic has compared the text, charitably, to the jokes of later twentieth-century writers like Raymond Queneau.[3] Most have preferred to look the other way. Prudently, the lines have been banished to the remote corners of the oeuvre, lest the evidence of bad taste mar Verlaine's pristine image—as one of the most musical voices in modern French poetry.

Verlaine's own story has, in a sense, encouraged the attitude. By the time he wrote this poem, his career was pretty much over. Even before the publication of his last serious collection, *Jadis et Naguère* (1884), he was checking in and out of public hospitals, alcoholic and penniless, while his stock with the younger generation was rising. Valéry remembered him in those years "angry and cursing . . . like a threatening tramp." Fauré told his American patroness in 1891 that Verlaine's closest friends had given up.[4] Under the circumstances, the Duvigneaux *Dédicace* reads like more bad evidence: an acerbic rhyme by a bilious old poet. Yet even without the trademark lyric charm, the verse does make an interesting sort of noise. The sheer candor—and topicality—of the lines speaks against the grain, suggesting that, if we listen carefully, we could get a different point. We just might hear how Verlaine, despite reduced circumstances, continued to be such an important voice for young writers in the 1890s.

Consider, for example, the opening address. The blunt "E coi" (*Eh, quoi*) already signaled a low register of speech, but the swallowed syllables and singsong rhythm also suggested a telling milieu. More like a chanson than a sonnet, the poem evoked the raucous atmosphere of the Chat noir cabaret and its house journal, which eventually preserved it. The spirit of populism—and anarchy—associated with Montmartre's café culture extended right to Verlaine's missing last word (*merde*).[5] Shouting all the louder in its absence, the expletive mocked both the dedicatee and the official matter he opposed: the case for phonetic spelling. But this, too, was a populist concern. As we know, debates over the reform of French orthography had been diverting socially conscious linguists for a few years. By 1889, the issue had become contentious enough to involve the entire Académie française.[6] If Verlaine's parting shot summed up his own attitude, it did so by underscoring his alignment with the unlettered classes who were the object of debate. At the same time, he managed to spoof another writer who had made his reputation imitating the vulgar tongue of "the people." Through the phonetic writing, the name of this celebrated literary figure (always "satisfied with a tart word") materialized in the penultimate tercet, naturally spelled *(zoi)zola*.

The orthographic joke was all in good fun, but the sense of play had a larger purpose. Verlaine's unorthodox sonnet summarized both his politics and his poetics as the medium became the message. The phonetic surface exposed the most crucial aspect of modern verse: its timbre. Appropriating the very writing it ridiculed, the *parole verde* became a perverse form of lyric sustenance, the slang word *verde* suggesting a pastoral pun that combined the bird's lunch—namely, worms *(vers)*—with the word for poetry itself *(vers)*. *Verde* also rhymed clamorously with *merde*, the deleted expletive of the last line. Reduced to phonic essentials, the text appeared as something new, a "fresh word" never before tasted. And yet this natural verbal state was what a writer like Verlaine had been cultivating for decades. With its multiple layers of verbal play and unfamiliar signs, this green little verse exposed the medium of poetry as Verlaine's followers understood it. These were the young French poets who styled themselves symbolists.

———

This chapter is about those young poets and the trouble they stirred up in the last decade of the nineteenth century, a trouble that has come to be known, for better or worse, as symbolism. It is a vexing coinage, to say the least. The origins of the term can be pinned to a self-promoting and widely disliked poet, Jean Moréas, who used it in a famous manifesto of 1886.[7] Narrating the evolution of modern literature as a series of isms, Moréas sketched a progressive history leading from Hugo's Romanticism through Banville's Parnassianism to Zola's Naturalism and arriving, by way of Decadence, at the movement he now called Symbolism. Despite the fictive genealogy, critics have not resisted the temptation to repeat it, and that tendency has only proliferated the sense of terminological vagueness. As the culmination of an ever more expansive literary history, symbolism had the potential, then as now, to mean everything and nothing at once. The word "is a bottomless pit," said Valéry.[8]

The vagueness of the movement complemented the face of its membership. The original symbolists were a mismatched group of poets from the 1890s, some now forgotten, many not even French. Moréas was a Greek immigrant, born Yánnis Papadiamantópoulos, who reportedly spoke with a heavy accent. There were also two Americans, Stuart Merrill and Francis Vielé-Griffin; four Belgians, Maurice Maeterlinck, Albert Mockel, Charles Van Lerberghe, and Réné Ghil; and one Alsatian, Gustave Kahn. Together with French poets such as Camille Mauclair, Edouard Dujardin, Jules

Laforgue, and Henri de Régnier (not to mention a very young Valéry and Claudel), they formed an unlikely aesthetic constituency. The Mallarmé critic Bertrand Marchal once went so far as to describe their output as a "lower-case symbolism [*symbolisme minuscule*] that hardly merits scholarly attention."[9]

Marchal was no doubt speaking for himself, but his comment belies the historical importance of these writers. It was their legacy that not only gave us the idea of symbolism but also put Mallarmé on the map. They were the ones, after all, who made the trek to his Tuesday salon on the rue de Rome. Mallarmé has often been described as a precursor to the symbolists, yet it may be more accurate to say that after the death of Hugo, he became a new kind of spiritual leader, alongside Verlaine and Rimbaud.[10] All three of these "cursed poets" (*poètes maudits*, as Verlaine called them) became heroes for the younger generation, in part through their failure to enter the literary establishment. If the youth movement called symbolism had one unifying trait, it was this antiestablishment stance. The young poets saw the overblown verse of the academic elites as too much hot air. They liked to call it "literature."

By 1891, when Verlaine had penned his own academic joke, this sense of youthful rebellion was as evident in the mainstream press as in the *Chat noir*. Jules Huret had just launched a series on the symbolists in *L'Echo de Paris*. No fewer than sixty-four interviews with France's most prominent writers formed his "Inquiry into the Evolution of Literature," which ran for four months between March and July.[11] The tone was so inflammatory that gauntlets were thrown down. Anatole France and Leconte de Lisle took to pistols. Francis Vielé-Griffin and Catulle Mendès crossed swords.[12] Artistic squabbles are always amusing, but among the stories, there is one that deserves closer attention. Following Verlaine's death in 1896, the *Nouvelle Revue* ran its own piece on style evolutions—this time, by the former parliamentarian (and ultraconservative) Jules Delafosse.[13] Delafosse was hardly a literary man, although that did not stop him from pronouncing on modern poetry, and on the faults of Vielé-Griffin, in particular. So the younger poet, again on the defensive, shot back the following month from the pages of the *Mercure de France*.[14] He portrayed Delafosse as a foolish, befuddled *Bonapartiste* shouting from the Senate floor. It was a bizarre comeback, perhaps, but it forms a useful companion piece to our opening anecdote, suggesting a broader, more political context for the evolution of French symbolism.

Delafosse was in good form. Vielé-Griffin lets him do the talking, quoting the offending opinions word-for-word from the *Nouvelle Revue*. There is just one embellishment. In the retelling, the Senator's red-faced pronouncements are punctuated with italicized stage directions. The screed now reads like this:

> Why, they stick together completely unknown words! They put ... unintelligible epithets with unknown nouns, transpose or reform the ordinary meaning of verbs, and generally lead our good French language (*approval sounds from the right*) toward the uncertain and stammering forms of primitive men (*laughter*). Sometimes the sentences they eke out sound like vague bleatings, (*animal cries from some central benches*) ... or, what is worse, like the scribbling that schoolboys scrawl in the margins of their notebooks!"[15]

Delafosse went on to link this youthful wordplay to what was for him the most regrettable legacy of the Third Republic—the democratic reform of education. With the memory of that recent victory fueling his rage, he launched an outrageous peroration: "the literary youth of today, freshly hatched from this education, show an equal ignorance of dead and living languages. It's no wonder they understand Maeterlinck! These writers ... they are all ... the descendents of Jules Ferry!"[16] The conclusion—too good to resist—became Vielé-Griffin's title: "Jules Ferry: Father of Symbolism." And it was the ultimate putdown.[17] Still, in a perverse way, the gesture also pointed to an important truth, one we need to take on board if we ever hope to understand what these younger poets really stood for. Their linguistic sensibility could not help but reflect their republicanism—or, at least, what they saw as their unique historical moment. When Ferdinand Brunot observed in 1899 that "the forward march of democracy" had brought about a powerful change in French literature, he was talking about the very sort of writing that now enraged Delafosse. In Brunot's words, "the average, neutral and correct language of the bourgeois classes" had been "dispossessed by ... [modern] writers" and "invaded by the free and colorful speech of the popular classes."[18]

Brunot may have been thinking of the realist novel, but Verlaine's sonnet supplied an equally vivid example. With its attempt to transcribe the voice of the boulevard or the cabaret, it evoked not just the low pleasures of song but the deformations of argot—what Marcel Schwob and others called the *langue verte*.[19] This more inclusive idea of language put a different spin on free speech and turned the heads of the younger generation. The most important legacy of the period—*vers libre*—said it all, highlighting the *liberté* that was this generation's true inheritance. Pulling poetry from hallowed halls, the youth took to the streets and to the countryside, in the hope of finding a more full-bodied expression, an accent that was in every way the opposite of "literature." And this accent—the noisy, candid, liberated, and, above all, physical commotion of words—pointed the way to a very different art. We could probably call it, as the poets themselves did, "music."

———

But should we? Of all the trouble stirred up by these poets, the idea of music has certainly remained most troubling, as vague and confusing as the symbolist movement itself. Music was, on the one hand, a symbol of the poet's newfound freedom. "Music before all things!" Verlaine proclaimed, and the line—it is true—has the sound of a manifesto. And yet the music of language also meant something far more discreet. The linguists we met in the previous chapter heard verbal nuances, phonetic impressions, timbres. So did Verlaine. Two conditions thus present themselves: clamorous libertarianism or silent materialism. Modern poetry happily mixed them up, and so shall I. Rather than skirting the confusion, I want to confront it, as a way of developing my argument from chapter 2. Even if Jules Ferry was not the "father" of the symbolists, the poets encourage us to connect the dots. The newer, freer poetry they wrote—with its heady mix of republican ethics and modern phonetics— bore the twin marks of liberal politics and liberated, positive science.

And where, exactly, was music? That is a different question, one that becomes all the more pressing in a study concerned with the very real forms of music that defined the *mélodie*. And so my argument in this chapter has to reach in one more direction. To give fuller consideration to the musical culture that symbolism embraced, I need to hear out some of the composers who embraced symbolism, which means, finally, returning to themes left behind in chapter 1. French poets of the period may have called out to music, invoking the exquisite instrument of speech, but French musicians responded in kind, putting that instrument to work in different ways. Examining this reciprocal relation in two sets of songs by Fauré and Debussy reveals how (and even when) that instrument began to work on song. The exercise also exposes another, more liminal space of sung language—a space that is not exactly "music," making it, for this reason, one of modern song's most meaningful realms. We shall continue, though, with the poets, and with Verlaine above all. His disarmingly natural voice set the stage, defining the liberties young writers and composers now dared to take in the name of a radical new art.

Poetry and the People

Verlaine did not approve of the term *symbolism* or, at least, was never known to have used it. By the time Huret interviewed him for his 1891 *Enquête*, he claimed complete ignorance of the movement:

Symbolism?...Don't know...that must be a German word, eh? What could it mean? Oh, I don't much care myself. When I suffer, when I feel joy, when I cry, all I know is, that's not a symbol. You see, all these distinctions, they're Teutonicisms, aren't they? What do they have to do with a poet—those things that Kant, Schopenhauer, Hegel and all the other Krauts think about human feelings!...When I am unhappy, I write sad poetry—that's all!"[20]

The response charmed Huret as much as it has amused later generations. The image of the naïve poet who simply writes what he feels was certainly an "anti-intellectual affectation," as Marchal puts it. But that affectation upheld the most important aspect of the poet's literary persona, the idea of his sincerity.[21]

It was this quality, far more than the epithets *symbolist* or *decadent*, that defined the value of Verlaine's poetry for the generation of 1890, for the idea carried distinctly republican overtones. When Legouvé, in *Les Pères et les enfants au XIXe siècle* (1878), declared sincerity the new democratic duty,[22] he effectively renounced the false charms of aristocratic discourse, its verbal *politesse*. The view persisted among the poets of the next generations, in the form of a distinct skepticism toward rhetoric and eloquence. "Words are indeed tricky and untrustworthy things," wrote the writer and music critic Georges Jean-Aubry in a 1916 essay on Verlaine. "They are soft and resistant material; they can be stretched, molded in a moment; they are what you want when you don't feel what you mean."[23] And yet there was "no untrustworthy music." Music's essence "is *sincerity*," he said, "which is also the principal element of the work of Verlaine....From the moment it comes into existence, good or bad,...perverse or mystic, it is the sincere cry of his soul or his flesh."[24]

That cry had been heard at the start of one of Verlaine's most famous poems, "Art poétique," just two years before Moréas trumpeted the arrival of symbolism. If the opening line was the rallying cry, the subsequent stanzas made the case:

De la musique avant toute chose,
Et pour cela préfère l'Impair
Plus vague et plus soluble dans l'air
Sans rien en lui qui pèse ou qui pose.

Il faut aussi que tu n'ailles point
Choisir tes mots sans quelque méprise:
Rien de plus cher que la chanson grise
Où l'Indécis au Précis se joint.

> . . . .
> Car nous voulons la Nuance encore,
> Pas la Couleur, rien que la nuance!
> Oh, la nuance seule fiance
> Le rêve au rêve et la flûte au cor!
>
> . . . .
> Prends l'éloquence et tords-lui son cou!
> Tu feras bien, en train d'énergie,
> De rendre un peu la Rime assagie.
> Si l'on n'y veille, elle ira jusqu'où?

(Let's have music before all things, / And for that, prefer the Odd / which is vaguer, and dissolves more easily in the air, / with nothing heavy or ponderous about it. // You also mustn't / choose your words without some misprision: / There's nothing dearer than the tipsy song / Where Undefined and Exact combine. // [. . .] For we want Nuance again. / Not local color, but Nuance! / Oh! Nuance alone binds dream to dream and the flute to the horn! // [. . .] Take Eloquence and wring its neck! You'd do well, in the process, / to hold your Rhyme in check / If you don't watch her, she'll go who knows where?//)

Verlaine called for a whole slew of quirky reforms. "Prefer the Odd," he said, and it is hard not to think of the peculiar phonetic sonnet from the beginning of this chapter. He meant odd meters, of course, as opposed to the more typical ten- or twelve-syllable lines of academic verse. ("Art poétique" featured lines of nine.) But that was not all. While arguing for the virtues of slack rhyme, he advised quashing eloquence for good: death by strangling. Forget French wit, he seemed to say. Leave behind the pearly word. Misprision beat precision. The real mot juste was nuance, a strange place of dreams where flutes and horns combined in unspeakable candor. The sentiment was hardly revolutionary, but it did suggest another sort of emancipation. Liberated by music to say nothing at all, the poem could take flight toward "other skies."

> De la musique encore et toujours!
> Que ton vers soit la chose envolée
> Qu'on sent qui fuit d'une âme en allée
> Vers d'autres cieux è d'autres amours.
>
> Que ton vers soit la bonne aventure
> Éparse au vent crispé du matin
> Qui va fleurant la menthe et le thym . . .
> Et tout le reste est littérature.

(Let's have music forever! So that your poetry might be a winged thing / Such as one feels when a soul alights / Towards other skies and other loves. // So let your poems be a happy venture / scattered in the brisk morning wind / flowering with mint and thyme . . . / Anything else is just literature. //)

The closing benediction painted a perfect image of such liberation. It enjoined fellow poets to make verses pure enough that they might be "scattered to the morning wind, smelling of mint and thyme," like a rustic chanson sung *en plein air*. Anything more (or less) than that, the stanza famously concluded, shouldn't be called poetry at all. The parting shot summed up the attitude of the idealistic poets of the 1890s. Verlaine linked the poetic art with a new more, natural voice—a voice that the younger generation now believed they heard in their midst: the unpretentious accent of the people.

Jean-Aubry picked up on such populism in 1916 when he described the deceased Verlaine as "something akin to a street singer." But the sentiment went back to the first generation of symbolists—the followers of Verlaine who saw their art, again, as a reflection of a new socialist sensibility. Most made their living not through poetry but through journalism. The newspaper and the revue became, then, the natural platform for their progressive literary ideas. I want to single out one of these figures, the poet Robert de Souza, who, though little known today, was a prolific apologist for his cohort. An "immaculate figure with a severe visage and a monocle,"[25] de Souza wrote essays for the most radical magazines, including *Mercure de France, Entretiens politiques et littéraires*, and *Gil Blas*. In the 1890s, under the auspices of the *Mercure de France*, he brought out an important essay on the subject of "popular" poetry, which exposes quite clearly the values of his generation. A new interest in folk poetry had sent all kinds of collectors into the field, "armed with their pens," he said, "just as magicians of old had their divining rods."[26] But the symbolists were the only ones to get it right. They had divined the true source, de Souza argued, the lyric current that could (and did) save modern poetry from itself. It is worth taking a moment to follow this argument, for it affords another, more pointed view of the politics of modern verse.

———

Where was the real attraction of rustic song? For the young poets, it was in the sound, with its "brusqueness of accent, [its] strong sensations coming from the throat." More conservative writers reacted differently to such full-bodied utterance. While charmed by the candor, they could hardly tolerate the cadence: in de Souza's words, they "take out their polishing cloth, remove all repetition, correct each rhyme, rearrange the strophes in a logical line, weigh and unify the syllables, thereby realizing a little masterpiece of bourgeois poetry."[27] One of the more notable polishers was the poet Gabriel Vicaire, a notorious pastiche artist who in 1885 had lampooned the moderns in his *Les Déliquescences d'Adoré Floupette*. This was a fictitious book of "decadent" poems that parodied the unorthodox forms and extravagant vocabulary of poets like Verlaine and Mallarmé.[28] De Souza now turned the tables, scoring a point against the parodist. Vicaire's chansons may have been rustic knockoffs, but his critical essays went straight to the point. Here is Vicaire discussing "the popular poetry of Bresse and Bugey":

> Certainly the verse is clumsy, but it nonetheless flows. The rhythm is not always easily distinguished, but one can be sure it exists. Rhyme is replaced by assonance, but the music loses nothing because of it. The feet are infinitely varied, but does it matter? *For what we have, it seems, is a malleable, almost fluid material, capable of lengthening or shortening at will.*[29]

De Souza considered it a brilliant insight, worthy of Julien Tiersot—the great collector whose modern editions of *chansons populaires* had been educating French audiences for more than a decade.[30] But the praise was double-edged. If Vicaire's last phrase rang bells (the italics are de Souza's), it was because it seemed to describe the increasingly free verses now being written by the younger generation, the very poets Vicaire had mocked. The sentence offered a neat formula for their modern poetics, while revealing the purity of its source. The bourgeois Vicaire unwittingly endorsed the sincerity of the symbolists.

Such pastoral ethics had, of course, informed Verlaine's own *art poétique*, from the simple music of *La Bonne Chanson* (1869) to the more confessional tone of *Sagesse* (1881). But the new poets had gone further. Fashioning their own verses out of a "malleable and fluid material" of mixed meters and flexible rhymes, the young writers of free verse did not merely mimic the forms of popular poetry. In de Souza's view, they had tapped into its source, a kind of primitive lyric unconscious. Younger poets like Mauclair liked to call this pure poetic stuff (as we saw in chapter 1) *le "lied."*[31] Vielé-Griffin heard it as "the authentic, distant and anonymous voice . . . of human emoting [*l'émotivité humaine*]."[32] The old chanson thus raised the stakes. Modern writers saw themselves digging into poetry's humble past, and the vision offered them just what they had been looking for: a way out of the stultifying world of "literature." Sense gave way to sensation; poetry found a brusquer tone. But the critics, of course, had missed all this by viewing the younger poets as decadents. That was the view de Souza was determined to change.

In a way, it still needs changing, which is why it seems useful to follow de Souza's argument to its end. Our modern histories continue to treat symbolism as a murky moment in French literature, filled with precious or difficult poets—most of whom we no longer take seriously. De Souza saw it differently. He considered the new poetry more precise than precious and thus called his book a "positivist" study (*une étude positive*). The writers he defended were sincere young men who, "with the aid of new techniques," had made a remarkable discovery: as he put it, "the simultaneous and immediate *refraction* of what we think through what we see, hear, taste, smell, and touch."[33] The image of refraction, the bending of light through a prism, may suggest the techniques of observation we commonly associate with painterly impressionism. As de Souza now insisted, it also defined the essence of what his generation called *symbolisme*.

Impressionism of thought implied democracy of feeling, and that implication, in turn, brought on de Souza's most radical claim. The new poetic techniques, he said, had led the symbolists to their "true audience." Who were these perfect listeners? Not conservatives like Vicaire or Delafosse, certainly, and not fellow poets, either. No, de Souza actually meant the unlettered masses—those citizens who "had no need of words for their feelings to be carried away by a color or a sound."[34] The sentiment recalls the populism of Verlaine's phonetic sonnet, with its "unlettered" orthography, though de Souza was poking no fun. By his logic, demoting letters and literature actually elevated verse. Of the three poetic registers—"art," "bourgeois," and "popular"—the bourgeois was the most unwelcome term.[35] And the symbolists had tried to do something about it. They had tried, he said, "to destroy its prosaic influence" by merging their art with the popular, embracing the knobby irregularities of the chanson, and refusing to produce those polished gems "dear to poets like Gabriel Vicaire."

> The new poets have not dragged a trunk load of old rules and old meters into the thatch.... They've not sought to offload their soul [onto the countryside].... They've simply led it into the solitude of the clearings and the furrows; and there, picking up the shepherds' flutes, they adjust their breath to the most subtle of rustic keyholes, and sing, like the wind in the trees, beneath the exaltation of mysteries that assault you when you openly and frankly abandon yourself to nature.[36]

The piping of the afternoon of a faun. Like Verlaine, Mallarmé had also spoken of the need to give the old poetic forms some air, especially the prosodic conventions that had dominated French poetry for two centuries.[37] The younger poets were merely following suit. Adjusting their breath to the task, trusting the natural sound of words to bring out deeper and somehow more intuitive meanings, they would eventually leave the rules behind— which meant, of course, abandoning classic prosody altogether.

I return later in the chapter to the precise forms taken by their newly freed verse. But for now it should be clear that the freedoms claimed by the young writers reflected, in a larger sense, the idealism of their generation. If detractors like Delafosse complained that the symbolists had taken undue liberties, perverting a "beautiful French language" that was supposed to unify the nation, the poets could answer that their work represented the values of the nation all the more deeply, for they embraced the idea of the people that France's liberal republic brought into view.

Richard Candida Smith has seconded the opinion. In his history of "Mallarmé's children," he observes some of the ways the symbolists mixed poetics with politics.[38] Through Mallarmé's example, Edouard Dujardin became a committed socialist; Camille Mauclair and Gustave Kahn, card-carrying anarchists. This radical stance may help to explain one aspect of their poetic production, the "considerable pride" they took, as Smith puts it, "in having narrowed the distance between poetic language and popular speech."[39] But according to Smith, such pride was false. "There is little evidence," he concludes, "that their work was shaped . . . by recording or studying contemporary usage."

The skepticism is apt. The hybrid accent de Souza discovered hardly resulted from intensive fieldwork, although he would later try to transcribe this sound directly, as we shall see. And yet Smith's objection says nothing about what (or how) the new poets *were* hearing. What of the flute and horn that materialize in the middle of Verlaine's "Art poétique"? More than a convenient pastoral topos, the orchestral image presents us with a different sort of clue, like a queer refraction of something heard. Verlaine called this refraction "nuance," and the word was more polemical than precious. The nuance was meant to disrupt the classic order of the verse in precisely the same way Verlaine's phonetic sonnet disrupted the order of the page. Even if this nuance was not, in any strict sense, a "recording of contemporary usage," it could nonetheless be seen as a kind of record. We might think of it as evidence of the very encounter the poets themselves were narrating: what remained when the French poetic tradition came face to face with its other. Verlaine obviously pointed the way to this encounter, but Rimbaud and Mallarmé met it head-on, revealing a poetry more fully "carried away by color and sound," to use de Souza's words. One early poem by Rimbaud is a rare case in point and, for this reason, worth looking at—and listening to—more closely.

Vibrations of Language

I am speaking of Rimbaud's famous sonnet from 1872, usually regarded as a textbook example of symbolist aesthetics. He called it "Voyelles" (Vowels).

> A noir, E blanc, I rouge, U vert, O bleu: voyelles,
> Je dirai quelque jour vos naissances latentes:
> A, noir corset velu des mouches éclatantes
> Qui bombinent autour des puanteurs cruelles,
>
> Golfes d'ombre; E, candeurs des vapeurs et des tentes,
> Lances des glaciers fiers, rois blancs, frissons d'ombelles;
> I, pourpres, sang craché, rire des lèvres belles
> Dans la colère ou les ivresses pénitentes;
>
> U, cycles, vibrements divins des mers virides
> Paix des pâtis semés d'animaux, paix des rides
> Que l'alchimie imprime aux grands fronts studieux;
>
> O, suprême Clairon plein des strideurs étranges,
> Silences traversés des Mondes et des Anges:
> —O l'Oméga, rayon violet de Ses Yeux!

> (Black A, white E, red I, green U, O blue: vowels, / Someday I will sing your secret births: / A, hairy black corset of bursting flies / That buzz around cruel stenches, // Shadowy gulfs; E, whiteness of vapors and tents, /Spears of proud glaciers, white kings, umbelled shivers; / I, purples, spit blood, laughter of pretty lips / In anger or in bouts of penitent drunkenness; // U, cycles, divine vibrations of verdigris seas, / Peace of pastures speckled with animals, peace of the ridges / That alchemy imprints on great, studious foreheads; // O, supreme Clarion full of strange, strident tones, / Silences passed through Worlds and Angels: /—O, Omega, violet ray of Your Eyes!)

"Someday I'll tell of your hidden births." The opening lines read like a hallucination, taking Verlaine's idea of nuance to new and extravagant heights. The impression is only strengthened in Rimbaud's notorious auto-biography, *A Season in Hell*. "I invented the color of the vowels!—black A, white E, red I, blue O, green U.—," he decreed. "I regulated the form and movement of each consonant, . . . flattering myself that I had invented a poetic word that might one day be accessible to all the senses."[40] The reminiscence finished with a tease, implying there was more to *Voyelles* than the reader might suspect. He simply said: "I withheld the translation." And a century's worth of commentators took the bait, trying to fill the blank the poet so enticingly left.[41]

I am no exception: the poem is hard to resist. It unfolds as a series of substitutions, a colorful chain of *correspondances* that turn the vowels into ever more fantastic forms. The black *A*, bottom of the alphabet, immediately morphs, for example, into another kind of fundament (in Latin, *anus*), carrying its own unexpected associations: rank, hairy, fit for buzzing flies. The *E* temporarily dispels this vision with a purifying whiteness, but it goes in two directions. The candor of that vowel the French call *e muet* (extended and intensified in the [oe] of *candeur* and *vapeur*) soon yields to the prick of another: the so-called acute *é* (of *glacier* and *fier*), with its thrusting diacritic, suggesting Rimbaud's noble lance.

Such graphic puns continue. If the *I* of *rire* recalls laughing red mouths, the slack *U* becomes a classic V, to produce, more pointedly, a whole cycle of "divine vibrations" (*vibrements divins*). These come to rest in more peaceful pastures (*pâtis*), a word whose conspicuous circumflex (ˆ), writ large, will produce one further association: a V-shaped wrinkle on an overlarge brow.[42] But the culminating *O* pulls together this fantasy on the material sign. The vowel is not only an evocative shape (in Latin, an *annulus*, or ring) but also a number (zero); not only a sound (*o*) but also a word (*Oh!*). The *O* thus completes the chain of correspondences—Alpha to Omega, anus to annulus—calling out to itself (Oh, O!) in an apostrophe the poem will never answer.[43]

Trumpeting the sonnet's ending, Rimbaud's *O* thus exhibits the same kind of hallucinatory nuance Verlaine had imagined, as "dream binds to dream and flute to horn." For Rimbaud, though, it is clearly a disturbing noise ("plein des strideurs étranges"), one that has been predicted already in the poem's second line: "je dirai quelque jour vos naissances latentes." Here the verb *dirai* is key, referring to a state somewhere between "singing" and "saying" (in Old French it meant both). It speaks to the vowel's "hidden birth" in the throat, suggesting the pure diction of language that makes letters of the alphabet come to life.

In this sense, the poem's clamorous end is doubly anticipated, for the buzzing flies of the first stanza are, after all, just as noisy. They form a shrewd aural metaphor for the sound of the *A* itself, the richest and most open vowel, a dark color produced from the "shadowy gulfs" of a very open mouth. In a similar way, passing through the blankness of the *oe*, the sharpness of the *é*, we can almost taste the grimace of the back-vowel *I*, pulling the lips into a questionable smile; we can feel the more complex vibrations of the French *U*, which modifies the *I* with a visible puckering of the lips. To *tell* the poem, to say it aloud (*dire*), is to experience its "color" in a directly physical way. The act of speaking, filtering noise through the mouth's chambers, yields not just words and images but distinct sonorities. And this colorful vocal nuance— the sound of vowels—is what acousticians and phoneticians like to call, more properly, *timbre*.

Timbre is thus the most hidden dimension of Rimbaud's vowel poem, and surely the most significant. Rimbaud, at least, appeared to be unmanned by this invisible aspect of his creation, and it is worth trying to understand why. Writing to Paul Demeny in 1871, he described exactly what poetry had done to him, beginning with the now infamous line: *JE est un autre*. The twisted sentence was followed by an equally twisted analogy, one that recalled the unsettling conclusion of *Voyelles*: "For 'I' is an Other. If the brass wakes up as a bugle, you can hardly blame it. This much is clear: I am attending the opening of my thought; I watch it, listen to it; I sound the first bow stroke: the symphony begins its soft murmuring from the back, or arrives all at once on the stage in a single bound."[44] Something strange is going on. Here, as in the last tercet of "Voyelles," Rimbaud conjures an uncanny bugle, a *clairon plein de strideurs étranges*, as if to say: "Oh, O!" Reveille has had a revelation. The poem, like Rimbaud's "JE," has come ear to ear with its other. This other is not exactly music. It is an obliquely sonorous quality of the self, like the bugle's brass,[45] the gut of strings. Taking up his instrument, Rimbaud in a single stroke becomes both concertmaster and versifier, and he discovers an unsettling resonance in the process: the blare or ping or pluck of poetic thought.

This is just the sort of resonance we need to hear in order to catch the full impact of Rimbaud's invention. And yet the condition leaves us in an interpretive bind. How do we appreciate this uncanny concert that Rimbaud himself attends? How, more basically, do we attend to timbre? The linguists we met in the previous chapter had one way of answering. If their graphic solutions were a kind of linguistic aide-mémoire, they did not resolve the more basic problem, because such pictures could not define, exactly, what timbre was. And it is no wonder. Timbre has always been resistant to definition.[46] It is probably worth taking another moment, then, to think about its meaning for French symbolism. Understanding timbre should offer us a new angle on both the aesthetics and the ethics of this poetry, for it created not just new standards of poetic conduct but a whole new impression of what French verse could be.

Part of the problem of definition may be that, as an acoustic phenomenon, timbre represents a second-order concept. That, at least, is what the etymology suggests. The Old French *timbre* derives from the Greek *tympanon*, or drum (from which we get *timbrel* and *tympani*), implying a physical form, a skin or parchment stretched across a frame. Like the sensitive skin of the middle ear (also called the tympanum, or eardrum), this taut surface, ready to be struck, is a site for both receiving and producing vibrations. In musical usage, timbre retains this two-sidedness. On the one hand, it is the sonorous property that distinguishes one sound from the next, a property deriving from a prior moment of impact: a unique pattern of overtones that strikes the ear and leaves its own "vibration impression." On the other, it suggests the actual material of the blow, the wood, gut, brass, or skin from which the impression emanates. Like the idea of the *tympanon* itself, timbre is both noise and source, drum and accent.

Jacques Derrida once famously explored this metaphor as a productive figure for the philosophical project of deconstruction. In the essay that opens his 1972 collection *Marges de la philosophie*, the tympanum appears as the site where philosophy catches its most crucial blow: in the attempt to think its "other" or, as Derrida puts it, "that which limits it, and from which it derives its essence, its definition, its production."[47] The analogy proves useful to a study of the deconstructive project we call symbolism, for symbolism defined itself on the same kind of threshold: the point where poetry dared to confront that other it called music.[48] What happens to a poetry that attempts to think music? And what happens to music in that thinking? This was, in essence, the twin question the young writers faced. Confronting it was a blow to the poetic imagination, producing a new threshold, one that redefined both music and poetry because it belonged properly to neither sphere. If Derrida marked philosophy's limit in the form of the tympanum, lying obliquely across inner and outer ear, the young symbolists sensed the edge of their own practice in an equally skewed space, one that remained both other to and constitutive of their experience of the poem: in short, as timbre.[49]

This was exactly the blow that struck Rimbaud, and the repercussions were shocking: "Look," he said to Demeny. "I is an orchestra." A statement of existential alienation became a confession about perception—about watching oneself hear something *else*, the obliqueness of a language. Soon enough, though, the new generation came to expect this sort of hearing, imagining with it a whole new poetic "instrument." One writer in particular is worth mentioning: a young Belgian called Réné Ghil. An admirer of both Rimbaud and Mallarmé, he is known today for a collection of essays he brought out in 1885 on symbolist poetics, the *Traité du Verbe* (*Treatise on the Word*).[50] The volume's final essay offered an elaborate case for what Ghil admiringly called "Poetic Instrumentation." Taking off from Rimbaud's orchestral hallucination, Ghil set out to define the idea of timbre—the "color of vowels"—not just as the common practice but as common sense.

Wagner played a distinctive role in this reinterpretation. Ghil, like Wagner, spoke of the expressive arts "losing themselves in total Communion" and of poetry as "the one Divinity." And if spectators tended to describe Wagner's music in terms of vision, décor, light, the same terms could apply to the effects of modern poetry. Ghil reasoned: "If sound can be translated into color, color can be translated into sound, and straightaway into instrumental timbre. That's the whole stroke of inspiration."[51] Writing verse, in other words, became like orchestration as vowels turned musical and the sound of poetry recalled the distinctive accents of brass, woodwinds, and strings. Rimbaud was to be praised for imagining his vowels in this way, but Ghil nonetheless thought the colors could use some adjusting. He proposed an alternative sequence (*A* black, *E* white, *I* blue, *O* red, *U* yellow) and insisted on a more precise instrumental translation (*A* organs, *E* harps, *I* violins, *O* brass, *U* flutes). And for that, he caught some flack. Verlaine quipped, "Ghil est un imbécile."[52] But Ghil himself remained unfazed and included a long footnote in the treatise's second edition to defend the claims. The orchestration fell in line, after all, with the "formidable discoveries" of Helmholtz. "Every musical instrument [has] its own harmonic series, from which it derives its timbre," he wrote. In this way "VOWELS ought to be compared to INSTRUMENTS, for the instrument of the human voice is a nothing but a reed ... completed by a resonator of variable resonance."[53] Through this fundamental connection between sound and color, voice and instrument, Ghil proclaimed a new poetic order in which "words might sound out in notes." Still, the ideal reed he had in mind was not the voice of Rimbaud. He had heard it piping, as de Souza did, in a work Ghil now held up on the final page of his treatise: Mallarmé's eclogue, *L'Après-midi d'un faune*.

Mallarmé thus had the last word in Ghil's *Treatise on the Word*. But he also had the first, for Ghil had convinced him to supply the book's preface. Mallarmé used the space to formulate a few rare claims of his own, producing a first take on a more important discourse, what would eventually become the end of his 1895 Oxford lecture, "Crise de vers." More than a century later, it may seem troubling to find Mallarmé in the company of a second-rate Belgian, promoting a kooky theory about vocal orchestration. But that trouble is key. Indeed, reading *through* Ghil, we may begin to see Mallarmé's poetic "instrument"—and its timbre—from a whole new angle.

———

Mallarmé began by praising Ghil, of course, but his preface addressed broader trends in modern poetry. "An undeniable desire of the present era is to separate, by virtue of different attributes, the double state of speech," he wrote, "raw and immediate on the one hand, essential on the other."[54] The passage, though much discussed in the Mallarmé literature, merits another look. It is tempting, for example, to read it as a kind of commentary on the new generation of poets, most of whom lived double lives (as Mallarmé himself did) as practicing journalists.[55] The "double state of speech" suggested two very different kinds of exchange for Mallarmé. Communication—the most "immediate" form—was the crudest. Language was commerce, he said, like taking a bit of change out of one's pocket and "placing [it] silently into another's hand." The word became common coin; poetry went begging. But the scenario also raised a question: "What good," he went on, "is the marvel of transposing a fact of nature into its near vibratory disappearance in the play of speech if it is not so that the pure idea, having nothing at all to pay back, might emanate from it?"[56]

Here, in effect, was the other side of the coin. Mallarmé's question imagined a purer language of vibration—speech's other—existing apart from the immediacy of representation or communication. He evoked the "double state" of the word in the very rhetoric of the passage, which played on the difference between an initial (grounded) statement and a second (floating) question, isolating the "free play of speech" from what he grimly called *reportage*. Then, as if to enact this difference, he changed course. Shifting his tone of voice in the next sentence, he offered an example. It is the best-known passage of the essay, perhaps of the whole Mallarmé oeuvre.[57] It begins: *Je dis: une fleur!* "I say: a flower! And, out of the oblivion where my voice banishes no contour, what rises up musically (as something other than the lilies I have known) is this laughing or perverse idea: the absent thing of all bouquets."[58] A long history of criticism has tended to focus on the absence, the negation, the virtuality of Mallarmé's lilies, reading the "something other" in these lines as a figure for the pure "idea" that supposedly formed the raison d'être of his verse. Without disrupting the critical consensus, we might read this absent thing in a slightly different way, taking our cue from Mallarmé's exclamation point, and also from his first two words: *je dis*. As we saw in Rimbaud's *Voyelles*, this verb, caught between singing and saying, suggests an object on the musical edge of speech. But Mallarmé's tense punctuation tells more. *Je dis: une fleur!* Between colon and exclamation point lies a taut, stretched space, on which another kind of flower will blossom: a poem. When deed is done, what remains of the poetic impulse is not just the page (which, like a drum, can be made to sound again) but something else: an accent, an outline, a distinct aural impression. This total sonorous imprint might also be called, once again, the poem's timbre.

In an essay on "Poetry and Abstract Thought," Paul Valéry made a very similar point in different terms, and the differences turn out to be instructive. Like Mallarmé, he, too. would begin by distinguishing the function (or fate) of utilitarian speech from that of poetry. In the first instance, he said, "Speech is completely replaced by its *meaning*, that is, by images, impulses, reactions, or acts that [now] belong to you."[59] This acquisitive aspect recalled Mallarmé's metaphor of currency and exchange, but Valéry elevated the comparison, connecting the goal of such speech to an ideal of transparent thought. "The perfection of this kind of language," he wrote, "consists in the ease with which it is transformed into something altogether different." The words themselves could disappear, that is, while making sense in someone else's mind. A poem never achieved that kind of transparency, and for Valéry, the failure defined its most admirable trait: "The poem . . . does not die for having lived. It is expressly designed to be born again . . . to become endlessly what it has just been. Poetry can be recognized by this property—that it tends to *get itself reproduced in its own form*."[60]

The idea of verbal reproduction suggested an impact of a different kind, as if a poem's form itself constituted a material "imprint," referring as much to something one can see on the printed page as to something one hears: the aural impression left by the poem, its *timbre*. The allusion to printing is, in this sense, doubly meaningful. The French word *timbre* also means stamp. This usage probably harks back to the *tympan* of the manual printing press, referring to the piece of material inserted between the platen and the type bed to even out the impression. As an object—a cloth or parchment stretched across a wooden frame—it forms an obvious connection to the frame drum or *tympanon* of antiquity. But it is the function of this skin that matters. To return to Derrida for a moment, one could say that this tympan works much like the threshold of the inner ear. Mediating the space between paper and metal, page and type, it marks the site of the first blow—of a powerful impression that nonetheless leaves no ink.

The connotation could hardly have been lost on Mallarmé, famous for his typographic fussiness. It is well known that as his career wore on, he became increasingly (almost obsessively) involved in the bibliographic production of his poems. The eclogue *L'Après-midi d'un faune* was an early but telling case in point. The poem mixed italic and roman type and featured unconventional white spaces that broke up lines of verse like page turns in a virtual book.[61] But Mallarmé's greatest coup was surely his last published work, *Un Coup de dès jamais n'abolira le hasard* (*A Throw of the Dice Will Never Abolish Chance*).[62] First printed in 1897 in the London literary magazine *Cosmopolis*, the venturesome prose text, with its extraordinary typographic freedoms, could be described as one of the first sustained projects of poetic deconstruction (Figure 3.1). As such, it offers another, more legible image of how Mallarmé's poetry was beginning to think, or rethink, the idea of music.

The magazine's editors put the matter bluntly: in this work, they said, Mallarmé had "endeavored to make music with words." The poet himself was more circumspect. True, he compared the poem's layout to a kind of music notation. The type was meant to convey both the character and intonation of the delivery, he said. But readers would be just as concerned with what the page did *not* say. The white surface struck first. "Versification requires it," he argued, "like surrounding silence, so that ordinarily in a piece of lyric poetry, or even in smaller forms, [the white space] occupies on average a third of the page." His next point was key: "I don't transgress this measurement," he said. "I simply disperse it. The paper intervenes each time an image, of itself, ceases or comes back."[63]

This scattering of words across a blank expanse has suggested many things to Mallarmé's readers: the trail of a ship's wake; the black and white of dice; nocturnal constellations. But the typographic dispersal of *Un Coup de dès* might also be read more basically—even primally—as the record of a moment of impact, a blow that has produced on the page a shock, like sound waves rising from a drum's vibrating surface. Mallarmé mused about a certain "simultaneous vision" afforded by the pages of his poem, allowing the text to be perceived all at once, as in an orchestral score. Still, the all-at-once-ness points to hearing as much as reading, not just the legible score but an audible symphony. The perception may even recall Rimbaud's symphony, "arriving all at once" on the stage of his thought. There, too, the symphonic noise represented a kind of shock or blow: in French, *un coup*. Rimbaud spoke of a "stroke of the bow" (*un coup d'archet*). Mallarmé imagined *un coup de dès*. In each case, the *coup* leads back to the ear, thus to the *tympanum* and the more primary meaning of *timbre*. Mallarmé's page becomes, all at once, like an eardrum: a taut white skin that, struck by language, strikes back (the brass rouses the bugler!), dispersing the poem in a shock of sound.

This is not exactly "music," of course. And that is the point. The musical quality that seems to haunt modern French verse in the last decades of the nineteenth century is strange, disturbing, even shocking, precisely because it is not exactly music. It can no longer be grasped, in all the easy ways, as the

c'était

issu stellaire

le nombre

EXISTÂT-IL
autrement qu'hallucination éparse d'agonie

COMMENÇAT-IL ET CESSÂT-IL
sourdant que nié et clos quand apparu
enfin
par quelque profusion répandue en rareté
SE CHIFFRÂT-IL

évidence de la somme pour peu qu'une
ILLUMINÂT-IL

ce serait

pire
non
davantage ni moins
mais autant indifféremment

LE HASARD

(Choit
la plume

FIGURE 3.1 Mallarmé, *Un Coup de dès jamais n'abolira le hasard.* Extract from first printing, in *Cosmopolis* (May 1897)

music of poetry. Nor does it sit comfortably among the more obviously musical elements of music, namely, pitch and rhythm. Timbre forms a kind of negative remainder, beginning where notions of pitch and rhythm leave off. As a perceptual quality, it is a queer boundary, poised at the limit of both poetry and music, informing and receding from both, like the "paper that intervenes," as Mallarmé put it, "each time an image, of itself, ceases or comes back." In other words, like a tympan.

This oblique threshold of the manual printing press is in some ways a perfect metaphor for the quality of music experienced by the symbolists. Site of an initial blow, the image of the tympan allows us to conceptualize, in a different way, the powerful refraction of poetic thought that worried the young poets of the 1890s. A piece of parchment, stretched between the type bed and the platen, made the impression stick in much the same way timbre aids in the perception of sound: enabling the production of multiple (sound) "types." It is, in fact, at the level of production that we begin to see how closely this impression connects to the other side of poetic performance, itself stretched obliquely across language and music: what the French call *diction*. We have already seen the significance of this word for Rimbaud and Mallarmé. In *Voyelles*, Rimbaud's *dire* signaled the speech act that gave birth to the vowel's presence: *Je dirai quelque jour vos naissances latentes.* For Mallarmé, it was almost a manifesto. *Je dis: une fleur!* The line reenacted in its material form the idea of the poem's sonorous impulse. The exclamation made diction (*je dis*) equivalent to this impulse, the *coup* producing the *fleur* we know as timbre. Here, however, what hit the ear was the not a single instrument or voice, but the sound of a whole tongue: in a word, its accent.

Accentus/ad cantus

A theory of modern poetry thus returns us to the same intangible material that captivated the phonologists of our previous chapter. The path from Rimbaud's *clairon* to Mallarmé's *coup* could be seen, in fact, as following a very similar trajectory. If, like Rimbaud, Paul Passy had fussed over the shading of vowels, the Abbé Rousselot, like Mallarmé, went on to capture whole sentences, developing instruments that made the spoken object hit the page all at once. Viewed in light of Mallarmé's typographic extremes, Rousselot's transcriptions, in fact, make quite a different impression. His reading of *La Chanson de Roland*, for example (Figures 2.6 and 2.7) offered its own version of an orchestrated speech act—a kind of *instrumentation parlée*.

Still more striking is the chronology. Rousselot was taking such readings in 1897, the very year Mallarmé set out to record the complex thrum of language in *Un Coup de dès*. I am not suggesting that Rousselot took inspiration from modern poetry, nor Mallarmé from a laboratory at the Collège de France. And yet it does seem significant that at the same historical moment, experimental scientists and experimental poets were tuning their ears, and their instruments, to the same elusive thing.

It was the generation of poets who followed Mallarmé—writers like Vielé-Griffin, de Souza, and Ghil—who tried, as we have seen, to bring this elusive thing down to earth. The accent of language, the "strong sensations coming from the throat," became the basis of their reformist practice and, more immediately, a brand new concept of rhythm. Marching to the beat of a different timbre, the symbolists also rethought conventional prosody, making it count in entirely new ways. And we may now be in a position to hear their counting differently. If the poetic stakes now had to do with the sound of a whole tongue, then the French accent would naturally affect not just poetry's sound but also its "beat." Timbre, in other words, offers us an even more productive way to understand the rhythm of modern poetry and thus to grasp what, exactly, the young poets of free verse were actually freeing.

Let's take the verse forms themselves. The alexandrine, for one, was about to be relieved of a few hundred years of baggage. Cornerstone of academic verse since at least the sixteenth century, its classic structure of two matched hemistichs (six syllables each) had undergone a well-known strain at the hands of the Romantics, who preferred more varied subdivisions without the binary split. The younger symbolists strained it further, to the point of breaking with convention altogether. Mallarmé pointed to this phenomenon, ironically, when he announced a "crisis" of French poetry in 1895. *On a touché au vers!* ("They have tampered with our verse!"), he exclaimed at the beginning of that famous lecture, predicting the end of the academic tradition. Two years later, on the heels of Mallarmé's *Coup*, Gustave Kahn put the matter more pragmatically. "We scan our poetry," he shrugged, "in the tone of conversation."[64]

According to the younger poets, then, it was plain talking that had produced the freer rhythms of their free verse, and Kahn saw the development as a very good thing. In his explanatory "Préface sur le vers libre" (1897), he defended the point at length, turning first to the poets of the great French tradition. Even Racine revealed more liberties when spoken aloud. The classic alexandrines of *Athalie*, for example, created an effect quite other than twelve equal beats cut by a central caesura. Kahn scanned the opening couplet: "Oui je viens—dans son temple—adorer—l'Eternel / Je viens—

selon usage—antique—et solonnel." The way he heard it, the cadence was a play of shifting strokes—phrases of three, followed by two and four (as his own notation tried to show). Following the "tone of conversation," rhythm became malleable, a function of the diction. The syllable, in this sense, was no longer a quantity but a quality, not number but timbre.

Once the symbolists had learned to follow the delicacy of their own ears, as Valéry once put it, they stopped counting syllables entirely, listening only to gently lapping waves. *Des mirages de leur visages garde le lac de mes yeux*: Kahn included this original line in his "Préface" as a telling example of the new verse, and of everything the alexandrine was not.[65] It was not twelve syllables, for one thing; the actual count could vary, depending on the speaker. Kahn advocated the most unpretentious diction, where the so-called mute *e* retreated, naturally, as in conversational French.[66] What counted in the end was the cadence, the five malleable beats:

1	2	3	4	5
˘ ˘ —	˘ ˘ ˘ —	—	˘ —	˘ ˘ —

Des mirag(e)s—de leur visag(e)s—gard(e)—le lac—de mes yeux.

The rhythm of free verse turned organic as poetry dug down to its source, remembering the accent of another time and place, not in far-off Alexandria but on native soil: the ancient lied of the French vernacular tradition. It was in following this lied that the poets believed they had come one step closer to music. The concept of *accentus* derived, after all, from the Latin *ad* + *cantus*, "toward song."

This was the same logic de Souza invoked, of course, when he linked the liberal practices of the free-verse poets to an ancient *poésie populaire*. But de Souza would eventually have much, much more to say about rhythm. The topic almost became a personal obsession as the century came to an end. Indeed, after the death of Mallarmé in 1898, when journalists were sounding a death knell for symbolism, and after poets like Henri de Régnier (and the fickle Moréas) were disavowing their own early experiments with free verse, de Souza redoubled his commitment to the cause. Casting about for more robust methods, he set out to prove what Kahn himself had claimed: that the free accent of *vers libre*—the material truth of symbolism—existed not just in theory but in practice, in the way people actually spoke the language.

He found what he was looking for in an unlikely place. Not in the countryside, nor on the street, but in a Parisian laboratory. That's right: de Souza finally made good on the desire to record and study contemporary usage by joining forces with the phoneticians. With Rousselot as his guide, he began conducting experiments to locate poetry's elusive accent and finally take its measure.[67] "Some people think," he joked, "that I have gone off to manufacture poetry at the Collège de France." But his concerns lay less with fabrication than with education. In a way, his complaint about the state of modern poetry echoed the chant of educational reformers. "They do not know how to read!" he would lament, speaking not of provincial schoolchildren but of his own educated generation, especially trained poets, "incapable of finessing the beats of the simplest alexandrine."[68] The whole controversy surrounding *vers libre* came down to this simple fact. Years of faulty teaching had destroyed the rhythmic sensitivity of the literate. The only remedy was to become resensitized—which was precisely what de Souza wanted. He would substantiate, with the aid of Rousselot's impartial machines, "the *reality* of the harmonic and rhythmic phenomena produced within the poet's song."[69]

His work began simply enough. A line by a younger poet, Paul Castiaux, became one test case, a verse whose liquid, ash-blue caress was meant to evoke, as de Souza put it, "the grace of a horizon in vaporous flight": *Fluide et douce caresse de cendre bleu*. The unconventional rhythm had annoyed at least one writer at the stodgy *Nouvelle Revue*.[70] The verse, it seemed, was impossible to scan. Was it decasyllable or alexandrine? Neither, de Souza said, and he turned to his lab partner to prove the point. The Abbé made an ideal experimental subject, in fact, because his conservative education had left him with virtually no feeling for free verse. Rousselot actually balked on seeing the line, declaring it unreadable, but de Souza egged him on, recording the attempts with the aid of an *inscripteur électrique de la parole*.

After these recitations came two more, performed this time by a savvier student of poetry, a researcher named Georges Lote, who was in the next room. Lote had recently embarked on his own experimental study of the French alexandrine. He was also interested in learning how people declaimed such lines and had found a large collection of willing subjects—from varied class backgrounds—from which to collect his data.[71] De Souza, for his part, seemed satisfied with just these four readings, which he collated as a stream of comparative data (Figure 3.2).

The natural scansion of the line was determined, then, by consensus—a democratic process, if a thin one. Despite very different performances, the collective articulation of the two speakers, figured in hundredths of a second, yielded evidence of two phenomena: a series of durational accents, which de Souza marked in boldface, and a less frequent accent of intensification, shown in italics. Their combined effect produced neither decasyllable nor alexandrine but a subtler, three-part cadence: *Flu-ide—et douce caresse—de cen-dre bleu*. The true basis for poetic rhythm emerged in this singular metaphor of touch, of impact: the "soft and limpid caress" of a speaking voice.

R {	1ʳᵉ fois	8	2	8̆	41	6	1̆1	12	2̄8	12	2½	9	1̄0	4	2̄6	11	3	5̆	5	6	1̄7	4	4	6̆	11	6	2̄3
	2ᵉ fois	20	8	15	25	5½	10	13	21	10	2	9	10	4	30	9	2	6	7	12	21	5	4	5	8	6	22
L {	1ʳᵉ fois	25	4	20	42	3		7	16	21	7		13	17		28	12	3	16	8	17	13	4	6	6	12	6	20
	2ᵉ fois	15	12	24	55	5		10	21	24	8		12	10	4	28	10	8	11	8	15	11	4	6	7	13	4	20

f   l   ü   i   d   e   d   u   s   œ   k   a   r   è   s   œd   œ   s   ü   d   r   œ   b   l   ẃ

FIGURE 3.2 Measuring the rhythm of free verse, from de Souza, *Du Rythme, en français* (1912). "R" stands for Rousselot; "L" for Lote

Just as significant was the impression left by the transcribed results. As we can see, de Souza took care to write the seven words of Castiaux's verse as an uninterrupted stream of phonetic characters, a perceptual trick that emphasized, as he put it, the "unbreakable continuity of the verbal line." Above this liquid frontier flowed a veritable river of numbers. Their sheer difference allowed one to perceive the accent as something "other": a fugitive reality extracted from the spoken word. De Souza later distilled this raw rhythmic content into the following essence:

˘ –   ˘ – ˘ –   ˘ – ˘ –

u *i*—é ou a *è*—e an e *eu*

The visible result of the Castiaux experiment almost recalled, in a perverse way, that marvel of poetic translation described by Mallarmé in 1885, in his preface to Ghil's *Traité du verbe*. ("What good is the marvel of transposing a fact of nature into its near vibratory disappearance in the play of speech if it is not so that the pure idea, having nothing at all to pay back, might emanate from it?") Here, too, we see an already transposed "fact of nature"—that is, a single line of poetry—transposed once again, right before our eyes, into the image of "its near vibratory disappearance," to use Mallarmé's words. The poetry has all but vanished, leaving behind only an image of its timbre. What remained, in short, was the poem's accent, that part of the verse that pushed the word "toward song."

De Souza himself moved closer to that ideal in a belated collection of free verse, *Terpsichore* (1920), a volume much admired by the young Ezra Pound. With its experimental typography, the pages could be said to reflect the twin influence of Rousselot and Mallarmé (Figure 3.3). Words climbed the page as if in a rising scale; tiny performance directions indicated the speed or character of the delivery; numbers marked the larger rhythmic cadence. But the volume as a whole ended with a few telling remarks about the limits of notation. "The author . . . makes do with writing because he has no other

LOLA

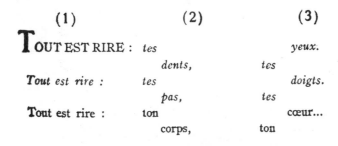

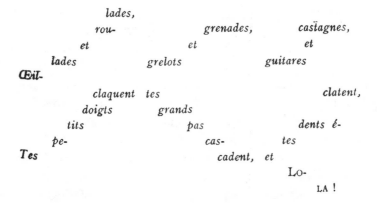

FIGURE 3.3 Robert de Souza, "Lola," from *Terpsichore* (1920)

choice," he wrote, adding that such *écriture* was "a faithless servant of the tongue."

> And whoever says "tongue" [*langue*] means language, speech, song, vibration, movement, and, finally, the harmonic or rhythmic organization of such movement. In truth, the expressive order that makes up the verbal work known as a *poem* could only be transmittable, in the absence of a voice, by means of phonograph records, especially if [such records] were one day to be perfected. But the day will soon come when the disc will replace the page.[72]

The passage brought the idea of a poem's "music" to its logical conclusion by predicting a time when the poem as we know it would disappear, replaced by a more foolproof transmission—one that preserved the original inflections intact. The disk became, then, the supreme *écriture* as writing became unreadable and verse turned to vibration: the imprint of a groove. In this capacity, the phonograph realized, belatedly, the ideal that the young poets had been seeking so many years before when they metaphorically took to the fields, armed with their pens, to reclaim their lyric heritage. As de Souza now put it, this was the instrument that would finally "lead them back to Homer."[73]

Music after All

With this image of poetry redeemed by a talking machine, our discussion of *vers libre* comes to an unlikely resting place. Our historical witnesses have led us down an oblique path from the open French countryside to a closed Parisian laboratory, in search of finer and finer impressions. Along the way, we have seen that the phonetic obsession figured by Verlaine in the Duvigneaux sonnet was no joke. Indeed, it should now be clear that the generation of 1890 had witnessed something extraordinary. As modern science rethought writing, exposing the accent of French in a new phonography, French poets rethought reading, dreaming of words released from the page and of verses perceived as the blind Homer heard them: in waves of harmonies and rhythms.

What, then, of French composers? It is time, I think, to stop and take their measure in order to consider symbolism from the other side. The concept of a poem made of waves of sound obviously affected the kind of harmonies and rhythms composers were themselves imagining. This is not news, of course: it is a convention of musicology to relate French musical style at the fin de siècle to the impact of poetry in general and of symbolism in particular. And yet it has remained difficult to say precisely—in musical terms—what this impact was. That is the question I now want to tackle, both to round off our discussion of poetry and to expand the story of *mélodie* I began telling in chapter 1. By focusing on more than one composer, and a different chronology, I hope, in fact, to enrich the historical context of that story. We will hear again from Fauré, though at a slightly earlier stage in his career, and for comparison, from an even younger Claude Debussy. The aim will be to observe the kind of musical language both were developing in the 1890s, a language Fauré would later memorialize in *La Chanson d'Eve*. The increasing freedom in the treatment of harmony and rhythm takes on a different tone when considered in terms of the literary history we have so far been exploring. Indeed, one might even say that—by a curious sort of reverse prophecy—the voice that proclaimed music *before* all things came back to musicians after all, and the result was completely unexpected.

———

Such a return seems clear enough in the case of Debussy. He has often been described as a literate composer, indeed, a "discriminating reader of contemporary poetry."[74] This tendency emerged with particular intensity in a set of songs he composed just before 1890, based on poems from Baudelaire's *Les Fleurs du Mal*. Baudelaire was enjoying a resurgence of popularity, having become a kind of honorary *poète maudit* for the young artists of Debussy's generation. In 1885, Théodore de Banville noted the "unprecedented explosive force" with which Baudelaire was spreading through the reading public and judged *Les Fleurs du Mal* "one of the most popular books of the century."[75] The protagonist of Huysman's *A Rebours* was so undone by Baudelaire's indescribable charms that he had to take his *Fleurs du mal* silently and in small doses. Elsewhere, though, one could hear Baudelaire being performed openly and often in drawing rooms and cabarets. In the early 1880s, the singer Maurice Rollinat found his fifteen minutes of fame by declaiming Baudelaire over his own piano accompaniments. A few years later, Debussy had outdone Rollinat, turning a small set of poems from *Les Fleurs du mal* into a musical tour de force. He called it the *Cinq poèmes de Baudelaire*.

I want to single out just one of these *poèmes*, the one Debussy called, after Baudelaire, "Le Balcon." This was the first of the set, composed in 1888 on the verge of two pilgrimages to Bayreuth, and the Wagnerian ambition is unmistakable. More than a few critics from Debussy's time considered it a bit too ambitious, complaining of "harmonic oddities, broken or disjointed rhythms, unsingable intervals without concern for vocal register . . . shocking modulations."[76] It is no surprise that Debussy had a hard time finding a publisher for these settings.[77] But even today listeners have demurred. "There are limits to the amount of sublimity that human throat and ivory keys can convey," declared Graham Johnson, suggesting that in "Le Balcon" Debussy simply went too far: "interpreters find it almost unrealizable," he went on, "wonderful to work on, almost impossible to perform."[78] And to a certain extent, he is right. There is something about the way "Le Balcon" pushes the limits—the way it attempts to exceed the category of song, one might say—that has made it challenging for interpreters of all kinds. Yet this difficulty turns out to be instructive as well, and so I want to allow the song to instruct us. I want to consider not only what Debussy's music might say about the new idea of poetry at the end of the century but also, more pointedly, how Baudelaire's poetry speaks to a new idea of music that the composer is himself working out: how, through Baudelaire, Debussy begins to rethink the idea of what French melody should be.

That Debussy was trying for something completely different is clear from even a cursory glance at both poem and music. The "waves of harmonies and rhythms" in the score capture a tone as impetuous as Baudelaire's own lines:

Mère des souvenirs, maîtresse des maîtresses,
O toi, tous mes plaisirs! ô toi tous mes devoirs!
Tu te rappelleras la beauté des caresses,
La douceur du foyer et le charme des soirs,
Mère des souvenirs, maîtresse des maîtresses!

Les soirs illuminés par l'ardeur du charbon,
Et les soirs au balcon, voilés de vapeurs roses,
Que ton sein m'était doux! Que ton coeur m'était bon!
Nous avons dit souvent d'impérissables choses
Les soirs illuminés par l'ardeur du charbon.

Que les soleils sont beaux dans les chaudes soirées!
Que l'espace est profond! Que le coeur est puissant!
En me penchant vers toi, reine des adorées,
Je croyais respirer le parfum de ton sang.
Que les soleils sont beaux dans les chaudes soirées!

La nuit s'épaississait ainsi qu'une cloison,
Et mes yeux dans le noir devinaient tes prunelles,
Et je buvais ton souffle, ô douceur! ô poison!
Et tes pieds s'endormaient dans mes mains fraternelles.
La nuit s'épaississait ainsi qu'une cloison.

Je sais l'art d'évoquer les minutes heureuses,
Et revis mon passé blotti dans tes genoux.
Car à quoi bon chercher tes beautés langoureuses
Ailleurs qu'en ton cher corps et qu'en ton coeur si doux?
Je sais l'art d'évoquer les minutes heureuses!

Ces serments, ces parfums, ces baisers infinis,
Renaîtront-ils d'un gouffre interdit à nos sondes,
Comme montent au ciel les soleils rajeunis
Après s'être lavés au fond des mers profondes?
—O serments! ô parfums! ô baisers infinis!

(Mother of memory, mistress of all mistresses, / oh, you who are my every pleasure, my every duty! / You will recall the beauty of our kisses, / The sweetness of the foyer, the charm of the evenings, / Oh mother of memory, mistress of all mistresses! //

The evenings illuminated by the heat of the coal, / And the evenings on the balcony, veiled in pink mist, / How soft your bosom! How good your heart! / We often said undying things / on those nights illuminated by the heat of the coal. //

How beautiful are the suns on warm nights! / How deep space! How strong the heart! / Leaning toward you, beloved queen, / I thought I breathed in the scent of your blood. / How beautiful are the suns on warm nights! //

Night thickened like a wall, / And my eyes saw your eyes in the blackness, / And I drank your breath, oh sweetness! oh poison! / And your feet slept in my brotherly hands. / Night thickened like a wall. //

I know the art of evoking happy moments, / And I see my past nestled on your lap. / For what good is it to look for your languorous beauty / Except in your dear body and sweet heart? / I know the art of evoking happy moments. //

Those vows, those perfumes, those infinite kisses, / Will they be reborn from a depth we are forbidden to sound, / As refreshed suns rise / after being washed at the bottom of the sea? / Oh vows! oh perfumes! oh infinite kisses!)

La Musique me prend souvent comme une mer, "music often pulls me like a tide," Baudelaire once wrote, and Debussy's "Le Balcon" suggests a similar sort of transport.[79] From the piano's surging cadences, the voice erupts on a top G before careening down an octave and up again, in an untamed arabesque (Musical Example 3.1). With wide leaps and sudden changes of direction, the melody takes us on an unexpectedly wild ride. The poem's list of memories— the beautiful caresses, the warm hearth, the charm of twilight—seems to connect through a form of melodic and harmonic free association that winds toward an improbable end, the phrase momentarily suspended on a top A. The effect is extravagant, if not exactly Wagnerian. Or perhaps one could say, it reminds us less of Wagner than of something Baudelaire once wrote about Wagner—the melody behaving like "a veritable arabesque of sounds sketched out by passion."[80] Still, just as quickly, the music takes a different turn and comes to its senses. To close the first period, the composer reproduces the song's opening measures, almost note for note, in a curiously literal "refrain."

Debussy fixes on this refrain, in fact, as an important organizing principle for his song, and it is easy to see why. Each of Baudelaire's five-line stanzas is

EXAMPLE 3.1 Debussy, *Cinq poèmes de Baudelaire*, "Le Balcon," first musical period, mm. 1–19

built in exactly this way, the first line returning as the last, to enclose an intervening tercet. In formal terms, the structure acts almost like a gloss on the poem's title image (*balcon* comes from the Italian *balcone*, which means

EXAMPLE 3.1 (Continued)

scaffolding). Leo Bersani has read these repeating lines in symbolic terms, as a reflection of the poet himself, caught up in an obsessive cycle of desire.[81] But we could just as easily understand them as a reflection of the poem's opening

figure, Memory. The very idea of poetic generation is written into this maternal image (*Mère des souvenirs*), in which ideas and feelings are both stored and *re*stored. "You will call them back," says the speaker in the third line. And the poem willingly responds to the command.

Debussy responded just as willingly, it seems, by "calling back" the exaggerated melody of the opening measures to close his first period. The gesture is ultimately true to the poem, but the literalness of the repetition also seems out of place amid the perfervid phrases, somehow more dutiful than expressive. Moreover, the pattern is repeated for each of the subsequent stanzas, as aimless or extravagant melodic lines find their way back, again and again, to an unlikely refrain. The process offers us an important clue about the nature of Debussy's musical reading, and a method in his madness. Debussy has preserved the opening poetic image ("Mother of memory") as the most literal—and memorable—element of his setting.

But this mother of memory turns out to be a mother of melody as well. The generative principle suggested by that opening figure is actually refigured in Debussy's music through a series of melodic tropes that themselves "recall" the song's opening image. Example 3.2 lays out the melodies Debussy conceived for five of the six stanzas to show the similarities between them. They are not exact likenesses, of course, but they share enough features to become blurred in one's mind as one listens. The recurring melodic idea, with its developments and digressions, seems to function in this sense less as a true refrain than as a kind of leitmotif.

In the fourth strophe, things change. Night falls, and, with it, the extroverted melody goes underground, as if the suns from the third stanza had now slipped into the sea. The melody is still there, in a sense, by its absence—implied in the piano part, which now replays the music from the opening, though more deliberately and in a different key. And the song turns another corner. An extensive interlude follows from the end of this period with its repeated line (*la nuit s'épaississait...*) and leads the song to a new place—a clearing—where the first person will be heard to speak for the first time in the present tense: "I know the art of evoking happy moments." At this point, Debussy does something very clever: he makes the first-person melody almost the mirror image of what it had been (see again Example 3.2).

It is a highly self-conscious gesture. "I know the art of evoking happy moments," says the poem, and Debussy seems to step in and say: "I do, too." The line calls attention to the composer in the act of reading, pointing not only back to the evocative piano interlude but also forward to the song's end, where the sun will rise again and we will hear another reminiscence of those happy moments as a final, wistful refrain. It becomes clear, then, how the refrain idea—through repetitions and mutations across this long song—works to evoke the poem's allegorical subject (memory) and to animate that subject in a particularly knowing way. But this level of self-awareness also offers a clue about the extent to which Debussy was also using Baudelaire to rethink the idea of melody in "Le Balcon," for many other aspects of the song are equally deliberate. What are we to make of the fact that Debussy sets each of the six refrains in an utterly different tempo and (more strikingly) different keys? And what can one say about the constantly changing rhythmic surface? In "Le Balcon," for the first time, Debussy drops the pretense of the four-bar phrase and opts for something different. The result is a curiously fluid and malleable declamation, intermingling phrases of three, four, five, six, or sometimes seven measures. These features may help to explain the criticism leveled against the song by critics of Debussy's day who complained of disjointed rhythms, unsingable lines, and shocking modulations. But they still do not explain exactly what Debussy was after. For that, we probably need to look again (as Debussy did) somewhere—anywhere—out of the music. We need to look again to Baudelaire.

We may as well start with the famous passage from Baudelaire's letter to Arsène Houssaye: "Who among us has not dreamed the miracle of a musical and poetic prose," Baudelaire wrote, "without rhyme and rhythm, supple and shocking enough to respond to the lyrical movements of the soul, to waves of reverie, to convulsions of conscience?"[82] The list sounds, in fact, like a plausible account of what Debussy has achieved in "Le Balcon." The song certainly represented a giant leap from the melodies of his *Ariettes*, published the same year. A song like "C'est l'extase langoureuse," which opened the collection of *Ariettes*, may have been suggestive in tone, but it still clung to the convention of the four-bar phrase. In "Le Balcon," Debussy refuses to contain the melodic thought within a regular frame and discovers in the process a new kind of lyric expression: a "prosodic and poetical" music exactly analogous, one might say, to the "musical and poetic prose" that Baudelaire dreams of.

Indeed, by creating such fluid and malleable form, Debussy seems to have reproduced an exaggerated image of the constantly changing timbres and rhythms pursued by the poets of his own generation. These were, after all, the same qualities Verlaine had placed "before all things" in 1884. As if fulfilling Verlaine's command, Debussy now showed his preference for odd measures over even (as Verlaine said, *préfère l'Impair*) and for nuance above all else (*rien que la Nuance!*). The extravagant setting of "Le Balcon" became, in this way, a manifestation of Debussy's very own *Art poétique*. Debussy looked to Baudelaire to find a different kind of music, one that was more musical precisely because it was more poetical. "True music can evoke analogous ideas in different brains," Baudelaire once said, speaking of Wagner's *Tannhäuser*, and Debussy might have said the same thing when speaking about the irregular, supple, and clangorous melody—the "true music"—he discovered in Baudelaire's "Balcony." Some years later, the French musicologist Louis Laloy would give Debussy's new kind of poetic expression a more obvious name: he called it "free melody" (*mélodie libre*).[83] And if this freedom of form suggested the influence of Wagner, the colors and rhythms of "Le Balcon" also revealed another equally plausible tendency: a music that was beginning to think and feel like free verse.[84] Debussy was never to write another set of songs quite like the *Cinq poèmes de Baudelaire*. But, then again, he never turned back.

———

Fauré, it turns out, welcomed Debussy's audacious new song cycle, calling it a "work of genius." And in its wake, he produced two venturesome collections of his own, the *Cinq mélodies de Venise*, completed in 1891, and *La Bonne Chanson*, in 1892. Both sets, based on poems by Verlaine, reflected a similar sense of freedom, featuring suppler rhythms and less predictable melodic lines. But it was in *La Bonne Chanson* that Fauré, like Debussy, created something grander than he had ever made before (or after), a watershed work that proved as challenging for audiences as Debussy's impulsive Baudelaire.[85]

Nothing in *La Bonne Chanson* quite reaches the declamatory excess of "Le Balcon," although a couple of songs come close. There was a notable concision in Fauré's songwriting that directed him to look for less long-winded poems or, at least, to cut down those with too much to say. Yet, despite the modest proportions, the songs of this collection loomed large, packed with big emotions and with rapidly changing harmonies that, as Johnson has remarked, often "pass by too quickly for the average ear to appreciate."[86] The skittishness reflected the feeling of the poetic cycle itself, which Verlaine conceived in 1869 as a too ardent bouquet for the sixteen-year-old Mathilde Mauté, with whom he had fallen hopelessly—and disastrously—in love. The poems displayed a huge range of affect, from eloquent alexandrines, to intimate, four-syllable whispers, to complex mixed meters, as if Verlaine were attempting to represent the depth of his ardor through metrical sophistication.

Such sophistication was to be felt even in more decorous poems, as we can see in "Une sainte en son auréole," the first song of Fauré's cycle. The text had all the marks of a *bonne chanson*, with its lilting *octosyllabes*, its uncomplicated syntax. Compared with the density of "Le Balcon," these airy lines come off a bit like greeting-card verse:

Une sainte en son auréole,
Une châtelaine en sa tour,
Tout ce que contient la parole
Humaine de grâce et d'amour;

La note d'or que fait entendre
Le cor dans le lointain des bois,
Mariée à la fierté tendre
Des nobles Dames d'autrefois;

Avec cela le charme insigne
D'un frais sourire triomphant
Eclos dans les candeurs de cygne
Et des rougeurs de femme-enfant;

Des aspects nacrés, blancs et roses,
Un doux accord patricien:

Je vois, j'entends toutes ces choses
Dans son nom Carlovingien.

(A saint surrounded by her halo, / a lady in her tower, / Everything that
human language contains of grace and love; / The golden note sounded
/ by a horn in the distant woods, / Mixed with the tender pride / Of
noble Ladies from times gone by; / Add to that the distinguished
charm / of a fresh, triumphant smile / Opening into the whiteness of a
swan / And the blush of a woman-child; / These pearly aspects, pink
and white, / A sweet patrician harmony: / I see, I hear all these things /
In your Carolingian name.)

The form amounts to little more than a list: a string of almost disconnected
metaphors that produce, like images on a tapestry, a charmingly medieval
picture of the beloved. Fauré, in turn, made the simplicity a virtue, setting the
lines amid a quaint triple-meter melody that recalled an ancient air, or a lied.

But if this was a folksong, it was more like one of those rustic chansons
cherished by the symbolists, for the *mélodie* of Fauré's "Une sainte en son
auréole" was every bit as *libre* as Debussy's liberated Baudelaire. Like Debussy, Fauré strove to create a different melodic line for each verse of this self-
contained song. And in his preference for both nuanced harmonies and oddly
measured phrases (with nary a four-measure phrase in sight), he took the
same sorts of liberties. The diminutive form of his two-minute song allows us
to examine those choices in more detail and thus to appreciate Verlaine's
music as Fauré himself did: by listening closely.

Three brief measures are all it takes for the song to establish both a key
(A♭) and an affect (Musical Example 3.3). A folklike air floats from the
pentatonic melody in the piano; it sounds like something we must have heard
before, although the fragment is too short to create more than a passing
impression. The voice casually utters the first image in the same pentatonic
breath (a "haloed saint") and then pauses while the piano retraces its steps. The
next item on the list, a "lady in her tower," is almost like a saint. Their
exchangeability is suggested by a new harmony that materializes, like a quaint
surprise, at the end of this phrase. The C♭ paints the tower (*tour*), with its clear
vowel, in a brighter shade than the dim *o* of *auréole*. But this tinge is just as
quickly forgotten as we move to the next, slightly overwrought metaphor:
"everything that human speech contains." A twisted, chromatic progression
leads us quickly (if unexpectedly) back to A♭ and sounds, in the context of all
this melodic naiveté, unnecessarily fraught. But the thought is incomplete,
and, as the melody continues in the next phrase, we stall on a little riff, a

thrice-repeated progression that cancels the confusion with a perfect picture "of grace and love": a refined French sixth resolving to its dominant.

Four tiny phrases, four rare musical images: Fauré's *mélodie* may be more restrained than Debussy's "Le Balcon," but the effect is, in its own way, equally mercurial. The music, in fact, continues like this for the rest of the song: each poetic image transposed into a fresh setting, as if being held to the light, or somehow turned over in one's mind, in contemplation. We cock an ear toward a sad "golden note" in the piano, like a distant horn call. We move through a charmingly archaic *fauxbourdon* sequence in a notably elevated key (A-natural), as if passing "noble ladies from times gone by." We hear the brassy brightness of an E-dominant seventh, showering us with a "triumphant smile" that marks the highest note of the piece. And we watch that glimmer disappear with a more demure image, made of just two sounds, one "pale," the other "blushing." In turn, this yields to a final "sweet patrician chord," another dominant chord on E, but this time in second inversion, a spelling that, like the aristocracy itself, is proud of its distant root.

After this surfeit of subtly changing impressions, it is almost a greater surprise to stumble on something familiar. To conclude the long list, and to tie up the open form, the chanson recollects itself in the final confession: "I hear all these things in your Carolingian name." The last line resolves the song's mystery by creating a context for its disconnected metaphors in the "grace and love" of the first musical period, while evoking a final, learned analogy: the name *Mathilde*, the speaker implies, sounds like the historical Clothilde, ancient Queen of the Franks (Musical Example 3.4). As Fauré spells it out, we hear this Carolingian sound in all its glory, as the singer lovingly caresses every syllable, extending the five phonemes into five delicious measures: *Car—lo—vin—gi—en.*

From the evidence of two songs, then, we begin to sense the change Mauclair summarized, with hindsight, in 1908, when describing the emergence of the modern French "lied." Something had happened between poets and musicians in the previous decade—"around 1890," as he figured it—and the change had fostered a new, more sympathetic dialogue. Mauclair acknowledged the ever-present influence of Wagner, but he gave just as much credit to Verlaine, for the way he had taught artists to be sensitive to "the musical elements of language," especially, as he pointed out, "the rhythm and timbre of its syllables."[87] The final phrase of "Une sainte en son auréole" suggests how quickly composers had learned that lesson. We hear the French language being broken down into precisely those elements, one delectable timbre at a time.

In the next chapter, we see how singers dealt with this new musical language, exploring the expressive possibilities of what Mauclair called "a new kind of diction." For now, it is useful to probe the critics' accounts a bit more deeply. Laloy, too, spoke of the "miraculous precision" of modern French prosody in this period, connecting the distinctly musical poetics of Verlaine and Mallarmé and even Ghil with the increasingly poetic music of contemporary French composers.[88] Paul Huvelin would later make a far more totalizing claim. The same forces that lay behind *vers libre* and *mélodie libre*, he said, had shaken up all the disciplines, from literature to the social and biological sciences, yielding the basic principles of socialism, positivism, even historicism. In the arts, it had brought on what he broadly—and idealistically—called "impressionism": "In this approach to art, the worker . . . no longer imposes his personality on the material. He merely *collects sensations from the outside world*, stylized, to be sure, but crystallized without conclusion. . . . The art is no longer *expression* but *impression*."[89] The image recalled de Souza's picture of modern poets in the field, "armed with their pens," as they collected the natural accents that would rejuvenate lyric poetry. Now modern composers had started to collect those accents for their own purposes. In the case of the *mélodie*, Huvelin concluded, the "impression to be collected" was that of the "*voix parlée*, transcribed in its essential inflections, with the greatest possible exactitude."[90]

Both Debussy and Fauré reached toward this goal with the freer melodies of the *Cinq poèmes de Baudelaire* and *La Bonne Chanson*, although neither one achieved the level of precision Huvelin's remark implies. Even with its apparently spontaneous declamation, its uneven phrases, a song like "Le Balcon" remained conventionally expressive. Fauré's concept in *La Bonne Chanson* was equally fulsome, resembling something closer to "a vocal symphony," as Nectoux put it, "in which voice and piano are an entity."[91] Within a few years, though, the two composers began to change their tune, toning down their song to create a stronger impression. Once again, just two pieces will suffice to demonstrate the shift. Both were composed in 1897, the year of Mallarmé's *Un Coup de dès* and Gustave Kahn's theory of free verse. Like these works, both show their authors attempting to record the accents of speech with even greater precision—scanning the poetry, as Kahn would advocate, with an ear for how the verse was spoken. If around 1890 Debussy and Fauré set out on a new path, by 1897, as we will see, they had landed in a very different place.

Transcribing the voix parlée

Debussy's *Trois Chansons de Bilitis* form a striking case in point. The texts, by his friend Pierre Louÿs, were themselves an unusual place to start: a collection of prose poems whose publication enacted a huge practical joke. When the edition first came out in 1894, Louÿs's name did not even appear on the title page. The initials (P. L.) pointed to the unnamed scholar who had translated the chansons "from the Greek, for the very first time." The same translator offered a few introductory remarks about the poetess ("Vie de Bilitis"), quoting from the work of a certain Professor G. Heim from Göttingen, who had not only discovered her tomb but also brought out her complete works (the *Bilitis sämmtliche Lieder*) earlier that year.[92] The German archaeologist was the crowning touch. A few gullible readers swallowed the story whole.[93]

Yet Louÿs may have had a more serious reason for the prank, one that related to the specific literary character of his text. In claiming to translate songs "from the Greek," the faceless P. L., in fact, sublimated his own poetic voice, creating the impression of a work standing between two eras (ancient and modern) and two alphabets (Greek and Roman), as well as two kinds of writing—namely, poetry and prose.[94] The ruse essentially solved the problem of the "prose poem," by suggesting that real verse did, after all, lie beneath the prosaic surface.

But what kind of verse? Did this woman who lived for a time on Lesbos sing in Sapphic forms? Louÿs's Professor Heim is notably silent on the subject, yet the translations offer their own reply, as the paragraphs of prose (when read aloud) parse into virtual stanzas. The beginning of "La Flûte," for example:

> Pour le jour des Hyacinthies, (8)
> Il m'a donné une syrinx (8)
> Faite de roseaux bien taillés, (8)
> Unis avec la blanche cire (8)
> Qui est douce a mes lèvres comme le miel. (11)
>
> Il m'apprend a jouer (6)
> assise sur ses genoux (7)
> mais je suis un peu tremblante. (7)
> Il en joue après moi, (6)
> si doucement que je l'entend a peine. (10)[95]

(For Hyacinth Day, he gave me flute, made out of well-hewn reeds, connected by white wax that was sweet as honey on my lips. / He teaches me to play seated on his knees, but I am a little nervous. He plays on it after me so softly that I barely hear him.)

Four unrhymed *octosyllabes* culminate in a line of eleven, followed by lines of six or seven yielding to one of ten. Reading the paragraphs, we may feel a bit like Bilitis herself, sensing a poem "so softly" in the background that "we can barely hear it." But the impression created by Louÿs's gently rhythmic utterances simply confirms the observation Mallarmé once made to Huret: "whenever there is an effort at style, there is versifying." It is as if a whole world of verse—free verse—were buried in those stylish sentences, ready for the taking. His fictional Bilitis thus symbolized much more than a scholarly hoax. Born in the undefiled space *between* prose and poetry, this imaginary voice from circa 600 B.C. came to proclaim the ancient purity and, in that respect, the classicism of modern *vers libre*.[96]

"Hers is the most persuasive voice in the world," Debussy wrote to Louÿs in 1898, not long after he had finished setting three of the poems to music.[97] They were the first songs Debussy had composed since the moment he threw himself into *Pelléas et Mélisande*, which occupied him obsessively from 1893 to 1895. Perhaps Debussy found the young Bilitis enough like Mélisande to write her a song of similar purity. Perhaps it was her antiquity that brought out, as Koechlin put it, "a certain atticism" in the composer's expression. In any case, his *Chansons de Bilitis* represented an entirely new approach to melody. Unfolding in simple cadences without meter or rhyme, this music assumed all the freedoms of free verse, capturing Bilitis's story very much "in the tone of conversation." No wonder Romain Rolland called the songs "miracles of 'speaking' French in music."[98]

The conversational tone, of course, had much to do with the rhythm. If in the *Cinq poèmes* we see Debussy avoiding the four-measure phrase, in the *Trois Chansons* he moved beyond meter entirely. The directions for "La Flûte de Pan" (based on Louÿs's "La Flûte") tell the performer to sing "slowly and without a strict rhythm" ("Lent et sans rigueur de rythme"), as if the composer were confirming something he once said to Guiraud: "rhythms cannot be contained within bars." Yet the song's notation puts the matter another way. A glance at the first few measures reveals, right from the start, a remarkably broad range of values. Each phrase has been set in a different rhythm, amid a meter that floats freely from three to four, without actually marking time (Musical Example 3.5).

Such nuanced notation in itself rules out the idea of "rhythmic rigor." In attempting realism, the score becomes more descriptive than prescriptive, the phrases notated as Bilitis herself might have spoken them. And in this way, Debussy managed to realize a larger poetic ideal, one written into the very concept of the *chanson* as the symbolists understood it. Uttered by a realistic Bilitis, the verses appeared in all their irregular rustic purity.

Théodore Gérold once observed that "the texts of Pierre Louys . . . [shared] a certain kinship with what one calls the *chanson populaire*."[99] Debussy captured this same sense of freedom in the contours of his vocal lines, reproducing the essence of the popular song that Mauclair called the *lied*

● EXAMPLE 3.5 Debussy, *Trois Chansons de Bilitis*, "La Flûte de Pan," mm. 1–12

EXAMPLE 3.5 (Continued)

-vec la blan - che ci - re qui est douce à mes lè - vres com - me le miel.

Il m'apprend à jou - er as - si - se sur ses ge - noux; mais je suis un peu trem-

blan - te. Il en joue a - près moi, si dou-ce - ment que je l'en-tends à

EXAMPLE 3.5 (Continued)

and that de Souza considered a prototype for free verse: a "malleable and fluid material capable of lengthening and shortening at will."

The fluidity was enhanced by the looseness of the accompaniment. Rather than shadowing the words, the piano moves along separately. In the process, it actually evokes another rustic image: a panpipe. The opening measures introduce a free-floating melody (in an antique Lydian mode) that will hover alongside the voice in its own time, like a memory of the flute-playing shepherd Lykas, Bilitis's first lover, who is the subject of her amorous tale. With its arabesques that weave in and out of the vocal part, it is the piano, in fact, that represents the more overtly expressive instrument in this song.

And yet the piano does not actually "express" anything. No one actually plays the flute in this pastoral vision, nor do frogs croak. Bilitis may remember such a sound near the end of her tale, the "song of the peepers" awakening the lovers from their passionate embrace (*Il est tard. Voici le chant des grenouilles vertes qui commence avec la nuit*). The piano even seems to answer the memory, with an odd, leaping gesture that jumps out of the texture as if on cue. But the noise is immediately recognizable as something else: not a frog, but the "Tristan" chord, recalling another, more famous pair of lovers and their nighttime assignation (Musical Example 3.6).

The failed mimesis speaks as much to Wagner as it does to Rousseau, who, in the *Essay on the Origin of Languages*, famously complained of harmony's inadequacy to express anything at all. "A musician who tries to render noise with noise errs," said Rousseau, thinking specifically of Rameau's frogs in *Platée* ("If he wished to make frogs croak, he would have to make them

EXAMPLE 3.6 Debussy, *Trois Chansons de Bilitis*, "La Flûte de Pan," mm. 17–30

EXAMPLE 3.6 (Continued)

sing"). Indeed, as Rousseau saw it, Rameau's modern idea of harmony had destroyed the possibility of authentic imitation:

> [harmony] eliminates the passionate accent in favor of intervals, it restricts to only two modes songs that should have as many modes as there are tones of voice, and it eradicates and destroys a great many intervals that do not fit into its system; in a word, it separates song and speech to such an extent that these two languages contend, thwart one another, deprive one another of any truth, and cannot be united in the treatment of a passionate subject without appearing absurd. That is why the people always find it ridiculous to have strong, serious passions expressed in song; for they know that in our languages these passions have no musical inflections at all.[100]

If the words were not Debussy's, they nonetheless formed an uncanny defense for the new kind of melody we observe in his *Trois Chansons de Bilitis*. As if in sympathy with Rousseau by way of his pseudo-Greek subject, Debussy looks to a time before harmony to find not only forgotten modes but also, more important, a forgotten melodic concept: an original "passionate accent" that had no need of intervals to make it sing. "We have nothing to say to each other," Bilitis mutters at the beginning of the third stanza, remembering her virgin flute lesson with Lykas, but the observation could just as easily be made of her own vocal line in relation to the piano's noise, for the voice, too, says almost "nothing." No leaps, no cries; just a steady syllabic chant that rises and falls, in the manner of the best French recitative, as Rousseau himself imagined it.

The expression is starkest in the song's final phrase. Bilitis gasps in mild panic: "my mother will never believe that I've been away so long looking for my lost sash" (*Ma mère ne croira jamais que je suis restée si longtemps à chercher ma ceinture perdue*). And Debussy sets the words as a breathless monotone, asking the singer to utter them "almost voicelessly" (*presque sans voix*). Through Bilitis, the composer would approach, in other words, a Greek ideal of *melos*, attempting to return song to its origins in speech. That may have been Rousseau's ideal, but it was also a symbolist dream, not to mention a phonetician's quarry. Transcribing the *voix parlé*, Debussy dared to reunite song with its original accent and achieved an utterly modern form in the process: a dispassionate *mélodie*, without expression, without imitation, and almost entirely without melody.

Fauré found his own solution to this classical problem in 1897, when he approached another, very different neo-Hellenist poet—Charles-Marie-Réné Leconte de Lisle—and his sonnet "Le Parfum impérissable." This was a text composed in classic alexandrines, representing the more pious sort of Greek purity cultivated by the so-called Parnassian poets. The lofty tenor of its first-person speaker could not have been more distant from the voice of the naïve Bilitis. And yet Fauré's song, while employing very different means, captured something of the same dispassionate accent. Indeed, as Koechlin saw it, Fauré's imperishable *mélodie* was but a step away from the "Greek serenity" that would characterize the perfect songs of *La Chanson d'Eve*.

Still, the liberated verses of a Van Lerberghe or a Louÿs would seem to have almost nothing to do with the chiseled perfection of this sonnet, whose form, like a crystal flask, becomes the pretense for a sentiment that will fill it like an expensive perfume:

Quand la fleur du soleil, la rose de Lahor,
De son âme odorante a rempli goutte à goutte,
La fiole d'argile ou de cristal ou d'or,
Sur le sable qui brûle on peut l'épandre toute.

Les fleuves et la mer inonderaient en vain
Ce sanctuaire étroit qui la tint enfermée,
Il garde en si brisant son arôme divin
Et sa poussière heureuse en reste parfumée.

Puisque par la blessure ouverte de mon coeur
Tu t'écoule de même, ô céleste liqueur,
Inexprimable amour qui m'emflammait pour elle!

Qu'il lui soit pardonné, que son nom soit béni!
Par de là l'heure humaine et le temps infini
Mon coeur est embaumé d'une odeur immortelle.

(When the sun's flower, the rose of Lahore / has filled the clay or crystal or gold flask / With its fragrant essence, drop by drop, / It can all be poured out on the burning sand. // In vain would the rivers and the sea engulf / The narrow sanctuary that holds fast the scent / Even broken, it keeps its divine aroma / Its very dust will be perfumed by it. // So do you, by the open wound of my heart, / Flow in the same way, oh celestial nectar, / Inexpressible love that enflamed me! // So let her be pardoned, and her name be blessed! / For by the hour of man and time everlasting / My heart is embalmed with an immortal perfume.)

The content indeed follows the form, as the verse inflates the opening quatrains, like air filling the lungs, in a single, continuous breath. The long-windedness sets the tone for the whole poem, which takes all fourteen lines to make its point. In the first two strophes, Leconte de Lisle sets up a cool philosophical proposition: once a perfume has penetrated its container, no amount of water will wash it out. But the more intimate tercets shift the focus, making the abstract personal. The "I" does not speak directly, although the subject analogizes the flask with his broken heart, and the perfume with the love that once flowed through it. The effort seems to relieve the pain. The final lines include, along with an oath, a purgative confession. "Let her be pardoned," says the wounded lover—stoically, generously—then exposes the beatific state his own heart, "embalmed with an immortal fragrance."

Younger poets must have cringed. With its rhetorical posturing, Leconte de Lisle's sonnet represented precisely the sort of verse Verlaine and his cohort dismissed as "literature" while raising the banner of a freer *Art poétique*. Fauré, however, seemed unconcerned by the formality of the older Parnassian, going straight to the heart of his impassive text.[101] This heart lay not on the sleeve, of course, but in a more refined idea of enclosure, the "narrow sanctuary" that held the poem's thought together. And it was precisely this image that would

EXAMPLE 3.7 Fauré, "Le Parfum impérissable," mm. 1–9

EXAMPLE 3.8 Fauré, "Le Parfum impérissable," melodic analysis of first quatrain, mm. 2–9

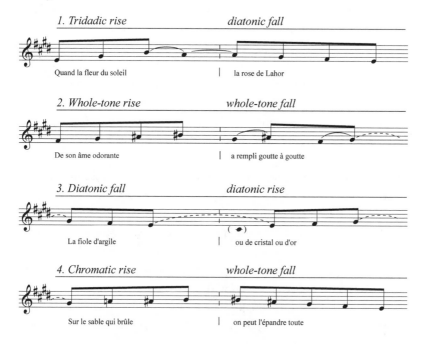

1. *Tridadic rise*   *diatonic fall*

Quand la fleur du soleil | la rose de Lahor

2. *Whole-tone rise*   *whole-tone fall*

De son âme odorante | a rempli goutte à goutte

3. *Diatonic fall*   *diatonic rise*

La fiole d'argile | ou de cristal ou d'or

4. *Chromatic rise*   *whole-tone fall*

Sur le sable qui brûle | on peut l'épandre toute

guide Fauré's hand as the composer, setting the sonnet to music, made such improbable containment the basis for a new kind of *mélodie*.

There was, once again, the question of the rhythm. If in *La Bonne Chanson* Fauré eschewed the four-measure phrase, in this song he, too, will rethink the very idea of measure. Debussy deployed an extreme form of notation in "La Flûte de Pan," where shifting time signatures and burgeoning note values announced a new temporal freedom. In "Le Parfum impérissable," Fauré took the opposite path, reducing the music to its barest essentials: a slow triple meter. Yet the simplicity was deceptive. Right from the start, we can hear how in this song, too, the rhythm spills beyond bar lines that can no longer contain it. The harmony creates an utterly mutable sense of time, shifting so quickly between metrical possibilities (3/2 to 3/4 to 3/2 to 2/2 to 2/4) that the notated measures almost become meaningless. Eventually, the downbeat loses its place, escaping the confines of the bar like a perfume from its bottle (Musical Example 3.7).

The vocal declamation was similarly deceptive. On the one hand, Fauré's phrases exhibit an obvious sort of Hellenism, permeated with anapestic rhythms that proudly display their "classic" heritage. On the other, the prosody seems almost free—with each alexandrine declaimed differently, according to its changing rhythmic content. Fauré will observe the pure *tétramètre* of the second line with an appropriately straight notation (*De son âme | odor-ante || a rem-pli | goutte à gout-te*). Yet the mixed meter of the third, with its rhythmic reversal on the conjunction *ou*, warrants a fresh nuance (*La fi-ol- | e d'ar-gil(e) || ou de cri-stal ou d'or*). In a similar way, Fauré's first phrase lingers on the expansive vowels of *fleur* and *soleil*, while skipping lightly over *la rose*. De Souza may have complained about modern poets "incapable of finessing the beats of the simplest alexandrine," but, in this song, Fauré appears to be a masterful reader, as if giving advance support for the claim Mauclair would later make to Marinetti: "the alexandrine is a free verse."[102]

The vocal melody enhances the declamatory freedom. In the first quatrain, the poem proceeds by a kind of exaggerated indirection: the initial preposition fills three full lines before the subject of the sentence is even stated. Fauré responds with an equally long-winded melody that not only mirrors the poetic thought but also respects the integrity of its individual alexandrines (Musical Example 3.8). The opening phrase, for example, balances a triadic rise from E (*Quand la fleur du soleil*) with an equal and opposite fall (*la rose de Lahor*). The return down the major scale neatly divides the melody into two opposed hemistichs, whereupon the process starts again, extending the thought directly into the second phrase.

A rising whole-tone scale now offers a whiff of the oriental fragrance (*De son âme odorante*) before falling in two stages, drop by drop, to its starting point (*a rempli goutte à goutte*). But this end becomes just another beginning. Sensitive to the poetic enjambment, the melody continues descending by whole tones to reach the object of the preposition (*la fiole d'argile*) and then equalizes that fall with another rise, pivoting on the conjunction (*ou*) that marks the second half of the line (*ou de cristal ou d'or*). And it keeps on rising. This time, the climb is by half step: a tense chromatic scale fills the first part of this closing phrase, which will end—once again—by falling, the melody returning to the tonic via yawning whole tones. The scalar conflict (ascending by closed intervals and descending by open ones) does more than expose the two halves of a symmetrical verse. It sounds a whole universe. Tight sibilants and back vowels (*sur le sable qui brûle*) disappear through the alexandrine's imperceptible join, as soft plosives and cavernous nasals flood the final cadence (*on p eut l'épandre toute*).

It was a finely calibrated approach to a highly calculated poem. And Fauré will measure his words in much the same way to the end, his close attention to language exposing the verse forms in all their nuance. Yet the approach yields, at best, a rather unassuming melody. Stripped of its words, the music

EXAMPLE 3.9 Fauré, "Le Parfum impérissable," mm. 18–24

of "Le Parfum impérissable" would be entirely forgettable—which is, in a way, as it should be. In the continuous rise and fall of the voice, Fauré has created not so much a memorable tune as an image of the poem's accent: the part of verse that moves toward song yet remains some distance from all-out "singing." Leconte de Lisle's sonnet comes across modestly, as Fauré himself might have spoken it. What lingers in the memory is not a melody, then, but an impression of reading, a kind of direct transcription of the *voix parlée*.

This made it, in effect, a song with almost nothing to say. Even more than the impressionistic phrases of *La Bonne Chanson*, where shifting textures and harmonies spoke to Verlaine's evolving metaphors, and more than Debussy's *Chansons de Bilitis*, where limpid piano lines evoke a bucolic paradise, Fauré achieved, in "Le Parfum impérissable," a wedding of word and music that utterly escaped mimesis. The most expressive moment of his song occurs, in fact, halfway through, as philosophical quatrains give way to more confessional lines. The voice leaps an octave as if in a cry of pain. And yet the abject cry does not paint anything so obvious as the open wound of the poet's heart. It occurs on the word *puisque* (Musical Example 3.9).

An extreme melodic gesture becomes, then, more functional than expressive, more deed than word: returning the word to accent. If the impassive *puisque*—the song's longest value—serves to express anything at all, it is, one could argue, something like emphasis itself, as in the expression *puisque je te le dis*: "I'm telling you *so*." In this singular act of uttering (*dire*), the song itself tells us: *so*. And by so doing, it actually tells us nothing. The refusal becomes a sign of the "not saying" that defined Fauré's mute subject: the inexpressible love (*inexprimable amour*) whose indelible impression, breathed in rather than pressed out, permeated the song's narrow form.

Such reserve looked forward to the Eve of Fauré's *Chanson d'Eve*. Her dying wish was also to be silenced, to reclaim the bliss of a wordless Paradise. Fauré anticipated the connection in the most prominent feature of "Le Parfum impérissable" by using the same, restrained texture he will later choose for Eve: a vaguely chanted melody accompanied by pulsing chords. This represented Fauré's purest song style, what Johnson called "the accompanied hymn." It is probably no coincidence, then, that the two songs share a telling metaphor. In the death chant of *La Chanson d'Eve*, "O Mort, poussière d'étoiles," Eve herself is figured as a "perfume," a divine aroma that will be poured into the abyss to "embalm the earth," just as an "immortal scent" here embalms the poet's heart. Without knowing it, Fauré has envisioned Eve's perfect end—and her imperishability—already in 1897, in the purified melody of "Le Parfum impérissable."

But the real connection between the songs lies not so much in a shared expression as in a shared attitude *toward* expression, an ideal of *melos* that was preserved—like Louÿs's fictitious Bilitis—through a fictive embalming of the lyric voice. Fauré's muting of Leconte de Lisle will confirm once again that real-life passions such as loving or dying have "no inflections at all in our languages." Even the silence of Fauré's expiring Eve would seem to make good on Rousseau's claim that real people "no more die singing than do Swans."[103] Modern composers like Debussy and Fauré may have gleaned this sensibility more from poets than from philosophers, but its basic truth was no less persuasive. As melodists, they learned to tone down melody, making their song a dying breath, and their singers virtually mute: "almost voiceless," as Debussy would write. And it was in this act of silencing that they, like the poets, dared to set song free.

Unsung Symbols

Our next chapter offers further evidence of this vocal liberation, as we trace the freer melodies of French composers further into the twentieth century. For now, I will close with one more figure, a less celebrated but equally significant composer, Ernest Chausson. Older than Debussy by several years and younger than Fauré by a decade, Chausson stands neatly between our two composers in both chronology and temperament, offering one more example of the expressive reticence that visited French composers of the later 1890s.[104] One notably understated song, completed three years before Chausson's untimely death in 1899 (and just a year before *Bilitis* or Fauré's "Parfum"), gives us occasion to reflect anew, and with particular poignancy, on the dying breath of the modern *mélodie*.

The song was called "Les Heures," the first of a set of *Trois Lieder* (op. 27) that Chausson wrote in collaboration with the poet we have already heard from several times, Camille Mauclair. Their exchange was remarkable in its reciprocity. Through it, Mauclair got a feeling for that elusive form he would call the modern French "lied"; Chausson, in turn, came to appreciate the freedoms of the new poetry. In fact, the song is interesting to consider as an early example of a setting based on free verse. "Write me a lied on a repeated rhyme," Chausson told Mauclair one day in 1896.[105] And the poet responded, returning the same evening with the following lines:

Les pâles heures, sous la lune, (7)
En chantant, jusqu'à mourir, (7)

Avec un triste sourire, (7)
Vont une à une (4)

Sur un lac baigné de lune, (7)
Où, avec un sombre sourire, (8)
Elles tendent, une à une, (6)
Les mains qui mènent à mourir; (7)

Et certains, blèmes sous la lune (7)
Aux yeux d'iris sans sourire, (7)
Sachant que l'heure est de mourir, (8)
Donnent leurs mains une à une, (7)

Et tous s'en vont dans l'ombre et dans la lune (10)
Pour s'alanguir et puis mourir (8)
Avec les Heures, une à une, (7)
Les Heures au pâle sourire. (6)

(The pallid hours under the moon, / Go singing til they die out, / With a sad smile, / One by one, / Over a moonlit lake, / Where, with a somber smile, / They extend, one by one, / Their hands that lead to death; // And certain ones, wan in the moonlight / With their unsmiling iris eyes, / Knowing that it is time to die, / Give their hands one by one, / And go all together into the shadow, and into the moon / To grow listless and then to die, / With the hours, one by one, / The pallid, smiling hours.)

Four very free quatrains: Mauclair had, in fact, organized the poem not so much around a "repeated rhyme" as around four repeated words, two pairs that chimed across the utterly simple form. With its short-breathed lines, its many one-syllable words and recurring sounds, the poem recalled the older pastoral tradition that stood behind the "free, polymorphous poetry" of the symbolists—precisely what Mauclair called the *lied*.

Mauclair once described the naturally singing *lied* as an "echo of the blessed region Shelley spoke of: 'Where music and moonlight and feeling are one.'"[106] And in writing this verse for Chausson, he seemed to take the formula literally. Not only did the poem's first word pair evoke this unified moonlit image: *lune—une*. The second pair also reinforced it, for the doubled syllable actually reproduced the single one of the first. To put this in other terms: the doubled vowel of *mou-rir—sou-rire* contained two musical timbres, *ou* and *i*, each producing a distinct feeling (sad or smiling, as Maucalir suggests). The *ou* was obviously the sad tone, formed by an actual pout, the literal "moue" of *mou-rir*, where the lips fall rounded and forward. The *i* of *ri(re)* was the laughing second syllable, where the tongue rises, and lips draw back. Put pout and smile together, and—as every first-year French student knows—you have a new thing, a uniquely French timbre: the *u* of *une* and *lune*. Mallarmé may have joked that French mixed up day and night, making *jour* dark and *nuit* bright,[107] but in this poem, Mauclair would resolve the contradiction. The quartet of rhymes fused to form a solitary, resonant note, a bright-dark color like moonlight. But that rich tone recalled, in turn, the purely French timbre of Mauclair's actual poetic subject: the tolling of a bell, announcing the monastic "hours" across a dark pastoral landscape.[108] Indeed, in medieval French, that is precisely what *timbre* meant: a bell that was struck by hand.

Mauclair's *lied* was all about that ringing. In this respect, it worked quite differently from the prose tale of Pierre Louÿs or the inflated alexandrines of Leconte de Lisle. His verse implied no speaking subject. There was only a sound, an eerie noise vibrating in the darkness. To catch its drift, the poet turned his own words into music, a sympathetic vibration that sacrificed grammar and meaning for sound. He imagined his verse, in other words, as if it were *already* singing—*en chantant jusqu'à mourir*, as he says in the second line. This image of "singing unto death" evoked the slow, dying envelope of a bell. But it also could stand as a telling metaphor for the condition of free verse, where the poet's desire to sing led to the death of poetic eloquence, of "literature." Mauclair's empty lines did not so much express the tolling of the hours as embody it, collapsing concept and sound into a single feeling, the space of one resonant word: *l'une, l'une, l'une, l'une*.

It was a sound that naturally suggested music. According to Mauclair, Chausson sat down at the keyboard after hearing the poem just once and improvised the perfect musical translation (Musical Example 3.10). Four offbeat octaves in the piano announced the song's beginning, "slow and resigned," as if reducing the minimal poem even further, condensing its emotion into a single tolling note. Certainly, the gesture can be heard as an image of the poem's evocative subject. And yet as it continues—through all twenty measures of the song—the mimetic character of the sound fades. The constant repetition turns the octave A into a mere vibration, a sensory background on which the poem will deposit its own accents.

Chausson's poetic reading, in fact, captures the same kind of accent observed in Debussy's *Chansons de Bilitis* or Fauré's "Parfum impérissable." Here again, we find a pared-down accompaniment with chiming purer than Fauré. Here again, we perceive a declamatory rhythm that "cannot be contained within bars." The sense of freedom emerges as much from the piano's continuous offbeats as from the vocal line's evaded downbeats, making the notated meter (4/4) seem arbitrary, a notational convenience.

EXAMPLE 3.10 Chausson, "Les Heures," mm. 1–5, with alternative barring to show collapsing phrase structure

The opening period of "Les Heures" can actually be heard as a telescoping form of constantly changing meters. A measure of five beats yields to another of four, then to three, then two, at which point the slowly descending vocal line reaches its lowest note. E♭ rings out conspicuously when the one-syllable verb (*vont*) lands for the first time squarely on the downbeat. Swelling to fill almost two beats, the dark, nasal timbre of this verb sounds for a moment like an exotic gong.[109] Yet the phrase will resume with a very different stroke. As we continue with the ever-narrowing progression—indeed, just at the point where the two-beat measure should collapse into one—Chausson gives us something else, a sort of musical pun. Instead of one beat, we get one word, which the voice delivers, clear as a bell, *in unison* with the piano's pinging A. It sings: *une . . .*

It was no doubt this kind of convergence that caused Mauclair to judge Chausson's *lied* a "model of musical translation," with its "identity of feeling, and rhythm, and syllabic chant."[110] But through its unique collapsing of word and tone and time, the song also idealizes the ethos of the *mélodie* around 1890. As we hear the poem's *une* rising to the surface, we perceive the extent to which the song's expression—like the poem's—was seeking to locate itself elsewhere. Just as Mauclair's verse manages to merge with its own vibration, the song becomes equivalent to its accent. To put this another way: the total musical expression of the song turns out to be nothing more (and nothing less) than its diction.

Our poetic journey may as well stop here, where two ideals meet face-to-face. Noisy song aspires to silence, and poetry to timbre. If the aesthetic conditions explored in this chapter—the envoicing of poetry (the *dire* of Mallarmé) and the silencing of melody (the *presque sans voix* of Debussy)—at first seemed like contradictory goals, placing them now side by side, we see how much they are the same. Mallarmé spoke of "transposing a fact of nature into its near vibratory disappearance," but this disappearance in poetry was exactly analogous to the disappearance of melody that we find in the later songs of Debussy or Fauré or Chausson. Looking for the purest possible expression, French composers discovered the *voix parlée* and, with it, a song that, like the "pure idea" of Mallarmé, had "nothing at all to pay back," a song that expressed almost nothing. And that discovery brought on one of the most unsung developments in the history of French music, a development I should like to call the unsinging of the *mélodie française*.

The clanging bell of "Les Heures" is a beautiful image of such unsinging, and it may also help to clarify what de Souza meant in 1899 when he described the uniquely materialist basis of symbolist poetry. He called it "the simultaneous and immediate *refraction* of what we think through what we see, hear, taste, smell, and touch." Singing has always promoted a physical display of thought, spelling out ideas through a flow of sensuous melody. But as should now be clear, the physical sensation de Souza caught was somehow different. By the late 1890s in France, the terms had been productively diverted, the order of expression twisted, through the very process of "simultaneous refraction" he now imagined.[111] As modern French poetry passed through a voice, music bent toward speech, the word toward song, and melody itself approached a form of that "pure idea" we might simply call *accent*. Neither musical nor verbal, the accent had nothing to say, so that song itself became more and more about the pure act of saying. The most profound lesson of symbolism surely lay here, in the *voix parlée* of the *mélodie française*. For on the eve of 1900, French song did conspire to think an "other" sort of music and in doing so produced, like French poetry, an uncommon musical result. It made its own language less expressive than simply expressed: inhaled, exhaled, tasted, felt, *dit*.

| *L'Art de dire*, or Language in Performance

The secret of our art consists in preventing the audience from recognizing it to be an illusion.

—*Sarah Bernhardt on "Pronunciation"*

O N THE OPENING PAGE OF his earliest published memoir, Reynaldo Hahn tells the story of a visit to one of his aging idols, the great diva of the Second Empire Pauline Viardot. The year was around 1900. Viardot was almost eighty, Hahn just twenty-five, although he had already established a reputation in Paris as a musician and *salonnaire* of considerable charm. He had become a lover of Proust, a confidant of Sarah Bernhardt, and a music critic for *La Presse*. He had published a fine collection of songs and mounted his first opera. Mostly, he was passionate about singing, a subject that not only would inform much future criticism but also figured into his conversation with Viardot that afternoon. As Hahn recalls it, the grande dame took the lead, posing an unexpectedly blunt question: "Do you really like the vapid manner in which your songs are sung?" she asked. "And is it necessary to have that pointed diction?" Hahn tried to deflect the criticism by launching into a discussion of French pronunciation, but Viardot changed the subject. "Sing me something," she commanded, and he consented with two songs: "Néère," from his *Etudes latines*, and "Cimetière de campagne," the latter at Viardot's request. When he had finished, she softened. "Yes, I like the way you sing," she said. "It's simple, it's good."[1]

There is no way of telling exactly what Viardot heard on that afternoon, but some of the recordings Hahn made later in life give an inkling. In the thirty years between 1909 and 1940, he recorded more than a hundred *mélodies* for French Gramophone, Columbia, Pathé, and Odéon, on disks featuring his own compositions, as well as those of Gounod, Chabrier, Fauré, Bizet, and Massenet—with an occasional chanson from the cabaret or countryside thrown in for good measure.[2] If he did not sing and play piano himself, he accompanied a favorite singer, tossing off the tunes in a single take as if entertaining friends. Indeed, the most conspicuous, or "pointed," aspect of his own performances had less to do with what he added, it seems, than with what he took away. There is a studied understatement in Hahn's singing, a tone that almost recalled the conversational style of the cabaret, where melody was little more than a vehicle for expressive declamation. One listens less to the voice itself than to the delivery, with its unusually clear vowels and consonants.

Viardot must have been at least somewhat prepared for what she heard that afternoon, for Hahn's declamatory singing was no secret in the Parisian salons of the day. In a lecture delivered at the Université des Annales in 1913, he confessed that, as a younger man, he had rebelliously cultivated this deliberately "antivocal" style.[3] Overcompensating for what he saw as the shortcomings of conventional voice lessons, he promoted realistic diction at the expense of everything else, and he referred disdainfully to those who worried over their voices as "merely" singers. "That went on for many years," he said.[4] Even later, he remained persuaded that good singing required little more than good speaking habits—the ability to *bien dire*, to use the French expression. For Hahn, the point of singing lay not in vocal purity but verbal sincerity, not in the artifice of the *chanteur* but the truth of the *diseur*.

The self-congratulatory tone of his memoir made that point especially clear, suggesting that even a figure as imposing as Viardot could not resist the charms of a well-spoken performer. And yet the anecdote also exposed a more general development in the history of French singing, a development affecting both musical style and, more basically, musical taste. Things had obviously changed in the salons of Hahn's day, enough to arouse the skepticism of a great performer from an earlier era. When the former diva asked her guest how he could possibly like "the vapid manner" in which people tended to sing his songs (*la façon mièvre dont on vous chante*), she did more than put him on the spot. She evoked the performance habits of a new generation and revealed her own historical distance in the process. In that sense, Viardot's question could easily be our own. How should we approach—at a remove of now more than one hundred years—this evidence of a changing performance practice for the French *mélodie*? And why *was* it necessary for singers of Hahn's generation "to have such pointed diction"?

The previous chapters have no doubt begun to suggest some answers, offering evidence of broad changes in the political, scientific, and aesthetic climate of Third Republican France, changes that would ultimately transform the ideology of the mother tongue. That French speech—and the varieties of its performance—had come to assume greater importance in the public imagination circa 1900 was as evident in the development of modern French phonetics as it was in the polemics surrounding modern French verse. Still, Viardot's question suggests something else again. It turns French diction into a specifically musical problem. And in the context of our own history of French melody, that problem proves to be unexpectedly significant, for the idea of diction, as it turns out, meant a good deal more to singers of Hahn's milieu than we might first suspect.

What *did* it mean? In the last chapter, we explored the poetic implications, but in practical terms, the French word is still difficult to translate. Take, for example, Paul Valéry's 1926 essay *De la Diction des vers* (On Reading Verse). English-language editions have avoided translating the title as *On the Diction of Verse* because diction, in English, connotes word choice, whereas in French it has more to do with uttering words aloud. When the context is singing, diction retains a more obvious sense of performance (from the Latin *dictio*, which, in rhetoric, signified the delivery of an oration), and yet, in most vocal pedagogy, the term is limited to the idea of accurate pronunciation. A translation of Hahn's 1913 lecture *Comment dire en chantant* thus renders the title *How to Enunciate in Singing* (and not, for example, *How to Speak While Singing*), as if pronouncing a language were merely a mechanical act, separable from expression in general.[5]

In French, though, the concept of diction is more comprehensive. It implies the condition of a text as it makes contact with a voice, a condition that yields two poetic possibilities: the emergence and the evanescence of the articulate word, or its "vibratory disappearance," to recall Mallarmé's apt phrase. The verb *dire* in Old French meant both "to sing" and "to say," and something of that doubling persists in modern usage. Like a slash separating the two speech acts, the verb embodies the difference between them, the friction between *vocalise* and articulate language. The testimony of Viardot and Hahn suggests that such friction had palpably increased in the years around 1900, as certain French singers sought to embrace more and more of the pleasures of speech.

Roland Barthes called this elusive space the "grain" of the voice. And his personal, idiosyncratic, and by now famous essay from 1972 still proves to be instructive. For Barthes, the novel term was meant to address not what the voice expressed but everything that hovered around expression. It encompassed, in his words, "the volume of the speaking and singing voice, the space in which the significations germinate 'from within the language and its very materiality.'"[6] This process of "signifying" had little to do with communication in the ordinary sense. It was "alien to communication," he said, and the distinction recalled the "double state" of Mallarmé's *parole*, where a vibration could escape the toil of common reportage. Barthes conjured a similarly liberated condition "where melody actually *works on* language" to express nothing at all. Summing it up "in a very simple word" that "must be taken quite seriously," he, too, called this phenomenon "the *diction* of language."[7]

Critics have tended to read all of Barthes's essays on voice as more evidence of the poststructuralist turn in his later teaching and writing. I find this essay telling, though, not just for the way it enlarges our concept of French diction but also for the way it focuses our sense of French history. After all, his very pointed description of a voice's encounter with language recalls many of the same values that informed singers of Hahn's generation—and it is hardly surprising. Barthes had a more or less direct link to such values as the pupil of Charles Panzéra, one of the most respected French baritones of Hahn's generation, who was known for his own understated and nuanced interpretation of *mélodies*. In that respect, we could say that Barthes came by his poststructuralism quite sincerely. Not only had he experienced this signifying through the sound of his own voice. He had also learned his lesson—the delicious possibility of a language unhinged from representation—from a singer even greater than Hahn, whose art and life depended on it.

———

It is this aspect of a language experienced *through* performance that forms the subject of this chapter. The focus is the ostensible art of speaking or singing words in public or private, known broadly in French as *l'art de dire*. I know of no better way to study this art than to listen to those who were said to have mastered it, which is what I propose to do, attending to the testimony—both the stories and the actual voices—of a select group of French singers who came of age after 1890 and preserved their art on record: not only Hahn and Panzéra, of course, but also Jane Bathori and Claire Croiza, Hector Dufranne and Camille Maurane, as well as foreigners: the Scottish mezzos Mary Garden and Maggie Teyte, and the Polish tenor Jean de Reszké. As it happens, most of the French singers were born after 1870: Bathori in 1877, Croiza in 1882.

Dufranne, born in 1870, came from Belgium, and Panzéra from Switzerland, although the latter moved to France permanently (and became a citizen) after he had volunteered in the French army in World War I. Hahn, born in Caracas just a few years before Bathori (in 1874), left Venezuela with his family when he was just four years old and essentially grew up Parisian.

The chronology is significant. For one thing, it places many of these singers within the reach of the new French school, suggesting that at a young age, they had collectively inhaled "the new breath (*le souffle nouveau*)," as Marcel Cohen put it, that enveloped the teaching of French in the early decades of the Third Republic.[8] To the extent that such teaching renewed the idea of French—the very *air* of the language they now learned to utter—we can imagine that it played some role in shaping the musical future. We have already seen how, in 1908, a poet like Camille Mauclair found reason to hold up singers like Bathori for "having developed the principles of a new kind of diction," a diction that supported and essentially defined what he called the complex "interior drama" of the modern *mélodie*. Bathori's almost uncannily flat and inward performances of the songs of Debussy, Ravel, and Satie (still available on record) more than bear this out.

But I will not, of course, be concerned only with singers. The art of the spoken word belonged as much to the theater as to the drawing room, as much to plays and verse as to opera and song. In a country whose national conservatory proposed to train both actors and singers under a single roof, we might expect to find connections between them. And we can: there is evidence in a number of contemporary treatises on the vocal arts. Léon Brémont, for example, who retired from acting to become an even more respected teacher, was fond of using musical examples to make his points. In his *L'Art de dire les vers* (1903), he referred frequently to the great baritone Jean-Baptiste Faure when explaining the proper manner to declaim a poem. We will see how Faure himself, in his treatise *La Voix et le chant* (1886), promoted certain classic techniques of elocution as the foundation of his singing method. And that was not all. In *Le Chant théâtral* (1911), the French bass Jacques Isnardon continued to pass on hints conspicuously drawn from the spoken theater, including comments from the renowned actors of the Comédie-française, Régnier and Got. In the 1920s, no less a figure than Paul Valéry, hoping to discover the secret of speaking verse, sought out the expertise (and the voice) of Claire Croiza, then at the height of her singing career.

In other words, we cannot really separate actors from singers in discussions of the French art of diction, for the performers themselves saw their paths as intersecting. And so we will listen to a few memorable *diseurs* and *diseuses* along the way, most notably, to Sarah Bernhardt, who took the time to record a number of poems and plays for posterity, some of them for the new Archive de la parole directed by Ferdinand Brunot. What do these recordings tell us? We know that Bernhardt's readings of Racine so captivated the public in her native France and abroad that she would eventually be awarded the medal of the Legion of Honor for her role in "spreading the French language throughout the world."[9] And yet in listening to her voice on a record today, we are more likely to be taken aback than taken in. A strange kind of *mélodie* emerges from her tremulous cadences, with pitches and rhythms so true that they can easily be transcribed. This melodious diction, moreover, did not stop with Bernhardt. The historian Theodore Zeldin relates the remarkable story of how René Viviani, who was minister of public instruction in 1914 (and who, as it happened, adored Bernhardt), actually "took lessons at the Comédie-Française in the art of declamation, and used to spend long hours practicing his parliamentary speeches as though they were songs."[10] Apparently, the lessons paid off, leading Viviani before long to the coveted post of prime minister.

Zeldin found Viviani's story curious, but the evidence suggests that the practice was not so unusual. Considering the sheer proliferation of self-help manuals after 1890 on what came to be known as "expressive diction," one could say that he was simply doing his job. All manner of experts—not just phoneticians but psychologists and doctors, actors and singers—began to theorize, it seems, about French pronunciation in this period, in books addressed to their own kind, as well as to orators, lawyers, schoolteachers, foreigners, and deaf people.[11] And that development, of course, makes a singer like Hahn appear differently, reframing the question Viardot posed on that afternoon in 1900. One can begin to see how the declamatory *mélodie* cultivated by Hahn's generation, with its apparently "studied" diction, in fact mirrored the melodious, lyric declamation cultivated by actors and other public officials. A uniquely modern ideology of expression emerges, as speaking and singing came to converge on the same object, which was French itself. As that object installed itself in the voice, the nuances of French pronunciation would not only become the subject of a new music. They would also come to represent the very rationale for a new oral pedagogy—the actual substance of voice lessons.

As a musicologist and a musician, I, too, have profited from these lessons, at a distance of more than one hundred years. In learning to hear, and to imitate, the diction of French performers, I have come to appreciate certain qualities that made the *mélodie* work—or, as Viardot would say about Hahn's singing, what made it "good." That, I suppose, is the aim of historical performance practice. And as we witness early music professionals of the twenty-first century work their way into more and more recent repertoires, this corpus of French song becomes an equally fitting candidate.[12] Yet my purpose in exploring the French *art de dire* is not to discover the "right" way of singing *mélodies*, nor to uncover the authenticity of spoken French circa 1900 as some kind of absolute value. I am more interested in the cultural meaning of a body of songs that offered "nothing" to sing and the values that motivated their performance. Is it possible, still, to taste the nuances of these reticent melodies? Or to feel their undeniable sincerity? French singers of the Belle Époque do not answer that question directly, but listening to their stories—and their diction—can usefully shift our perspective. Indeed, this twin testimony turns the work of the language scientists on its head, as the sounds of French become refigured in singers' mouths not as material quantities but as aesthetic qualities, or even objects of rare and fragile beauty.

Venetian Glass and Marqueterie

Hahn once again brings us straight to the point. In one of his more memorable lectures on song, he conjured exactly this sort of object as he likened singing to a work of Venetian glass. The glassblower was an artist who always worked in the heat of the moment, he said, subjecting his material "to infinite manipulations." "He turns it in spirals, pulls it out, flattens it, makes a ball; from this ball, he pulls out tendrils and fashions them in turn; he inflicts on this malleable outline more sinuous conceits, protuberances, hollows, creating the most variable and imaginative shapes, all while the glass continues to burn."[13] Hahn explained that he could never watch such artists without thinking of the singer "in the moment of singing." The analogy was meant to evoke the public face of the performer, who like the glassblower always worked before an assembled audience. But it also embodied, more pointedly, the pure sensation of the song. Singing, Hahn suggested, involved the same sorts of manipulations in sound: pulling and then crystallizing not just notes but nuances—the myriad colors and shapes of the spoken word—from the "heat" of a malleable melody.

He certainly knew that sensation firsthand.[14] But to illustrate his point, he called on other witnesses as well, performers whose French reputations were built on the same kind of verbal artistry. Among them were the Polish tenor Jean de Reszké and his predecessor Jean-Baptiste Faure, "grandfather of baritones."[15] Neither had an active career by the time Hahn was writing. De Reszké had retired from the stage in 1903, Faure in 1886, but their legacy lived on in memory and especially in their teaching. The cosmopolitan de Reszké, whom Hahn knew personally, had risen to prominence in Paris in the 1880s by creating roles for Massenet and Gounod; he was admired not only for his perfect French (like many well-bred Poles he was multilingual) but also for his dramatic flair. Hahn called special attention to the nature of his vocal technique, founded on what the tenor himself called the *voix parlée*. The concept could be traced in part to de Reszké's Parisian studies in the 1870s with the tenor Giovanni Sbriglia (teacher of Pol Plançon and Mary Garden), who stressed the fundamental importance of diction for acquiring proper vocal resonance.[16]

The older Faure had established a reputation for intelligent, well-spoken singing a good generation before that. By the time de Reszké was making his mark, in fact, Faure had already become something of a legendary figure in operatic circles,[17] with tales of his triumph in Gounod's *Faust* acquiring almost mythical status. Hahn was too young to have attended that opera, of course, but he did describe the rare experience of hearing the great baritone much later in life. Actually, he had gone to eavesdrop at "a certain church" where the elderly Faure (who lived until 1914) used to attend vespers:

> Standing behind a pillar, I listened with profound emotion as a voice rose beneath the vaults, a voice I would not call marvelous, but which, to the ear of one who loves singing, even venerates it, was deeply moving. It seemed, as I listened to Monsieur Faure, that I was observing a remarkable and transcendent work of sonorous *marqueterie*. Each tone, each fragment of tone, was classed, encrusted, fitted, in the most astonishing way.[18]

If the image was a shade less exotic than the swirling colors of Venetian glass, the art it evoked was all the more French. Hahn's marvelous metaphor called to mind a sound where the incisive articulations and pearly timbres of the *voix parlée* were perfectly inlaid into the grain of the singing voice. Faure's own method book, *Le Voix et le chant*, offered clear advice about how to achieve such effects. Perhaps for this reason Hahn thought it "the most captivating book ever written on singing."[19] Published in 1886, the year of Faure's retirement, it represented the art of a singer whose star had risen long before the period of our own study. And yet his pedagogy was, as we shall see, remarkably germane. Not only did Faure develop a technique that could be considered, in many of its elements, distinctively French but he also framed his pedagogy in terms that would resonate with the ideals of a new, more liberal French education. It may not be hard to imagine the reasons why, but it is enlightening to see exactly how.

———

Faure opened his book with a curious story, relating his attempts at the beginning of the previous decade to reform vocal instruction at the Conservatoire. That was, he tells us, in 1870, following a general directive from the minister of the beaux arts. The purpose of the decree was not entirely clear from the context, but it seemed to recall similar initiatives by the Ministry of Public Instruction in the same period, initiatives that would, as we know, have important consequences for the future of education all over France. In just a few years, the enterprising young Buisson would set sail for Philadelphia to study primary schooling in America and the teaching of the mother tongue. And soon after his return, Ernest Legouvé would bring out, at the ministry's request, the influential primer on public speaking that we examined in chapter 2, *L'Art de la lecture* (1877).

The connection between these disparate political events is strengthened when we learn that Legouvé sat on the Conservatoire's advisory committee.[20] In this position, he proved instrumental for Faure's novel ideas. Like Bréal, who stressed the value of "talking, talking, always talking," or even those French commissioners who would admire America's open classrooms and their lessons in "imitative elocution," Faure seems to have wanted the conservatory to open its traditionally closed studios. He objected to the secrecy of the private lesson and proposed that the conservatory establish a new public course, where teachers and students would come together for mutual instruction. "We must not forget," he explained, "that singing, like declamation, is an imitative art, and that . . . students should hear absolutely everything they can."[21]

Faure's plan was officially adopted by order of the commission in June 1870, and yet by 1886, he admits, its effects were no longer much in evidence, the teachers having soon returned to their old ways. By using his treatise to recall this forgotten history, Faure accomplished several goals at once. He not only established himself in a class apart,[22] aligning his singing method with a nobler educational mission, but also he capitalized on his earlier political success, "seizing the opportunity to present his case once again." Indeed, he believed now more than ever that to elevate the art of singing, one would have to "emancipate education," replacing the conservatoire's "little chapels" of private interest, as he called them, with "the impersonal teaching of a true École."[23] Heard in 1886, in the aftermath of the Ferry laws, the remark no doubt had a special ring. It implied that even an art as subjective as singing might benefit from the emancipated (and secular) ethos of the new French school.

Of course, in many other respects Faure's teaching, like most vocal training, remained strongly traditional.[24] I shall not be concerned, then, with outlining his entire method. I am more interested in tracing the origins of a few ideas taken up by later generations, especially younger readers like Hahn. At the very start of Faure's exposition, for instance, we find a telling question: Was it necessary to have a big voice in the theater? No, he said, a singer should strive instead for nuance: "Have we not in fact seen many singers who, after struggling on stage next to artists endowed with much bigger voices, ultimately surpassed them with charm, with sweetness, with expression?" One suspects that the retired baritone was thinking of himself.[25] But the remark also made clear that his concept of *La Voix et le chant* would involve a good deal more than vocalizing.

It involved, for one thing, a thorough study of French pronunciation. And here was where Faure's goals began to resemble those of Legouvé, who had placed the French voice, and the art of elocution, at the very foundation of a liberal primary school. "One of the most precious elements of vocal resonance (*coloris*)," Faure claimed, lay not in the singer's tone but in "in the diversity of vowel timbres, open and closed, nasal and oral," without which "song [was] but a succession of monotonous sounds."[26] Like Legouvé, he, too, advocated elocution as the basis of a sound technique, and he urged his students to begin by reading *à haute voix*. "Take the text of the piece that you want to perform," he said, "and read it aloud in fragments. Then immediately try it again while singing, to reproduce, with the most scrupulous fidelity, the sounds of the *voix parlée*."[27] The approach left no doubt about the foundation of Faure's art because it placed the speaking voice at the very core of singing. Indeed, Faure developed some elaborate exercises to help students develop this core. The most innovative was a new—and, it seems, very French—twist he brought to the classic *vocalise*. He called them *Exercises-Vocalises avec paroles* (Vocalise-exercises with words).

The title was a contradiction in terms, of course, because *vocalise* refers by definition to singing *without* words, usually on a single, open syllable. And yet it was precisely this activity, often considered "the Palladium of the singer's art," as Faure put it, that he deemed potentially harmful. The judgment seemed to pose a sly challenge to classic Italian pedagogy, with its focus on the warmth of the singer's *ah*. Here is what Faure has to say: "Vocalizing on *ah* can be one of the most painful exercises. Over time, it promotes the contraction of the muscles of the larynx, a condition that, in a different genre, suggests an analogy with what we call "writer's cramp" (*la crampe des écrivains*)."[28] Singing, the analogy implied, was a liquid expression of language analogous to beautiful penmanship. Almost a century later,

Roland Barthes would make a strikingly similar point in "The Grain of the Voice," when he described the true achievement of the French *mélodie* as "the sung writing of language."[29]

Faure's *vocalise* exercises were designed to develop the singer's control over this unique writing instrument. The exercises looked unimpressive on the page, resembling little more than folk songs, but the simplicity was deceptive. Students were, in fact, told not to attempt words until they had thoroughly practiced the melodies on solfège syllables and then on several different vowel sounds. The point was eventually "to train singers to give the proper sonority to all those sounds, especially the back vowels or nasals they seemed to dread so much."[30] Musical Example 4.1 shows one such exercise, a hymnlike melody based around the interval of the second, designed "to exercise the voice on the *o bref, ah, au ô, é, e muet.*" Practicing it, we begin to get the point. It gives us an idea, at least, of what Hahn might have heard as he eavesdropped on the unsuspecting Faure, singing in "a certain church" sometime after 1900. Through these simple songs, Faure taught the singer to engrave all the delicate curves and angles, all the nuanced shadings of French, directly *into* the singing voice, one colorful syllable at a time.

It went without saying, of course, that before embarking on such studies, the singer would have to get rid of all speech defects. That meant the ordinary, pathological ones like lisping or stuttering, as well as circumstantial ones, like a southern accent. Faure made the requirement explicit in his chapter "Pronunciation and Articulation." Once again following the example of Legouvé, who had ridiculed the provincial twang in *L'Art de la lecture*, Faure went on to describe how "certain southerners" readily mispronounced common words ("saying *tronne* for *trône, jonne* for *jaune, fâme* for *femme*"). He thus recommended, as the only acceptable alternative, "the pronunciation of the north and center of France," that is, the pronunciation of Paris.[31] The linguistic centrism may be familiar, but Faure's rationale was delightfully poetic: this was the only accent, he claimed, in which one could hear all "the secret . . . sonorities, and infinite delicacies of our language."[32]

———

Faure's *La Voix et le chant* offers striking evidence of a modern vocal method founded on the ideal of sonorous French speech. Inscribing the *voix parlée* directly into the singing voice, it not only reflected the orality of the new French school, with its emphasis on reading as an art, but also revealed the basis for a specifically French concept of diction, a phonetic concept that would inform the practice of singers in future generations. Jean de Reszké, as Hahn tells us, maintained much the same ideal of the spoken word in his own teaching, an ideal we may recognize in the voice of one of his more celebrated

foreign students, the soprano Maggie Teyte.[33] And we hear it, of course, in the voice of Hahn himself, through writings and recordings that reveal the persistence of such values well into the twentieth century.

Nor are these our only witnesses. Jacques Isnardon would take modern phoneticism to much greater lengths in his own enlightened singing method, *Le Chant théâtral* (1911), which touched on the new-fangled studies of Dr. Marage. Isnardon continued to pay homage to Faure's *Le Voix et le chant* in his teaching, and the French baritone Camille Maurane followed suit a generation later. Remembering his own lessons with the venerable Claire Croiza in the 1930s, Maurane described how she—like Faure—had required all her pupils to declaim their texts aloud, and to chant them on a single note, before allowing the melody to cross their lips. And it apparently worked. Listening to Maurane's postwar recordings, one is reminded of that felicitous image of sonorous marquetry that Hahn first ascribed to Faure.

This is not to say that Faure established the foundations of a new French school, for there were certainly other singers and other methods. But he and his disciples were instrumental in establishing a new singerly discourse centered on the speaking voice. By making speech the center of their singing method, they brought the French accent into the realm of aesthetics, revealing not just the reality but the beauty of that accent. And as French sounds began to be appreciated in terms of their unique *coloris*, or resonance, French eloquence itself would acquire a new dimension—the ideal of sonorous elegance. Understanding this ideal leads to a different kind of voice lesson, one that puts French letters, and the modern *art de dire*, into a distinctly new light.

Vibrant Noise, Expressive Elegance

That lesson emerges most clearly in discussions of one sound in particular. Complaints about it cropped up again and again. Too many Parisians did not pronounce this sound "naturally." The unacceptable alternative that rumbled in their throats seemed to pose a threat to the beauty of the tongue. There was a name for this inelegant noise: Legouvé, Faure, and others called it *grass-eyement*. The word may well strike twenty-first-century readers as strange. My own informal survey of Parisian friends suggests that the term is hardly known today, nor is it to be found in most dictionaries, and with good reason. It describes a pronunciation error that in our day defines the norm: the unique Parisian way of saying *r*. Or perhaps I should simply say the French way of saying *r*, for that is how we think of it today. It is a sound that most foreigners find awkward to imitate, requiring the speaker to produce a sometimes muffled, sometimes scraped, sometimes gurgled articulation at the back of the throat. Linguists call it the "dorsal" or "uvular" *r*, depending on how far back you put it. But in the nineteenth century, French people of taste considered any variety of this articulation objectionable, an inelegant and lazy habit. The verb *grasseyer* (from which the noun *grasseyement* is derived) conveyed such offense by its very form, constructed as it is from an adjective (*gras*) that means not only "fat" but also "coarse" or "crude." Certainly, those who belonged to the best Parisian society did not learn to *grasseyer*.

What did they learn to do? In a word, *vibrer*, to vibrate. They executed this phoneme not at the lazy back of the throat, but in the front, just behind the teeth, with a gently sonorous flip of the tongue. This fact alone is pertinent to a history of song, simply for what it tells us about older performance practices. Other historical witnesses offer ample testimony that Parisians pronounced their French differently before 1900. Already in 1887, for example, Darmesteter had become aware of the erosion of the spoken tongue, and Rousselot had tried to help on this score. If he had designed new phonetic tools to teach about shifts in pronunciation, his colleagues at the Conservatoire played another role. He, in fact, pointed out in his *Principes de prononciation française* (1902) that although the "*r grasseyée ou parisienne*" had essentially become the norm, the "traditional *r*" was "still very common," largely because "professors at the Conservatory [had] continued to teach it to Parisians destined for the theater."[34]

Today classically trained performers also treat the *r* as a special case in whatever language they happen to be uttering, for the rolled variety has always seemed more suitable for vocal projection and placement.[35] And so we could probably leave our history at that. Yet in pursuing this idea of the "traditional" Parisian *r*, one soon discovers that for turn-of-the-century witnesses, it had a character all its own, subtly different from the traditional *r* in other regions of France let alone in other romance languages. Listening to the accounts of this difference, we begin to see how the study of pronunciation, even of a single phoneme, can resolve into larger issues, reflecting broad cultural ideals of taste, deportment, even temperament. Rousselot placed this *r* at the very head of his discussion of consonants and created a category—as far as I can tell, a uniquely French category—that he called *vibrantes* ("vital" or "resonant" letters).[36] But the artists of his era tell us something else again, showing us both the significance of this letter in the French imagination, and the extent of its vitality.

Legouvé is ever enlightening. He devoted an entire chapter of his 1877 *Art of Reading* to the execution of this pesky phoneme ("Some peculiar defects of pronunciation"), offering a remedy used by the great actor Talma to teach lazy actors how to "vibrate" properly:

> Talma's idea was first to pronounce [the letters *d* and *t*] rapidly and alternately; as in *de te de te*, etc. Then by degrees joining *r* to them, he pronounced the new combinations also rapidly and alternately, *dre, tre, dre, tre*, etc. By this contrivance, it struck him, that he could fish up the letter *r* from the depths of the throat where it seemed to prefer keeping itself; that he could compel it, as it were, to answer the call of its companions inviting it to dance.[37]

It was certainly an imaginative approach to speech therapy. But the image of the shy, retiring *r* just waiting to be transported to the dance floor tells us more. Legouvé developed the idea in another anecdote, this one about a frustrated young actor who happens to discover his *r* on the same day he finds true love. As the story goes, almost as soon as the girl says yes, the as-yet-unheard vibration surges forth, arriving suddenly and effortlessly on the actor's lips. Excited by his success, he stays up for hours, walking the streets and rolling his *r* endlessly into the night, "as if," Legouvé concluded, "in a grand triumphal procession!"[38] The allegory thus linked the recalcitrant letter, in its enunciatory *éclat*, with the young man's vital fluids—and it is not surprising: the French verb *vibrer* also meant "to thrill."

Hahn himself had thrilled to this vibration. In an essay published just two years before his death, in 1946, we find him waxing just as poetic about the *r vibrée*. He was answering the query of a disgruntled correspondent who had asked him "why a detestable pronunciation in the spoken language" should still be "admissible in singing."[39] The nature of the question offers even clearer evidence that the *parler Parisien* of the 1940s was no longer what it once had been. Hahn was the first to admit it, complaining of the *grasseyement* he now regularly heard at the conservatory's vocal juries. Yet, to his interlocutor's question, he demurred. This vibrant phoneme, he said, was far from detestable. It still rolled naturally off the tongues of a good portion of the population. The people of Touraine, Normandy, Burgundy, and the Southwest used it in "infinitely subtle ways." It had given "light and joy to the language of the troubadours." Among those living in the Pyrenees, it had "the gentle sound of a bubbling spring." Hahn even recalled how, on a recent trip to Toulouse, the "ravishing" pronunciation of his taxi driver, whose *r*'s were "at once so shining and so sweet," had caused him to take a long and costly ride around the city just "for the pleasure of hearing him talk." Nor would he let us forget the "rich and unctuous sound" of the Perigord *r* or, heaven forbid, those inimitable *r*'s of the great actor Mounet-Sully, with their "unspeakable nuances ranging from the most soothing suavity to the most terrible violence."[40]

We get the picture. Hahn positively longed for this letter, a sound that had all but disappeared from Parisian parlance (as well as from the diction of singers) by the end of the Third Republic, a letter that once upon a time had been so "natural" on the Île de France. The nostalgia made clear how much the sounds of the language—indeed, a single letter of the alphabet—had come to mean in the mouths of performers of his generation, how much physical and emotional weight they carried, how much, in short, the basic units of the tongue had turned into discrete objects of desire. The phoneticians of the 1890s might have worked to make such objects visible. Performing artists made them lovable. Charles Panzéra put the matter most succinctly, perhaps, when discussing that fine little letter in his own handbook on singing from the 1950s, *L'Art vocal.* He called the *r*, simply, "the most beautiful of all the consonants."[41]

———

Such images of sonorous beauty would enhance, in turn, the larger picture of the tongue, extending to more general ideas of French expression. It soon became a point of deep significance that these sounds, which made a strong impression on the ear, often left no mark upon the face, no trace of effort in the expression of the speaker. Phoneticians described the pronunciation of the traditional *r*, for instance, as a matter of the tongue acting quickly and efficiently behind scarcely parted teeth and stationary lips. But this was characteristic of the language as a whole. A 1914 handbook on pronunciation by the linguist Maurice Grammont tells us that "in French, the work is done almost entirely *on the inside,* and it is intense work, indeed, the muscles remaining extremely taut. But from the outside most of the effort remains unseen. The checks are almost immobile, the lips half-opened, the face calm."[42] This picture of impassivity contrasted starkly with the description of France's neighbors on each side, those speakers of German or English, who, as Grammont would have it, moved their jaws when speaking as though "masticating with great effort." The Gallic temperament evidently recoiled at such exhibition. If the language was hard work, the French did not let on. It was this measure of control that led to Grammont's most telling observation, forming the basis for an accepted linguistic "fact": such exterior calm was responsible, he concluded, for "the supreme elegance of French diction."[43]

The elegance of the tongue was now a matter of restraint. This truth would find its way into musical performance, in sometimes startling ways, as we shall see. Singers, too, learned to keep their efforts to themselves. Hahn had said as much in his previously mentioned lecture on diction (*Comment dire en chantant*), calling attention to his own infamous habit of smoking through a song. "Unfortunately, I am so addicted to smoking," he admitted, "that the cigarette has become part of my body." Yet the little vice concealed a greater virtue. To keep the cigarette in one's mouth—even in the midst of a performance—showed a certain mastery of diction: it proved that Hahn barely moved his lips. All the real work took place, as Grammont himself asserted, *à l'intérieur*. The external calm not only ensured consistency of vocal tone but saved the audience, said Hahn, from a "grotesque spectacle" of pronunciation.[44] In much the same way, Croiza counseled students to maintain a noble visage while on stage. But the critic Georges Jean-Aubry would take the idea one step further, revealing the true value of such interior control. His encomium on the singer Jane Bathori in *La Musique française d'aujourd'hui* (1916) praised the "discreet and human art" of her singing, dismissing those who judged her manner as cold, those who preferred to see "a body trembling," or to listen to "rending cries." They obviously had missed the point, and it was "too bad for them," he said. "It's still a French virtue to understand the half-said thing (*C'est encore une vertu française que de comprendre à demi-mot*)."[45]

À demi-mot: the expression recalled the opening image of Valéry's 1912 *Psaume sur une voix*, a free-verse poem that paid homage to the voice of another discreetly human artist, the long-deceased Mallarmé:

> A demi-voix
> D'une voix douce et faible disant de grande choses:
> D'importantes, d'étonnantes, de profondes et justes choses
> D'une voix douce et faible. . . .
>
> (With muted voice / a soft and faint voice, speaking of great things: / Important, astonishing, profound and righteous things / In a soft and faint voice. . . .)[46]

Valéry described the poet's voice as containing all "the menace of thunder, the presence of absolutes / in the fine detail of a flute, the delicacy of pure sound."[47] Next to the account of Bathori's singing, the comment takes on greater resonance. In each case, the *à demi* is meant to signal the highest mark of refinement, as if raising a physical trait of French pronunciation, where words escaped from "half-opened" lips, to the level of a discourse where discretion reigned supreme. Tales of such virtuous understatement would appear again and again in the annals of French performance in our period, curious stories about great singers or actors who had triumphed in just this way—by holding their expression in reserve.

Hahn recalled a night when Jean de Reszké, for example, stricken with a bout of tracheitis, had mesmerized his audience with a performance of Lohengrin, his execution all the more exquisite as he performed with diminished faculties, "concealing his illness behind the beauty of renewed interpretation."[48] Legouvé relayed a very similar tale in his *Art of Reading*, explaining how "resources of articulation" were often brought forth "by a fortunate hoarseness." He told a story about the great actor Hugues-Marie-Désiré Bouffé, who, in a performance of *Père Grandet*, became not merely hoarse but mute, forced "to recite his words in dumb show," as Legouvé expressed it. This vocal weakness proved, once again, a strength, for the actor "was actually more natural, more affecting, and far more impressive," said Legouvé, when "distinct articulation took the place of indistinct sound."[49]

The stories offered an unexpected twist on the beauty of the French speaking voice, which stirred the listener all the more, it seemed, by falling silent. Jacques Isnardon would draw much the same conclusion in his *Le Chant théatral* (1911), remembering his experience of hearing the Flemish soprano Marie Heilbronn at a time when she, too, was suffering from some minor vocal ailment. It was 1885, and she was preparing what would in fact be her final role,[50] Cleopatra in Massé's *Une Nuit de Cléopâtre*:

> In the second act, if my memory is correct, there is a phrase where Cleopatra warns a slave, who is in love with her, of the terrible fate that awaits him. Heilbron [*sic*], whose vocal abilities were restrained on this occasion, nonetheless delivered these few measures with a perfect evenness of tone, a fullness and force of expression that were extremely moving.
>
> On another day, truly suffering this time, she asked if she might spare herself during the rehearsal. So she uttered her phrase without any voice at all. The effect was far more stunning than before. Freed from the distractions of the voice, the interpretation itself was liberated, and so too the formation of the words. Moreover, as sound failed her, the singer experienced that necessity of replacing its effect with a redoubling of articulation. Knowing how to realize all the nuances [in this way]...she *doubled her emotion*...and mine as well.[51]

A song that proved more powerful when mute? It was a strange conclusion, to be sure, and yet it also shed light on things we have already observed in another context. Remember Debussy's unusual performance direction in the *Chanson de Bilitis*, which asked the singer of "La Flûte" to conclude *presque sans voix*, with almost no voice at all. The notation seemed to serve the same purpose, the enforced muting of the singer producing a more sincere and "natural" diction—and a more affecting delivery. Debussy had anticipated the point in a letter he wrote to Chausson in 1893, just after he had begun work on *Pelléas et Mélisande*. "I've found myself using," he explained, "and quite spontaneously, too, a means of expression which I think quite unusual: namely silence (don't laugh)." As he conceived it, silence had the potential to realize an effect very similar to the one described by Isnardon, a notable increase of feeling. In the composer's words, "it is perhaps the only way to give the emotion of a phrase its full value."[52]

His Mélisande, of course, would die in silence, and so, too, Fauré's Eve, as we saw in chapter 1. Yet we are now in a better position to understand how those idealized endings reflected, in more than one sense, a condition of the spoken language. The silent death was the epitome of restraint, a muting of drama that ensured the naturalness and elegance of the denouement. But such silence, we should not forget, also haunted a very specific sound in French, evoking yet another order of expressive significance. For if muteness figured in the half-said word, defining the virtuous temperament of French performers, it also defined, more pointedly, the central timbre of the tongue, a sound that was said to distinguish French from all the other European languages. I refer to that paradoxical vowel we have encountered many times by now: the half-silent phoneme the French call *e muet* (mute *e*). I want to take it up again, this time from the perspective of its performance, to explore the greater consequence of this vowel *à demi-voix* for the modern arts of diction. We shall see how this *e*, more than just a letter, embodied in its less-than-vibrant tone larger questions of French expression: evoking not just the muteness of modern music, but the very "genius" of the language.

Dir(e)

That was what the linguist Albert Dauzat more or less implied in a postwar primer on French, *Le Génie de la langue française* (1954). The apparent point of the book was to uphold the central values of the French tongue and to preserve the language from ruin. In the opening pages, Dauzat complained, as Hahn had done, that the once elegant language of French was beginning to lose its clarity and distinction, as speakers chose "the path of laziness." Lost along that path was a sound that, in his view, proved indispensable for the clarity of French diction. Dauzat announced it, in boldface, as the very first item on his agenda: "the role of the mute e." Here is what he said:

This little sound—the shortest, most neutral, most unstable sound—disappears and reappears depending on the context of the word, or on the needs or quality of the elocution. It is a sound that on its own amounts to so little, yet is enough, in the capricious play of speech, to modify the architecture of words and phrases, materializing to separate consonants . . . or evaporating to permit elision. It is one of the most typical elements of French pronunciation. And yet it is not so easy to characterize, not even for specialists.[53]

He attempted to characterize it nonetheless, asserting first what it was not: not the French *è* or the *é*, certainly not the *eu*. By process of elimination, Dauzat would arrive at the unusually poetic definition cited already in chapter 1: "in reality," he said, "it is the neutral vowel *par excellence*, a confluence where all the vowels meet *to be silenced*."[54]

The description called up the familiar triangle of vowels, as if to depict, in a more tangible way, the natural "inwardness" of the French language. The pale gray sound defined the most interior point of the scheme, located inside the two axes, at the very center of the mouth. It was thus the most hidden and discreet of all the vowels, lying at the still point of the tongue, where timbre was effaced. Voltaire once wrote teasingly to an Italian friend: "you reproach us for our mute *e*'s, as a sad and veiled sound that dies upon our lips, but it is precisely in these sounds that lies the great harmony of our poetry and prose."[55] Filling the spaces of an utterance with its almost voiceless "air," this vowel brought out, in its very neutrality, all the harmonious elegance of French words, representing the single most characteristic feature of *la diction française*.

No wonder it attracted so much attention from those modern guardians of the tongue, the phoneticians, poets, and performers of the Third Republic. No wonder, indeed, that essays extolling the virtues of this letter became increasingly prominent in reputable journals of the 1890s. To take just one example, the progressive *Mercure de France* opened its January 1895 issue with a long piece on "The Role of the Mute E in French Poetry" by Robert de Souza, pointing out the letter's musical variety and complexity and its importance for free verse.[56] But De Souza's conclusions had been inspired by an even more interesting figure—a contemporary actor and singer named Léon Brémont.[57] A popular performer of his time, Brémont's stage career peaked in 1897, when he played opposite Sarah Bernhardt in Rostand's hit *La Samaritaine*. But his lasting contribution to the stage came only after his retirement, in a series of pedagogical studies on the declamatory arts. The work that made his name was a much reprinted how-to book he published in

1903, *L'Art de dire les vers*.[58] As a text that draws together a number of the themes that we have so far encountered, it deserves a closer look.

———

Interestingly, there was a market for this kind of book. In the 1870s, after Catulle Mendès first launched his Parisian *matinées poétiques*, public readings of verse had become hugely popular affairs, drawing enthusiastic crowds to the Odéon, the Théâtre Sarah-Bernhardt, and eventually to the Comédie-Française. Brémont hoped to improve the quality of these occasions by offering practical advice to would-be *diseurs*. As he saw it, even the most experienced readers had something to learn: if poets tended to psalmodize their delivery, professors had weak or colorless voices. But it was the actors who needed the most help, for, despite talent and training, they often did not know the difference between drama and lyric. What Brémont called the *manie d'extérioriser*—the zeal to act everything out—had ruined many a poetic reading, and so he advised actors to tone it down. Just as a great singer learned to "speak the song" (*parler le chant*), he said, a good actor had to know how to "sing poetry" (*chanter les vers*).[59]

The advice recalled the *voix parlée* of Faure, and the connection was not accidental. Like Hahn, Brémont adored Faure's artistry, and he pointed to the baritone's performances as "unforgettable lessons" in the art of diction. In a chapter on consonants and vowels, for example, Brémont described Faure's ability to hold back certain plosives for expressive effect, and chided actors for never thinking of doing the same. "When you insist on acting everything *out*, you never dream of holding anything *in*," he said, "and yet what delicacies are to be found by doing so!"[60] Successful *diseurs* had to develop a sense for the "exact prolongation of syllables," monitoring "the balance between the quality of articulation and the quantity of sound." Which syllable had the greatest potential to affect this internal balance? It was the *e muet*, of course. Brémont devoted three entire chapters to this nuance, which represented, in his words, the absolute "touchstone for a good *diseur* of lyric verse."[61]

The extra attention was necessary, it seems, to clear up misunderstandings. Foreigners often made spurious judgments about French poetry "because of their inability to feel the suppleness with which our mute *e* enriches [it]." To feel this quality properly, he said, "one had to be born on French soil, or at least cradled in the love of our national rhythm."[62] Indeed, those who judged French poetry as "nothing but a play of rhyme, without rhythm," had not recognized that the "longs and breves, those values that our poetry supposedly lacks, are in fact *created* by this vowel." Yet the vowel elicited similar confusion at home. Brémont was especially impatient with phoneticians who wished to unburden French verse of these so-called silent letters. He eventually ended up, like de Souza, at the Collège de France in the laboratories of the Abbé Rousselot, hoping to verify his intuitions about the French alexandrine.[63] Brémont used phonetics against the phoneticians, that is, to reveal not the nullity but the nuance of the *e muet*: its subtle power to make French poetry speak. Perhaps, he mused, the vowel should be given a completely different name: "Call it veiled, supple, soft, attenuated, variable, colored, poetic, feeble—anything but mute!"[64]

All mute *e*'s were evidently *not* created equal, and, with that knowledge, Brémont made a simple rule of thumb. "For an ear capable of enjoying finely and fully the treasures of our prosody," he said, "the mute *e* at the interior of a line of poetry, when it is not elided to a neighboring vowel, *always* has a value, however minimal it may be!"[65] The values were difficult to capture in writing, but Brémont made an attempt, conceiving an auxiliary notation with a sliding scale. He used the number 1 to indicate an *e muet* receiving its full weight, equal to that of other syllables; 2 for a sound more murmured than pronounced; and 3 for an *e* that was more or less unspoken but still suggested—by a puff of air, perhaps, or a slight lengthening of the syllable before it. In later editions of the treatise, Brémont called this final form a "compensatory value" (*valeur de compensation*), offering several examples from modern poets, including these lines from Mallarmé's *Apparition*:

3
La <u>lune</u> s'attristait. Des séraphins en pleurs

　　　　　　　　　　　　1　　　2
Rêvant, l'archet aux doigts, dans le calme des fleurs

(The moon saddens. The seraphim in tears / Dreaming, bow in hand, in the stillness of the flowers . . .)

Brémont underlined the word *lune* to indicate its subtle rhythmic pull, the bright-dark *u* sounding a momentary complaint, before tumbling voicelessly into the sad and sibilant verb. In the next line, the two *e*'s of the second half, one longer than the other, produce a gentle murmuring. The moment calms the rhythm of the line whose first half flexes—tensely—like archer's fingers poised on a bow. De Souza offered an explanation of this attenuated effect when he described the importance of the mute *e* for French poetry: "When we speak we make ourselves understood as much by the *movement* and *tone* as by the specific meaning of the words. From these two elements are born the diverse rhythms whose allure and color govern pronunciation, making it rushed or expansive, depending on the situation."[66]

The observation puts a slightly different spin on what we might think of as the normal declamatory order. Here, it is not pronunciation that controls rhythm, but the "movement and tone" of the line, which, producing its own rhythm, governs pronunciation. Brémont would make this rhythmic order even more explicit by transcribing several poetic readings into musical notation. Musical Example 4.2 reproduces his take on a line from "Un Evangile," a poem by François Coppée, showing two possible readings. The subtle mixing of duple and triple values in both may remind us of the increasingly realist prosody we find in Debussy's songs of the same period, or even in certain *mélodies* of Hahn, whose *Etudes latines* included rhythmic details as fussy as Brémont's little grace note (Musical Example 4.3).

But Brémont wanted to teach another kind of lesson with this example, and so he used the notation to contrast the two readings, one bad, one good. A quick glance makes the differences obvious. In the first (4.2a), the vocal line literally acts out the line, emphasizing the importance of every word with dramatic shifts of tone and register. The effect is an exaggerated singsong—a bit like a schoolteacher telling a children's story. In any case, for Brémont, it was flawed because it brought out the wrong genre: a feeling for the anecdotal, the familiar. The proper way to read poetry, he countered, was shown in the second notation (4.2b). There, a single tone produced quite a different effect: a monotone. This kind of delivery had all the solemnity of a chant, suggesting the hieratic and exalted. It suited poetry not (or not merely) because it was lofty, but because it drew attention to the purely sonic character of the words—to form, rather than content. Through this sort of intonation, Brémont said, the words preserved "their simplicity, their sweetness, their tranquility, their mystery—in short, their *poetry*."

EXAMPLE 4.2 Two readings of Coppée, "Un Evangile," example (a) not recommended; example (b) recommended. From Brémont, *L'Art de dire les vers* (1903)

(a)

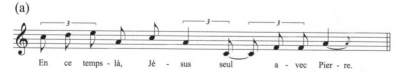

En ce temps - là, Jé - sus seul a - vec Pier - re.

(b)

En ce temps - là, Jé - sus seul a - vec Pier - re.

EXAMPLE 4.3 Hahn, *Etudes latines*, extract from "Lydie" (1900). Note the different rhythmic values ascribed to the line's four mute *e*'s: *blanch*(e), *lyr*(e), *mod*(e), and *Laconienn*(e)

The examples present us, then, with a somewhat different notion of what it meant to *chanter les vers* around 1900. Here, in effect, was a striking image of poetry's "music." And yet Brémont's ideal verse seemed determined to put a mute on melody in the conventional sense, producing something more like that empty sound Mallarmé had once imagined from the flute of his dejected Faune (*une sonore, vaine et monotone ligne*, Mallarmé had called it, "a sonorous, meaningless, monotone line"). We have encountered this ideal before, of course: in the allegorical muteness of Van Lerberghe's Eve, in the disappearance of Mallarmé's *fleur*, in the discreet unvoicing of Debussy's Bilitis. Now it makes a different kind of sense, preached from the mouth of a real, live performer who would extol such unvoicing as the pinnacle of his art. The monotone of Coppée's "Evangile" exposed in a very basic way the restraint that was again and again proclaimed as the highest virtue of French, manifested, as we have seen, in Brémont's own refusal to "exteriorize" the sentiment of poetry, in the exquisitely held-back consonants of a Jean-Baptiste Faure, in Reynaldo Hahn's immobile cigarette, or in the sheer tact of Jane Bathori's singing, with its intimations of "half-said" things.

This restraint was most thoroughly embodied, of course, in the sound of the mute *e* itself, that uniquely French vowel whose blankness stood as the central value of the tongue. It was the *e muet*, we are told, that defined the "national rhythm." It was the *e muet* that served to regulate what de Souza called the movement and tone of French poetry. It was the *e muet*, this most inward phoneme, that ultimately produced within a line of verse the same effect as the silence that Debussy desired within a musical score. This was where the real music of French could be found: as Brémont put it, in "the relation words and sounds should have to play off one another."[67] And yet, as if by poetic irony or some queer dictate of the tongue, that music would take the form of its most hidden and interior vowel, unfolding in a neutral air that promised to say nothing at all. Intoning that droning string of As, we begin to sense, finally, what Barthes may have meant when he described the *mélodie* as an ideal space "where the language works on itself *for nothing.*" Brémont offered a final observation about this zero-degree of diction: "In the end it is the rhythm that makes us hear such melody," he said. "And by rhythm good *diseurs* are made. It would be wise, then, for us to give up the expression *chanter les vers*, an expression that has led to so many pointless discussions, and say, more correctly, perhaps, that we must *rythmer les vers.*"[68]

Many genres of French vocal music after 1900 reflected this concern for finding *le rythme juste*, and the rest of the chapter considers some notable examples. But before shifting our attention to musical performance, I want to consider one last *diseur* from Brémont's milieu. I am thinking of a great French artist, perhaps the greatest of them all, with whom Brémont had the privilege to work at the end of his own career: *La Grande Sarah Bernhardt*. And I have a particularly telling performance in mind, indeed, a reading of the same poem Brémont found so exemplary: "L'Evangile" by François Coppée. Bernhardt recorded it for French Gramophone in 1903—the very year Brémont published his *Art de dire les vers*—and her performance turns out to be more instructive than we might have guessed.[69] Taking up Brémont's challenge, then, I will attempt to *rythmer* these lines of Bernhardt, in an effort to grasp more clearly, and more than a century after the fact, the significance of her marvelous, historic performance.

Expressions Lyriques

I admit that I had something of a shock the first time I heard the voice of Sarah Bernhardt. I was sitting in the audio room of the new Bibliothèque national, listening through headphones, when it came: the poem by Coppée.

> ◐ En ce temps-là, Jesus, seul avec Pierre, errait
> Sur la rive du lac, près de Génésareth,
> A l'heure où le brûlant soleil de midi plane,
> Quand ils virent, devant une pauvre cabane, . . .

> (At that time, Jesus, alone with Peter, was roaming / Along the bank of the lake, near Nazareth, / In the burning, flat sun of midday, / When they saw, in front of a poor shack, . . .)

One might wonder what the Jewish Bernhardt was doing in 1903, recording this sentimental gospel by an anti-Dreyfusard poet. But it was not the poem that threw me off. It was the reading itself. I thought I knew something about Sarah Bernhardt, but nothing I knew had prepared me for that sound.

Trembling, pathetic, uncanny, her voice evoked in me that mixture of horror and fascination we often associate with the dead. Here was a figure from the past, speaking directly into my ear, but the words I heard hardly mattered. I was listening to something more alien: a strange, murmuring cadence like a lament or a mad lullaby, a cadence that sounded almost (but not quite) like singing. In an age of flat, Hollywood diction, where the postproduction voice of film has come to stand for naturalness of expression, this was an impossible sound, indeed.

And yet listeners from Bernhardt's time evidently felt quite differently. Brémont considered this reading so exemplary that he recommended aspiring actors to do exactly the same thing. This, at least, is what is implied by the notations he included in his *L'Art de dire les vers*. The monotone reading Brémont recommended (Musical Example 4.2b) corresponds almost exactly to what we hear on this record (Musical Example 4.4). Where his notation indicated a string of repeated A-naturals, Bernhardt begins a step lower, on G. But the rhythms line up almost note for note, suggesting that Brémont may well have followed her record as a guide. We find the same initial triplet figures, neatly marking the parallelism of the two hemistichs (6 + 6, En ce temps-là, Jé-sus, seul a-vec Pier-re er-rait). Brémont stops transcribing after the word "Pierre," although here Bernhardt's rhythm becomes more interesting. She pronounces rather than elides the mute *e* of Pierr(e), following with a tiny silence to mark the clause. This sets apart the verb whose *r* she makes doubly vibrant (errrrait), as if anticipating the enjambment that will drive the thought into the second line. Making the two verses into one long period, she finishes with a decisive melodic drop, reinforcing the cadence with an extra punch: a healthy (unwritten) mute *e*, affixed to the final syllable: Génésareth-e.

Interestingly, Brémont was not the only pedagogue to make use of Bernhardt's recording in this way. There was at least one other listener from the period who considered it just as exemplary, a listener who transcribed the reading even more carefully to teach a different lesson about French performance. The listener I am referring to was a French schoolteacher, Marguerite de Saint-Genès, and the lesson appeared in an unusual place: tucked within the folds of a brand new magazine called the *Revue de phonétique*. This was a publication we learned about in chapter 2, inaugurated by the Abbé Rousselot to celebrate the new science of experimental phonetics. Both technical and populist by turns, the magazine included an educational insert—something the editors called the "Gramophone Course" (*Cours de gramophonie*)—prepared each month by Saint-Genès, who happened to be Rousselot's cousin. Once a month, she transcribed a recording by a famous

En ce temps - là, Je - sus seul a - vec

Pier - re er - rait Sur la ri - ve du lac (e),

près de Gé - né - sa - reth (e) A l'heure où le brû -

lant so - leil de mi - di plane, Quand ils

vi-rent de-vant eux, un - e pauv - re ca - bane, ----

actor into phonetic notation, so that readers could learn to perfect their French at home. Who did Saint-Genès choose for the magazine's inaugural issue? It was Sarah Bernhardt, of course, reading Coppée's *Un Evangile* (Figure 4.1).

This transcription represented something like the B-side of Brémont's music notation. Where his efforts devolved on pitch, Saint-Genès fussed over the timbres, specifying the nuances of spoken French through a precise, alternative orthography. The phonetic notation was in one sense egalitarian, designed to make the sounds visible—and accessible—to the widest possible readership.[70] And yet the alternative writing was also strange, more unfamiliar, at any rate, than Brémont's music. In his example, musical symbols floated above conventional writing; in hers, phonetics took over, replacing familiar French with something impossible to read in the normal way. The only way to comprehend this gospel, in fact, was to sound it out.

I

ãn évãjílœ

dœ Frãswá Koppé,

di par madam Sára Bernàr. [5″]

lent

ã sœ tã la, Jézu, sœl avek pyèrœ, èrè,

súr la rív du lakœ; prè dœ jenézaretœ;

a l'èr u lœ brúlã solèy dœ mídi planœ;

kãt il vír dœvãt [é] unœ póvrœ kabanœ;

5 *la vœvœ d ã péeèr, ã lõ vwàlœ dœ dœyœ;*

ki s etè tristœmãt asízœ súr lœ sœyœ;

rœtœnã dã sèz yé, la larmœ ki lè muyœ;

pur bersé sõn ãfã, e filé sa kœnuyœ.

nõ lwœ d el; kaeé par dè figyé tufú,

10 *lœ mètr e sõn ami, vwayè sãz ètrœ vú.* [48″]

sudẽ, ã dœ sè vyé, dõ lœ tõbó s aprètœ,

ã mãdyã, portãt ã vázœ súr sa tètœ;

vẽt a pásé, é dit a sèl ki filè : [19″]

plus lent

famœ, jœ dwa porté sœ vázœ plẽ dœ lè;

15 *céz ãn omœ, lojé dã lœ proeẽ vilàjœ.*

mè tu lœ vwa; jœ süï fèbl e brízé par l ájœ.

lè mézõ sõt ãkòr a plú dœ mil pá;

é jœ sã byẽ kœ, sèlœ, jœ n akõplíre pá

sœ travay, kœ l õ dwa mœ beyér un obòlœ. [22″]

lent

20 *la fam sœ lva sã dír unœ parolœ,*

lèsa sãz ézité, sa kœnuyœ dœ lẽ

e lœ bersó d ózyé u plœrè l orfœlẽ;

pri lœ vázœ; e s ã fut avek lœ mízerablœ.

FIGURE 4.1 Phonetic transcription of Coppée, "Un Évangile," as performed by Sarah Bernhardt. Published in *Revue de phonétique* (1911)

As Saint-Génès explained, the records contained all "the nuances, inflections, changes of tempo, pauses—all the qualities that make good diction."[71]

In other words, the records revealed not just timbres but rhythms. And if Saint-Génès's written transcription did not show those rhythms directly, it did expose one declamatory error that may reveal, indirectly, how Bernhardt was feeling the lines. In line 2, for example, we hear the verse begin to swing, the rhythmic snap of the first half (ri-v(e) du lac[e]) creating a broad upbeat that resolves into the triplet tattoo of the second half (près d(e) Gé-né-sa-reth[e]). As the verse continues, however, the duple urge becomes stronger. In the next line, Bernhardt burns through the first part, peaking late on *soleil*, only to pull back the tempo with the image of the "flat midday light" (de mi-di plane). And in the fourth line, caught in the flow, something happens: an extra syllable creeps in. "Quand il vir-ent de-vant eux u-ne pau-vre ca-bane," she says, adding a word that is not part of the original text.[72] The slip has the effect of shifting the emphasis toward the end of the line, as if to bring out both the impoverishment of the image and its pathetic lyricism.

Francis Sarcey, a devoted fan and critic, once called Bernhardt's voice "music incarnate."[73] And we can now see why. Treated with the natural music of her *voix parlée*, this reading begins to sound like those not so very melodic *mélodies* that French composers were conceiving in the years around 1900. All that is missing, it seems, is the piano accompaniment. But even that ingredient is not so hard to imagine. I tried, as a test, to compose one myself in a style that sounds plausible against Bernhardt's recorded delivery (Musical Example 4.5).[74] On the page, this added element makes the poem's "music" appear quite obvious. But when played, the result is even more startling. With its naturally resonant dominant ninths, the piano brings out the inner harmony of the spoken syllables. Still, even as it seems to enhance the music of the voice, it has another effect. Through an odd sort of supplemental logic, the added music actually reduces the exteriority of the declamation. By giving the line a sense of direction, the piano diminishes the perception of Bernhardt's tremulous reading as an alien thing. The nearly sung words sound, in effect, more natural, the rhythm clearer, the pitch truer.

———

Taken collectively, these transcriptions suggest something about the close kinship between poetry and song during Bernhardt's era, when an actor's preference for "singing verse" came strangely close to a singer's tendency to "speak song," as Brémont put it. But in doing so, they also, unwittingly, expose a broader picture of lyric performance around 1900. As it turns out, the accompanied monotone would become a more and more common feature of modern French performance practice. A notable setting by Reynaldo Hahn

● EXAMPLE 4.5 Musical transcription of Coppee, "Un Évangile," as performed by Bernhardt and supplied with piano accompaniment

EXAMPLE 4.6 Hahn, "La Paix," opening measures, as printed in Isnardon, *Le Chant théâtral* (1911)

of Banville's "La Paix" is worth mentioning in this context (Musical Example 4.6). Isnardon recommended the piece in 1911 as an edifying vocal workout, and with good reason. The voice part features nothing more than a single note—a repeated A-natural—declaimed over a cyclic chord progression in a marchlike rhythm that follows the basic scansion of the poetry. The melody conveys all the pomp of a processional, all the humility of a whispered secret, as each repeated A takes on a new color through the changing harmonies of the syllables. Performed by the baritone Guy Ferrant accompanied by Hahn on a recording from 1937,[75] the song seems to accord Brémont's rhythmic mono- tone—the central tenet of his "art" of reading verse—a new musical dignity.

Even Brémont himself seems to have imagined the greater musical potential of his semichanted diction. In one edition of his treatise, he included a long discussion of something he called "musical adaptation," a form of poetic melodrama that turned out to be a personal specialty. The idea behind the "adaptation" was to enhance the already musical delivery of a poem with evocative accompaniments, tailored to the verse's changing moods. Brémont was quick to explain how his performances had nothing to do with the more vulgar form of poetic recitation, popular at the time, where an actor declaimed a famous text over the Egmont Overture or some other well-known orchestral work. In those ill-begotten readings, the music remained the main event, the words a mere ornament.

With the *adaptation musicale*, the roles were effectively reversed: the accompaniment entered only to sustain the poem or, as he put it, "to reinforce and complete it, to make a frame, a foundation, an envelope." Brémont had developed a comfortable working relationship with the pianist and composer Francis Thomé (dubbed by Sarcey the "father of the musical adaptation"), who apparently had a knack for playing just the right music to accompany the actor's subtle intonations. Because their performances were largely improvised, the collaborators left behind no record of their work, even though Brémont did attempt to publish some pieces after Thomé's death in 1909.[76] Still, the actor's testimony gives an idea of the popularity of the practice, which earned an entry in the *Dictionnaire encyclopédique du Conservatoire* in 1910 after attracting a number of composers to its ranks, as figures like Gabriel Pierné, Paul Vidal, and Benjamin Godard grasped the potential for writing new music to *vers à dire*.

The best known, perhaps, was Massenet, who had begun sketching the uncommon settings he called "Expressions lyriques" already in 1902. This was a collection of ten pieces, published posthumously in 1913, that took an innovative approach to the verses of some minor salon poets, freely mixing song with spoken declamation. As mentioned in chapter 1, Massenet had experimented with a similar mixture of recitation and song many years earlier, in his 1866 *Poème d'avril*. But by 1900, he had become far more systematic in his treatment of the *voix parlée*. Speaking nearly outweighed singing in this new collection, as the composer strove to integrate recitation directly into the songs, with many more passages of what he called *déclamation rythmée*. The eighth song offered one of the more minimal, and effective, treatments, based on a diminutive poem in free verse—the only anonymous text in the set. With its deliberately flat and repetitive lines, the setting conveyed the desolation of its melancholic subject.

Sur les flots de la vie
Suivant ce qui me tient
Suivant ce qui me lie
Je m'en vais, pauvre rien
Le temps est gris . . .
Qu'importe! . . .

Va, mon coeur, suivant ce qui t'emporte
Chante ou pleure les jours
Mon coeur, va toujours
Suivant ce qui t'emporte
Va toujours. . . .

EXAMPLE 4.7 Massenet, *Expressions lyriques*(1913), "Mélancolie," first verse and refrain

VIII

Mélancolie

EXAMPLE 4.7 (Continued)

(On the waves of life / Following what holds me / what binds me / I leave, a poor nothing / In gray weather . . . / What does it matter! . . . / Go, my heart, following what takes you / Singing or crying all the day! / My heart, always go / following what takes you. / Always go. . . .)

Massenet matched the "gray atmosphere" of the poem with the deliberate monotone of the voice part, asking the singer to speak the opening lines flatly, and in rhythm, over an almost static piano (Musical Example 4.7). The score actually featured two forms of notation. One showed the desired rhythm with noteless stems, the other a melodic variant, provided "for singers who preferred not to do the spoken declamation." And yet this alternative melody looks exactly like what we have seen (and heard) before. With its line of static pitches, it reminds us of the ideal monotone of Brémont's art of diction, or the actual sound of Bernhardt's affecting "Evangile."

Following this confessional opening strophe, spoken in halting half-phrases, the vocal line opens out to a sung refrain. An arpeggiated dominant chord beneath the throwaway line "Qu'importe!" (What does it matter!) announces the contrasting melody, which carries the conviction of the refrain's repeated command, "Va!" (Go!). The speaker self-consciously turns inward, addressing her own heart. But in the end, the "singing" is as listless as the speech, the sad descending line sounding like something straight out of Edith Piaf, with its music hall accordion, its strained voice uttering the negligible melody "voicelessly" (*sans voix*), as Massenet writes. By the time the refrain rolls around a second time, even this minimal melody has disappeared, erased and replaced by the deliberately colorless rhythms of a melancholy *voix parlée*.

Frits Noske ultimately dismissed Massenet's collection as "unsatisfactory."[77] But in revealing his own taste, he failed to recognize the true significance of these experiments for a history of French song. Alongside the evidence of Brémont or Bernhardt, the score offers even clearer evidence of the ways in which the spoken word had impinged on musical thinking. In the last chapter, we saw how French composers had "discovered" the timbre of the *voix parlée* in a search for the purest poetic expression. But these essays in lyric declamation suggest that the field of discovery was larger than one might suspect, reflecting not just a compositional feature but a genre of performance. Nor is Massenet's collection the only evidence we have of such performance. There is, for example, a charming (if little known) set of piano accompaniments by Reynaldo Hahn that materialize, unexplained, in Proust's first book, *Les Plaisirs et les jours* (1896). The four compositions, lithographic reproductions in Hahn's own hand, appear silently in the middle of the volume to conclude a quartet of poems about painters.[78] Apparently, the two lovers used to entertain friends with poetic recitals of their own, with Reynaldo installed at the keyboard, accompanying Proust's pretentious verses with music. A little practice is all one needs to discover how the poem Proust called "Antoine Van Dyck" might fit together with Hahn's composition of the same name (Musical Examples 4.8a and 4.8b).

But there is a more interesting example of this sort of lyric expression, completed just a year before Massenet began composing his collection. I am thinking of the second collaboration between Debussy and Pierre Louÿs, early in 1901. That was the year they staged twelve more poems from Louÿs's cycle, this time not for a singer but for a *diseuse*.[79] In their new concept, which received but one performance, Louÿs's texts were declaimed in alternation with an appropriately Hellenic instrumental ensemble (two flutes, two harps, and celesta) punctuating the verse with ephemeral

EXAMPLE 4.8A "Antoine Van Dyck," poem by Proust, as published in *Les Plaisirs et les jours* (Paris: Calmann Lévy, 1896)

ANTOINE VAN DYCK

Douce fierté des cœurs, grâce noble des choses
Qui brillent dans les yeux, les velours et les bois,
Beau langage élevé du maintien et des poses
— Héréditaire orgueil des femmes et des rois! —,
Tu triomphes, Van Dyck, prince des gestes calmes,
Dans tous les êtres beaux qui vont bientôt mourir,
Dans toute belle main qui sait encor s'ouvrir;
Sans s'en douter, — qu'importe? — elle te tend les palmes!
Halte de cavaliers, sous les pins, près des flots
Calmes comme eux — comme eux bien proches des sanglots —;
Enfants royaux déjà magnifiques et graves,
Vêtements résignés, chapeaux à plumes braves,
Et bijoux en qui pleure — onde à travers les flammes —
L'amertume des pleurs dont sont pleines les âmes
Trop hautaines pour les laisser monter aux yeux;
Et toi par-dessus tous, promeneur précieux,
En chemise bleu pâle, une main à la hanche,
Dans l'autre un fruit feuillu détaché de la branche,
Je rêve sans comprendre à ton geste et tes yeux :
Debout, mais reposé, dans cet obscur asile,
Duc de Richmond, ô jeune sage! — ou charmant fou? —
Je te reviens toujours : Un saphir, à ton cou,
A des feux aussi doux que ton regard tranquille.

interludes, while a cast of naked female models, directed by Louÿs himself, executed suggestive tableaux.

Needless to say, it has not become Debussy's best-known setting. The piece is hardly programmed today. But the problem is not the obviously dated erotic content. Audiences, after all, still respond with pleasure to the unambiguous eroticism of Debussy's *Trois Chansons*. The problem with the 1901 version is the denuded recitation itself: Debussy never bothered to notate a vocal part. Like most "musical adaptations," the

EXAMPLE 4.8B "Anton Van Dyck," *adaptation musicale* by Hahn, as published in *Les Plaisirs et les jours* (Paris: Calmann Lévy, 1896)

declamation was simply left in the hands (and voice) of the actress engaged for the occasion. And that missing information not only makes the work now seem incomplete but also leaves us at a loss.[80] A satisfied reviewer for *Le Journal* may have spoken of "the pleasure of savoring" Louÿs's lines in 1901, "marvelously declaimed (*merveilleusement dites*)" by one Mlle Milton. Yet actors and musicians today, unaccustomed to savoring any kind of poetry, have little idea of what such marvelous diction might feel like.

We are certainly not likely to feel much pleasure, for example, listening to the 1989 recording of these *Chansons* by Deutsche Grammophon, in which Catherine Deneuve does the honors with the Ensemble Wien-Berlin.[81] In one respect, Deneuve was an interesting choice, given her legendary role in Buñuel's 1967 *Belle du jour*, where she, like Bilitis, played both a lover and a prostitute. But as a voice, she seems strangely miscast, her film experience at odds with Louÿs's suggestively musical text. Deneuve rushes through the lines, the prose tumbling swiftly and impassively from her closely miked speaking voice. *"Il faut chanter un chant pastoral, invoquer Pan, dieu du vent d'été"* (We must sing a rustic song, invoking Pan, God of the summer wind). The rustic proclamation is rattled off like a list of things to do. In that context, Debussy's sweet Arcadian music sounds out of place, as if the players had somehow barged into the wrong recording session.[82] In short, the whole concept of Deneuve's recitation, wan and without rhythm, could not be further from the beguiling cadences of Bernhardt. And without that more musical concept of diction, the fragile phrases of these *Chansons* fall to pieces.

My point is not to malign a popular actress of our time. Nor am I making a pitch for informed historical performance—although I could. I will admit to being intrigued by the possibility of using Massenet's or Brémont's notations as a kind of guide to inspire a more deliberate rhythmic reading of these *Chansons*. But my interest in the Deneuve reading, and its failure, hinges on a more general problem of music history. It is the problem of lyric itself, that "other" manner of speaking, that returns us, once again, to the questions raised at the beginning of this chapter. How are we, in the twenty-first century, to imagine this paradoxical accent, at once spoken and sung, declamatory and mute? More pointedly, how do we feel the pleasure it once produced? In Deneuve's performance, the idea of the lyric monotone has been reduced, it seems, to pure ennui. But there is a big difference between flatness and tedium—one quality suggesting presence, the other a lack. Only in sorting out that difference—two ways, we could say, of doing "nothing"— can we begin to appreciate the particularly *motivated* flatness that defined the ideal voice of the French *diseuse* circa 1900, which was the voice of Bilitis herself: halfway between poetry and prose.

Debussy described that voice as "the most persuasive in the world," and for once, we might take him seriously. Valéry heard Mallarmé's speaking, and Jean-Aubry, Bathori's singing, in much the same way. Even Sarah Bernhardt was known to provoke similar reactions in her fans. The writer Jules Renard described Bernhardt's acting as "something more like the song of the trees, or an instrument's *monotone noise*," something so natural, he said, that "we don't even notice it."[83] Freud went further, writing to his fiancée after seeing Bernhardt in Sardou's *Théodora*: "After the first words of her lovely, vibrant voice," he said, "I felt I had known her for years. . . . I believed at once everything she said."[84] The remark is hard to take seriously, but the questions it raises simply point to the imaginative crux of our whole historical project.[85] Making sense of this music means not just reconstructing an idea of its lost lyric accent. No, our first and greatest historical challenge is to relive that experience of Freud: to hear this voice and *believe* it.

Once we do, the 1901 *Chansons de Bilitis* should appear more exemplary than extreme, like a naked version of those other sincere songs Debussy had conceived during the very same years: not only the earlier *Trois Chansons de Bilitis*, those "miracles of 'speaking' French in music" discussed in the last chapter, but also, more obviously, the earnest declamations of *Pelléas et Mélisande*, staged just a year later, in 1902. This singular opera, occupying a decade of Debussy's creative life, could be described as one of the sincerest things he ever wrote and as a remarkable outpouring of "expression lyrique." Brémont considered it a notable example of "musical adaptation," and he had a point.[86] No work better exemplified the significance of the lyric monotone, the *demi-voix* of French expression, than *Pelléas et Mélisande*.

For this reason, the opera forms a fitting conclusion to a chapter about the French language in performance. Over the course of five acts, Debussy offers an even more complete range of styles of expressive declamation than Massenet: from the pure recitation of the letter scene (Act I) to the unaccompanied folksong of the *scène des cheveux* (Act III). A contemporary actress like Deneuve could easily have consulted this score for hints about how to conceive her Bilitis. But the drama of *Pelléas* will add one more dimension to our lessons in the *art de dire*, as we see the idea of lyric expression—and its sincerity—take on a new dramatic meaning. Here, the problem of declamatory "truth" becomes not just a matter of performance but, in many ways, the crux of the opera's story.

Forget That You Are Singers

That Debussy's *Pelléas* forever changed the nature of French vocal music has become a truism of music history, but the commonplace harked back to the composer's lifetime as well. Louis Laloy, who was voluble on the subject of Debussy and on *Pelléas* in particular, considered this work "at least as important as . . . the first Florentine operas"[87] because, in his view, it had brought about an analogous reform. Liberating melodic expression from "those great gestures, those upward leaps modeled on the rough accentuation of German," Debussy had arrived at a more restrained, more affecting, and ultimately more French expression in *Pelléas*, learning to capture real emotion, as Laloy put it, "by virtue of a free melody modeled on the *voix parlée*."[88]

Romain Rolland may not have shared Laloy's enthusiasm for Debussy, but he touted the historical significance of *Pelléas et Mélisande* in no less extravagant terms. In an essay from 1907, he judged the work "a fatal—even vital—reaction of the French spirit against . . . the Wagnerian art," suggesting, as Laloy had, that "the declamation of Wagner, with its great vocal leaps and massive, resilient accents," proved especially "unpleasant" to a French sensibility. The comment may be difficult to balance with what we know of Wagnerian aesthetics, where a musical declamation based on prose was supposed to intensify the possibility of dramatic truth. These were, after all, the same ideals that had inspired the new French aesthetic of free verse. And yet, according to Rolland, the Debussyian reaction was understandable, coming from a "French mind" that could not help but reject "all emphasis, all excess, all expression that exceeded the thought."[89] He went on to characterize the unique dramatic solution of *Pelléas*:

> The love that grows in the hearts of the unfortunate couple is expressed by imperceptible tremblings of the melodic line: from the timid "Oh! Pourquoi partez-vous?" of the end of the first act, to the tranquil "Je t'aime aussi," of the next-to-last scene. How different the savage lamentations of the dying Isolde from the wordless, noiseless death of Mélisande, without cries, without sentences!

Here was the French difference. No prose; no noise. In *Pelléas*, he concluded, all "the passions were expressed *à mi-voix*."[90]

The remark tellingly recalls an ideal of performance we have by now encountered in many forms, an ideal bound up (as the critic here seems to realize) with the "natural" elegance of French itself. But Rolland suggested two more precedents for this expressive reserve: the reforms of theatrical declamation promoted by André Antoine, and the renewal of French recitative imagined by Jean-Jacques Rousseau. Indeed, the kind of recitation Rousseau envisioned, in which the vocal line would "roll between very small intervals without raising or lowering the voice" and with "no shouts or cries of any kind," was, as Rolland noted, exactly what Debussy had accomplished in *Pelléas*.[91]

That observation, as it happens, took on a life of its own, becoming the preferred rationale for Debussy's unique approach to text-setting *Pelléas*. Future commentators took up Rolland's remark and enhanced it, like a game of musicological telephone, in each retelling. By 1926, Maurice Emmanuel was willing to say that, in listening to *Pelléas*, "one could believe that [Debussy] had strictly applied the precepts of Jean-Jacques." He even pointed out that, in 1888, the pedagogue Bourgault-Decoudray had taught an open course at the Conservatoire, where he "read from both the 'Letter' and the 'Dictionary' to an auditorium of about three hundred amateurs and less than half a dozen students." Although Emmanuel acknowledges that Debussy (who left the conservatory in 1884) was not likely to have attended these classes for a general audience, he nonetheless paints Debussy as having fulfilled Rousseau's prophecy. By the 1960s, Edward Lockspeiser would massage the same speculative details into an outright claim that Bourcault-Ducoudray *had* taught such things during the years Debussy attended the Conservatoire, implying that the young composer learned his recitative straight from the philosopher's mouth.[92]

Rousseau's significance is hard to deny, but there are certainly other ways to explain Debussy's novel experiments in prosody. Why, for example, have historians fixed on Rousseau rather than Rolland's equally suggestive remark about André Antoine?[93] He was the director who in 1887 established the *Théâtre-Libre*, an experimental company in Montmartre dedicated to producing brand new works in brand new ways. Antoine's name is associated with a number of modernist innovations that continued well into the twentieth century, among them, the exploitation of "real" stage props and gestures and, more radically, the use of untrained actors.[94] Never having attended the Conservatoire, the director believed that such unofficial artists always performed more naturally, free of those artificial habits accrued from years of thoughtless practice. Yet he did not exactly reject the classic *art de dire*. He admired the "truly modern" performances of Got, "for their simplicity and truth," as well as Mounet-Sully's *Hamlet*, "one of the most curious conceptions of his career," for its "opposition of simplicity and near triviality."[95] He sought the same truth by different means, encouraging his actors to skip the mannerisms, to replace what Brémont called the *manie d'extérioriser* with a more thoughtful and interior declamation—in short, to speak their roles more like real people.

Antoine's reforms seem all the more relevant when we recall what Debussy himself had to say about his aims in composing *Pelléas*. In a well-known program note from 1902, written at the request of the Opéra-Comique, he explained not only how his "doubts about the Wagnerian formula" had led him to Maeterlinck's play but also how his setting had observed one "law of beauty" generally forgotten in opera. He had tried to make "the characters of his opera," as he put it, "sing like normal people, and not in an arbitrary language of outdated traditions."

> That's where the reproach comes in about my so-called prejudice for monotone declamation [*déclamation monotone*], where nothing ever seems melodic. In the first place, that's untrue. In the second, a character's feelings cannot be expressed continually in a melodic fashion. And finally, the dramatic melody ought to be something entirely different from melody in general.[96]

The turning away from "outdated traditions" smacks of Antoine, but the confession is significant in a number of other respects, not least for what it implies about *mélodie*. Most intriguing is the threefold rebuttal, with its dangling demurral, "that's untrue (*cela est faux*)." What is false is not Debussy's "so-called prejudice" for monotone but the idea that "nothing ever seems melodic" in such declamation—which, of course, we already know. The experience of listening to Sarah Bernhardt showed precisely how musical such diction could be and how very close to *mélodie*. The realization helps us to grasp what Debussy may have meant by his term "dramatic melody."[97] This *mélodie à demi* was, in effect, the voice of the "normal" theater. And by exploiting it as the normal voice of his opera, he seemed to ensure the credibility and sincerity of his own dramatic music.

Debussy stated the point more baldly in an interview for *Le Figaro* in the same year. When the critic Henri Gauthier-Villars (or "Willy") publicly expressed his disappointment that the vocal parts of Debussy's new work contained "no melodies," the composer expressed his dismay, in return, at such critical stupidity. "Melody," he countered, "is antilyrical. It cannot express the varying states of the soul, or of life."[98] It would be easy to pass off the remark as another instance of the composer's well-known cheek. Yet, almost in the same breath, he goes on to praise another dismissive reviewer for calling *Pelléas et Mélisande* a mere "declamation in notes, scarcely accompanied." And we begin to get the point. The idea of lyric, as Debussy understood it, meant anything but "melody" in the conventional sense. As in Brémont's *art lyrique* or Massenet's *expressions lyriques*, he was thinking of poetry, not opera; of a voice that relinquished full-blown singing for a more muted diction. He was thinking, in short, of a very different performance practice. And Debussy was intent that his singers understood that difference. According to Mary Garden, he faced the cast at the first rehearsal and, before anyone had uttered a sound, announced solemnly: *"Mesdames et Messieurs. . . .* Everyone must forget that he is a singer before he can sing the music of Debussy. *Oubliez, je vous prie, que vous êtes chanteurs!"*[99]

What the composer wanted, evidently, was a cast of *diseurs*, and he more or less got his wish. I have often wondered whether Debussy considered Mary Garden the perfect Mélisande not just because she was beautiful but because she was foreign and therefore exotic in more than one sense. It is certainly suggestive, at any rate, that Debussy's first two Mélisandes—Mary Garden and Maggie Teyte, both Scottish by birth—were inclined to speak their French in a studied, even exaggerated way, having learned it as a second language. Yet even more significant was the general verdict on Garden's singing. As William Ashbrook has pointed out, "some claimed her instrument was a mirage, that she was at best a sort of inspired *diseuse*."[100] Although such criticisms can easily be refuted (recordings from 1911, for example, reveal a serviceable coloratura in Verdi's "Sempre libera"), the point is nonetheless apt. What appeared to be a vice became a virtue for Debussy, especially in an opera where the singers were required, above all, to *dire*.

———

That requirement emerged most strongly in one extended scene from *Pelléas*, where the question of diction was paramount. This was the so-called Letter scene, from Act I, in which Geneviève, in her only meaningful appearance, reads aloud a letter Golaud has written not to her but to his half-brother Pelléas, confessing his fateful meeting and marriage to the princess Mélisande. Performances of this scene drew the attention of at least two commentators close to Debussy. In 1905, Laloy reviewed a revival of the work with (more or less) the original cast and expressed relief that the concept had "not greatly changed. Mademoiselle Garden [Mélisande], Messieurs Périer [Pelléas], Dufranne [Golaud] and Vieuille [Arkel] are equally excellent as artists and singers." His only regret lay with "Mademoiselle Passama," the new singer who played Geneviève. In Laloy's view, this poor soul simply didn't get it: "she sings her role too much and does not *say* it enough (*{elle} ne le* dit *pas assez).*"[101] Many years later, Désiré-Emile Inghelbrecht would make a similar judgment, in his cranky account of "How Not to Perform *Pelléas*":

One discovers, in reading the score, that Debussy never intended to offer posterity the Air of Geneviève any more than the Cavatine of

Yniold, or even the Stanzas of Arkel. . . . Geneviève says "Voici ce qu'il écrit à son frère Pelléas." And then she reads Golaud's letter, *simply and without nuances*, as Debussy explicitly indicated. But that is what singers used to proclaiming Werther's letters . . . fail to do.[102]

It is worth pointing out that, in Inghelbrecht's lifetime, there was a singer who had succeeded beautifully in the task, one who knew the difference, so to speak, between her Charlotte and her Geneviève. And her success should not be surprising, for her own vocal pedagogy was based, as we know from her students, on this very art of reading aloud. I refer to Claire Croiza, born Claire Connelly in Paris to an American father and Italian mother in 1882. At the time of the premiere of *Pelléas*, Croiza was just completing her vocal studies, soon to have her horizons opened with a few lessons from Jean de Reszké. Making her debut in Nancy in 1905, she established a fine reputation during several seasons at the Théâtre de Monnaie in Brussels, where she played, among other roles, Charlotte in Massenet's *Werther* and, in 1913, the title character of Fauré's *Pénélope*, roles she would later bring to the Opéra-comique. In Paris during the war, she sang concerts with both Fauré and Debussy and, in the 1920s, went on to launch an important series on French poetry and music at the Théâtre du Vieux-Colombier and at the Salle Érard, premiering works by Honegger, Caplet, Roussel, and Cocteau. In 1927, she sang Geneviève in a performance of *Pelléas* conducted by Pierre Monteux, alongside Dufranne and Panzéra. Signing an exclusive contract with Columbia in November of the same year, she made her first sound recordings over the next few months. One of them was the letter scene from *Pelléas*.[103]

It is, needless to say, a precious historical document, worthy of our close attention, and so I intend to read it closely. Croiza's performance offers a remarkable illustration of the French art of reading as it was still being practiced before the end of the Third Republic. Yet I hardly need to transcribe her phrases (as I did with Bernhardt) to discover the secrets of her art, for Debussy has, in a sense, already done it for us. That is how closely Croiza's musical reading matches his notation. In a recent essay on Debussyian performance practice, Richard Langham Smith looked to this same recording of the Letter scene with a different aim, pointing out places where he believed Croiza had strayed from the notation.[104] And yet this somewhat single-minded approach to listening may obscure the most interesting aspect of the scene, which has to do as much with Debussy's concept as with Croiza's realization: in this scene of public reading, performance and composition have become uncanny reflections of each other. In imagining Geneviève's reading, the composer, in other words, has produced a plausible image of the

EXAMPLE 4.9 (Continued)

art de dire, setting down the rhythms as if he had already heard them in real life. The scene reveals the same obsession with the performance of French that we have observed again and again in this book: a strange convergence of an utterance and its representation, of *vox* and *nota*. And it is precisely this merger that gives the Letter scene its peculiar force.

Debussy's written-out reading relied, for one thing, on a few of the same musical conceits that we observed in the *Chansons de Bilitis*. The measures shift from 4/4 to 9/8 to 4/4 to 3/4 and back again, through a neutral melodic line

EXAMPLE 4.9 (Continued)

whose minimal inflection can only be described as monotone (Musical Example 4.9). Most striking, however, is the subtle push and pull of the prose. And here it is worth noting a few details whose significance we can now appreciate more fully. The suppleness of the rhythm was helped along, certainly, by the composer's evident sensitivity to one of the more affecting dimensions of the spoken language: the changing value of the mute *e*'s. Right from the start, we can see, for example, how Debussy has set "frèr(e)" as a single quarter note, as if expecting its final mute syllable to emerge simply as a result of pronouncing the vibrant *r.* Yet in the next two phrases, he notates the terminal *e*'s of "fon-tai-n(e)" and "a-g(e)" as leftover values tied to the preceding beat.

Such distinctions suggest the different expressive "weight" of each *e* and could easily be represented by using the same cipher notation recommended by Brémont in his *Art de dire les vers*: where 1 indicates a fully pronounced *e*; 2, a murmured value; and 3, one barely uttered. In that case, the beginning of Geneviève's recitation might look something like this:

3
Voici ce qu'il écrit à son frère Pelléas:

1   1   2
Un soir, je l'ai trouvée tout en pleurs au bord d'une fontaine

1
Dans la forêt ou je m'étais perdu

1 1   2   1   2
Je ne sais ni son age ni qui ell' est, ni d'où elle vient et je n'ose pas
    l'interroger,

2   3   2
Car elle doit avoir eu une grand' épouvante,

2   3 2
Et quand on lui demande ce qui lui est arrivé,

1   1   2
elle pleure tout à coup comm' un enfant et sanglote,
si profondément qu'on a peur.

Marveling at Debussy's sensitivity to the rhythm of this scene, Croiza once exclaimed to her singing class, "What a pity that poets do not indicate the rhythm of their poems by a kind of alphabet of signs analogous to those in music!"[105] The marvel was that through his meticulous attention to such notation, the composer had essentially made the letter "literal." He had captured its accents as faithfully on the page as he expected singers, so to speak, to write them with their voices.

This is how we should probably interpret, then, the somewhat confusing performance direction Debussy writes in the vocal score, *simplement et sans nuances* (simply and without nuances). He seems to ask the singer to perform the reading not with feeling but, in short, as literally as she possibly can. The demand implied two conditions at once. Most obviously, it suggested a close attention to diction—the actual "letters" of this recited Letter. But such careful pronunciation implied its own emotional reserve, the same restraint associated with the act of speaking French itself, where all the work, as Grammont tells us, took place on the inside, "the cheeks immobile, the lips half-opened, the face calm."[106] In a sense, the role of Geneviève represented a more dramatic manifestation of this natural French reserve, this expression *à l'intérieur*. As we listen to the words, the meaning unfolds not through the singer's expressiveness—the manic desire to "exteriorize," as Brémont would have it—but simply through the clarity of the (invisible) articulation. Aided by the underscoring orchestra, it is this dimension of the letter that carries the greatest weight. Indeed, once uttered aloud, the words seem to reveal certain meanings hidden even to Golaud himself.

Croiza acknowledged this condition again and again, when speaking of the enormous importance of articulation for the singer's art. In a class on the "expressive value of words," she quoted that elemental and elementary definition by Abbé Rousselot we have already learned, the maxim that "speech is made up of musical sounds and noises." "Are these 'musical sounds' respected enough in our ways of talking?" she asked. "I don't think so."[107] And she went on to stress the work necessary to achieve this music in song. "Singing must acquire muscle," she said, "and that is the role of articulation."[108]

> The accent in singing is given by the attack of the consonants, but an energetic articulation...does not mean a brusque articulation.... Learn to pronounce well, to pronounce in a noble way.... [Singers always underestimate] what can be achieved in interpretation by the way in which a consonant is pronounced.[109]

The bass Jacques Isnardon had made much the same point in his own treatise, chiding singers who fretted that strong articulation would mar their vocal placement. "They do not understand," he wrote, "that to pronounce the consonants is to give each syllable an instantaneous clarity, a force, a significance, a color, that are precious to it."[110] He called the consonant the "strike of the hammer that places the vowel, and the stroke of the brush that colors it." This vivid definition, which obviously challenged the idea of singing as an art of *vocalise*, may help us to comprehend Viardot's objection to the "pointed diction" she was hearing around 1900. But it also helps us to hear what Croiza herself is doing in her recorded performance of the Letter scene. Attending more closely to the singer's remarkably thoughtful consonants, we begin to appreciate (as Viardot eventually did) the sincerity of this more articulate style. Croiza's Geneviève reveals the remarkable expressive possibility contained in the simple act of pronunciation, giving us a whole new purchase on the actual material of "expression" in the French *art de dire*.

A few examples will illustrate the point. Interestingly, each one involves the singer's treatment of the two most "vibrant" sounds of the French alphabet: the letter *r* and its companion, the letter *l*.[111] Croiza's letter-perfect diction demonstrates exactly what happens whenever these letters are joined by another consonant. For one thing, we discern the most basic function of the mute *e*, as enumerated by Dauzat: epenthesis. This neutral sound materialized continuously in Croiza's recitation "to separate the consonants," as he would say. Its presence is so audible that we could almost rewrite her opening lines:

   1   3   3   3

Voici ce qu'il éc(*e*)rit à son f(*e*)rèr(*e*) Pelléas:

   3 1   3   3   1   2

Un soir(*e*), je l'ai t(*e*)rouvée tout en p(*e*)leurs au bord d'une fontaine

   1   3

Dans la forêt où je m'étais per(*e*)du

Still, the rhythmic value of this added vowel is negligible. A minuscule puff of air seems to subdivide the note, and yet the *e* is so neutral in timbre it doesn't really count. More like a verbal shim slipped in around the letter, the added vowel simply lets the *r* vibrate properly.

Which is to say, oh so discreetly. Croiza indulges in no fiery rolling. Hers is an elegant *r* "without nuance," sounded with a single flip of the tongue. And yet, in each case, the tiny, compensatory value generated by the vibration is different. For example, when Geneviève reads that Golaud hasn't learned anything about the woman he has just married, only that "she must have suffered some great fright" (*Car elle doit avoir eu une grande épouvante*), the rapid-fire rhythm clearly leaves little room for expression. A plaintive oboe takes up the slack, sighing sadly over the rationalization, just as the voice rises a half-step from E to F to accent the word *grande* (Musical Example 4.10). But Croiza does something a little different with the line. She shaves off a tiny portion of the *e* of *un(e)* to make room for the mute value that will follow [*g(e)rand'*]. Then she adds it back in the form of an audible appoggiatura on E that makes the arrival to F, together with the oboe's fall, just a wee bit more *grande*.

Hairsplitting it may be. And yes, I admit to feeling a little like Abbé Rousselot, searching for the secret of Croiza's singerly "accent." I certainly

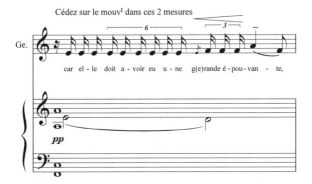

Cédez sur le mouv¹ dans ces 2 mesures

Ge. car el - le doit a - voir eu u - ne g(e)rande é - pou-van - te,

pp

took advantage, as Rousselot would have done, of some modern technology: in this case, a bit of audio software that displayed an image of Croiza's diction on my computer monitor and allowed replay of tiny verbal segments. But this audiovisual microscope also teaches a very useful lesson, one that should be of interest to anyone wanting to comprehend the precise, speechlike diction developed by the great singers of French *mélodie*. Indeed, I began to hear what I never expected: in Croiza's mouth, the consonant is no longer just noise. It has acquired musical value, becoming a discrete object of melodic desire.

The melody of these utterly judicious letters emerges more clearly in the next phrases, as Golaud goes on to explain in the letter how his new wife, when questioned about her past, "cries like a child, and sobs so deeply it's frightening" (*elle pleure tout à coup comme un enfant et sanglote, si profondément qu'on a peur*). In evaluating Croiza's recording of this scene, Langham Smith isolated this phrase for particular comment, pointing out "two successive portamenti" that, as he expressed it, she "indulges in" when singing the word *sanglote*.[112] If we listen closely, however, we discern that the issue, once again, is less a matter of portamento than of pronunciation—now impinging, almost imperceptibly, on the melodic line itself. A sudden lower neighbor on *p(e)leure*, a swift passing tone on *sang(e)lote*, another dip on *p(e)rofondément*: Each one is extremely precise in its execution; each serves, finally, to bring out the vibrant consonant (Musical Example 4.11). That the interpolated *e*'s have now made these consonants more active suggests some increase of expressive tension, consistent, perhaps, with the dominant thirteenth chord that has unexpectedly arrived on the scene. But the expression is restrained, at best.[113] The added melodic values—ornaments, really—are stifled sounds, imploded rather than exploded in Croiza's reading. Coming from somewhere deep inside the mouth, they are swallowed by the singer like a discreet sob, or a tear.

"From the point of view of expression," Croiza claimed, "everything is in the attack of the consonant." And now we see what she means. She certainly treats the consonants of this phrase in a completely new way, adding inflection to the mix. But the idea that the liquid *l*'s of *pleure* and *sanglote* might deserve some special attention in a line about Mélisande's tears was not just a singer's whim. It defined a whole area of linguistic study— sometimes referred to as "expressive articulation" or even "sound symbolism"—of great interest to French poets, writers, phoneticians, and psychologists of the Belle Epoque, not to mention the *chanteurs* and *diseurs* themselves. We glimpsed this phenomenon already in Van Lerberghe's *Chanson d'Eve*, where echoes of Eve's name represented a secret, transcendent quality within language—the capacity of sound to recall the object it named. There are many other examples. Leaving Geneviève mid-sob, I am not in a position to survey the full range, which included French writers as diverse as Mallarmé and Otto Jesperson.[114] But a single striking instance may help to suggest the importance of this way of thinking. Take, for example, the distinguished linguist Maurice Grammont, who somehow found it appropriate to conclude a comprehensive (and scientific) treatise on phonetics with a long exposition on what he called *phonétique impressive*—the phonetics of pure impression.[115]

As a faithful student of Saussure, Grammont could not begin without rehearsing the Saussurian doctrine we all know: that the linguistic sign is an "arbitrary" value, that languages, as Grammont put it, "are essentially composed of semantically inert phonic elements." And yet, he also could not dismiss (as Saussure had done) the compelling evidence of onomatopoeia. The existence of words "whose phonemes imitate[d] the noises of nature" encouraged the view that all words must harbor, at some level of association, such primary meanings, a kind of symbolic content based on their sound. Grammont called this residue the *valeur impressive des mots*, to denote a more universal (indeed, cross-linguistic) quality based on the capacity of sound to evoke the feeling of objects.

It is this *valeur impressive* that Croiza awakens, we could say, in her subtly emphatic report of Mélisande's sobbing. The singer does not sob herself; that would go too far. She simply gives us an inkling in the quality of her *l*'s. Grammont actually described the *l* as the only consonant "capable of expressing liquidity" and offered all the "flow" words as evidence: *couler* (to flow), *glisser* (to glide). Yet the "limpidity" of the *l* also gave rise to other associations, he said, noises like clapping (*applaudir*) or yelping (*glapir*). The noisy liquidity of Mélisande's tears (*pleurs*), her sobs (*sanglots*)—evoked in the near voiceless gulps of Croiza's consonants—was thus a telling sound. And the *r* was equally telling. A truly vibrant letter, it had the potential (said Grammont) to evoke something like "rumbling" (*grondement*), when attached to a dark vowel—a description that is striking in the context. Indeed, the terror of Mélisande's emotion seemed to surface in that little tremor that Croiza opens up with the word *profondément*, as if to expose, with a flick of the tongue, the depths of Golaud's fears.

Such emotion was even more overt in the most "profound" line of this primal scene of letters. I speak of the moment, halfway through the recitation, when Geneviève reads Golaud's fraternal confession: "But I'm afraid of Arkel (*Mais j'ai peur d'Arkel*)." Here the singer rides her lowest tessitura, a true contralto. And in a way, there is nothing more to say: the vocal register already evokes the dark sentiment; the words (not intended for Arkel's ears) are already too honest. Modern singers who exaggerate the pronunciation of *peur* as if they themselves were experiencing fear—as if this admission were their own—miss the point. What Geneviève reads, after all, is a purloined letter, destined for another's eyes. And for that reason, it can never be expressive in a conventional way, delivered, as it is, by a third party, to the wrong audience. Croiza obviously knew better. The only suggestion of discomfort comes with the name of Arkel, registered not just by a change of harmony, as bassoons and horns moan a low dominant chord that will shift the tonality toward G-minor (Musical Example 4.12). The distress is also conveyed in Croiza's voice, by an audible expulsion (more like a *ugh* than a *e*) on the final *l*: *J'ai peur(e) d'Arkel-(e)*. The doubly underscored emission

EXAMPLE 4.12 Debussy, *Pelléas*, Letter scene, *Je sais que ma mère …*

signals not fright but something more like shame—the indignity of naming the one who was never meant to hear.

And in this moment we may finally understand what Brémont meant when he called the mute *e* the "touchstone for a good *diseur* of lyric verse." We may glimpse how the most silent and interior vowel could be conceived as the most meaningful material of the French language—how, indeed, a nonletter could become so crucial to the (non)expression of this decisive scene of letters. Showing up as it did, in the cracks between the consonants, the sound carried no direct emotion. It represented something more like feeling once removed, like evidence that something had happened in that space, that an emotion had passed through, leaving its trace. In that respect, the mute *e* could be said to play a role very similar to that of the orchestra underpinning the opera as a whole: filling the gaps in expression, defining its silences, it signaled emotion without really "saying" it. Both phenomena, in other words, spoke to an ideal of French as a language where everything happens "on the inside," a language where the impression of feeling, its accent, mattered more than expression itself.

A Bird in a Branch

Geneviève's Letter and Croiza's remarkable reading of it thus stand as further evidence for a new aesthetics of diction in Debussy's mature vocal music. From the perspective of its symbolism alone, the scene could be read as a somewhat startling representation of what Saussure himself had called (in another context) the "tyranny of the letter." Symbol and performance uncannily converge in this moment, in the form of a virtual restraining order on the tongue that mandated, as Inghelbrecht had advised, how not to approach the act of singing in *Pelléas et Mélisande*.

And yet Geneviève's scene is also, unmistakably, a special case. Not only does it represent the only set piece for the opera's most marginal female character. It is also the only setting in which an act of *indirect* discourse is fully staged, as if to suggest, through the figure of the blind Arkel, the significance of overhearing in a drama that centers on never knowing enough. From this perspective, the foregrounded Letter can make us appreciate the calculated way Debussy has staged the diction in other parts of the opera. Although Geneviève's singing certainly informs the declamatory ideal throughout much of Debussy's opera, it also represented just one manner of speaking. What Debussy called the "dramatic melody" involved a whole range of expressions from speech to song to silence.[116] It is by observing this expressive scale at work within the larger drama that we may begin to see not only the limits of theatrical diction but also how Debussy pleads the special case of *mélodie* itself. To complete our review of *Pelléas*, then, and to bind the opera more tightly into the larger concerns of this book, I want to conclude by looking closely at one final scene.

It is the famous solo number for the opera's other female, the song that initiates the so-called *scène des cheveux* (III, i). Like Geneviève's monologue, this moment also constitutes a tiny scene of overhearing, although in a less obvious way. As the curtain opens, Mélisande is alone in her tower, combing her hair and singing to no one in particular (Musical Example 4.13):

EXAMPLE 4.13 Debussy, *Pelléas*, Hair scene, III, i, *Mes longs cheveux*

Mes longs cheveux descendent
Jusqu'au seuil de la tour.
Mes cheveux vous attendent
Tout le long de la tour,
Et tout le long du jour.
Saint Daniel et Saint Michel,
Saint Michel et Saint Raphaël,
Je suis née un dimanche,
Un dimanche à midi.

(My long hair falls / to the door of the tower. / My hair awaits you / all
down the tower, / and all the live-long day. / Saint Daniel and Saint
Michael, / Saint Michael and Saint Raphael, / I was born on a Sunday, /
on the Lord's day at noon. . . .)

This obscure and fanciful tune could not be more different, of course,
from Geneviève's restrained recitation. Indeed, its charming cadence leaves us
in no doubt about the different "registers" these two women occupy in the
drama, not just as characters but, we could say, as *diseuses*. With her spontaneous half-phrases, Mélisande comes across like nature's child, an oddly naïve
creature next to her well-spoken *belle-mère*. The difference is especially
marked in the third scene of Act I, when we find the women together, for
the first and only time, on the castle's grounds. Geneviève's grave pronouncements about the vegetation and the weather, about time and responsibility
("I've been living here for over forty years . . .") clearly identify her as
Mother—indeed, as the mother of the utterly worldly Golaud. By contrast,
the relatively speechless Mélisande, a newcomer to Allemonde, appears free as
a bird.

And she is. Or so Pelléas thinks, when he hears the princess trilling in
her tower at the start of the third act: "What are you doing up there singing
like some exotic bird?" he asks (*Que fais-tu là, à la fenêtre, en chantant comme
un oiseaux qui n'est pas d'ici?* [literally: a bird that is not from here]). Carolyn
Abbate has read this exchange, astutely, as a representation of the two
different kinds of hearing that operate in the scene, a doubling that locates
Mélisande's song both here and "not here" at the same time. On the one
hand there is the actual melody, "the phenomenal reality in the theater,"
and on the other, "Pelléas's experience of it, as expressed through his
poetic figure."[117] Abbate rejects the "trite" notion that Pelléas's question
is simply a reflexive trope, giving voice to our own experience of the music,
as we sit in the opera house, listening. The difference between his simile

and her song suggests, instead, "that Pelléas hears something concealed from us, something his characterizations cause us to posit or imagine, a sound not literally there, not subject to capture. Like the sound of an alien bird."[118]

What Abbate articulates as a problem of hearing reflects back, in interesting ways, on what we have already encountered as an ideal of poetic diction. Indeed, her description is especially moving in light of what we know about the culture of verse, and of the voice, in the era of Maeterlinck. When Jules Huret, for example, interviewed Verlaine in the course of his serialized "Enquiry into the Evolution of Literature," he had some trouble (as we know) getting a straight answer from the washed-out but still hugely influential poet. Huret did manage to finagle a response to a question about Verlaine's significance for the younger generation. The poet's words are worth quoting in the context: "I myself am a bird (as Zola is an ox). There are some wicked tongues out there who say that I have even founded a school of canaries, which isn't true. The symbolists are birds, too, with a few exceptions."[119] The remark, however impertinent, is illuminating. It implicates Maeterlinck as one of those symbolist "birds" who had learned alongside Verlaine to sing in a new key and with a new, more natural accent. Maeterlinck certainly revealed an inclination toward such naturalness in the stripped-down prose that defined most of his *Pelléas et Mélisande*. But he displayed it even more directly in these verses from the tower in Act III, where he managed to channel, through the voice of Mélisande, a poem that stood miles away from the brutish "naturalism" of a contemporary (ox) like Zola. What his ancient princess sang, in fact, was nothing other than an ancient *lied*.

Or a chanson. Call it what you like. Formally speaking, "Mes longs cheveux" is even more naïve than the typical Verlainian romance, although it speaks to the ideal "art poétique" with its strong sense of music, its uneven lines (of six, or seven, or eight syllables), its inconsistent rhymes. The non sequiturs, the repetitions—all these suggest a "brusqueness of accent" that de Souza, as we saw, ascribed to rustic song in general, that original lyric form whose strong, throaty sensations so attracted the younger generation of symbolists. "When there were no books, when there were no cities, where then was poetry?" Mauclair had asked, longing for the truth of a purer and more spontaneous verse. Like many of his generation, he believed he had found it in an ancient and exotic tradition of popular song.[120] Our discussion of *vers libre* in chapter 3 casts a strangely luminous shadow on Abbate's alien bird, singing in the night, for it is clear, already from its form, that the *chanson* perched in the center of this drama was definitely "not from here."

Drawing on the free and fluid material—the *melos*—that was Mélisande herself, Maeterlinck fashioned a song that would represent the play's lyric Other and, in doing so, exposed the drama's most musical strain.

Indeed, the watery Mélisande—the free spirit of the fountain, the girl of copious tears, the foundling by a forest spring—stands as a compelling symbol of that gushing underground source, that "natural" song, that poets of Maeterlinck's generation believed they had discovered with their own free verse. The view may even help to explain the curious nature of her diction throughout the play. In every scene, she speaks in the same non sequiturs, the same truncated lines that rarely exceed an *octosyllabe*, and most notably, in the same deliberate repetitions that turn her thoughts into miniature refrains. That is why her utterance turns out to be so ungraspable for her literalist husband. That is why he can never get a straight answer. With Mélisande, words are always a strain. We have already heard Golaud's puzzled confession, in the letter from Act I, about his wife's inexplicable bouts of crying. The sad voice from the tower at the start of Act III now gives us, it seems, a different purchase on the remark. Maeterlinck and Debussy were determined to expose that crying for what it was: a very real act of singing (Abbate calls it "hyper-real"), a music that poor prosaic Golaud could never understand. In fact, he never hears it. Debussy appeared to sympathize with this spousal deafness when he described the impossibly pure Mélisande, flippantly, as a girl made from "nothing,"[121] for her cry couldn't mean much more than that to Golaud. Standing for a purer and more liberated sort of expression, this sound from on high was simply over his head, harboring a truth (*la vérité*) that would remain continually out of reach, right to the end of the play.

Yet the spousal conflict also helps us see Debussy's treatment of the two women in a new light. Representing the difference between prose and poetry, real speech and ideal song, the voices of Geneviève and Mélisande mark a similar opposition, as if enacting, through their symbolic positions, the drama of that "double state of the word" we observed in the last chapter. They show us, in effect, two kinds of talking, two forms of diction that make up the same musical coin, and thus, two conflicting ways of hearing that, according to Abbate, make Mélisande "not here" for all those stuck on the flip side—stuck, that is, with explaining things or (as Mallarmé would have it) "exchanging" common currency. On the one hand, there is the *demi-voix* of the Letter scene, the literal declamation that effectively silences melody, and on the other, the *je dis* (or, perhaps, the *je suis*) of the Tower scene, the pure envoicement that mutes meaning, like a strange, foreign note that has "nothing at all to pay back." If in the Letter, melody disappears into declamation, *sans nuances*, in the Tower, the word disappears into vibration, timbre, linking Mélisande's *moi*, then, to "pure" poetry as the symbolists understood it. She embodies everything implied on both sides of the colon in that tiny Mallarméean dictum (*je dis: une fleur!*), both *diseuse* and flower, voice and poesy. She is a near *vocalise* to Geneviève's near monotone, a liberated vowel soaring above the earthbound and articulate consonant. And from the opera's other, more prosaic side (the side of Golaud's Letter), she is simply inaudible.

But not to Pelléas, nor to Debussy himself, it seems. And it is tempting to transfer this purely symbolic scenario of Maeterlinck's play—with its intrigue of hearing and the impossibility of hearing—to our understanding, once again, of the opera's "real" performance, that is, to the alien historical creature that was the 1902 *Pelléas et Mélisande* of the Opéra-Comique, a work whose now inaudible accents are, of course, the point of this chapter. Indeed, when I think about Pelléas's unique on-stage experience of Mélisande's voice, a tremulous sound coming from some out-of-reach, invisible place, I cannot help being reminded of my own experience of listening to Sarah Bernhardt for the first time, over headphones in the Bibliothèque nationale. It was about as foreign a sound as I could imagine, a totally unfamiliar French, coming, as it did, from the crevices of history, a place that was very much "not here." It is possible that Debussy, inventing an exotic plainchant mode for Mélisande's unaccompanied song,[122] was trying for a similar effect in 1902, a frisson of difference that would place her out of the normal range of musical hearing and thus "elsewhere" for his French audience. And yet we can no longer hear it that way. The song has simply become too familiar.

Even when I return to the ancient Gramophone recording of "Mes longs cheveux" that Mary Garden made with Debussy (at the instigation of Louis Laloy) in 1904, I do not hear it.[123] There is a certain charm to be found in Garden's trembling soprano, with its pitches so pure and true; there is even something marvelously birdlike in her warble. But the sound does not create the same sense of surprise or wonder. Indeed, in listening, I begin to wonder if Debussy were not a bit like Pelléas himself, hearing something in Mary Garden's voice that made her, for him, the "ideal" Mélisande—something that we, of course, will never hear.

And yet there *is* one place where I begin to sense what that voice might have meant. It is a moment, at any rate, when Debussy seems to reveal its irresistible effect on Pelléas, not through poetic figure but through another, touching scene of music—the only true solo for Pelléas in Act III. A few, brief minutes allow us to experience the palpable seduction of this sound "not subject to capture," for the sound *is* captured. The lover cages his elusive bird for a glorious instant, symbolically pinning her down so we can sense what he might be hearing. This moment amounts to the most symbolic, and most poignant, declamatory act in the whole opera, one in which Debussy will ultimately disclose a secret. What we discover in that precious interval is not just the power of an impossible, ideal voice, but something like the delicious art of illusion lying at the heart of the French *mélodie*.

———

This bird is trapped in her tower, not long after we hear her pure, enchanting song. Pelléas, like a cat, wants in, but he simply cannot reach. He begs Mélisande to lean forward so he can see her hair unbound, so he can kiss her hand. She can't, or won't. He says he must leave; she says no kiss unless he stays. It's the usual kid stuff, all very delicately handled. But then, while he is desperately stretching, she precariously leaning, it happens: her hair falls and inundates him head to toe. At first, Pelléas doesn't know what hit him. When he does, he is overcome. He finally has his bird in hand. Or perhaps the bird has ensnared him in her massive golden nest. It hardly matters. For, as he says, now that she is within reach, he is never, ever going to let go.

This arresting moment brings on a new way of talking. Pelléas begins to speak in the same refrain-like forms that had characterized most of Mélisande's diction in the play so far. Caught in her hair, he catches her cadence and begins to improvise what could be a little chanson all about his newfound pleasure. Indeed, if we untangle the prose, his fulsome appreciation begins to resemble the freest sort of free verse:

Je les tiens dans les mains
Je les tiens dans la bouche
Je les tiens dans les bras
Je les mets autour de mon cou.
Je n'ouvrirai plus
Les mains cette nuit.

(I have it in my hands / I have it in my mouth / I hold it in my arms / I put it round my neck / I will never again / open my hands tonight.)

He has never spoken this way before. Debussy responds to the poetic turn with a new kind of musical accent. One could imagine the scene continuing with the same sort of playful shouting that came before—each one of these phrases set with an exclamation point, like great gasps of amorous good fortune. But the music takes a different turn. Pelléas's sudden urge to versify

causes Debussy to smooth out the prosody, to write a "slower and passionately contained" line (*moins vite et passionément contenu*) that will represent the lover's bliss (Musical Example 4.14). Louis Laloy pointed to this very moment in his long exposition on the opera from 1905, citing it as an instance of real singing in a work that privileged discourse over descant. "This is a true melody," he said, "but its shape and rhythm are the very motions of the impassioned words; it is a melody that palpitates with controlled emotion, and starts up again, and becomes elated, and improves on itself, in a sweet, impetuous frenzy."[124]

The sense of "true melody" comes in part from the new feeling of continuity in the orchestra, which features a languid clarinet over liquid eighth notes in the strings, flowing over the scene like a stream of pleasure or, perhaps, like tears. The new, plaintive note suggests, in any case, how much our weeping bird has begun to affect her captor. But as Laloy's description makes clear, the free melody that Pelléas starts up at this point will actually stop and start in interrupted intervals that become more impassioned as they

EXAMPLE 4.14 (Continued)

go. A whole, untapped melodic source flows from this point, one that will not be depleted until Golaud appears at the Tower's door several minutes later. Following the course of this spontaneous melody, one can easily see how it ends up, as Laloy says, "improving on itself."

EXAMPLE 4.15 Debussy, *Pelléas*, Hair scene, III, i, *Non, non, non …*

Pelléas is interrupted almost immediately, right after his initial arabesque. Mélisande calls out, "Let me go! You'll make me fall," with a sad,
falling line that suggests more resignation than resistance as it resolves into a
new key. It is Pelléas who resists, his thrice-repeated *non* outlining a diminished triad that is a more compressed version of the same gesture sung by
Mélisande earlier in the scene (Musical Example 4.15). He even snatches the
clarinet's descant, repeated from the previous phrase (*je les tiens* ["I hold it"]),
while singing his oddly homonymic exclamation, *Je n'ai jamais vu de cheveux
comme les tiens* ("I have never seen hair like yours"), as if linking the two
strands of possession in a melodic braid. And with this self-possessed act of
imitation, his lyrical determination grows stronger. Over a fresh, pulsing
rhythm, he delivers an ever more colorful bouquet. First, a virtual tercet of
nine-syllable lines:

EXAMPLE 4.15 (Continued)

Vois, vois, vois: ils viennent de si haut
Et ils m'inondent encore jusqu'au coeur
Ils m'inondent encore jusqu'au genoux!

(You see, you see? It comes from so high / and yet it still floods me
right to my heart, / It floods me to my knees!)

EXAMPLE 4.15 (Continued)

Then, a decasyllable:

    Ils sont doux comme s'ils tombaient du ciel.

    (It's soft, like [a gentle rain] falling from the sky.)

Then, a perfect, classic alexandrine:

    Je ne voix plus le ciel à travers tes cheveux.

    (I can no longer see the sky through your hair.)

This moment of wonder is appropriately underscored in Debussy's setting, not only through the vocal rhythm, which clearly marks the alexandrine's two hemistichs, but also through a colorful sigh in the full orchestra. Two symbolic chords (C and F#) surround the verse like a luminous shadow, drawing out the reverent sentiment. And that gesture brings on yet another change of key, along with a more declamatory rising line. Pelléas marvels that his two hands cannot begin to hold the luxuriant hair, extending, as it does, as far as the willow tree. Indeed, in his most unexpected ornithological metaphor, he shouts that this delicate quivering mass feels "like living birds in my hands," which "love me more than you do" (*Ils vivent comme des oiseaux dans les mains, et ils m'aiment, ils m'aiment plus que toi!*). And with this outburst, he warbles a high A, the highest note of the scene (extremely high for a baritone),[125] reaching, one presumes, the "frenzy" that Laloy was referring to. Yet this cry of passion does not say it all, for the most remarkable moment is yet to come.

One last time, Mélisande interrupts; one last time, Pelléas demurs. But now, instead of rising in excitement, he pulls back. "I shall not deliver you tonight; you shall be my prisoner, all night long" (*Je ne te delivre pas cette nuit; Tu es ma prisonnière cette nuit, toute la nuit*). No longer overcome, he calculates, planning his act of possession in a deliberately hushed line that falls to his lowest note so far. A lonesome call from the captive bird, sad as a mourning dove (Pelléas, Pelléas . . .), is his sign. At this sound, he begins to perform the most fraught act of the scene, possibly of the whole opera: he forms a glistening golden cage, tying her hair to the branches of the willow (Musical Example 4.16). And as we all know, from this symbolic knot (*noue*) will come the opera's tragic *dénouement*.

> Je les noue, je les noue aux branches du saule
> Tu ne t'en ira plus, tu ne t'en ira plus
> Regarde, regarde, j'embrasse tes cheveux
> Je ne souffre plus au milieu de tes cheveux. . . .
>
> (I tie [your hair], I tie it to the willow branches. / You will never get away now, you will never get away, / Look, look, I'm kissing your hair. / I no longer suffer when I'm in your hair. . . .)

The versifying once again recalls Pelléas's original "poetry," the refrains that erupted spontaneously with his first flood of pleasure (see Musical Example 4.14). Yet here the verse is all the more well formed. Forgetting the exuberance of his earlier, short-breathed lines, he begins with a quatrain of virtual alexandrines, producing a fulsome rhythm, a more captivating

EXAMPLE 4.16 Debussy, *Pelléas*, Hair scene, III, i, *Je les noue …*

"music." At least, that is how Debussy reads the sentences. Pulling back the tempo, muting the strings, he replaces the sighing clarinet with an unmuted viola, whose more tremulous voice imbues the moment with unaccountable melancholy. Most significantly, he brings back the harp, largely silent since the falling of the hair, and gives it a prominent solo role, as if to suggest—through a *valeur impressive* of the orchestration—the presence of those shimmering golden strands strung in the willow tree. With its luminous timbre, its more continuous scoring, the harp now has the most prominent role. Leading the muted ensemble of strings, it almost becomes a figure for Apollo's lyre. And the orchestral symbolism makes a certain sense, for in binding himself to Mélisande in this way, Pelléas is indeed manned with a new "instrument," and a new orphic power.

Charles Panzéra seems to have understood the point. On an unforgettable recording from 1927,[126] he sings this music of the willow with a broad and noble air and yet with audible tears in his voice. The singing is so poignant, in fact, that we can believe Pelléas has been fully infected with the ethos of Mélisande's alien poetry, the sad, melancholy strain of her exotic birdsong. And yet he does not exactly sing *in* her voice. These are not the candid accents of "Mes longs cheveux." Pelléas's song of binding lives, it seems, in a space

EXAMPLE 4.16 (Continued)

between his possessiveness and her purity. Indeed, the phrase rhythm of this song, driven by a more stable harmony and a more articulate accompaniment, is both bound and free. The sense of musical time has completely transformed. In Panzéra's performance, the tempo slows to a point of pure languor, creating an utterly imaginary space in which he seems to float weightlessly above the orchestra. "Look," says Pelléas, "no hands."

It is in that suspended interval that the vocal line itself becomes liberated from the burden of representation. Infected by a strain of "pure" poetry, but speaking in his own voice, Pelléas could almost recall the condition of Orpheus, suspended between gods and mortals. And that condition may help us recognize, in turn, something about the special status of his diction, which, caught in a rhythmic braid, neither resembles the free flow of Mélisande's "unbound" melody.[127] Nor does it quite imitate the cadence of natural speech. What we hear in this sad song of the willow is, it seems, a marvelous mediation of the Tower and the Letter, a place in which the idea of the natural chanson comes into focus—indeed, into the range of our hearing—by being tied to a unit of time: the alien bird is bound to the conductor's branch. In this way, the scene offers us a perfect, symbolic representation, a kind of allegory, in fact, of the origins of a uniquely French form of musical expression. Arresting *melos* in Allemonde's forest, Pelléas reveals the secret of French *mélodie*.

This allegory is a slight revision of our story from chapter 1, offering a phenomenological twist on the theme of *La Chanson d'Eve*. In that cycle, we discovered the desire for a song so pure it turned expression into silence. Here we are shown, in a sense, the illusionism of such song. The hair scene, in other words, defines the fulfillment of that desire *as* an illusion—a moment of intense pleasure, but an illusion nonetheless. It is Orpheus all over again: the lover may talk his way into the world of the gods, but he cannot have his Eurydice forever, not as long as he is bound by human time. When Pelléas cries, "You can never abandon me again," we feel the full weight of this orphic condition, for we already know this is one wish that will never come true. In fact, his willow song—a blissful moment of communion in music—comes to an end, right there.

——————

And this is where we should perhaps bring our own argument to a close. Debussy's *Pelléas* has taught enough lessons for one chapter, offering yet another view on a musical art whose meaning we have been seeking since Eve's first words. Suspended in the branches, Pelléas's song marks, in fact, the only real *mélodie* in the whole opera. And for this reason we are able, for once, to see that song itself for what it truly is: a moment of pure, poetic fantasy, a magic bubble of time that will inevitably be broken.

The revelation offers a small but important refinement to our view of this modern genre and its much-discussed naturalism. At this point, there should be no doubt that the years before 1900 saw a change in the face of French song, as composers renounced melody to catch the natural "accent" of speech. If our previous chapters sought to unpack the cultural and literary meanings of this development, here I have probed its aesthetic implications. Examining a variety of historical performance practices, I have attempted to trace some of the ways in which the French accent did infiltrate the idea of song: in the singing "instrument" itself, in concepts of muteness and restraint that governed French diction, and in actual genres of poetic recitation, true *expressions lyriques*, that celebrated the hushed music of the spoken word. But the allegory of *Pelléas*, with its song of the willow, puts an even finer point on this aesthetic development and puts the French accent, so to speak, in its place. It reveals one critical element previously hidden from our historical view of song. It shows us, in short, how this *mélodie*—as an aesthetic form—will always be bound by another sort of accent: a beat, or pulse, that fixes the voice in time and thereby makes "natural" speech a welcome dream.

This point is not sharp enough to burst the bubble of the *voix parlée*. But it does make us tune into this voice with new sensitivity. In that respect, it gives new meaning to that "natural" Rousseauian melody we have encountered again and again in discussions of modern French prosody. The French lyric arts may have been fascinated with the *melos* of declamation, "rolling between very small intervals," but in phenomenal terms, something had to change for *melos* to become *mélodie*. By adding a piano accompaniment to my transcription of Bernhardt's "Evangile," I could demonstrate the thin line separating her "sung" poetry from Debussy's or Fauré's or Chausson's "spoken" melody. But it is now clear that in turning the songlike into the sung, the piano does more than bring out the harmony of poetic accents. The accompaniment also creates a temporal frame for the diction, slowing and stretching the words to a point of desirable *un*reality. Through an attenuation of speech, the song's phonetic elements become rare aesthetic objects. And that transformation, paradoxically, brings out their "truth." What is unreal, in fact, goes unnoticed; the bubble remains intact. This pretense, lying at the core of the French *mélodie*, is precisely what Sarah Bernhardt addressed in her *Art du théâtre*, when explaining the importance of pronunciation. "The secret of our art," she said, "consists in preventing the audience from recognizing it to be an illusion."[128] The audience is protected from the secret, encouraged *not* to hear the apparently natural accent for what it is: an intensely beautiful work of art.

If Debussy's *Pelléas* momentarily breaks that rule, offering us a glimpse of the illusion, it is only because the opera's single, symbolic *mélodie* is already a representation, deftly woven into the fabric of an opera that made naturalistic declamation the norm. But this glimpse also helps us peer into the last act of the opera with greater insight. I am thinking about the scene of Golaud's anguish and his insatiable desire for truth at the end of the play. The role was immortalized by Hector Dufranne, who created Golaud for the 1902 premiere at the Opéra-Comique and went on perform in almost every revival until 1939, more than 120 performances in all. Listening to his unpretentious *voix parlée* on the 1928 Columbia recording he made with Claire Croiza, we can believe him to be, as Debussy wrote in 1907, "the most profoundly human Golaud one might ever hear."[129] When he kneels by Mélisande's deathbed in the last act, the sad, betrayed husband presses her one last time to break the spell and tell him what he has wanted to know all along: "We must out with the truth at last, do you hear?" All she can do is echo back his words: "*la vérité... la vérité....*" Setting the first as a question, with an upward cadence that does not resolve, Debussy makes these virtually the last words spoken by his beloved Mélisande.

One could easily wonder about the broader impact of this quizzical response in 1902, in an era when the question of "*la vérité*" burned on the lips of so many French citizens. Mélisande's equivocation could even be seen to reflect the composer's own questionable stance on the Dreyfus Affair, about which, as Jane Fulcher has shown, he remained decidedly on the fence. But I hear Mélisande's unanswered question as a warning about the nature of art itself, especially the musical art that consumed Debussy while he composed his *Pelléas*, an opera whose truthful accents ultimately changed the meaning of French musical prosody. Debussy may have tried, as he tells us, to write an opera where "his characters would sing like normal people," but he also reminds us, with Mélisande's dying question, that the point was not to make art be absolutely true but to make the truth an art. In our next chapter, we have occasion to explore the larger consequences of this idealistic stance. Examining songs composed by Debussy and others in the decades that followed, we shall begin to see the fraught nature of this quest and how it played out as part of the natural history of the *mélodie française*.

CHAPTER FIVE

Farewell to an Idea

A FTER *Pelléas*, Debussy's music turned a corner. Or so it appeared to Louis Laloy. In his essay "Debussy and Debussyism," he described the "perceptible change" he heard in the composer's style, starting with the songs from 1904 that would become the second set of *Fêtes galantes*.[1] Writing in Debussy's lifetime, Laloy was cautious about naming a reason and spoke only of "a certain sense of diligence" that seemed to visit the new works. Later critics would be bolder. Lockspeiser, for example, connected the change directly to Debussy's scandalous circumstances in 1904: the tryst with Emma Bardac, the attempted suicide of Lilly Texier, and the prolonged emotional turmoil that followed.[2] Graham Johnson conjectured along similar lines that Debussy, "deserted by his erstwhile friends," never recovered, and the damage showed up in the music. "His songs became less easily accessible," he said, "like the man himself."[3]

Conclusions like this are hard to resist, though the new sense of remoteness Johnson perceives may require another explanation. For one thing, Debussy was not the only one to show it. If his style appeared more studied in the music after *Pelléas*, the same was true for others of his cohort. We learned in chapter 1, for example, about the shift in Fauré's style in 1906 as he embarked on *La Chanson d'Eve*, a cycle that betrayed a similar sense of diligence and, in a way, a similar connection to *Pelléas*. Not only did Fauré take pains to demonstrate in this cycle what a French *mélodie* should and should not do but the first song he completed was actually built on top of a melody—a song for Mélisande—that he had written, but never used, as part of his incidental music for Maeterlinck's play. I am not saying that Maeterlinck should now be blamed for the change in style, any more than

Emma Bardac. But the self-reflexive turn we witness in both composers in this "post-Pelléas" moment does suggest that something was going on, something that had changed the idea of what a song, or *mélodie*, could be. This final chapter, simply put, is about that transformation. The bird of *Pelléas*'s central scene may have been a harbinger of truth, but as the century moved on, that bird, now caged, begins to look and sound a little different.

La vérité

The difference is easy to catch in Debussy's reading of "Les ingénues," which opened the new *Fêtes galantes*. If the poems he chose for his first set, in 1891, tended to flaunt the antique moonlight and sensual melancholy of Verlaine's Watteau-inspired landscapes, those of the second are more knowing. It is as if the composer returned to the collection and discovered a whole cast of unexpected characters hidden there, jaded and disenchanted.[4] In "Les ingé-nues," the most disillusioned is the first person itself, recounting sexual exploits of more innocent times:

Les hauts talons luttaient avec les longues jupes,
En sorte que, selon le terrain et le vent,
Parfois luisaient des bas de jambe, trop souvent
Interceptés!—et nous aimions ce jeu de dupes.

Parfois aussi le dard d'un insecte jaloux
Inquiétait le col des belles, sous les branches,
Et c'était des éclairs soudains de nuques blanches
Et ce régal comblait nos jeunes yeux de fous.

(High heels struggled with long skirts / In such a way that, depending on the terrain or the wind, / The low portions of legs sometimes gleamed, too often / Intercepted!—and we loved this dupe's game. // Sometimes also the sting of a jealous insect / Bothered the necks of beauties, under the branches, / And there were sudden flashes of white napes, / And this treat gratified our young fool's eyes.//)

Debussy's music is knowing in a similar way. The setting turns around a repeated riff in the piano: a deliberately artificial mode in D♭ whose hybrid surface, both augmented and chromatic, keeps its tonal distance (Musical Example 5.1). The text is declaimed impassively alongside, in nearly uniform note values. Falling in with the piano's obsessive rhythm, the monotone melody emphasizes the speaker's cool. Only the thought of a stolen glance

EXAMPLE 5.1 Debussy, *Fêtes galantes* (1904), "Les ingénues," mm. 1–36

breaks the pattern, and the composure. The memory of animal whiteness—a flash of neck—in the poem's second stanza causes the piano to slip impetuously toward black keys and a more primal sort of pentatony (*Et c'était des éclairs soudains de nuques blanches*), while the voice rushes headlong toward a climax of its own. In a sense, the gesture reads in two directions. The pentatonic rush may have painted the unabashed eroticism of the game, "gratifying young fool's eyes," but it functioned self-reflexively as well. This

EXAMPLE 5.1 (Continued)

EXAMPLE 5.1 (Continued)

was, after all, a very "Debussyian" effect. The knowing first person could just as easily speak for the composer, calling attention to the music's pentatonic foolishness as if to question the facile effects of his own style. Was that, too, a dupe's game?

The next measure seems to make it so. A return of the opening riff—collapsed in thirds and slowed to half the speed—damps the excitement in preparation for the final stanza (Musical Example 5.2):

> Le soir tombait, un soir équivoque d'automne:
> Les belles, se pendant rêveuses à nos bras,
> Dirent alors des mots si spécieux, tout bas,
> Que notre âme depuis ce temps tremble et s'étonne.

> (The evening fell, an equivocal autumn evening: / The lovely ones, hanging dreamily on our arms, / Said such specious things, so quietly, / That ever since our soul has trembled, astonished.//)

The song's augmented Db mode now comes across more clearly, as aloof and "equivocal" as the autumn night. But once again the impression is fleeting. With the start of the next phrase, the piano stalls on a plangent minor-major seventh, reinterpreting that Db as it reconsiders the lovely girls, hanging dreamily on boyish arms. And then, as if unable to resist their words (*des mots si spécieux*), it slips once more—back into the specious pentatony it left behind in measure 36. This time, black keys have been exchanged for white, though the effect is no less touching. Indeed, in the piano's languid turns, we can almost make out the echo of another, more familiar pentatonic theme—that of Mélisande herself, the exotic bird who once upset the universe of Allemonde.

This near quotation, recalling music from another place and time, is far more knowing than the previous gesture, and the final phrase will reveal exactly how much more. A snap of the G-string in the piano's left hand brings on the chilling conclusion. "Our souls have been trembling ever since," the first person admits, and an utterly arresting Gb minor ninth sounds three times, like a bell tolling for the dead. The chord's dark certainty will shut the door on the memory of Mélisande, as well as the song's ambiguous Db harmony, providing the augmented chord with an unexpected root. But in quelling one vibration, it simply starts up another, for this was a chord with deeper repercussions. Debussy had used it once before, in fact, in the final act of *Pelléas*. There it appeared—at the very same register and pitch—to punctuate Golaud's anguished confession, the moment he implored Mélisande, finally, to tell the truth (Musical Example 5.3).

EXAMPLE 5.2 Debussy, *Fêtes galantes* (1904), "Les ingénues," mm. 37–53

EXAMPLE 5.2 (Continued)

On its own, the chord could be called a *valeur impressive* within the setting, analogous to the dark tremor written into the poem's quaking verb, *tremble*. As a self-quotation, though, its trembling has another implication. The song's first person is affected, it suggests, by the same kind of trouble that visited Golaud: a problem of sincerity, *la vérité*, which was the trouble with Mélisande herself. It may be easy to imagine Debussy identifying with his opera's guilty husband in the midst of his own marital troubles in 1904.[5] But the self-reflexivity of "Les ingénues" may have just as much to do with the truth of song and poetry, with *melos* in the broadest sense. If for Debussy the goal of writing music was "to arrive at the naked flesh of emotion," as he once put it,[6] this poem turned the whole game on its head. Speaking through its knowing "we," the composer seems to raise a different question: about what it meant, not for himself, but for a piece of music to be true.

It is a concern that will resonate throughout this chapter, just as it haunts the *Fêtes galantes*, and so it makes sense to follow the question to the cycle's end. The faux "Faune" of the second song, "laughing at the center of the garden," may seem to scoff, constructed as he is not out of truth but out of terra-cotta. But "Colloque sentimental," Debussy's final *mélodie* in this set and his final testament to Verlaine, will deal with the question more openly, through a text that was actually a series of questions, a discourse about love spoken by two ghosts on a frozen landscape. Johnson saw this ghostly dialogue as "utterly truthful" in its depiction of the nature of human relationships.[7] What Debussy expressed even more truthfully, though, occurred between the lines of dialogue. The final song of *Fêtes galantes* became an occasion to interrogate voices from his own musical past, voices that would begin to teach a starker lesson about the limits of the *mélodie*.

The poem was a haunting bit of theater. Beginning and ending in narration, the scene it captured was staged in lonely couplets, floating on a cold, white page:

Dans le vieux parc solitaire et glacé
Deux formes ont tout à l'heure passé.

Leurs yeux sont morts et leurs lèvres sont molles,
Et l'on entend à peine leur parole.

Dans le vieux parc solitaire et glacé
Deux spectres ont évoqué le passé.

—Te souvient-il de notre extase ancienne?
—Pourquoi voulez-vous donc qu'il m'en souvienne?

—Ton coeur bat-il toujours à mon seul nom?
Toujours vois-tu mon âme en rêve?—Non.

—Ah! Les beaux jours de bonheur indicible
Où nous joignions nos bouches!—C'est possible.

—Qu'il était bleu, le ciel, et grand l'espoir!
—L'espoir a fui, vaincu, vers le ciel noir.

Tels ils marchaient dans les avoines folles,
Et la nuit seule entendit leurs paroles.

(In the old, frozen and lonely park / Two forms just passed by. // Their eyes are dead and their lips soft, / And their words are barely audible. // In the old, frozen and lonely park / Two ghosts recalled the past. // "Does it remind you of our old passion?" / "Why would you have me remember that?" // "Doesn't your heart still beat at the sound of my name? / Don't you still see me in your dreams?" "No." // "Ah! The beautiful days of unspeakable happiness /When we kissed!" "Possibly." // "How blue, the sky, how great our hope!" / "Hope has fled, defeated, toward the black sky." // Thus they walked in the wild oats, / And only the night heard their words.//)

Debussy catches this sense of isolation as his song begins (Musical Example 5.4).[8] Aimless figures in the right and left hands pass by in contrary motion, coupling but not communicating. Like the verse forms, they prescribe the ghost's encounter as an eerily failed communion, in sterile two-part counterpoint. The tableau soon changes, though, as the cold present gives way to the heat of memory, and narration to dialogue. A repeated A♭ in the piano, like a ritual drum, signals the new temporal space, while a chord above rustles and

vibrates. The warmth breaks the ice, and from the fissure, an arabesque alights (Musical Example 5.5). One ghost hears and remembers. "Does that remind you of our former passion?" What follows is not so much an answer as a kind of twin refusal. The other ghost not only poses another question, replacing the familiar second person (*tu*) with a formal *vous*. But this question also keeps its distance through the subjunctive mood (*Pourquoi voulez-vous donc qu'il m'en souvienne?* "Why would you have me remember that?"). A low half-diminished chord clinches the rejection, silencing the more nostalgic, fully

EXAMPLE 5.4 (Continued)

EXAMPLE 5.5 Debussy, "Colloque sentimental," mm. 19–50

EXAMPLE 5.5 (Continued)

EXAMPLE 5.5 (Continued)

diminished harmonies of the previous phrase.[9] One cannot help recalling the kind of failed dialogue that reigned in the opening scene of *Pelléas*, where an eager Golaud asked his hopeful questions, and Mélisande refused, in her way, to answer. Could it be that Debussy saw in Verlaine's ghosts the afterlife of the two figures he left behind in *Pelléas*'s last act?[10]

The impression is strengthened as the dialogue continues. Impervious, the first ghost follows the arabesque toward an even more powerful erotic reminiscence—the memory of a kiss—and the song's sole moment of lyricism at the word *indicible*. And here something marvelous happens: the second ghost gently yields. Its equivocal *C'est possible* sounds unexpectedly sincere through the pure Db triad that resolves the previous measure's dominant. A sigh from within the pulsing accompaniment candidly echoes back this answer, and a whole world of possibility opens: the two spirits, for the first time, communicate. "How blue the sky, how great our hope / Hope has fled, defeated, toward the black sky." While the visions are opposed, the chiasmus in the poetry forges a tenuous connection, which Debussy strengthens by joining the two phrases into one six-measure period, antecedent and consequent. He also complicates the second ghost's reply, shading it with a suggestion of reconciliation, or regret. For this time the response is not quite so distant, accompanied as it is by the same, fully diminished harmony that had provoked the first ghost's memory and started up their dialogue. Still, the communion is fleeting; A♭ falls silent; memory soon dissolves (Musical Example 5.6). The narrator, in the historical *passé simple*, reenters the scene to close with an eerie thought, like the conclusion of a macabre tale by Poe: "only the night heard their words." And from the blackness sounds a final death: a fading arabesque; a cadence; curtain.

That ending—a startled, A minor gasp—is the thing we ought to question. Through it, the song seems to enter into a dialogue of its own, one that goes well beyond *Pelléas* into the music of a very different time and place. Debussy knew another A-minor setting of Verlaine's poem, by Charles de Sivry. Or at least, he seems to have known it, for he recalls the opening notes of the vocal line almost verbatim (Musical Example 5.7). Whether conscious or not, the theft was significant, for the old song must have carried with it a memory of Debussy's bohemian youth. Years before, de Sivry had been a cabaret musician, playing nightly at the old Chat noir, where his life had brushed both poet and composer. De Sivry was the son of Debussy's first piano teacher, and—more important—the brother of Mathilde Mauthé. That made him Verlaine's brother-in-law, a connection that suggests a story of its own. In calmer days, we know, Verlaine had given his bride-to-be a *Bonne chanson*, before entering into a famously hopeless marriage. Mathilde, in turn, had often sung for Verlaine's pleasure. The real-life history invoked by Debussy's knowing citation thus reproduced the same kinds of questions raised by Verlaine's ghosts: a spooky tale of love gone wrong, and hints of darker times.

The song's trilling arabesque had much the same effect. It, too, was a quotation, and a more obvious one, at that. This time, Debussy looked back to music he himself had written, in 1892, for his very first collection of *Fêtes galantes*. In the first song, "En sourdine," a similarly warbling melody, sounding in the opening measures, played a clearer role as sound effect. The explicit erotic tableau of "En sourdine" included the sonic signature of a nightingale that appeared as a future portent, foretelling a time when passion would be dead. "And when the night falls from the black oaks—oh voice of our despair!—the nightingale will sing." Debussy made his night bird sing on all the black keys, in a chirping pentatonic flourish (Musical Example 5.8).

When that melody shows up on the cold frontier of "Colloque sentimental" (Musical Example 5.6), it is a shadow of its younger self. The pentatonic

EXAMPLE 5.6 Debussy, "Colloque sentimental," final measures

freshness has withered, shrunk into a diminished mode that now sounds hollow and depleted. It was a technique Debussy had used before, and once again, it was in the last act of *Pelléas*. A weakened Mélisande, cold as the ghosts in "Colloque sentimental," lies in her bed as the harp and strings make a gesture to her sickness, outlining a diminished version of her once frankly

EXAMPLE 5.7 Charles de Sivry, "Colloque sentimental," opening measures

EXAMPLE 5.8 Debussy, *Fêtes galantes* (1891), "En sourdine," final phrase

pentatonic theme (Musical Example 5.9). "It's as if her soul had frozen," says Arkel. The birdsong in the final *Fêtes galantes* is withered in the same way, fulfilling the first song's dismal prophecy. It has become the voice of the lover's despair, for it expresses the future "En sourdine" could only hint at: its diminished form reflects the missing plenitude, the passion, whose death the ghosts themselves personify. A melody transposed from a different time and sung by no one, it haunts the setting like another "bird that is not from here," to recall Pelléas's words at the Tower.

This time, though, the bird has really flown. And that realization brings up one more difference, for when we compare the two settings not as stories but as songs, we see something else the later one lacks. Gone is the long, sobbing climax heard in "En sourdine" (*Voix de notre désespoir*). No such vocal arabesque animates the second set of *Fêtes galantes*. The ghosts, though sentimental, keep their cool. Even at its most passionate, "Colloque senti-mental" remains on the side of colloquy: declamatory and discursive rather than conventionally "expressive." In that respect, the avian call could be said

EXAMPLE 5.9 Debussy, *Pelléas*, Act V, orchestral opening: Mélisande's theme "diminished"

to do two things. It does not merely represent the condition of a failed romance. It also stands in for a voice—an entire way of singing— that the ghosts have now forgotten. The sensuous line recalls the very thing the later song cannot or will not do: it will not turn real feelings into full-blown tunes. I can just imagine Debussy, reminded of a song like "C'est l'extase langoureuse," demurring with the second ghost: "Why would you have me remember that?"[11] In "Colloque sentimental," he refuses in just this way so that he can say something else, something whose modernity we may now recognize more clearly. He has withheld expression to make his words ring true. He has fashioned a *mélodie* quite deliberately without melody.

The difference, of course, is the refusal. That is why these songs from 1904 stand out and why they become crucial to a history of *mélodie*. They introduce an attitude we have not quite seen before, an attitude I want to trace now through a longer span of time, as a way of fleshing out that history. We could call it simply a new awareness (or "diligence," to use Laloy's word) about the nature of expression. But it is the quality of this awareness that interests me, for it now turns on a subtle negation, an idea about what expression can no longer be. Significantly, there was none of this negation in Debussy's *Trois Chansons de Bilitis* from 1897. Quite the contrary: those modern settings were explicit about their sensuality and their sincerity, full of the affirmation—and the youthful idealism—that permeated poets in an era when verse was supposed to be free, and music itself the liberator. By 1904, the idealism was not completely gone, but what remained had shrunk, it seems, into the second ghost's wary "c'est possible." "I feel nostalgia for the Claude Debussy who worked so enthusiastically on *Pelléas*," the composer wrote to André Messager in 1904.[12] What had happened? That is what we need to figure out.

If, as I have suggested, Debussy's life cannot provide a satisfactory answer, we have to look to larger trends. Here it becomes tempting to wonder again about the effect of an event like the Dreyfus Affair on musicians of the period. What can be said about the import of this crisis? I do not pretend to have an easy way of linking its politics to the tastes of individual composers. Jane Fulcher showed the delicacy—and the difficulty—of that task many years ago. But the extended public trial, which after Zola's intervention in 1898 took on national proportions, obviously played some part in quashing the idealism of a younger generation, especially the youth culture of the 1890s that had absorbed the Republic's rhetoric of freedom, equality, brotherhood. The deaths of Verlaine and Mallarmé, coming at just this time—in 1896 and 1898, respectively—could only reinforce the sense of disillusionment. These poets, of course, represented for the younger writers the same cherished idealism brought to the realm of art. Their passing, which suggested (to some, at least) the death of symbolism itself, may have brought on impassioned defenses by devotees, as we saw with Robert de Souza. But such actions also revealed how much a generation's confidence had been shaken. Indeed, the collection of currents suggests an interesting analogy to the aftermath of a similar moment in the twentieth century, that period commonly known as May 68. This was, at least, another point in French history where a powerful youth culture had formed briefly and intensely under the banner of *liberté, égalité, fraternité*. The idealism of that moment was also quashed—and quickly, too—in the Republic of Pompidou and Giscard that followed, leaving only a dim sense of the transforming possibilities that had fueled the previous decade's social explosion.[13] In the years after 1898, crossing into a new century, the musical and literary youth in Paris seem to have experienced much the same diminishment.

Of course, the composers were never so helpful as to tell us directly. And so we are forced to look for our history in other places. I shall continue as I have begun, staying close to the music. In the very texture of the songs, we can, I think, read a kind of history: the traces of a change that affected more than one composer in the period. I will not be offering anything like a survey of the *mélodie* from this point on, although a sampling of pieces written after the premiere of *Pelléas* until about 1920 (the year of Fauré's retirement) can begin to show the extent of what I mean. I am looking neither for individual styles nor for harmonic novelties. What I am after involves something far more basic: one might call it the "grain" of the song or, more simply, following the discussion in the previous chapters, its diction. In any case, I want to show how the *mélodie* itself, as a musical practice based around an act of telling (*dire*), becomes implicated in its own history, not just through what it tells but how. By listening to the diction, a different kind of story emerges, not reported but felt, in the very texture of the language. As before, Fauré and Debussy will continue to offer enlightening testimony, but I also want to consider some songs by Fauré's student Maurice Ravel to try to catch the accent of a younger generation. As we shall see, there is perhaps more resignation than disillusionment in the music Ravel wrote after *Shéhérazade*, his singular testament to *Pelléas*, but he is no less self-conscious about the problem of sincerity or truth in art. Indeed, one set of songs from 1907 reveals, even more pointedly than Debussy, how important these problems had become.

Natural History

These were the *Histoires naturelles*, a collection of animal portraits Ravel conceived around Jules Renard's tiny prose tales. With their odd stories of four birds and one defenseless cricket, the songs were more comical than Debussy's chilly *Fêtes*, but in some ways, they were just as knowing. Critics have been quick to ascribe the tone, as they did with Debussy, to something within Ravel's own nature, especially the ironic temperament that caused him, as Laloy once put it, ever to "remain an observer."[14] And it is hardly surprising. The collection does seem to bring out Ravel's wittiest and most observant qualities, even as he turns an ironic mirror on himself. Benjamin Ivry was certain he recognized the composer in the peacock-dandy of the first song, but there are other telling resemblances. One might wonder, for example, about the fastidious cricket of no. 2, winding his little watch, or the swan of no. 3, gliding on impressionistic pools. Johnson even heard Ravel's accent coming through the vocal line.[15]

All these references could point back to Ravel himself, but they tell us even more about his craft. Calvocoressi reports that listeners often reacted badly to the composer's apparent lack of sincerity, to "the care he took," as Calvocoressi put it, "to exclude from his music all that might resemble a direct expression of emotion."[16] The first performance of the *Histoires naturelles* bore this out. The audience balked. According to Jane Bathori, who sang the premiere, the reason was simple: the songs "represented a complete break with what one normally thought of as *mélodie*."[17] And yet Ravel himself insisted otherwise. In fact, when Calvocoressi pressed him to cite pieces from his oeuvre that showed real feeling, he pointed immediately to a song from the *Histoires naturelles*. One could interpret this response, of course, as another instance of his ironic nature. But taking the comment seriously brings another possibility into view. This queer set of nature songs from 1907 can, in fact, tell us something significant about the nature of song, of *mélodie*, as Ravel now understood it. I want to take the time now to find out what they have to say.

And I want to begin with Jules Renard. After all, Renard is the one historical witness who offers a first-person account of what Ravel was trying to do in these songs, and the testimony is intriguing. Ravel apparently visited the writer on the day of the premiere in 1907, and the conversation was recorded in Renard's diary for posterity. As the story goes, Ravel explained to his host that in setting the *Histoires naturelles,* he had attempted to "say with music," what Renard had "said with words."[18] This remark, too, can be interpreted in many ways, but critics have tended to read it as more evidence for Calvocoressi's claim, revealing the lengths to which Ravel would go to avoid the "direct expression of emotion."[19] But here, perhaps, the critics are too literal, or at least they sell Ravel short, for the composer surely knew that there was more between the lines of Renard's prose than might at first appear.

The stories, in fact, came with a big moral attached—one that was quite self-conscious about the goals of modern art. If that message was not lost on the idealistic artists of Ravel's generation, it should not be lost on us.

It helps to know that Renard was not only a prominent Parisian writer but also a socialist who, by 1907, had become mayor of his provincial hometown and friend to two important republican leaders, Jean Jaurès and Léon Blum. Almost twenty years earlier, in 1889, he had also helped to found the *Mercure de France*, that new journal of the literary avant-garde created to support the idealistic artists I was just talking about: the same generation we met in chapter 3, those who believed they could democratize poetry by restoring, as Kahn said, the unpretentious "tone of conversation." Renard thought he had done just that with his own book of *Nature Stories*, whose first edition appeared in 1896. The author was no poet, of course, but his prose works cultivated the same rural and populist ethos through a radically stripped-down style. "When a truth goes on for longer than five lines," he liked to say, "it's already a novel."[20] He had a horror of inflated sentiment. Like the younger symbolists, he saw "literature" (always *entre guillemets*) as a bourgeois pastime, destined to tell lies. He wanted to become, with his peasant neighbors, a man of fewer words. He confessed it again and again in the pages of his journal: his greatest desire was "to seek true impressions, and to express, in precise language, feelings that have the *taste of truth*."[21]

The *Histories naturelles* spoke directly to that desire. The collection opened with a vignette called "Le Chasseur d'images," a term that invoked his ideal truth seeker in more than one sense (Figure 5.1). Literally an "image hunter" (or "shutterbug" in slang), the figure introduced the reader to a *flaneur* of the open air, wandering the fields like a photographer or a poet in search of fresh material. It was he who would become the book's omniscient narrator, collecting the impressions for all the stories that followed: the cow, the magpie, the rooster, the bull. But as a figure for Renard himself, his eye could also be brutal. Consider, for example, the story of "Le Cygne" (The Swan):

> Il glisse sur le bassin, comme un traîneau blanc, de nuage en nuage. Car il n'a faim que des nuages floconneux qu'il voit naître, bouger, et se perdre dans l'eau.
>
> C'est l'un d'eux qu'il désire. Il le vise du bec, et il plonge tout à coup son col vêtu de neige.
>
> Puis, tel un bras de femme sort d'une manche, il le retire.
>
> Il n'a rien.
>
> Il regarde: les nuages effarouchés ont disparu.

Il ne reste qu'un instant désabusé, car les nuages tardent peu à revenir, et, là-bas, où meurent les ondulations de l'eau, en voici un qui se reforme.

Doucement, sur son léger coussin de plumes, le cygne rame et s'approche.

Il s'épuise à pêcher de vains reflets, et peut-être qu'il mourra, victime de cette illusion, avant d'attraper un seul morceau de nuage.

(He glides on the pond like a white sleigh from cloud to cloud. For he's hungry only for the snowy ones he sees appearing, moving and vanishing in the water. / It's one of those he wants. He aims at it with his beak and, suddenly, plunges in his snowy neck. / Then, like a woman's arm coming out of a sleeve, he pulls it out. / Nothing. / He looks around: the startled clouds have gone.

He's disillusioned only a moment, for the clouds are hardly slow to return, and there where the waves are dying, he sees one. / Softly, on his light feather cushion, the swan paddles closer.

He's exhausted fishing for vain reflections and perhaps he'll die a victim of this illusion, before catching a single bit of cloud.)

The prose impression might be fresh, but if you look more closely, there is also something wrong with this swan picture, for the tone is deliberately double-edged. For one thing, the opening images seems somewhat glib for the taciturn Renard, the words gliding a bit too easily from the tongue. The sentences almost suggest the refinement of verse, scanning naturally into "free" alexandrines (twelve syllables, more or less), punctuated by half lines. Indeed, if he had wanted to, Renard could easily have written the text in the manner of the young poets of the *Mercure de France*:

> Il glisse sur le bassin, comme un traîneau blanc,
> De nuage en nuage.
> Car il n'a faim que des nuages floconneux
> Qu'il voit naître, bouger, et se perdre dans l'eau.
> C'est l'un d'eux qu'il desire.
> Il le vise du bec, et il plonge tout à coup
> Son col vêtu de neige.

But he didn't. Or he wouldn't. And in not doing so, he seems to comment on that poetic affectation. By opting for the frankness and directness of prose, the first-person narrator of these stories becomes, then, something like the poets' conscience, sounding a cautionary note to all those would-be writers of the open air. "Get real," he warns. And that is exactly what his story does. The speaker wakes up—just in time—to catch the "true impression" of the swan.

> Mais qu'est-ce que je dis?
> Chaque fois qu'il plonge, il fouille du bec la vase nourissante et ramène
> un ver.
> Il engraisse comme une oie.

(But what am I saying? / Each time he goes down, he digs into the healthy mud with his beak and brings back a worm. / He's getting fat as a goose.)

Get your head out of the clouds, the speaker says. There is nothing poetic about digging for worms. The well-aimed parting shot is even more pointed by ear, for in French, as we know, the word for worm (*ver*) sounds just like the word for poem (*vers*). The riposte played on the old Verlainian gag of symbolist birds feeding off the earth, not simply to dispatch the conventional swan of "literature," but to give the poets themselves a reality check. For what, in truth, is a *ver*? Renard will tell us that, too, elsewhere in his book. 'Tis a funny little thing, he suggests, that "stretches out and lengthens like a noodle" (Figure 5.2). The definition recalled de Souza's now familiar account of free verse, as a "malleable and fluid material capable of lengthening and shortening at will." But Renard's down-to-earth worm ultimately looped back to something more basic: his own prose style, flexible and starchy. The moral of the story? Don't ever forget the taste of truth.

We can guess how the poets reacted to all this in 1896, but the warning seems to have affected Ravel just as strongly ten years later—at least, if music offers any indication. His readings of the *Histoires naturelles* were a stylistic about-face. The songs represented a turning away from the lush impressionism of a cycle like *Schéhérazade* toward something more disciplined and "true." It is hard to gauge what role Ravel's socialism might have played in this sympathy to Renard's pastoral politics, but he clearly picked up the author's implied critique of the symbolists—and again it is no surprise. Connected to the circle of the *Mercure de France* through his friends Tristan Klingsor and Léon-Paul Fargue, Ravel knew how to read the signs. One prominent feature of the *Histoires naturelles* suggests, in fact, that he knew more than we might think.

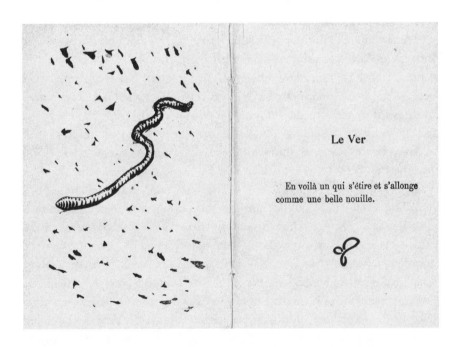

Le Ver

En voilà un qui s'étire et s'allonge comme une belle nouille.

FIGURE 5.2 Renard, *Histoires naturelles*, "Le Ver," with drawing by Bonnard, 1904 edition

I am talking about his treatment of the prosody. Every commentator mentions it: Ravel chose to set the texts of this cycle with a relentless realism. What is interesting, though, is that he did not quite follow Debussy's example. He actually went further, making the rhythms so natural and casual that he was tempted to drop the occasional syllable, especially that syllable we have come to know so well by now, the *e muet*. The opening song of the set, "Le Paon," is a case in point, with its partly funny, partly sad portrait of a celibate peacock all dressed up for a wedding that will never come.

Il va sûr<u>e</u>ment s<u>e</u> marier aujourd'hui.

C<u>e</u> d<u>e</u>vait êtr<u>e</u> pour hier. En habit d<u>e</u> gala, il était prêt.

Il n'attendait qu<u>e</u> sa fiancée. Ell<u>e</u> n'est pas venu. Ell<u>e</u> n<u>e</u> peut
   tarder. . . .

(He's surely getting married today. / It was supposed to be yesterday. He was ready, dressed in his finery. / He was waiting only for his fiancée. She didn't come. She can't be long. . . .)

The impatience of the strutting bird is mirrored in the clipped diction, and Ravel fashions an equally brusque vocal line for his setting (Musical Example 5.10). See how he handles the rhythm of the text, especially the subtle accents of its half-silent syllables, underlined in the text.

He certainly did not learn this kind of text setting from his teacher Fauré, and critics have argued that there was more than a bit of cheek in his compositional choice. About the mute *e*'s, Johnson has commented that because they would normally be dropped when one read aloud, Ravel dared to drop them, too, "to the horror of even old friends."[22] Nichols saw the setting, with its apparently low diction in the voice and its high French overture in the piano, as throwing down the gauntlet, openly challenging "the barrier between the popular and the serious."[23] But what kind of challenge was it? Listening to Jane Bathori's impeccable singing on a recording from 1929 reminds us that this was not, after all, a working-class accent.[24] The flap following the premiere had to be about more than a missing letter, for, in truth, the *e*'s were not dropped. A closer look at the notation shows how carefully Ravel has preserved them: he either assigns each one a separate note or ties the value over from the previous syllable, as Debussy had done in his setting of Geneviève's letter scene. True, we find no note for the second *e* in "Ell*e* n'est pas venue," but that is because the sound would be there anyway, in performance. Jane Bathori does it beautifully in her recording, putting the tiniest puff of air between the vibrant French *l*, spoken close to the teeth, and the *n* that follows. The whole approach showed

EXAMPLE 5.10 Ravel, *Histoires naturelles*, "Le Paon," opening measures

Ravel remaining "true" to Renard and, by extension, to the idealistic poets of free verse that the writer himself had addressed. He scanned the text not in the edgy voice of the faubourg or the music hall, but in the unaffected "tone of conversation."

Still, it must be said that the overall effect is strange, defamiliarizing. This kind of diction may have been perfect for Geneviève's recitation, but it was a bit too stingy for a song—which was part of Ravel's game, I think. Here he makes his vocal line perform too much like Renard's omniscient narrator. The diction has acquired a "taste for truth," but such truthfulness puts a clamp on singing. To put it another way: the trouble with realism is that it never permits excess. A truth longer than five lines is already a novel, said Renard, already fiction. This is precisely what Ravel's hyperreal rhythms expose in the realm of melody. The prosody polices expression, throws song off balance. If the French overture sounding through the piano part of *Le Paon* sounds pompous and exaggerated, it is because the voice itself will not go that far. The song's comic effect comes less from overture's mechanical rhythm than from the difference between the melody and the accompaniment. Terse and tight-lipped, the vocal line makes the piano's music seem loud, verbose: the musical equivalent of "literature." Ravel has essentially created the condition whereby song can observe *itself* going too far—as in the text of Renard's swan. This is one way he manages, brilliantly, to "say with music" what Renard has "said with words."

The effect redoubles when it is the voice that crosses the line. It happens rarely enough, but one passage in "Le Paon"—halfway through the song— makes the blunder unmistakable. The otherwise noble peacock forgets his prenuptial preening and, showing his true animal nature, calls out to the fiancée that will never appear. "Léon! Léon!" It is the song's only moment of direct address, a bestial cry uttered at the top of the range (Musical Example 5.11). It also cries out for comment, for the absent fiancée bears a man's name, indeed, a name with some significance for Ravel. There were a couple of important Léons in his life, namely, the two poets just mentioned, Léon-Paul Fargue and Tristan Klingsor (whose real name was Léon Leclère). By accident or design, the song turns personal, confessional.

Again, I am less concerned with what this birdcall might say about Ravel's life than with what it tells us about singing. And if Ravel has built a form of autocritique into his cycle, the songs become our most reliable source. As the example shows, the first-person speaker tells part of the story. It drops an octave and, reclaiming its focus, mocks the bird in a mordant aside, just like the narrator in "Le Cygne" ("Leon? *That's* what he calls his fiancée?"). But the self-conscious comeback is not quite enough. Not enough,

that is, to stop the impact of the cry or to check its diabolical effect. Where does all the feeling go? A quick perusal of the other songs will tell us straightaway and bring us closer to the point.

At first, the feeling shows up quite nearby. The cricket hears it, in the next *histoire*, echoing at his door as he returns home, to his tidy music box domain (Musical Example 5.12). At least, it seems that he hears it, because the intruding sound—like an unwanted memory—makes him react in a typically neurotic way. He starts to clean: raking, filing, dusting the threshold to "repair the disorder" in his house. But the effort does not have the desired effect. Even with his house in order, the sad feeling hangs around (Musical Example 5.13). The cricket feels unsafe, the story says. Repression seems to be the only answer, so in the end he burrows down, deep enough to block it out completely.

The cricket's denial will become the swan's oblivion. In the third song, the nagging call goes missing, although it is actually there, hidden inside the

EXAMPLE 5.12 Ravel, *Histoires naturelles*, "Le grillon," with the cry of the peacock, mm. 1–6.

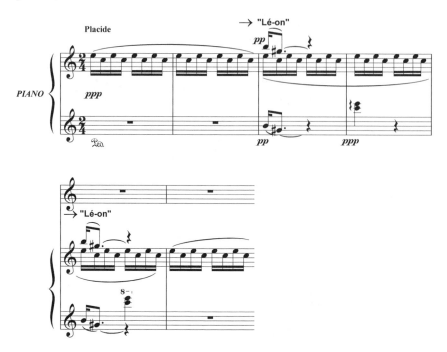

EXAMPLE 5.13 Ravel, *Histoires naturelles*, "Le grillon," the peacock's cry returns, mm. 51–53

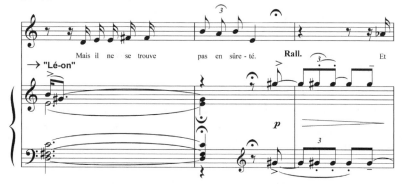

pentatonic clouds that make up the bird's foolish diet (Musical Example 5.14). Ravel here speaks to cloud-eating composers as pointedly as Renard spoke to the poets.[25] And like Renard, he, too, will break the spell, brutally, at the end of the song, pulling the speaker back to his earthy diction as the swan is pulled into

EXAMPLE 5.14 Ravel, *Histoires naturelles*, "Le Cygne," opening measures

the mud. But this happens only after he has dealt a lower blow. He exposes impressionism as a questionable coping mechanism. Scratch an impressionist, and you'll find a Romantic, he seems to say. When the speaker reflects on the swan's sad state, Ravel will make the vocal line swell, turning the pentatonic clouds chromatic, in a gesture of pure bathos. The passage is marked *très expressif*, and we can almost hear the quotation marks around it, when an echo of the peacock's cry returns in the vocal line, slowing to the end of the phrase (Musical Example 5.15).

The melodrama will be made even more noticeable by the change of affect that is to come, as the first person comes to his senses. *Mais qu'est-ce que je dis?* is the question he poses, and it might as well be our own. What is he saying, indeed? The songs so far present us with a double bind: parched realism or comic excess. Words either stick to the teeth or fly out of bounds. And yet those alternatives do not, in themselves, resolve the basic problem—the problem of expression raised by an unwitting peacock. As we see, the bird's unanswered call keeps showing up, looking for a home, haunting the other settings, as Debussy's nightingale did, like a guilty secret. Here it is again at the end of the cycle, screaming from the piano (in its original scoring and register) to announce "La Pintade," the guinea hen: a very foul-mouthed fowl acting out her rage (Musical Example 5.16).

Only one bird in Ravel's menagerie will not act like this. No loud decor, no unwanted cry comes to mar the surface of his song. It is the "Martin-pêcheur," the discreet and poignant creature perched in the middle of the set. This is, incidentally, the song Ravel pointed to when he told Calvocoressi that he, too, could be sincere. It enters and leaves the *Histoires naturelles* without making much noise at all, which means we have to listen even more carefully to find out what it has to say, and why.

EXAMPLE 5.16 Ravel, *Histoires naturelles*, "La Pintade," opening measures

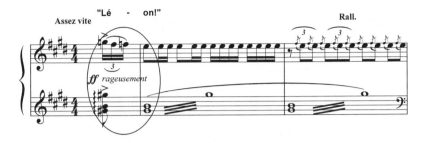

Ça na pas mordu, ce soir, mais je rapporte une rare émotion.

Comme je tenais ma perche de ligne tendue, un martin-pêcheur est
venu s'y poser.

Nous n'avons pas d'oiseau plus éclatant.

Il semblait une grosse fleur bleue au bout d'une longue tige. La perche
pliait sous le poids.

Je ne respirais plus, tout fier d'être pris pour un arbre par un martin-
pêcheur.

Et je suis sûr qu'il ne s'est pas envolé de peur, mais qu'il a cru qu'il ne
faisait que passer d'une branche à une autre.

(Nothing biting tonight, but I'm bringing back a rare emotion. / As I was
holding out my fishing pole, a kingfisher came and perched on it. / You'll
find no more brilliant bird than this. / He seemed like a great blue flower
at the end of a long stalk. The pole bent under his weight. / I stopped
breathing, so proud was I to have been taken for a tree by a kingfisher. /
And I'm sure that he didn't fly away in fear; he just thought he was passing
from branch to branch.)

The opening words say it all: "Nothing biting." For once, the diction is not
mordant. The speaker neither bares his teeth nor tries to stop the flow of words.
First- and third-person mix freely in this *histoire*, much like instrument and singer
do in Ravel's laconic setting (Music Example 5.17).[26] The pianos of the other songs,
with their vulgar rhythms, have vanished: a shy descending phrase is the only
unlikely refrain. The singer almost holds his breath. No one watches. Nothing
happens. The expression police have gone fishing. The peacock, too, has fallen
silent, and we wonder why until we see it—right at the end of our pole. A lonely
"Léon" is hiding in that chromatic subject, falling from D♯ to C at the song's
beginning, or from A♯ to G in the middle, or from G♯ to F (and beyond) at the end.

In not calling attention to itself, this almost silent musical subject behaves, in
a way, like the first-person of Renard's story, who stops breathing so the kingfisher

EXAMPLE 5.17 Ravel, *Histoires naturelles*, "Le Martin-pêcheur" (complete)

EXAMPLE 5.17 (Continued)

won't hear *him*. The tale offers the only true alternative to the swan, whose false impressions made the bird a mirror of the poet: "a fisher of vain reflections" (*un pêcheur de vains reflets*). The kingfisher does not fish in vain; it is he who catches the poet, unawares. Ravel underscores this difference by linking the two songs with a sob. The singer poet pouted a maudlin "Léon" when realizing his swan would never catch the clouds (see Musical Example 5.15). In "Le Martin-pêcheur," the sound returns to mark the loss not of a metaphor, but of the bird itself, passing "from branch to branch" (*d'une branche à une autre*). Same sounds, different affect, and the difference is key: caught by the bird, the writer can finally be "true" to his surroundings. It's an accident, really. For one magical moment, he is no longer an observer but a participant in the wood, blending in completely with the land-scape. The bird has taken him for a tree.

Both the accident and the mistaken object were necessary to this extraordi-nary song, for together they became the pathway to true feeling. Ravel's friend Roland-Manuel suggested one reason this was so. In a review of *L'Enfant et les sortilèges*, he explained, revealingly, that "a certain discretion" had always informed Ravel's sensibilities, making him "grant more of a heart to clocks than to clockmakers; more of a soul to trees than to humans."[27] Renard apparently shared a similar feeling. In fact, the most touching story in his collection of stories was the one he saved for last. He called it "Une famille des arbres," "A Tree Family," and in the context, it is worth quoting in full:

> After crossing a sun-drenched field, I meet them.
>
> They don't live at the edge of the path, because of the noise. They're in the uncultivated field, on a stream known only by birds.
>
> From afar, they seem impenetrable. As I approach, their trunks relax. They welcome me cautiously. I'm able to rest here, to refresh myself, but I sense they're observing me all the same, mistrustful.
>
> They live together as a family, the oldest among the youngest— those whose first leaves are just starting to come out. They're scattered all over the place, without ever straying from each other.
>
> They take a long time to die, and they keep their dead standing until they fall in dust.
>
> They stroke each other with their long branches, to make sure they're all here, like blind people do. If the wind ever tries to uproot them, they shake their fists. But they have no argument with each other. They murmur only in harmony.
>
> I feel that they should be my real family, so I quickly forget the other one. And these trees adopt me. To deserve this kindness, I learn what you have to know:

I now know how to watch the passing clouds.

I know how to keep still.

And I almost know how to be silent.

To be silent, almost: The conclusion speaks to the truer sort of impressionism Renard desired in 1896. It also tells us something about song as Ravel experienced it in 1907—or, at least, it gives new meaning to what he apparently told Renard on the night of the premiere. Let us return to that famous passage from the writer's journal and read it again, this time including the part most commentators leave out. What Ravel is reported to have said was actually quite strange. The entry reads: "I have tried to say with music what you say with words, when, for example *you're in front of a tree.*"[28] After reading Renard's final story, we can now guess what this remark might mean. Ravel implies that, like the author, he, too, had tried to learn the lessons of nature. He, too, had tried to keep still and sing a *mélodie* no bird would ever notice. He, too, had acted out the strain, by showing, as Renard had done, what his birds ought *not* to do. For it was not (as we now see) a hyperreal diction that would make a song fall silent, but a more mysterious effect: a holding of the breath, an unintended act of blending in.

This was, of course, what Fauré knew how to do, and Ravel saw that. Many years later, in an article about Fauré's songs, he praised his former teacher for this same silence and discretion. "The materials of Fauré's oeuvre are uniquely his own," he wrote, "and will remain useless in the hands of imitators or plagiarists. In fact, Fauré's mysterious techniques captivate us even more and fatigue us less, owing to their subtlety and quiet demeanor; their discretion is their strength."[29] Poised atop his accidental pole, the kingfisher offers similar testimony from inside the music, for the truth of this *histoire* from 1907 lies in the way the songs have told it. Ravel did not speak directly of such things, but from this interior perch, we begin to get the picture. More poignantly than Debussy's nightingale, his kingfisher shows us what this art—his teacher's art—once was, and what a precious bird it has become.

Une voix du passé?

The "Martin-pêcheur" could thus be read as a sign of extreme respect for the older Fauré, a sign that also marks the distance separating him from the idealistic cohort Ravel would refer to in hindsight as the "younger composers of 1895"—that is, his own generation.[30] In achieving a state of near silence, the song represents the truest tale of all these *Nature Stories* and, in many ways, the only true *mélodie*. But that achievement is short-lived, as we know, for the silence is broken—shattered, really—by the scream of the "Pintade" that marks the end of the cycle. No wonder the audience was horrified. The violence of the gesture repeats the brutality of Renard's *chasseur d'images*, breaking the beautiful illusion of the swan. The kingfisher's *mélodie* offered a similar illusion, one that the composer evidently could not sustain. "But what am I saying?" he seems to ask, as the guinea fowl performs its impertinent about-face. This was "the complete break," as Bathori put it, "with what one normally thought of as *mélodie*."

It is a complicated refusal, one that acknowledges both the beauty and the difficulty of a song that came so close to nature. And the complication, I think, had something to do with a condition, or a capacity, that has been evoked already many times in this study: the capacity for sincerity. This was a quality Ravel was famously said to have lacked, but the *Histoires naturelles* prompts us to think again, to reconsider the meaning of the term not only for him but also for his whole idealistic generation, for it was also, as we have noted, a buzzword of Third Republicanism. And so it may be useful for us to pause for a moment to see, finally, what the buzz was about, and what it had to do with *mélodie*.

Philip Nord has commented, for example, that in the early years of the Republic, the term *sincerity* tended "to describe upright conduct toward others," and in that sense, it carried not only social and political but also artistic resonances. "A candid manner in dress or expression bespoke a sincerity of being, a willingness to make the self transparent without the cloaking of affectation," writes Nord. "The building of a republican order required a new kind of man, one who eschewed pose in favor of sincerity."[31] The young symbolists certainly eschewed that pose they called "literature," preferring a freer verse uttered in the tone of conversation. And composers of the 1890s advocated an unencumbered melody modeled on the accents of "normal people." Like the so-called *plein air* painters of the same decade, all of these artists imagined their work not only in the space of the countryside but also, as Nord says, in the "language of republicanism."[32] To make their own art more democratic, they wanted to become, above all, more honest.

This kind of talk was common in the early days of France's Third Republic. But what the historical context may help us see is how such rhetoric served to shape a new concept of art that was both modern and French. A catalogue for a one-man show by Manet put it best: "Come and see sincere work," it said, announcing both the painter's unorthodox manner and his democratic stance in the same breath.[33] De Tocqueville had anticipated this rhetoric already in the 1830s when describing the influence of democracy on etiquette: democratic manners, he said, were "neither so tutored nor so uniform" as aristocratic ones, but they were often "more sincere."[34] Some three decades later, Ernest Legouvé made the point more forcefully in his own study of modern French mores, when he defined sincerity not merely as the result, but as the duty, of democracy: "if the charm of the ancien régime was to be polite," he claimed, "the duty of democracy is to be sincere."[35] As Nord has pointed out, the young impressionists took this duty to heart, representing a new kind of democratic subject by painting men in casual poses—with their feet drawn up—to show "the unmannered freeness of the milieu in which they lived."[36] Composers like Ravel and Debussy took it to heart as well, for they showed just as much diligence when they worried over the potential hypocrisy of their own work, struggling to capture, as Renard had put it, "feelings that had the taste of truth." This meant, in short, striving to make their songs more transparent through a melody that had fallen silent.

But this sort of idealism obviously had its limits. An imperative of truth would, over time, have to place greater and greater burdens on the artist. By 1912, the poet Robert de Souza ended up in a language lab, let us not forget, in order to validate the accentual basis of French poetry—in effect, to prove the sincerity of his own free verse. That alone reflects an increment of doubt that had crept into the practice, a questioning of the limits of poetic truth or of poetry's relationship to the real world, which came to touch the *mélodie* as well. The sense of disillusionment suggests, once again, an intriguing analogy to May 68. We might even push the analogy a bit further and think for just a moment about what eventually happened to the heroes of both countercultures. Was not the fate of Verlaine or Mallarmé or Debussy by 1920 similar to that of an artist like Godard in the 1980s or 1990s? In each case, what was first embraced as an art founded on cherished values of free speech came, over time, to be seen as a kind of special case: either precious or pretentious, it had turned into an art of connoisseurs. That, in a sense, is the view I have been working against throughout this study of the *mélodie*. I have wanted to find a moment when French melody meant something different—when its form of expression actually stood for a value that listeners recognized and embraced as true. Ravel, like Debussy, was trying to find the same thing, it seems, trying to find a place on the tongue where the truth that Renard could taste so palpably in 1896 might still exist in song. From the evidence, it appears that, by 1907, his task had become more difficult.

Even Fauré would recognize the difficulty. The older musician, whose melodies had once "indicated 'the most charming path'" to the younger generation,[37] had to have known, when he took over as director of the

Conservatoire in 1905, how much the path had shifted in the intervening years. In fact, by 1906—just after the *Fêtes* of Debussy but before Ravel's *Histoires*—he had begun to work out his own story about the nature of this art. It was the one with which our study began: *La Chanson d'Eve*. An idealist of a different kind, Fauré made a powerful case for song, as an "unofficial" composer at the head of the Conservatoire. As we saw, his allegory of Eve exposed what was essentially a radical idea—that of a musical art based on silence—in terms that obviously pleased a leftist writer like Barthes half a century later.[38] In that sense, *La Chanson d'Eve* could be said to teach a more affirming lesson about French song than the work produced by Debussy or Ravel around the same time. And yet when we reconsider the songs within the more contested space I am now exploring, a slightly different quality emerges, one that draws Fauré closer to his younger colleagues, with their darker outlook and their doubt.

Seen from this perspective, Fauré's cycle proved just as somber, and the first song he composed sounded the darkest tone. That was the one he called "Crépuscule," his revision of a number originally meant for Mélisande in the incidental music to *Pelléas*. The new text had some of the eeriness of Verlaine's ghosts, turning around a set of unanswered questions. "Who is sighing?" someone wonders. "What is weeping?" The questions seem to issue from an invisible narrator, but as we learned, it is Eve, the poem's "I," who asks them. Divided by self-consciousness, she is listening to herself. That, at least, is how I read the text first time round. And yet returning to it in light of what we have just witnessed—in the more knowing songs of Debussy, the hyperaware Ravel—I begin to see how that reading might be developed. For here, too, the self-conscious first-person could speak for someone (or something) other than Eve. I argued in chapter 1 that *La Chanson d'Eve* was bound up with Fauré's idealistic hopes to promote the modern lied within the Conservatoire curriculum. The implication makes the next question in "Crépuscule" all the more telling: *Est-ce une voix future, / Une voix du passé?* Is this a future voice, it asks, or already a voice of the past? And it could just as easily be Fauré—or the lied itself—questioning the fate of a music that once spoke so easily to the "younger composers of 1895." Would it, in fact, still make sense?

The fear seems to have been that it would not or could not. Why else would Fauré have spent the next three and a half years working out his alternate solution? The story of *La Chanson d'Eve* did try, as we saw, to make sense of the *mélodie*, but it did so by showing, in elaborate allegorical terms, all the ways it could go astray. The result was thus quite different from his first and most optimistic cycle, *La Bonne Chanson*, from 1891. Although both harbored a unifying theme, the point of including the "Eden theme" in this new work was ultimately to watch its undoing in the dark night of "Crépuscule." "What just fluttered on my heart like a wounded bird?" the subject asks over that theme not long before the rising figure *will* be crushed: bent, just like another bird we have heard, into a diminished version of itself (chap. 1, Musical Example 1.17). Like Debussy's nightingale and Ravel's swan, this bird of Eden would have to confront—even before the cycle started—a vision of her own negation.

Stated in these terms, the musical attitude seems unmistakably modernist, although perhaps not quite disenchanted. There was still, after all, the *C'est possible* of Debussy's second ghost; there was still Ravel's kingfisher; there was still, at the end of Fauré's *Chanson d'Eve*, the monotone line recalling the purity and promise of Eve's first words. In short, there was still a space in which sung language—especially the near silent expression of the *mélodie*—was posited as making sense. But that space had somehow become very narrow. What interests me is not only the constraint but also the consensus. Recognizing the collective acknowledgment discourages easy answers based on the personal lives of individual composers, for it draws out a different kind of explanation, one that, speaking across the "grain" of the song, addresses not just the art but the social situation that made it speak the way it did.

An example from the visual arts may help to elucidate the problem. I am thinking of a particular discussion about modern painting from 1912. The writer is Jacques Rivière, and the subject is a rationale for one of the most burdened visual forms of the early twentieth century: cubism. "Nothing is more hypocritical," he writes, "than perspective":

> For on the one hand it pretends not to know that the picture is a plane surface, and on the other it imitates depth solely by means of a system of profiles, all of them established on the same plane—precisely that of the picture. *To represent depth sincerely*, the painter will first have to acknowledge that he works on a flat surface; that is what he will do if he establishes all his objects next to one another, side by side. From then on he will have to try to imitate depth with something that has more of the nature of depth than a play of flat profiles.[39]

The aspect that interests me here is not the account of cubism per se but the imperative that drives it: the need, as Rivière puts it, "to represent depth sincerely." The end of hypocrisy for Rivière meant a greater and greater awareness of the material limits of representation. It involved painting depth "as though it were a material thing," with "transparent planes of shadow" issuing "from all sides of the object." Depth, he writes, would then "appear as a subtle but visible slippage keeping the objects company."[40]

In other words, the "sincerest" representation would have to include on its surface an acknowledgment of all it could not do. The represented thing materialized elsewhere—in a slippery dance between the object and the forms of its negation. Whether cubism ever honestly fulfilled this contract is not my concern.[41] Rivière's discussion is useful, I think, because it offers a kind of analogy for a problem in French music—and French *mélodie*—at this same moment. Here, the object in question would be spoken language, and the hypocrisy, singing. Histories of musical modernism have traditionally waited for the rhetoric of Cocteau to give voice to this sort of hypocrisy. And yet our understanding would be considerably enhanced if we admitted that such rethinking of music's means had actually begun earlier, in less noisy repertories that had just as much at stake. The *mélodie*, to the extent that it has something of its own to "tell," is the most significant. Was it still possible, the songs wondered, to catch the true impression of sentiment? And if so, what would it now take?

The awareness of what both linguists and singers called the *voix parlée* was part of the problem, placing an increased burden on the idea of melody. This did not cause the composers to abandon their ideals, only to try harder. At the time of *Fêtes galantes*, for example, Debussy began experimenting with alternative accents, trying his hand at old French poetry and a stripped-down, neomedievalist style in works like the *Trois Chansons de France* (1904) and the *Trois Ballades de François Villon* (1910).[42] Ravel, in a similar vein, threw himself into folk song, with the *Chants populaires* (1910).But in 1913, both composers would find a very different solution to the problem of melody. At this point, though, their efforts would include another burden, that of fidelity to the deceased poet for whom they now wished to speak: Mallarmé. Reading him "sincerely"—trying to remain true to the master's terms—would produce a very different kind of song indeed.

Realism Revisited

There is none of the expected irony in Ravel's *Trois Poèmes de Stéphane Mallarmé*, the next major vocal work he would attempt after the *Histoires naturelles*. That is probably because these ultramodern settings were bound up, in a sense, with the world of the Ballets Russes. They followed hard on two Diaghilev projects that occupied Ravel during this period: the premiere of his *Daphnis et Chloé* in 1912 and the orchestration, with Stravinsky, of

Mussorgsky's *Khovantchina* in 1913. Ravel traveled to Switzerland for the second project, where he got his first glimpses of *Pierrot lunaire* and Stravinsky's *Japanese Lyrics*. The scores gave him ideas. Ravel had acquired permission to set some poems from the new edition of Mallarmé's *Oeuvres*, published that same year by the *Nouvelle Revue française* (N.R.F.). When he turned to that project in Switzerland, he followed Stravinsky's lead, arranging them for a Pierrot-like ensemble of two flutes, two clarinets, string quartet, and piano. By April, he had drafted two of the songs, then began planning a "scandalous concert" in which they would be programmed with the Stravinsky and the Schoenberg.[43] Four months later, in France, he added a third.

The turn to Mallarmé was as retrospective as it was advanced. The release of the new edition by the *N.R.F.* solidified the poet's historical reputation while simultaneously bringing him up to date. In 1912, devotees of Mallarmé witnessed two even more progressive treatments: Albert Thibaudet's *La Poésie de Stéphane Mallarmé*, the first comprehensive study of the oeuvre,[44] and Nijinsky's outré *L'Après-midi d'un faune*. The latter was a study of a wholly different order, whose scandalous choreography, based on Debussy's still popular *Prélude*, caused the predictable public scuffle. But like Thibaudet's coolly objective critique, it, too, put a new face on symbolism, planting Mallarmé solidly within the purview of the prewar avant-garde. "The spirit of Mallarmé lives with us tonight," Odilon Redon pronounced to Diaghilev the night of the premiere. Ravel responded to this spirit with characteristic craft, making his Mallarmé read in two ways at once: retrospectively melancholy in the first two *mélodies*; severely modern in the last. It is the final song—"Surgi de la croupe et du bond"—that I want to read more closely, for with its austere attitude, it can tell us not only how French song had changed by 1913 but also how Mallarmé had changed, as well.

The poem was a sonnet, its subject a curious vessel of glass:

Surgi de la croupe et du bond
D'une verrerie éphémère
Sans fleurir la veillée amère
Le col ignoré s'interrompt.

Je crois bien que deux bouches n'ont
Bu, ni son amant ni ma mère,
Jamais à la même Chimère,
Moi, sylphe de ce froid plafond!

Le pur vase d'aucun breuvage
Que l'inexhaustible veuvage
Agonise mais ne consent,

Naïf baiser des plus funèbres!
À rien expirer annonçant
Une rose dans les ténèbres.

(Sprung from the croup and from the bounce / Of an ephemeral glassware / Yielding no flower for the bitter watch / The ignored neck is interrupted. // I do believe two mouths have not / Drunk, neither its lover nor my mother, / Not ever, from the same Chimera, / I, sylph of this cold ceiling! // The pure vase without any drink / but its endless widowhood / is dying but allows // nothing to expire [nothing to breathe out] announcing / —The most mournful of naïve kisses! —/ A rose into its darkness.)

The piece of glass is scrutinized in this poem from at least three points of view.[45] In the first quatrain, it appears as a peculiar, even monstrous, form. A short and slender neck springs too eagerly from glassy buttocks and then stops short. Suspended in its act of leaping, this neck is left wanting: it yields no hoped-for flower. But the vision, too, is quickly interrupted, and the second quatrain sees the form anew. It is a sylph's-eye view. The neck is glimpsed as if from the end point of its imaginary leap, where a ceiling lies. Spied from this cold place, the empty vessel becomes a cup, the eager neck a mouth, though with nothing to offer. No lover of this glass has drunk from it, not even the mother of the sylph who speaks to us from the page's cold ceiling. No, this vase is pure, the next line says, to begin and end the sonnet. And there, at the boundary of the tercet (every sonnet's golden section), the form is imagined from inside out. It is a "widowed" form, both dry and dark, whose only rose is the one it continues to refuse.

Ravel could hardly have picked a more unlikely poem for a song. With its multiple points of view, it suggested a way of seeing—in fact, an extreme form of realism—that might easily be called "cubist." Robert Greer Cohn described the opening line in just those terms: it was, he said, "a graphic, almost Braque-like, image of the vase, with round bottom . . . and linear neck."[46] Mallarmé was long dead by the time the proponents of cubism came to prominence; still, the anachronism makes a certain sense. In the wake of a painting like Picasso's *Glass of Absinthe* (1911), the modernity of Mallarmé's own vision—at least in this poem—must have seemed all the more prescient. And the analogy worked both ways. If Picasso (as it is claimed) came to Paris in part because of what he knew about Mallarmé, a poem like "Surgi de la croupe et du bond" begins to show us why. With its twisted syntax and tripled perspective, it "saw" the vase much as Picasso might have seen it: as the node of several conflicting possibilities. For Mallarmé, what lay in those contradicting lines, in the folds of the poem, was not a symbol, as it is often confusingly said, but the opposite: an object represented with so much fidelity that it materialized elsewhere, at the oblique point where material reality and verse collided. In chapter 3, I defined this space as timbre, or *l'absente de tous bouquets*, in Mallarmé's memorable phrase. But one could just as easily use the terms of the cubist criticism advanced by Rivière in 1912 and call it "a slippage keeping the [poem] object company."[47]

In any case, this angle was certainly not lost on Ravel, whose difficult setting featured, some have said, "the most 'advanced' music he ever wrote."[48] The difficulty came in part from the instrumental premise. The song's extended Pierrot ensemble (including piccolo and bass clarinet) provided no easy footing for the voice. Tonal ambiguity was the least of it. The instru-

EXAMPLE 5.18 Ravel, *Trois Poèmes de Stéphane Mallarmé*, "Surgi de la croupe et du bond," first musical period

EXAMPLE 5.18 (Continued)

ments themselves sent vexingly mixed signals. The piping that opens the piece, for example, seemed tailor-made for *Shéhérazade*, with its breezy suggestion of the orient (Musical Example 5.18). But are we not also meant to catch a whiff of Nijinsky's Faun in that upward surge of flutes? Certainly, Mallarmé's suggestive (even crude) image of a figure springing from shapely haunches brings to mind a picture of the Russian dancer himself, famous for his ability to leap—straight up—from a standing position. The exotic impression is quickly interrupted, though, and the slender flute soon "ignored," like the too eager neck of Mallarmé's widowed vase. The introduction stops short, without properly flowering, on an incomplete cadence.

EXAMPLE 5.18 (Continued)

What happens next sounds, by contrast, utterly disenchanted. Like the poem, the music turns a corner, offering a new perspective on its object. Horizontal becomes vertical; lush counterpoint turns to static chords. *Je crois bien*: with the entrance of the first-person, the piece begins again, rewriting the flute's upward flourish into an angular vocal line—half octatonic, half pentatonic (Musical Example 5.19). It is a strange beast to sing. The texture reverts to that of a conventional *mélodie* as the winds fall silent, leaving the piano to support the voice. And yet the piano does not do its job. It tolls away on empty octaves, while strings produce the "cold ceiling" of the chord, a cloud of high harmonics. The song essentially falls askew, separated into elements (bass note, harmonics, voice) like the mythical Chimera (made from the parts of three animals, lion, goat, and snake). Indeed, the most arresting

EXAMPLE 5.19 Ravel, *Trois Poèmes de Stéphane Mallarmé*, "Surgi de la croupe et du bond," second musical period

thing about this passage is the way it appears to deconstruct the central premise of the *mélodie*. The rarified expression of French song may have issued from the timbre of the *voix parlée*, but here the equation has flipped around: the *voix* now seems to issue from an expression of the timbre. Ravel has scored the string harmonics to read, almost literally, like the partials of a hypothetical sound—stacked up over the piano's bass note as if on some imaginary spectrogram.

If this scoring makes us "see" the melodic object differently, that could be the point, and this becomes another way that Ravel, as Rivière might say, avoids hypocrisy. His difficult setting will preserve the idea of *mélodie* much

EXAMPLE 5.19 (Continued)

EXAMPLE 5.20 Ravel, *Trois Poèmes de Stéphane Mallarmé*, "Surgi de la croupe," final musical period

like Mallarmé's vase: by making the flower of speech occur elsewhere—as a supplement, or a slippage, keeping melody company. The song's remarkable ending works just this way. When the full ensemble comes together at the turn of the last tercet, the singing voice is now heard in relation to a wind that cannot sustain it, with "nothing to breathe out," *à rien expirer*, as the poem says. Ravel has the piccolo take up its opening line, playing a sad, deflated version from the introduction's end (Musical Example 5.20). The

EXAMPLE 5.20 (Continued)

voice will try to rise to the occasion, but flowers on a dying verb (*agonise*). As the instrumental line descends, following bass clarinet to the grave, the voice falls in with an inversion, groaning a melancholy sigh. But in the end, it is instrumental sound that carries this modern *mélodie*. The singing remains in the shadow of the wind, *dans les ténèbres*, which is exactly how the voice preserves its truth.

We will look in vain, of course, to find evidence of such intention in the words of Ravel himself. He had characteristically little to say about these extraordinary songs, as he did about all his works. And yet an interview from some years later casts an interesting light on what their composition might have

EXAMPLE 5.20 (Continued)

meant. Admitting that the poems were "very obscure," he went on to make a judgment that is pertinent to our present history. Mallarmé, he said, was "not merely the greatest French poet, but the *only* French poet, since he made the French language, not designed for poetry, poetical. It is a feat in which he stands alone. Others, even that exquisite singer Verlaine, compromised with the rules and the boundaries of a most precise and formal medium."[49] The remark gives an even more pointed sense of how times had changed, especially for the "generation of 1895" for whom Verlaine, as we know, had been the supreme exemplar of sincerity. From the vantage point of a new century, that once exquisite singer began to seem a little sloppy. Mallarmé, on the other hand, had struggled with his craft, wrestling with the materials of a "precise and formal medium." The image spoke to Ravel's own work ethic, and also to his concept of sincerity. "Sincerity," Ravel claimed, was "of no value unless one's conscience helps to make it apparent, [and] conscience compels us to turn ourselves into good craftsmen."[50] These were, of course, the very terms that would fuel the modernist view of Mallarmé, a poet whom Valéry once described as "the purest, the most intransigent, the hardest on himself of all those who have held a pen."[51] In chapter 3, I tried to resuscitate the Mallarmé of the 1890s as socialist poet, putting him and all the symbolists in their place. It is now clear why that move was necessary. The modernist view of Mallarmé, a view emerging already in 1913, would eventually come to obscure his powerful connection to a populist poet like Verlaine. And that was not all: it was at the very point Mallarmé got teeth, so to speak, that the idea of *mélodie* began to lose its bite. French song would no longer be the free expression of the tongue celebrated by a liberal (and liberated) generation. It had now become, it seems, hard work.

In the Shadow of the Faun

The same sense of struggle can be heard in the settings of Mallarmé that Debussy completed in 1913. These, too, followed on the heels of a Diaghilev commission: Debussy's music for the ballet *Jeux*, which premiered in May, exactly one year after Nijinsky had unveiled the precise gestures of his updated Faun. The composer minced no words when it came to the merits of the modernist choreography. "I gather it's called the 'stylization of gesture,'" he wrote to Robert Godet in June. "It's awful!"[52] Later that summer, he consoled himself with music, returning to the original author of the Faun to embark on what would be the last set of songs he ever wrote. He called them the *Trois Poèmes de Mallarmé*. He had no idea that Ravel had beat him to the punch and was none too pleased to find out that the younger composer, quite by chance, had chosen two of the same texts, "Soupir" and "Placet futile." When the Mallarmé heirs, who owned the copyright, hesitated to grant permission twice, his annoyance reached its limit. Ravel eventually intervened but not before Debussy had fired off a revealing remark to his publisher Jacques Durand. "Perhaps they are afraid," he quipped, "that Nijinsky will invent some new choreography for these three songs?"[53]

Though the fear would be unfounded, the joke may help explain where Debussy stood in taking up this project. He, like Ravel, would craft some very modern settings. Still, the songs he created were nothing like the modish sort of modernism represented by the Nijinsky circle, whose popularity (Debussy thought) was an expression of bad taste. An eternally gullible public, he said, always preferred "lies to sincerity."[54] And the comment was significant. With its telltale opposition, it expressed the composer's notorious high-mindedness—his determination to hold fast to the truth in art. As such, it hints at the attitude inscribed in these new works. Halbreich described the *Trois Poèmes* as an "exceptional case, a summit, and also an impasse."[55] But the impasse had to do, it seems, with Debussy's own struggle to remain true to Mallarmé. If these settings closed the book on *mélodie*, it could be for this reason. They were just about the truest melodies he could ever hope to write.

Such *vérité* provoked a new austerity in Debussy, as well, and once again, the effect was strongest in the last song of the set. Although the opening melody, "Soupir," retained some marks of Debussy's naïve pentatonic style,[56] and "Placet futile" clung to the antique rolling cadence of his more recent neomedievalism, the richness of the final poem, "Eventail," seems to have brought forth something unique.

> O rêveuse, pour que je plonge
> Au pur délice sans chemin
> Sache, par un subtil mensonge,
> Garder mon aile dans ta main.
>
> Une fraîcheur de crépuscule
> Te vient à chaque battement
> Dont le coup prisonnier recule
> L'horizon délicatement.
>
> Vertige! Voici que frisonne
> L'espace comme un grand baiser
> Qui, fou de naître pour personne,
> Ne peut jaillir ni s'apaiser.
>
> Sens-tu le paradis farouche
> Ainsi qu'un rire enseveli
> Se couler du coin de ta bouche
> Au fond du l'unanime pli!
>
> Le sceptre des rivages roses
> Stagnants sur les soirs d'or, ce l'est
> Ce blanc vol fermé que tu poses
> Contre le feu d'un bracelet.

(O dreamer girl, so that I might plunge / Into pure, directionless delight, / Know how, by a subtle lie, / To keep my wing in your hand. // A twilight freshness / Comes to you with each beat / Whose captive gust / Delicately pushes back the horizon // Vertigo! Here is how the space trembles / Like a great, wild kiss, / which, born for no one in particular, / Can neither erupt nor abate. // Don't you feel the savage paradise— / As you might a stifled laugh / Flowing from the corner of your mouth— / At the heart of the unanimous fold! // The scepter of stagnant pink shores / On top of golden evenings: this is it, / This closed white wing that you place / Against a bracelet's fire.//)

It was a poem about a fan. And it was a poem in a fan—or *on* a fan—the lines having been transcribed by Mallarmé directly into the folded form as a gift to his daughter Geneviève. This convergence of subject and object contributed to the vertigo announced at the poem's central fold, for right from the start, we are presented with at least three points of view. There is the fan, the material poem, which is also the poem's material. Then there is the person who holds it, the poem's reader (who is presumably looking at the inside). Finally, there is the person who gave it away, the poem's writer, who may speak through the fan but also stands apart, on the other side. The convergence of perspectives creates a vision at least as skewed as that of the vase in "Surgi de la croupe."

In the first stanza, it is the poem-fan who speaks—asking to be held, and opened, in order to experience the pleasure of being moved. From the fan's perspective, this is a little like flying, plunging aimlessly through space, and it is also a little like lying, because the fan does not really take off. It moves only while grounded: the poem's flight remains in the hand of the (be)holder, with the winged word (*aile*) folded into, and out of, the fan's wind (*vent*): e + vent + ail{e}. So the poem makes a deal. This is what you will get, it says, by doing as I ask. The pleasure of the text works both ways. By moving me, a delicious *coup de vent* carrying the evening's freshness will be moved back toward you. This gust issues from the object in more ways than one, for, as we know, the *coup* in Mallarmé was also the stroke of the tongue that caused the verse to sound: as music, rhythm, timbre. And in this poem of sweet *octosyllabes*, that sound is, quite literally, an *air*. So a bigger question hovers on the horizon, not real but implied: does this air move the fan (poem), or does the poem (fan) move it? The oscillation of subject and object yields a tiny moment of vertigo, which, rather than answering, complicates the question with a pun. This "poem-stem" (*vers + tige*) becomes just another way to grasp the whole suggestive form that fans out, like a flower, from the dreamer's clutch.

But "here," on the other side of the exclamation point, is where the perspective subtly shifts. The space—this *air*—is trembling, the line says. What is happening here is no longer exclusive to you and me. It lies somewhere else, or in-between, like an air kiss (very French!) proffered to no one. This dispersal of the subject into the indefinable "here" is irreversible, and it makes the next verse very strange, indeed. Another question, this time a real one: Do you feel the pleasure within you, like a giggle seeping from the corners of your mouth? The fan itself is being questioned. But who is asking? This object that has been addressing the reader is now addressed *as* an object, one whose endless delights are bound in its "unanimous fold." We have moved past the here, to the place where the absent author stands. Ah yes, *this* is it. Or so we are told, as that other "I" looks back, presumably observing the dainty scene painted on the paper front—a pink sunset, an oriental shore. Then the folds are closed for good, lain to rest on a pretty wrist where just a bracelet shines.

While presenting some of the same abstraction as the widowed vase in Ravel's last song, this poem is certainly a lot more fun. And why shouldn't it be? It was written as a gift, and the lines produce an equivalent kind of pleasure—like the delight one feels on opening a package. Such a feeling could hardly have been lost on a reader like Debussy, but his choice of "Eventail" seems fitting in more than one respect. With its implicit sugges-tion of physical acts, of an *air* guided by an accompanying hand, it offered a neat image of song, or *mélodie*, as Debussy had come to know it. Indeed, a composer who once so carefully transposed the world of Mallarmé's Faun into music could easily have heard the implied command in this poem ("go ahead and move me") as one issued directly to him. As a famous musical dreamer, Debussy already knew how to take a paper form in hand and push it toward that elusive space where the air trembled with audible vibration. Knowing that this "Eventail" was an actual, material gift from Mallarmé could only make that imperative, for Debussy, seem all the more real and true.

In any case, his song *is* true to Mallarmé, achieving a level of realism no earlier song had found. This is especially evident in the opening period. After a minimalist introduction—a lighthearted fanning up black keys, a delicate descent by white—the piano steps aside. The voice declaims the text without instrumental support, its phrases punctuated by dry gusts of noise, more like Morse code than music (Musical Example 5.21). But the declamation is still more alien. Moved by an indeterminate chromaticism and a rubato rhythm, Debussy's melody sounds closer to the *voix parlée* than any he had made before: closer than the letter of Geneviève, the colloquy of *Fêtes galantes*, or any of his medievalist chansons. All those melodies, of course, followed the conventions of diatonic tuning. Here the intervals formed no clear-cut mode. They floated instead in an indefinite space between the diatonic and chro-matic, exactly like the "melody" of spoken poetry.

Sous le pont Mir - a - beau cou - le la Sei - ne

Et nos a - mours Faut - il qu'il m'en sou - vien - ne

La joie ve - nait tou - jours a - près la pei - ne

Or perhaps I should say like poetry spoken in 1913, for the opening lines of "Eventail" bore an uncanny resemblance to a recording made by Guillaume Apollinaire that year, when he put "Le Pont Mirabeau" on gramophone (Musical Example 5.22).[57] The sound was subtly different from what we noted in Bernhardt's diction ten years earlier, and this level of subtlety is what Debussy brings to his own setting. Whereas Bernhardt brought the verse of Coppée close to singing, increasing the tension of the verse, here Apollinaire does the opposite—as if starting with the thought of song and letting the voice droop toward the spoken word. This was exactly the kind of delivery Valéry argued for, incidentally, in his essay "De la diction des vers."[58] It was also, I think, the kind of sound he had in mind when he wrote the melancholy poem mentioned in the last chapter: the *Psaume sur une Voix* of 1912, com-memorating the low and lilting voice of Mallarmé ("*A demi voix* / D'une voix douce et faible disant de grande choses . . ."). And in that context, Debussy's 1913 melody seems all the more significant. The sound he captures at the start—neither diatonic nor chromatic but lying somewhere *à demi*—speaks as much to the poem's captive fan as to the voice of Mallarmé himself.

This self-effacing *voix* holds back its shy request (*garder mon aile*) until the quatrain's final line. When it comes, the vocal line fans out, and the piano does, too, bringing back its own black-note glissando. And—voilà—the perspective gently shifts: a new verse, a fresh sound, a clearer sense of movement (Musical Example 5.23). Right and left hands now scan the measures one by one, while the voice intones a two-note ditty, simple as a child's. This is indeed the fresh air promised by the poem, and it raises the same sorts of questions. Does the air itself create the sense of movement, or

does the movement create the air? From the song's point of view, these questions are less abstract, pointing to the heart of the act of composition. Who *is* responsible for the movement we now feel—as speech becomes "air," and poem turns to melody? The piano suddenly drops its beating for a delicately rising figure, as if to pose the question by itself. Is this the poem pushing the composer? Or does the composer now have the upper hand?

The next strophe offers no easy answer. At first, the composer's "hand" seems all too evident in the bombastic piano figuration (Musical Example 5.24). A run of showy chromatic triplets cuts off the previous question and tumbles quickly down the keyboard, treating the exclamation mimetically ("Vertige!"), like the intertitle of a silent film. And yet the mumbling phrase that follows sounds quite different. Less mimetic than automatic, it has an odd mind of its own. The left-hand melody recalls the slippery voice of the opening period, singing in the distance (*doucement en dehors*), although the rhythm is as straight as the second stanza's air. *Voix parlée* and *voix chantée* have strangely folded in on one another. Add to this the nervous perpetual motion of the right hand's whole-tone clusters and the aimless, almost drunken declamation, and the result is a kind of poetic vertigo. If this space seems to tremble, it is because it offers no single horizon of interpretation. The right hand no more "knows" what the left is doing than the piano knows the singing voice, or melody the poem. With all these unseen implications, enfolding mutually divergent possibilities, the passage almost prefigures the playfully folded *cadavre exquis* concocted by the surrealists.[59] The unique space it oversees is "born for no one," like this poem's crazy kiss.

Debussy will soon bring back the piano's questioning figure (now a half-step lower) as the voice prepares to utter its first real query: "Do you feel it?" (*Sens-tu . . .*). And yet, as in the poem, the one who does the asking is unclear. That the composer himself might feel addressed is suggested by what happens next. The irrepressible pleasure that is the question's object (*le paradis farouche*) is likened to a "stifled laugh." At once, the piano's rising fifth (F to C) becomes a fleeting pentatonic paradise. If such a musical transformation was a "dupe's game" in *Les ingénus*, it is now presented as a more obvious joke—though one the composer still, it seems, cannot resist. And the familiar black-note sweep returns to confirm the gesture's playfulness, while also signaling that the end is near (Musical Example 5.25). But here the song takes an unexpected turn. The whole scherzando setting, with its curious question, goes begging. There is something beyond this playfulness, it seems, a world as remote as the pink shore and golden sunset that inhabit the poem's last lines. "This is it," the song and the composer and the poet announce together, while the setting comes to rest improbably on E. What "it" is, though, remains undecided, as two hushed chords are left to oscillate, in wonder.

With its multiple, conflicting points of view, Debussy's handling of this folded form shows a certain kinship with Ravel's obscure glass vessel. In each,

EXAMPLE 5.24 (Continued)

EXAMPLE 5.25 Debussy, *Trois Poèmes de Mallarmé*, "Eventail," final period

the poem's strophes present a different angle on its object. Each *mélodie*, in turn, offers a peculiarly shifting musical perspective whose contradictory planes kept expression safe, in effect, by concealing it. We might understand this strategy as a cubist sort of realism, a form of representation trying so hard for truth that it embodied the conflicts posed by the material itself. The music suggests, in any case, that painting was not the only art that was trying to square the real with its forms of representation. In the case of the *mélodie*, that kind of squaring produced a strange result, as the pure material of the voice confronted the *noir et blanc* of a keyboard fanning out beneath fingers. Debussy's *Eventail* tried to show the poem's inflections in all their purity, to be sure, but there was clearly more behind this gesture than the exactitudes of a language lab. What the song as a whole was trying to safeguard was another sort of truth, one more in line with the substance Valéry himself memorialized in 1912.

This was Mallarmé's "muted voice," a voice containing, as Valéry put it, "the presence of absolutes in the fine detail of a flute, the delicacy of pure sound." Debussy had, of course, discovered such delicacy already in 1894, in his orchestration of the *Prélude à l'Après-midi d'un faune*.[60] And I cannot help but feel that in 1913, in the wake of Nijinsky's unseemly appropriation of that prelude, he was still trying to hold onto it, even if that meant now hiding the flute in the folds of what would be his final testament to the poet. Was there not, after all, a trace of that sound in the repeated pentatonic sweeps of *Eventail*, with their more obvious suggestion of Pan's pipes? Or in the hushed chords at the end, where the piano's rising question oscillates from G-natural to C#, as if referencing, in reverse, the trajectory of that earlier flute? Or perhaps even in the unexpected final cadence, which comes to rest, as Debussy's *Prélude* did, on E? And yet the remoteness of this cadence (now uttered in the *mode mineur*) also shows us, all too poignantly, how very far away that world now was. By 1913, the Faun-like poet, and the exquisite *mélodie* he inspired, belonged to a different time. The delicate and pure flower of sound that once blossomed from his flute had not quite died. But it had been stepped on, in the meantime, by a dancer.

Mirages

The stark conclusion suggests we have perhaps reached the beginning of the end of our story, that we must now prepare to bid farewell to the "most sincere art" lauded by Henri Fellot in 1904. And in a sense, we must. It is hard, at least, to imagine this art being sustained much beyond 1912, when the advent of a world war would put a value like sincerity in even shorter supply. But Gabriel Fauré, the composer whom Fellot held up as father of this art, did not give up quite yet. There is a final set of songs we should probably hear out before we close the book on the *mélodie*. It was not Fauré's last but his second-to-last collection: the late opus he called *Mirages*. These melodies would continue to project a confidence, or optimism—even a sincerity—that neither Ravel nor Debussy could any longer seem to muster. Unlike these younger composers, Fauré had continued undaunted on his path, neither looking ahead nor looking back, as if unwilling to acknowledge the pressures the twentieth century now imposed on a composer from a former time. A letter from his beloved old teacher Saint-Saens in 1915 suggested as much, warning of the "atrocities" perpetrated by the likes of Debussy. "We must at all costs bar the door of the Institut against a man capable of such [things]," he fomented, adding that Debussy's most recent atrocity, *En Blanc et noir*, "should be put next to the cubist pictures."[61] There is no telling what Fauré himself thought about the newer music, but the final song of *Mirages* gave a hint that he was perhaps more alert to the new century than one might suspect and that he knew exactly what was at stake.

It is interesting, too, that Fauré, unlike his younger colleagues, had managed to steer clear of the trappings of the Ballets Russes, which may account for his different point of view.[62] And yet in the years immediately after *La Chanson d'Eve*, he was consumed by an equally large-scale project: his opera *Pénélope*. Following its premiere in 1913, he turned again to melody and to Charles Van Lerberghe, setting eight poems from Van Lerberghe's *Le Jardin clos* for his next cycle. Johnson saw this work as "an infinitely moving farewell . . . [from] the revered old Goethe of French song," but the melodies themselves suggested a different greeting. In the fifth ("Dans la nymphée"), an image of a maiden waking in a blue garden forged an unmistakable continuity with the earlier Eve—one that Fauré drew out by using not just the same key but the same hymnlike style that had marked "O Mort, poussière d'étoiles." And Eve's song would exert an influence for several years to come. As late as 1919, for example, the composer found himself accompanying the young soprano Madeleine Grey in a "gala performance of *La Chanson d'Eve*."[63] The success of the performance prompted Grey to beg Fauré for something new. By August of that year, he had written her the four songs of *Mirages*.

This time he drew on a different poet, a minor talent and society figure, the Baroness of Brimont.[64] The choice could not have been further from Ravel and Debussy's 1913 run with Mallarmé. Reading Renée de Brimont was hardly a difficult task, and this alone could explain the speed with which

Fauré completed his new collection. Still, the Baroness's poems produced a similar kind of soul-searching. Their reflective tone addressed the situation of this seventy-four-year-old composer, who shortly after Debussy's death (and just before his own retirement) felt himself coming to the end of the line. In March, he had gone to Monte Carlo to work on his Watteau-inspired *Masques et bergamasques*. This was a *comédie lyrique* (as Fauré called it) that combined new orchestral dances with pieces going back to the 1880s, producing what was, in effect, a staging of his own musical life. Included were the *Pavane* (op. 50), the *Madrigal* (op. 35), and the songs *Clair de lune* and *Le plus doux chemin* (op. 46 and op. 87). The last, composed in 1904 to a text by Armand Silvestre, was "still hardly known," Fauré wrote to his wife, Marie, that month, adding bitterly: "for just as pianists play the same eight or ten pieces, singers all sing the same songs."[65] The *Masques* were thus as much artistic summation as reality check, and the sobering lesson would soon extend to the melodies of his newest cycle. Indeed, as the last cycle Fauré ever publicly performed,[66] *Mirages* could be seen as the aging composer's swan song.

The opening *mélodie*, "Cygne sur l'eau," brought that message home almost literally, with its image of a swan on troubled waters:

Ma pensée est un cygne harmonieux et sage
Qui glisse lentement aux rivages d'ennui
Sur les ondes sans fond du rêve, du mirage,
De l'écho, du brouillard, de l'ombre, de la nuit.

Il glisse, roi hautain, fendant un libre espace,
Poursuit un reflet vain, précieux et changeant,
Et les roseaux nombreux s'inclinent quand il passe,
Sombre et muet, au seuil d'une lune d'argent;

Et des blancs nénuphars chaque corolle ronde
Tour à tour a fleuri de désir et d'espoir . . .
Mais plus avant toujours sur la brume et sur l'onde,
Vers l'inconnu fuyant, glisse le cygne noir.

Or j'ai dit, "Renoncez, beau cygne chimérique,
À ce voyage lent vers de troubles destins;
Nul miracle chinois, nulle étrange Amérique
Ne vous accueilleront en des hâvres certains;

Les golfes embaumés, les îles immortelles
Ont pour vous, Cygne noir, des récifs périlleux;
Demeurez sur les lacs où se mirent, fidèles,
Ces nuages, ces fleurs, ces astres et ces yeux.

(My thought is a wise and harmonious swan / Gliding slowly on banks of boredom / On bottomless waves of dream and delusion, / Of Echo and fog, of shadow and night. // It glides, an arrogant king, dividing an open space, / Pursuing a vain reflection, precious and ever-changing, / And the ample reeds bow down when it passes, / Somber and mute, on the sill of a silver moon. // And each round corolla of the white water lilies / Has blossomed one by one with hope and desire . . . / But further along, on mist and wave / Toward the fleeting unknown, the black swan still glides. // So I said, "Oh beautiful, chimerical swan, / give up this slow voyage toward uncertain destinies; / No Chinese miracle, no strange America / Will welcome you into safe harbors; // The perfumed gulfs, the immortal islands, / Are for you, black swan, perilous reefs, // Remain on these lakes that faithfully reflect / These clouds, these flowers, these stars, and these eyes."//)

Here again was the swan of "literature," and here again it carried a cautionary tale. Unlike Renard, whose graceful bird had warned against an ill-begotten symbolism, Brimont presented the opposite scenario. As Nectoux points out, her poetry was recognizably old-fashioned by 1919, harking back to the style of the 1890s. Where Renard warned symbolists to watch their step, Brimont herself was stepping back. Her warning, then, concerned the seductions of a later, more modern time. An ever-watchful first-person materialized to say "turn back," and its reasons were as strange as they were impassioned. "No Chinese miracle, no foreign America / Will welcome you into safe harbors," the poem reads. The lines could be heard as a nostalgic gloss on Rimbaud's drunken boat, but they harbored a topical reference, too. There was, after all, the Russian ballet's most recent debacle, *Parade*, with its queer Chinese magician, its "little American girl." Written into a poem published in 1918, the same year as Cocteau's noisy apology for *Parade*,[67] the connection could hardly be missed. Nor could the poem's moral have gone unnoticed. "Turn back," it said, as it urged a path toward calmer shores. For Brimont, that meant a glassy lake to mirror back old symbols: "these clouds, these flowers, these stars, these eyes."

As backlash poetry, it almost worked, or at least, it seemed to work on Fauré as he sat in the lakeside room where he composed his new song cycle.[68] The opening melody deftly mirrored the poem's melancholy warning. Beginning with a suggestion of his own (now signature) hymnlike style, Fauré's setting also comments on that style (Musical Example 5.26). The song soon becomes slipperier as it follows the arrogant bird in its pursuit of "vain reflections." A churning accompaniment arrives to launch the second musical period (*Il glisse,*

EXAMPLE 5.26 Fauré, *Mirages*, "Cygne sur l'eau," first three musical periods

EXAMPLE 5.26 (Continued)

EXAMPLE 5.26 (Continued)

roi hautain . . .) and produces a kind of harmonic undertow pulling the melody on a downward slide that finally delivers the black swan, some twenty-two measures later, on an E♭ cadence and a froth of black keys—one whole step lower than it started. Then, a change of voice. Dry, pulsing chords arrive to underpin the poem's new command, *Renoncez*: "Turn back" (Musical Example 5.27). And the song backpedals, forgetting the treacherous harmonies of the previous period and eventually finding its way back to safer shores, the home key of F and the unpretentious hymn of the opening measures. The gesture rounds off the form, while also fulfilling the poem's final command. Recovering his purest form of song, Fauré remains faithful to his own reflection.

The next two songs stayed close to home as well. In the second melody ("Reflets dans l'eau"), the swan's resigned gesture of turning back is developed through a grand apostrophe to the Past: "O dear mysterious Past, you who are reflected in my eyes like a cloud, / It would be so sweet for me / To embark with you on the long voyage!" The speaker then imagines crossing that divide, slipping into the mirroring water (again, like a swan of the opening song). Fauré turns this vision into a stunning sound effect, the piano producing a swirling, glistening pool series that now disturbs the clarity of vision (Musical Example 5.28). Orledge called it "the only passage of illustrative accompaniment" that Fauré had ever written, but we know his piano had painted like this at least one other time, in the liquid waves of "Eau vivante," the sixth song of his *Chanson d'Eve*. In "Reflets dans l'eau," the effect was more extreme, appearing unexpectedly, like a musical mirage, between the spoken phrases. Indeed, the voice at this moment is reduced to a pure monotone, announcing the watery visions like the intertitles of a silent film, while the song moves into a very different musical time and space. But clarity eventually returns as the song regains its footing. "The enchanted mirror again grew limpid," the voice announced, and Fauré's melody, too, retrieves its original flatness, a serenity that would be sustained through the end of the placid "Jardin nocturne."

Only the final song, "Danseuse," would break this studied calm. And it is with its accents I want to close, for this poem brought out a very different feeling from Fauré. Here at last, the composer looked away from the reflecting glass, it seems, to glimpse the modern world that lay beyond. "I spend my time saying to myself: make way for the young ones!" he wrote to his wife in July. And in this last melody of *Mirages*, that is exactly what he did, for the music now seemed to address a very different cohort. With its mechanical ostinato, denuded style, and squared-off phrases, it had more in common with the values of those "young ones" who belonged to Cocteau's immediate circle. The opening measures, for example, introduce an angular two-step that will dominate the texture, a clanging pedal tone in the piano's right

EXAMPLE 5.27 Fauré, *Mirages*, "Cygne sur l'eau," final two periods

EXAMPLE 5.27 (Continued)

EXAMPLE 5.28 Fauré, *Mirages*, "Reflets dans l'eau," rippling pools

hand, snapping accents in the left. Then the voice falls in with its monotone command, "Sister of sisters, weaver of violets . . . dance!" (Musical Example 5.29). Such austerity continues unbroken into the second period, as the image of the dancer comes into clearer focus: *Vase svelte, fresque mouvante et souple.* The flat, rhythmic surface makes the dancer two-dimensional, a (neo) classical figure captured on an ancient urn.

Soon not just the music but the poem turns repetitive:

Sois la fleur multiple un peu balancée,
Sois l'écharpe offerte au désir qui change,

EXAMPLE 5.29 Fauré, *Mirages*, "Danseuse," mm. 1–24

Sois la lampe chaste, la flamme étrange,
Sois la pensée!

(Be the multiple and barely swaying flower, / Be the scarf offered to a
changeable desire, / Be the chaste lamp, the strange flame, / Be thought
itself!)

The anaphora is mesmerizing, and the music sways along in turn. Tight
accents are now exchanged for suppler harmonies, rising in a fluid sequence
(Musical Example 5.30). The gliding passage recalls both the agitation of the

EXAMPLE 5.29 (Continued)

EXAMPLE 5.30 Fauré, *Mirages*, "Danseuse," third musical period

"Cygne" and the ripples of "Reflets dans l'eau," as if pointing to the dreamy premise that first served as the swan's analogy: "*ma pensée*." But if this flowing movement promises a return of the old dream, it does not deliver. Now, at last, it is Fauré's turn to refuse. As the sequence crests on the culminating thought, all churning vanishes. The stark ostinato reappears on cue, as if to say: there is no getting there from here. In the deserted musical world of this "Danseuse," the water can be no more than a mirage.

The commentary was almost worthy of Cocteau, whose *Le Coq et l'arlequin* (1918) had staged a similar refusal, famously rejecting the foggy mists of Debussy. And the next moment in the song nearly clinches the verdict. The poem's speaker issues one last command: "Dance, dance to the song of my rude flute." And something odd begins to sound. A piping starts up among the piano rhythms, quoting an iconic tune by that now deceased composer. That's right: Fauré slips in the opening measures of the *Prélude à l'après-midi d'un faune* (Musical Example 5.31). The melody is in some ways hard to hear. Coming through the rhythm as if through some queer distorting lens, the tune sounds both more distant and more caustic than it should. What is one

EXAMPLE 5.31 Fauré, *Mirages*, "Danseuse," end

FIGURE 5.3 Vaslav Nijinsky as the Faun with Lubov Tchernicheva as startled nymph, photographed by Baron Adolf de Meyer in 1912. Courtesy of the Jerome Robbins Dance Division, New York Public Library for the Performing Arts, Astor, Lenox, and Tilden Foundations.

to make of it? It is true that Debussy and Fauré had always had kept their distance, but the aging Fauré was certainly no Cocteau. He had no ideological bone to pick. And especially after Debussy's death, he had even less cause for ill will. Fauré had written sad condolences in 1918 to the widowed Emma, and her touching reply must have been hard to forget. "He was so happy last summer to study *La Bonne Chanson,*" she explained, recalling Fauré's own music from the 1890s. But her concluding words about Debussy were ones she knew Fauré alone would understand: "People," she said, "were unaware of his sincerity."[69]

In an era when irony had become the new sincerity, the remark seems all the more melancholy, and in that respect, it may suggest a different way to hear Fauré's unexpected (and unexpectedly ironic) reference to the Faun in this final song of *Mirages*. The quotation could be understood as a kind of extended farewell: to a deceased composer, to an idealistic era, and finally to a value that belonged to both, a value that Debussy—like Fauré—had made the basis of an art. It was a younger Nijinsky, after all, who had first challenged the sincerity of the Faun back in 1912, when he moved so knowingly against the grain of Debussy's *Prélude*. And Fauré, though he had never dealt directly with the Russian dancer, shows himself here to be just as knowing. Was Nijinsky not the voice that spoke in Brimont's poem, commanding this *danseuse* to move to the sound of his flute? Fauré seems to have thought so. And why not? With its images of a female nymph—palms extended flatly in a frieze, scarves offered fickly to desire—the poem offered a shrewd picture of the infamous choreography or, at least, one of the famous photos taken by Baron Adolf de Meyer in the same year (Figure 5.3). Fauré called up this picture in turn, taking the central motif of Debussy's *Prélude* and flattening it, as Njinsky had done, through the distorting lens of rhythm. Indeed, one might even say that, in Fauré's posthumous retouching, Debussy's once supple and languid flute melody turned, well, a little cubist. And yet this distorting gesture was somehow all the more poignant, made as it was in the summer of 1919, a year that marked a death for Nijinsky as well: the moment of his official retirement from the stage.

Through a cunning aural reminiscence, Fauré's *danseuse* spoke, then, to not one or two but to all three versions of Mallarmé's captivating Faun—as told, as heard, and as seen—thus bidding farewell to the single most powerful icon of music and poetry of the 1890s. That is why it serves as such a fitting conclusion to our own story. The citation would turn out to be Fauré's first *and* last word on Mallarmé, a poet he had otherwise never ventured to set during his long career. And in saying it now, his *mélodie* perhaps tells the profoundest thing of all. The edgy modern dance may have tipped the composer's hand, as he tried to "make way for the young ones." But it also seemed to announce that, soon enough, Fauré would have to say goodbye (just as we ourselves must now do) to a beautiful idea of song—one whose time had already come and gone.

Preface

1. Vladimir Jankélévitch, *La Musique et l'ineffable* (Paris: Editions de Seuil, 1983). See especially chap. 2.

Chapter 1

1. Dujardin-Beaumetz, *Journal officiel de la République française* (4 August 1905), 4799–4800. Cited in Gail Hilson Woldu, "Fauré at the Conservatoire: Critical Assessments of the Years 1896–1920," in *Regarding Fauré*, ed. Tom Gordon (Amsterdam: Gordon and Breach, 1999), 106.

2. *Le Temps* (7 August 1906). Cited in Hilson Woldu, 109–110.

3. Henri Fellot, "Lieder français," *Revue musicale de Lyon* 1, no. 23 (23 March 1904): 265–269.

4. Robert Brussel, "Les 'Lieder' de Fauré," *Musica* 77 (February 1909): 21–22.

5. Charles Koechlin, "La Mélodie," in *Cinquante ans de musique française, de 1874 à 1925*, ed. Ladislav Rohozinski (Paris: Librairie de France, 1925), 2:25, 1.

6. Ibid., 2.

7. See Koechlin, Ibid.; Frits Noske, *La Mélodie française de Berlioz à Duparc: Essai de critique historique* (Paris: Presses Universitaires de France, 1954); trans., Rita Benton, *French Song from Berlioz to Duparc* (New York: Dover, 1970); Marie-Claire Beltrando-Patier, "Le Lied et la mélodie," in *Histoire de la musique* (Paris: Bordas, 1982); David Tunley, "Mélodie" in *The New Grove Dictionary of Music and Musicians* (London: Macmillan, 2000), 16:356–360; Graham Johnson and Richard Stokes, *A French Song Companion* (New York: Oxford University Press, 2000).

8. The texts for Berlioz's songs were Thomas Gounet's very free French adaptations of Moore's poems. When the collection was reissued in 1850, it appeared with the title *Irlande.*

9. The best account of this word history is Noske's. See his *French Song from Berlioz to Duparc*, chap. 1, especially pp. 22–25. Most twentieth-century accounts have been

content to repeat the story in abbreviated form. Johnson simply reports that Berlioz put "voice and piano in equal partnership" and called it "melody," and that somehow "the label stuck." See Johnson and Stokes, *A French Song Companion*, xix.

10. Marie-Claire Beltrando, "La Mélodie à la recherche de sa forme et de son style," in *Autour de la mélodie française*, ed. Michelle Biget (Rouen: Université de Rouen, 1987), 139–148.

11. In his essay on song for the Lavignac encyclopedia, Théodore Gérold remarks on Berlioz's particular susceptibility to foreign influence, pointing out that "it was not French authors who made an impression on the young Berlioz, it was always foreigners: Goethe, Shakespeare, Walter Scott, Byron." See the article "Monodie et Lied," in *Encyclopédie de la musique et dictionnaire du conservatoire*, Part 2, vol. 2, *Esthétique*, ed. Albert Lavignac and Lionel de la Laurencie (Paris: Delagrave, 1930), 2854.

12. L. Quicherat, *Adolphe Nourrit, sa vie, son talent, son caractère, sa correspondance* (Paris, 1867). Story cited in Noske, *La Mélodie française de Berlioz à Duparc*, 28.

13. Antoine Romagnesi, *L'Art de chanter les romances, les chansonettes, et les nocturnes et généralement toute la musique de salon* (Paris, 1846). Cited in David Tunley, "Mélodie," in *The New Grove Dictionary of Music Online*, ed. L. Macy, at http://www.grovemusic.com. Noske notes that the second edition of this volume (also published in 1846) appeared with the alternate title *La psychologie du chant*.

14. Ernest Legouvé, *Soixante ans de souvenirs* (1885). Cited in J. G. Prod'homme, "Schubert's Works in France," *Musical Quarterly* 14, no. 4 (October 1928), 497–498.

15. Noske apparently found it frustrating that, even in 1878, the Academy dictionary "still lacks this new meaning of the word" and that Littré's 1885 *Dictionnaire de la langue française* insisted that the word was used—incorrectly—"as a synonym for *romance*." See his *French Song from Berlioz to Duparc*, 22.

16. *Dictionnaire de l'Académie française*, 6th ed. (Paris: Didot, 1835), 2:185.

17. Johnson, xx.

18. Noske, 211.

19. Ibid., 281.

20. "Car notre idiome, à nous, rauque et sans prosodie, / Fausse toute musique; et la note hardie, / Contre quelque mot dur se heurtant dans son vol, / Brise ses ailes d'or et tombe sur le sol." Gautier, "La Diva," from *La Comédie de la mort* (1838).

21. For an account of Gounod's experiments with the prose libretto, see Steven Huebner's *The Operas of Charles Gounod* (Oxford: Oxford University Press, 1990), 223–244.

22. Koechlin, 9.

23. Noske, 294.

24. Here are the opening sentences of his essay: "Ce n'est pas sans raison que nous évitons ici le terme de *lied*. Plusieurs, il est vrai, ont préféré l'emploi de ce mot, maint critique musical notamment; et le traité de composition de M. d'Indy parle souvent de la 'forme-lied.' Néanmoins, la *mélodie française* pour piano et chant reste bien différente du *lied* allemand" (Koechlin, 1). In a shorter account of the "humble genre of the *mélodie*" for Lavignac's encyclopedia in the same year, Koechlin makes a similar opening gesture but adds, somewhat defensively, that his avoidance of the German term was not at all motivated by nationalistic sentiment ("non du tout de faire acte d'un nationalisme"), which he considered "puérile." It was only, he continued (protesting a bit too much),

because of the profound difference between French and German music. See his "Tendances de la musique française moderne" in *Encyclopédie de la musique et Dictionnaire du conservatoire*, ed. Albert Lavignac and Lionel de la Laurencie (Paris: Delagrave, 1925), 2:1, 130.

25. Brussel, "Les 'Lieder' de Fauré," 21. Note how Brussel suggestively encloses both "lied" and "mélodie" in quotation marks.

26. Ibid.

27. Camille Mauclair, "Le sens du lied," in *La Religion de la musique* (Paris: Fischbacher, 1938), 51–64. Collection originally published in 1909. Camille Mauclair was the pseudonym of Camille Laurent Célestin Faust (1872–1945). After becoming friends with Mallarmé in the 1890s, Faust adopted his nom de plume, evidently exchanging one loaded surname for another. "Mauclair" is a very clever pun, indeed, fusing the word *maudit* (as in Verlaine's famous collection of essays from 1883, *Les Poètes maudits*) with the poetic ideal of luminous speech, exemplified by the "mot clair." Nor is it far-fetched to imagine such patronymic word games, especially when we recall the far more outrageous examples in Mauclair's *Le Soleil des morts*, a tattletale roman à clef in which he provided a whole generation of French poets and musicians (his colleagues) with similarly evocative pseudonyms. See Susan Youens, "*Le Soleil des morts:* A Turn-of-the-Century Portrait Gallery," in *Music at the Turn of Century: A 19th Century Music Reader*, ed. Joseph Kerman (Berkeley: University of California Press, 1990), 151–166. Richard Candida Smith offers a more equivocal reading of the novel and its author in chapter 3 of *Mallarmé's Children: Symbolism and the Renewal of Experience* (Berkeley: University of California Press, 1999), 40–48.

28. Mauclair, I might add, spoke from actual experience, having provided the texts for Ernest Chausson's 1896 collection, *Trois Lieder*, op. 27. These songs will be discussed in chapter 3.

29. Mauclair, "Le sens du lied," in *La Religion de la musique*, 55–56.

30. Ibid., 57.

31. Ibid., 62. Or as he says earlier in the essay (54), "all true verse is free, like every true individual."

32. As should be obvious, Mauclair takes the metaphysical claims of Herder one step further, as it were, cleverly updating the German Romantic ideology of the lied in order to transform it into an acceptably modern and French concept. It was the later, grimmer history of the twentieth century, and the aftermath of two world wars, that led twentieth-century critics from Koechlin on to refute the connection. Hence Vladimir Jankélévitch: "the populism [of the German concept] remains deeply foreign to French music; and if it is true that, following Franck, the *Scholistes* developed their own taste for folklore, the *mélodie française* nonetheless never ceased to develop toward more and more refined forms, without any relation to the Lied." See Vladimir Jankélévitch, *Gabriel Fauré: Ses Mélodies, son esthétique* (Paris: Plon, 1938), 3.

33. Fellot, "Lieder français," 265.

34. Fellot's judgment reveals his own bias as a member of the Schola Cantorum, for, among the most significant results of this revolution in French music, he lists four, in the following order: "the modern symphonic poem, the . . . Wagerian music drama, . . . the *Schola cantorum* [under Vincent d'Indy and Charles Bordes] and the *Lied* français." Ibid., 266.

35. Camille Mauclair, "Le 'Lied' français contemporain," *Musica* 7, no. 74 (November 1908): 163–164.

36. Ibid., 163.

37. Edouard Dujardin, *Les Premiers Poètes du vers libre* (Paris: Mercure de France, 1922), 63.

38. André Barre, *Le Symbolisme: Essai historique sur le mouvement symboliste en France, 1885 à 1900* (New York: Burt Franklin, 1968, reprint; orig. published, Paris, 1911), 18.

39. Ibid., 164.

40. As Guizot put it in an 1828 lecture on "The General History of Civilization in Europe," "there has hardly been any great idea, any great principle of civilization, which, seeking to spread everywhere, has not first passed through France." Cited in Theodore Zeldin, *France, 1848–1945* (Oxford: Oxford University Press, 1977), vol. 2, chap. 1, "The National Identity."

41. Fellot, "Lieder français," 267.

42. Ernest Legouvé, *Les Pères et les enfants au XIXe siècle* (Paris, 1878), 243. Cited in Philip Nord, *The Republican Moment:Struggle for Democracy in Nineteenth-Century France* (Cambridge: Harvard University Press, 1995), 230. Carlo Caballero opens his book *Fauré and French Musical Aesthetics* (Cambridge: Cambridge University Press, 2001) with a long meditation on the "question of sincerity" but does not discuss the significant political resonance of the term.

43. Mauclair, "Le 'Lied' français contemporain," 164.

44. Hilson Woldu, "Fauré at the Conservatoire," 109.

45. Brussel, "Les 'Lieder' de Fauré," 22. Not everyone was as enthusiastic about the change of style. In a review of a 1912 performance of the cycle, Félix Gaiffe expresses some regret about what he calls Fauré's "dernière manière." See "Les Petits Concerts," *Revue française de musique* 10, no. 2 (15 March 1912): 96–100. Jankélévitch predictably divides Fauré's career into three periods, the last commencing with *Chanson d'Eve*. See *Gabriel Fauré: Ses Mélodies, son esthétique*, 16.

46. Albert Mockel, "Charles Van Lerberghe," *Mercure de France* 4, no. 50 (April–June 1904): 32–33. Mockel's review functioned as a kind of advertisement for the book of poems, which had itself been published by the press of the *Mercure de France* in 1904. I suspect that Mockel's detailed reading of Van Lerberghe played a larger role in Fauré's conception of the cycle than has so far been recognized by critics, because it was, after all, Mockel himself who personally introduced Fauré to the poetic cycle, when Fauré traveled to Brussels in 1906. See Jessica Duchen, *Gabriel Fauré* (London: Phaidon, 2000), 160.

47. Jean-Jacques Rousseau, "Essay on the Origin of Languages," in *The First and Second Discourses and Essay on the Origin of Languages*, trans. Victor Gourevitch (New York: Harper and Row, 1986), 246.

48. Mauclair, "Le sens du lied," in *La Religion de la musique*, 56.

49. Mockel, "Charles Van Lerberghe," 24.

50. Mauclair, "Le sens du lied," in *La Religion de la musique*, 53.

51. Donald Flanell Friedman describes the effect of this verse: "Lerberghe orchestrates a fluid, malleable language of variable meter and often muted or absent end rhymes intended to convey the unspoiled vision of the first being." See his "Belgian Symbolism: A Poetry of Place and Displacement," in *An Anthology of Belgian Symbolists Poets*, ed. Donald Flanell Friedman (New York: Garland, 1992), 4. Mockel would put the matter

far more simply, saying that Van Lerberghe was inspired in *La Chanson d'Eve* "to sing freely the freest verses of all" ("Charles Van Lerberghe," 19–20). It is probably just as significant to note that, after this experiment with free verse, Van Lerberghe returned to writing in more classical forms.

52. This is the formulation of André Barre, discussing the symbolism of Verlaine. See *Le Symbolisme: Essai historique*, 197.

53. Laurence Porter, following Genette, has discussed Mallarmé's belief in the "age-old doctrine of Cratylism, [which] postulated that language in and of itself, as a divine creation, bears an ultimate signification. Its shape and sound constitute the outward and visible sign of an inward and invisible transcendence." And he offers, as one explanation for this poetic orientation, "the rapid development of historical linguistics in the nineteenth century . . . that traced Western languages back to an Indo-European root." See his *The Crisis of French Symbolism* (Ithaca, NY: Cornell University Press, 1990), 9–10. See also Gérard Genette, *Mimologiques: Voyages en Cratylie* (Paris: Seuil, 1970).

54. This picture of Eve bringing an ancient, dormant language to life almost functions as a poetic defense of the younger poets and one of their favorite esoteric activities: restoring archaic words. See Barre, *Le Symbolisme: Essai historique*, 397, who gently criticizes this tendency among the symbolists. Its most passionate defender was Rémy de Gourmont, *Esthétique de la langue française* (Paris: Mercure de France, 1913, reprint; orig. published 1899).

55. Mockel, "Charles Van Lerberghe," 32.

56. C'est en réalité la voyelle neutre par excellence, confluent où toutes les voyelles se rencontre pour assourdir." Albert Dauzat, *Le Génie de la langue française* (Paris: Payot, 1954), 15.

57. "Quand nous ouvrons la bouche sans intension [*sic*] bien marquée [par exemple quand nous sommes embarrassés pour répondre], c'est [e muet] que nous prononçons. Paul Passy, *Les Sons du français* (Paris: Firmin-Didot, 1899, reprint; orig. published 1887), 88.

58. Carlo Caballero discusses Fauré's choices in "Fauré's Religion and *La Chanson d'Eve*," in Gordon, *Regarding Fauré*, 310.

59. Jankélévitch, *Gabriel Fauré*, 190. A sound recording featuring all ten songs in *La Chanson d'Eve* is available on the companion Web site for this book ◐.

60. Eve's water birth is not mentioned explicitly in any of the poems, although it is certainly implied by the end of the cycle, where (as we shall see) Eve begs to return to the place whence she came, imploring her God to turn her back into the foam splashing off the waves.

61. "Gabriel Fauré (1845–1924)," in Johnson and Stokes, *A French Song Companion*, 169. The description pertains specifically to "Dans la nymphée" from Fauré's next Van Lerberghe cycle, *Le Jardin clos* (1914), a song Johnson calls the "apotheosis of the chordally accompanied hymn," although the sentences serve perfectly well in capturing the character of "Prima Verba."

62. For a slightly different reading of the metrical ambiguities of this song, see Caballero, *Fauré and French Musical Aesthetics*, 229–232.

63. "On sait maintenant, grâce à Gabriel Fauré, qu'il peut y avoir dans un simple *lied* plus de *vraie* musique que dans tout un opéra" (emphasis in original). Brussel, "Les 'Lieder' de Fauré," 22. It should be pointed out that Brussel was familiar with only five songs from *La Chanson d'Eve* at the time of his 1909 essay: "Crépuscule" (1906), "Paradis"

(1906), "Prima Verba" (1906), "Roses Ardentes" (1908), and "L'Aube blanche" (1908). Evidently, "Comme Dieu rayonne" (1909) had not yet appeared at the moment he wrote the review.

64. I should probably explain this slightly playful translation, which attempts to bring out the pun in the text linking the verb *luire* (and its third-person conjugation *luit*) to the pronoun *lui*. Graham Johnson and Richard Stokes (in *A French Song Companion*, 203) translate the line, "I raise my eyes a little toward it," which is literally correct but fails to deal both with the evident personification of the sun in the poem—as a figure for a male God—and with the aural equivalence of "him" to the shining "light" that causes Eve to wake in the first place.

65. Mockel, "Charles Van Lerberghe," 24.

66. This poem (sans title) was also taken from Van Lerberghe's first chapter, "Premières Paroles." That Fauré will slant his reading toward the story of Eve's ultimate temptation is further evidence of the influence of Mockel on his reading.

67. Jankélévitch, *Gabriel Fauré: Ses mélodies, son esthétique*, 198. In the context of a long rhythmic analysis of "Eau vivante," Caballero also noted that "the piano part, for all its abstract calculations in the metrical and harmonic dimensions, embodies the bubbling, endlessly changing sameness of the flowing water that Van Lerberghe's poem salutes" (*Fauré and French Musical Aesthetics*, 235).

68. Barbara Meister, *Nineteenth-Century French Song* (Bloomington: Indiana University Press, 1980), 141.

69. Koechlin, "La Mélodie," 1.

70. Ibid. Koechlin himself puts the word *evocation* in quotation marks, calling attention to its own more evocative sense: "Avec les temps modernes, [notre musique] c'est une 'évocation' plus profonde."

71. Koechlin, "Tendances de la musique française moderne," 130.

72. Koechlin, "La Mélodie," 1.

73. Porter, *The Crisis of French Symbolism*, 30.

74. "Veilles-tu" is, as it happens, the only poem Fauré drew from Van Lerberghe's "La Tentation."

75. The verbal pun reflected the tendencies of a whole generation of modern French writers. When Flaubert asserted that "le mot harmonieux est le mot juste," he seems to have been defending this sometimes questionable practice of neologism, suggesting that the poet must sometimes favor the "rightness" of the relation of sound to that of meaning, even to the point of resorting, when necessary, to invented words. See Ferdinand Brunot, "La Langue française de 1815 à nos jours," in *Histoire de la langue et de la littérature française des origines à 1900*, ed. L. Petit de Julleville (Paris: Colin, 1899), 8:796.

76. The text (also drawn from the first chapter of Van Lerberghe's book) happens to be the only verse among the twenty-eight poems that make up "Premières Paroles" set in italic type.

77. The words come from Meister, *Nineteenth-Century French Song*, 145. Caballero has also explored the whole cycle as a reflection of what he takes to be Fauré's own pantheistic leanings in "Fauré's Religion and *La Chanson d'Eve*."

78. The curious text of the original number, which Fauré had set in English for the London production, has all the impenetrable strangeness we have come to expect from Maeterlinck's brand of symbolism:

The King's three blind daughters sit locked in a hold.
In the darkness their lamps make a glimmer of gold.
Up the stairs in the turret the sisters are gone.
Seven days they wait there and the lamps they burn on.
"What hope?" says the first and leans on the flame.
"I hear our lamps burning, O yet if he came."
"O hope," says the second, "was that the lamp's flare?
Or the sound of low footsteps, the Prince on the stair?"

79. Mockel, "Charles Van Lerberghe," 33.

80. Ibid.

81. Ibid.

82. Caballero, "Fauré's Religion and *La Chanson d'Eve*," 319.

83. Housed in the library of the Harry Ransom Humanities Research Center, Austin, Texas. The autographs for the other nine songs are located in the Fonds Bibliothèque Nationale, MS17748.

84. Noske, *French Song from Berlioz to Duparc*, 22.

85. Brancour, "Mélodie," in *La Grande Encyclopédie* (Paris: Société Anonyme de la G.E., 1885–1902), 23:613.

86. Jean-Jacques Nattiez, *Wagner Androgyne: A Study in Interpretation*, trans. Stewart Spencer (Princeton, NJ: Princeton University Press, 1993), 40. See also Marcel Beaufils, *Musique du son, musique du verbe* (Paris: Presses Universitaires de France, 1954).

87. Barthes had long ceased his lessons, although Panzéra was still alive (he did not die until 1976). The whole story of his vocal training becomes all the more poignant when we realize that Barthes was himself the longtime victim of a form of tuberculosis, a disease that eventually forced him to quit singing. It is impossible to say (although tempting to contemplate) whether this debilitating physical ailment had anything to do with the development of his highly nuanced concept of the voice's "grain." In any case, his infirmity seems to provide a telling context for one of the more cryptic remarks of the essay, when he calls the lung "a stupid organ (the lights of cat food!)." See Roland Barthes, "The Grain of the Voice," in *The Responsibility of Forms*, trans. Richard Howard (New York: Hill and Wang, 1985), 271.

88. Ibid., 275.

89. Johnson and Stokes, *A French Song Companion*, 161.

90. Beltrando-Patier, "Le Lied et la mélodie," 395.

91. Ibid.

92. Barthes, "The Grain of the Voice," 275.

93. Ibid. Emphasis in original.

94. Panzéra was born in 1896, Claire Croiza in 1882, and Jane Bathori in 1877.

95. Arsène Darmesteter, *République française* (3 November 1887). Cited in H. Michaelis and Paul Passy, *Dictionnaire phonétique de la langue française* (Hanover, Germany: Carl Meyer, 1897), vii.

96. Reynaldo Hahn, *L'Oreille au guet* (Paris: Gallimard, 1937).

97. Koechlin, "La Mélodie," 61.

98. Ibid. Emphasis in original.

Chapter 2

1. Jean-Paul Sartre, *Les Mots* (Paris: Gallimard, 1964); trans. Bernard Frechtman, *The Words* (New York: George Braziller, 1964), 139.

2. Ibid., 135.

3. Ibid., 142.

4. Michel Leiris, "Alphabet," in *Biffures*, vol. 1, *La Règle du jeu* (Paris: Gallimard, 1975; originally published 1948), 40–76. Leiris became attached to the surrealists in 1924 and produced the poems of *Simulacre* in 1925. Later, in 1939, he brought out the volume of word games he called *Glossaire, j'y serre mes gloses*, after he had undergone psychoanalysis, and after his first trip to Dakar in the 1930s. The twin experiences—of discovering Africa and his own psyche—eventually led him to the Musée de l'homme, where he worked as an ethnologist until 1971, undertaking the study of man at the same time he was studying himself.

5. Ibid., 40–41.

6. Leiris was born in 1901, Sartre in 1905.

7. François Furet and Jacques Ozouf, *Lire et écrire: L'alphabétisation des français de Calvin à Jules Ferry* (Paris: Minuit, 1977), 9; trans. Maison des Sciences de l'Homme, *Reading and Writing: Literacy in France from Calvin to Jules Ferry* (New York: Cambridge University Press, 1982).

8. Ibid., 3.

9. Michel Bréal, *Quelques Mots sur l'instruction publique en France* (Paris: Hachette, 1872), 2.

10. Just one year after taking up his post at the Collège de France, Bréal would establish the Société linguistique de Paris.

11. Decree of 10 August 1807. Cited in Bréal, *Quelque Mots*, 2.

12. Ibid. As George Weisz has pointed out, the idea that "German universities had been responsible for the national renaissance of Germany which followed the Napoleonic wars" was a common trope in the 1870s. Paul Bert, a scientist, statesman, and founding member of the Société de l'Enseignement Supérieur, made more or less the same point before the French Chamber in arguing for the necessity of university reform in "a recently vanquished and politically divided France." See Paul Bert, *Discours parlementaires, 1872–1881* (Paris: G. Charpentier, 1882), 93. Cited in Weisz, *The Emergence of Modern Universities in France, 1863–1914* (Princeton, NJ: Princeton University Press, 1983), 10, n. 9.

13. Eugen Weber, *Peasants into Frenchmen: The Modernization of Rural France, 1870–1914* (Stanford, CA: Stanford University Press, 1976). See especially chap. 6, "A Wealth of Tongues," 67–94. Weber's statistics, taken from an 1863 survey conducted by the minister of public instruction, are the subject of some mild skepticism on his part. As he notes at the outset (67): "Some of the data are suspect on their face, but one would want to accept them with caution in any event, since the Minister...had every reason to exaggerate success and to conceal failure. Apart from the internal evidence, other official statements show that the survey in fact underestimated the situation."

14. Ibid., 67.

15. Bréal, *Quelques Mots*, 32.

16. Ibid., 39–40.

17. The topic was developed as the subject of an entire chapter titled "Du Goût de la lecture."

18. The claim is buttressed with a passage from Gabriel Monod's essay, "Allemands et Français; Souvenirs de campagne," *Revue chrétienne* (5 December 1871): "At Ouzouer, among one hundred wounded, I found no more than four or five who had a taste for reading, and only two who liked being taught." Cited in Bréal, *Quelque mots*, 72, n. 1.

19. Ibid., 41.

20. Ibid., 42.

21. Ibid., 45.

22. Ibid., 42.

23. Ibid., 43. On this point, he goes on to conclude (44): "vous reconnaîtrez bientôt que nos jeunes paysans ne sont pas la race prosaïque dont on nous parle, et que si leurs pères sont devenus trop souvent étrangers à la poésie, c'est qu'on leur avait laissé ignorer ou qu'on leur avait appris à dédaigner les chants populaires, par où se transmet, chez tous les peuples de l'Europe, la veine poétique. Là-dessus, comme sur tant d'autres points, il faut qu'avec l'aide de l'école que nous renouvions la tradition qu'un mépris imprudent du passé a rompue à notre détriment."

24. Sanford Elwitt, *The Making of the Third Republic: Class and Politics in France 1868–1884* (Baton Rouge: Louisiana State University Press, 1975), 19. If Philip Nord sometimes raises an eyebrow over the heavy-handedness of Elwitt's Marxist readings, his own thesis does not differ, on the whole, with the Elwitt's premise of the IIIe République as a bourgeois success story. See Philip Nord, *The Republican Moment: Struggle for Democracy in Nineteenth-Century France* (Cambridge: Harvard University Press, 1995), 2–5.

25. Durkheim, *Éducation et sociologie* (Paris: PUF, 1966), 91–92. Cited in Elwitt, *The Making of the Third Republic*, 170.

26. Gambetta goes on to note—at least a century before Bourdieu—that "*manual capital* reinforced with...*intellectual capital* become the wellsprings of leisure and wealth." Speech delivered June 15, 1878, to a meeting of the people's library in the thirteenth arrondissement. Cited in Elwitt, *The Making of the Third Republic*, 197.

27. Ferdinand Buisson, *Dictionnaire de pédagogie et d'instruction primaire* (Paris: Hachette, 1882). A one-volume abridged edition was brought out in 1911. Pierre Nora laments in that the staggering work is hardly known today except by specialists. See his essay "Le 'Dictionnaire de pédagogie' de Ferdinand Buisson: Cathédrale de l'école primaire," in *Les Lieux de Mémoire*, ed. Pierre Nora; Quarto edition (Paris: Gallimard, 1997), 1:327–347.

28. Buisson was named president of a committee comprising the following members: Messieurs Berger, first inspector of the Seine; Laporte, inspector of Rochechouart; Olagnier, public school instructor in Boulogne-sur-Mer; Valens, adjunct public school instructor in Paris; and Rauber, who is listed as a "free" teacher ("instituteur libre") in Paris.

29. Ferdinand Buisson, *Rapport sur l'instruction primaire à l'exposition universelle de Philadelphie en 1876* (Paris: Imprimerie nationale, 1878), 1.

30. The subjects treated, in order of appearance, are: reading (chap. 10), writing (chap. 11), teaching the mother tongue (chap. 12), geography (chap. 13), history (chap. 14), and arithmetic (chap. 15).

31. "Lecture," in Buisson, *Rapport sur l'instruction primaire*, 235. The essay is signed by Valens (see note 28).

32. Ibid., 235–236. Emphasis mine.

33. Ibid.

34. "'Reaction speaks Bas-Breton,' insisted the Jacobins. 'The unity of the republic demands unity of speech, . . . Speech must be one, like the Republic.'" Cited in Weber, *Peasants into Frenchmen*, 72.

35. Ibid., 674. The findings would gain a more public airing when at the Exposition Universelle de Paris, in 1878, more than two thousand teachers would attend presentations on modern teaching methods, including one by Buisson himself on what he called intuitive instruction. See Pierre Boutan, *La Langue des Messieurs* (Paris: Armand Collin, 1996), 16.

36. Legouvé (1807–1903) gained his seat in the Academy, in 1856, for his stage works. He earned a popular reputation through the series of lectures he delivered in 1857 at the Collège de France (and later published) on "The Moral History of Women" and on "Parents and Children in the Nineteenth Century." No stranger to the world of music, he was also the author of several opera librettos and a biography of Maria Malibran.

37. Ernest Legouvé, *L'Art de la lecture* (Paris: Hetzel, 1877).

38. *The Art of Reading*, trans. Edward Roth (Philadelphia: Lippincott, 1879), 9. A second edition was issued in 1885.

39. Legouvé, *Petit Traité de lecture à haute voix, à l'usage des écoles primaries* (Paris: Hetzel, 1878); *La Lecture en action* (Paris: Hetzel, 1881). A much abbreviated version of these arguments later reappeared in Legouvé's essay, "Lecture à haute voix," prepared for the second volume of Buisson's *Dictionnaire de pédagogie*, 1st ser, 2 (Paris: Hachette, 1887), 1551–1553.

40. Legouvé, *Petit Traité*, 3.

41. Ibid., 3.

42. Ibid., 78.

43. See Françoise Mayeur, *Histoire générale de l'enseignement et de l'éducation en France*, vol. 3, *De la Révolution à l'école républicaine* (Paris: Nouvelle Librairie de France, 1981); also, François Furet, ed., *Jules Ferry, fondateur de la Republique* (Paris: Editions de l'Ecole des hautes etudes en sciences sociales, 1985); Alfred Rambaud, *Jules Ferry* (Paris: Plon-Nourrit, 1903); Jean Foucambert, *L'école de Jules Ferry* (Paris: Retz, 1986); Jean-Michel Gaillard, *Jules Ferry* (Paris: Fayard, 1989); Pierre Chevallier, *La Séparation de l'Eglise et de l'école: Jules Ferry et Leon XIII* (Paris: Fayard, 1981); Jean Cotereau, *Laïcité, sagesse des peuples: anthologie des grands textes de la laïcité, de Jules Ferry à nos jours* (Paris: Fischbacher, 1965).

44. This criterion has made the new school appear less "democratic" than it was touted to be, for there was no real possibility, within the system, for peasants to raise themselves up to the level of the bourgeoisie. Still, the reformers themselves would argue that the lower classes now had the opportunity to escape their agricultural drudgery by becoming primary school teachers.

45. The law of 1882 listed the following subjects as part of the obligatory primary schooling: moral and civic instruction; reading and writing; French language and literature; geography (especially that of France); history (especially French history); law and political economy; natural sciences, physics, and math; elements of drawing, sculpture, and music; physical education (*la gymnastique*).

46. Alfred Rambaud, "France," in Buisson's *Dictionnaire de pédagogie*, 1st ser., 1, 1090.

47. *République française* (25 March 1882). Cited in Rambaud, Ibid.

48. Rollo Brown, *How the French Boy Learns to Write: A Study in Teaching the Mother Tongue* (Cambridge: Harvard University Press, 1922), 4. Ironically, Brown seems not to have known of the French commission who traveled to America forty years earlier, nor that many of the techniques he observed in France had been adapted from those used in his own country in 1876.

49. Legouvé is, in fact, cited in one of the classroom dialogues (a lesson in reading Lamartine) that the American professor has meticulously transcribed. See Brown's *How the French Boy Learns*, 144.

50. Ibid., 120.

51. Ibid., 5–6.

52. Antoine Rivarol, *Discours sur l'universalité de la langue française* (Paris: Librairie Delagrave, 1929). Originally published 1784.

53. Ferdinand de Saussure, *Cours de linguistique générale*, ed. Charles Bailly and Albert Séchehaye (Paris: Payot, 1995), 53.

54. Saussure arrived in Paris in 1880 to study, among other things, comparative grammar with Michel Bréal. As early as October 1881, the brilliant student (only twenty-four years old) was named *maître de conférences* at the École des Hautes Études, where he would, over a period of about ten years, influence an international community of linguists. See "Notes biographiques et critiques sur F. de Saussure" in Saussure, *Cours de linguistique générale*, 335.

55. Ibid., 54.

56. Arsène Darmesteter, *République française* (3 November 1887). Cited in Hermann Michaelis and Paul Passy, *Dictionnaire phonétique de la langue française*, rev. ed. (Berlin: Mayer, 1914), vii.

57. Ibid., 38.

58. Passy was born in 1859; Saussure in 1857.

59. The group first called itself the Phonetic Teacher's Association, adopting the more cosmopolitan name in 1897.

60. The first version of the alphabet was collectively developed by Alexander Ellis, Paul Passy, Henry Sweet, and Daniel Jones, from a concept proposed by the Danish linguist Otto Jespersen.

61. Paul Passy, *Les Sons du français* (Paris: Firmin-Didot, 1887). All subsequent quotations will be taken from the fifth edition (1899).

62. Ibid., 5. The orthography, he noted, was that used in the newspaper *Le Réformiste*.

63. The whole, confused story of this reform movement and the conflicting ideologies that motivated it is chronicled by Yannick Portebois in *Les Saisons de la langue: les écrivains et la réforme de l'orthographe de l'Exposition universelle de 1889 à la Première Guerre mondiale* (Paris: Honoré Champion, 1998).

64. Ibid., 14.

65. Hermann Helmholtz, *Die Lehre von den Tonempfindungen* (Braunschweig: F. Vieweg, 1863). The best known English translation was first produced by Alexander Ellis, one of the founding members of Passy's *Association phonétique internationale*, based on the third edition of Helmholtz's book: *On the Sensations of Tone as a Physiological Basis for the Theory of Music* (London: Longmans, Green and Co., 1875).

66. Twentieth-century research into speech synthesis has determined that vowels have, in fact, several "peaks" in the spectrum. The relatively rude nature of the nineteenth-century instruments made it almost impossible for German acousticians like Helmholtz, as well as the English and French scientists who followed him, to isolate more than one.

67. That the "natural" sequence of timbres turned out to be a dominant seventh chord has equally suggestive implications, one might add, for the progressive development of modern French harmony. A sound recording featuring a live demonstration of this vowel sequence is available on the companion Web site for this book ◑.

68. Passy, *Les Sons du français*, 70, note 1.

69. This is how Passy put it in the "Avant-propos" to the third edition (1892), printed in subsequent editions: "L'étude des sons du langaje est un préliminaire indispensable de la fonétique historique, à laquèle èle rent les memes services que la jéografie à l'histoire." Ibid., 5.

70. "Our language does not inherit [this vowel] from Latin," he reminds us. Barthes makes the remark in the context of his discussion of Panzéra's rendering of this ultra-French phoneme, commenting on "the virtually *electronic* purity [of the sound], . . . so taut, raised, exposed, tenuous." See Roland Barthes, "The Grain of the Voice," in *The Responsibility of Forms*, trans. Richard Howard (New York: Hill and Wang, 1985), 272.

71. Passy, *Les Sons du français*, 82.

72. Letter to Minna Bernays, 3 December 1885. In Ernst L. Freud, ed., *Letters of Sigmund Freud*, trans. Tania and James Stern (New York: Dover, 1992), 188.

73. Passy does, however, use the expression *letres muètes* at the end of the treatise, in describing the advantages of a phonetic writing system that would leave them out.

74. "Le son ə, c'est donc la *voyèle neutre* du Français." Passy, *Les Sons du français*, 89. Emphasis in original.

75. Ibid.

76. Ibid., 90.

77. Henry Sweet, "Phonetics," in *The Encyclopædia Britannica*, 11th ed., vol. 11 (New York: Encyclopædia Britannica, 1910–1911), 466.

78. "Tout ça contribue à doner à notre langue un remarquable caractère de nèteté." Passy, *Les Sons du français*, 90.

79. Sweet, "Phonetics."

80. Ibid., opening paragraph.

81. Michaelis and Passy, *Dictionnaire phonétique de la langue française*, viii.

82. Passy, *Les Sons du français*, 136.

83. Ibid., 137.

84. Eduard Koschwitz, *Les Parlers parisiens: anthologie phonétique* (Paris: H. Welter, 1893). A second revised edition was issued by Welter in 1896; all subsequent citations are drawn from this second edition. Parts of Koschwitz's study were also published (in German) in his *Zur Aussprache des Französischen in Genf und Frankreich* (Berlin: Wilhelm Gronan, 1892).

85. See note 81 in this chapter.

86. Koschwitz, *Les Parlers parisiens*, 33.

87. Ibid., xxii.

88. From this perspective, the book also seemed to pose a direct challenge to an earlier anthology produced by Passy (*Le Français parlé. Morceaux choisis à l'usage des étrangers avec la pronociation figurée* [Heilbronn: Henninger, 1886]), which included certain apparently questionable transcriptions of some of the same speakers and texts, which Koschwitz was now prepared to correct.

89. Koschwitz, *Les Parlers parisiens*, xxvi.

90. According to Rousselot, Koschwitz had audited his classes at the Institut Catholique from 1890 to 1891 and, impressed by the priest's methods, fought for their acceptance at his own university until his untimely death in 1904. See Pierre-Jean Rousselot, "Phonétique experimental ou 'Instrumentalphonetik,'" *Revue de phonétique* 1, no. 1 (1911): 11. Koschwitz would use Rousselot, incidentally, as an additional "informant" when he completed a revised edition of his study in 1896 (*Les Parlers parisiens*, xxix, 1).

91. In 1881, the Ecole des hautes études had created a new chair of *dialectologie*, hiring Jules Gilliéron to fill it. Gillérion later made an important contribution to patois studies with his 1917 compendium on the highly pastoral idea of the "bee" as it was expressed in every region of France, *Généologie des mots qui ont désigné l'abeille*. See Marcel Cohen, *Histoire d'une langue: le français* (Paris: Editions sociales, 1967), 284.

92. Etienne-Jules Marey, *La Méthode graphique dans les sciences expérimentales et principalement en physiologie et en médecine* (Paris: G. Masson, 1878).

93. Ibid., 144. Cited in Pierre Jean Rousselot, *Principes de phonétique expérimentale* (Paris: H. Welter, 1902), 48.

94. Rousselot, *Les Articulations parisiennes étudiées à l'aide du palais artificiel* (Paris: Welter, 1899). This study was later abridged in Rousselot and Fauste Laclotte's *Précis de prononciation française* (Paris: Welter, 1902).

95. L'Abbé Pierre-Jean Rousselot and Fauste Laclotte, "La Prononciation française," *La Revue phonétique* 1, no. 1 (1911): 85.

96. Ibid., 86.

97. Marey, *La Méthode graphique*.

98. Readers of my first book may recognize a similarity between Abbé Rousselot's ideas of direct transcription and those of Dom Mocquereau, the Solesmes monk of the same generation (just three years younger than Rousselot), who desired to capture the living reality of the Gregorian phrase in a similarly evocative chirography. See *Decadent Enchantments: The Revival of Gregorian Chant at Solesmes* (Berkeley: University of California Press, 1998), esp. chap. 4, "Reading, Writing, Singing," 92–142.

99. Rousselot and Laclotte, *Précis de prononciation française*, 7.

100. The Alliance française had been incorporated, in the same spirit of Republican reform, in 1884. See Maurice Bruézière, *L'Alliance française: Histoire d'une institution* (Paris: Hachette, 1983); and Constant Roy, *Le Livre de propagande de l'alliance française* (Paris: Armand Colin, 1894).

101. Rousselot and Laclotte, *Précis de prononciation française*, 10–13.

102. Ibid., 13. "L'enfant né à Paris est Parisien, et même l'enfant qui y arrive le devient très vite, à la condition qu'il fréquente une école populaire."

103. Ferdinand de Saussure, *Cours de linguistique generale*, 32.

104. See "Exercises sur les articulations isolées et les syllabes," in Rousselot and Laclotte, *Précis de prononciation français*, 206.

105. "La parole se compose de sons musicaux et de bruits." Ibid., 13.

106. See Hélène Abraham, *Un Art de l'interpretation: Claire Croiza; les cahiers d'une auditrice, 1924–1939* (Paris: Office de centralisation d'ouvrages, 1954). In the notes for her class of 24 May 1933, on the "Expressive value of words," Abraham transcribes Croiza as saying "M. Rousselot says: 'speech is composed of musical sounds and of noises'" (p. 193). It is worth pointing out that Paul Valéry admired Croiza not just for her singing but for her expressive declamations of French poetry. See Valéry, *De La Diction des vers* (Paris: Emile Chamontin, 1933).

107. George René Marie Marage, *Petit Manuel de physiologie de la voix, à l'usage des chanteurs et des orateurs*, 4th ed. (Paris: Gauthiers-Villars, 1925). As announced on the title page, Marage's wife compiled the book from his course materials. I am extremely grateful to Emanuele Senici, who, on one of his shopping expeditions for antiquarian books in Oxford, found a copy of this text and bought it for me.

108. Marage supplied a celebratory foreword to Isnardon's subsequent treatise, *Le Chant théatral* (Paris: Vieu, 1911), a document I discuss more thoroughly in chapter 4.

109. Docteur Marage, *Petit Manuel de physiologie de la voix*, vi.

110. Ibid., 92.

111. Ibid., 94.

112. Ibid., 99.

113. This work had, in fact, been developed by Marey's assistant Georges Demeny (1850–1918). As Marta Braun writes, "In 1891 Marey turned over to Demeny a project that would be his introduction to moving pictures—a study in the mechanics of speech initiated at the request of Hector Marichelle, professor and director of the National Deaf-Mute institute, who saw the possibility of using filmed speech for the education of deaf children." See Marta Braun, *Picturing Time: The Work of Etienne-Jules Marey* (Chicago: University of Chicago Press, 1992), 176.

114. Ibid., 184.

115. Legouvé, *Petit Traité de lecture à haute voix*, 34.

116. Cited in Hubert Pernot, "L'Institut de phonétique de Paris," *Revue de phonétique* 5, no. 1 (1928), 31. A complete audio recording of the address can be found online at the digital archives of the Bibliothèque nationale de France (http://gallica.bnf.fr/) as Brunot, "Discours d'inauguration des Archives de la parole" (Paris: Archives de la parole, 1911).

117. Ibid.

118. Mary Garden did leave one fleeting trace of her singing on a recording from 1904, which I discuss in chapter 4.

119. Barthes, "The Grain of the Voice," 275.

120. Cited in Pernot, "L'Institut de phonétique," 32. For an extended meditation on the airplane in the French imagination, see Glenn Watkins, *Proof through the Night: Music and the Great War* (Berkeley: University of California Press, 2003), esp. chap. 10, "Neoclassicism, Aviation, and the Great War."

121. Furet and Ozouf, *Reading and Writing*, 315–317.

122. The lessons were prepared by Rousselot's cousin, Marguerite de Saint-Genès. See Pernot, *Revue de phonétique* 1, no. 1 (1911): 93–102.

123. Charles Koechlin, "La Mélodie," in *Cinquante Ans de musique française, de 1874 à 1925*, ed. Ladislav Rohozinski (Paris: Librarie de France, 1925), 2:25, 1. See also chapter 1, note 72.

124. For more on Koechlin's left-wing sympathies, see Robert Orledge, *Charles Koechlin (1867–1950): His Life and Works* (London: Harwood Academic, 1989).

Chapter 3

1. The deleted expletive, of course, is *merde* ("shit"), which just happens to rhyme with *verde*. Paul Verlaine, *Oeuvres poétiques complètes*, ed. Jacques Borel (Paris: Gallimard, 1962), 610.

2. The *Chat noir* was a weekly published under the roof of the famous Montmartre café of the same name, owned and operated by Rudolphe Salis and home in the 1880s to numerous up-and-coming young writers. Verlaine's poem apparently first appeared with the title "À S. Du Vigneau" and was later printed posthumously in a volume of wicked poems Verlaine's editor titled *Invectives*. The Pléiade edition corrects the spelling to "À A. Duvigneaux" and includes the poem among the *Dédicaces*.

3. Michel Barlow, *Poésies: Verlaine* (Paris: Hatier, 1982), 53.

4. "It appears that the torch now throws only a feeble light and that that light falls on some pretty dismal things!" The comment came from an 1891 letter to the Princesse de Polignac, née Winaretta Singer, daughter of the American sewing machine manufacturer. Cited in Jessica Duchen, *Gabriel Fauré* (London: Phaidon, 2000), 96.

5. It was an expletive in more than one sense: in poetry, the term *expletive* refers to a word added to fill out the meter of the line.

6. Yannick Portebois presents an exhaustive survey of this spelling debate as it was carried out publicly in the French press in *Les Saisons de la langue* (Paris: Honoré Champion, 1998).

7. Jean Moréas, "Un Manifeste littéraire: Le Symbolisme," *Le Figaro*, 18 September 1886, 150. Five years later, the publicity-hungry Moréas would, even more cheekily, turn around and reject the movement he had just invented in favor of what he dubbed the new "Roman school" of poetry. Moréas's story is engagingly told by Richard Candida Smith in *Mallarmé's Children: Symbolism and the Renewal of Experience* (Berkeley: University of California Press, 1999); see chap. 2, "The Production of Symbolism," 17–39.

8. Paul Valéry, *Existence du symbolisme* (Maestricht: A. A. M. Stols, 1939), 5. See also Bertrand Marchal, *Lire le symbolisme* (Paris: Dunod, 1993); and Richard E. Goodkin, "Zeno's Paradox: Mallarmé, Valéry, and the Symbolist 'Movement,'" *Yale French Studies*, no. 74, Phantom Proxies: Symbolism and the Rhetoric of History (1988): 133–156.

9. Marchal, *Lire le symbolisme*, 5.

10. After making a precocious splash on the Parisian literary scene (which included his scandalous affair with Verlaine), Rimbaud had essentially renounced literature in 1880, when he left, improbably, for North Africa, living out the next ten years as a gun runner.

11. Published as Jules Huret, *Enquête sur l'évolution littéraire* (Paris: Charpentier, 1891).

12. Richard Candida Smith explains that fights were caused "by aspersions on their personal honesty." *Mallarmé's Children*, 36.

13. Jules Delafosse, "Les Evolutions du style," *La Nouvelle Revue* 18, no. 100 (May 1896), 42–69.

14. Francis Vielé-Griffin, "Jules Ferry: Père du symbolisme," *Mercure de France* (June 1896), 321–326.

15. Ibid., 322. The passage he cites can be found in Delafosse's "Les Evolutions du style," p. 54.

16. Vielé-Griffin, "Jules Ferry: Père du symbolisme," 323; Delafosse, "Les Evolutions du style," 67.

17. It is worth pointing out that Delafosse's deeper complaint about Ferry had to do with the suppression of Latin in favor of "modern languages." The young French writers, he said, now knew common English better than their Latin declensions. The point must have particularly stung Vielé-Griffin, who was American by birth and citizenship. But in another respect, the younger poet, who had resided in France from the age of nine, remained impervious to the criticisms. Vielé-Griffin's fancy Parisian education (which, in fact, predated the Ferry reforms) included a hefty dose of the classics. His first schoolboy verses were Latin poems.

18. François Brunot, "La Langue française de 1815 à nos jours," in *Histoire de la langue et de la littérature française des origines à 1900*, ed. L. Petit de Julleville (Paris: Colin, 1899), 8: 829.

19. Marcel Schwob, *Études sur l'argot français* (Paris: Emile Bouillon, 1889).

20. Huret, *Enquête sur l'évolution littéraire*, 67.

21. Marchal, *Lire le symbolisme*, 3. See also James R. Lawler, "Verlaine's 'Naïveté,'" chap. 2 of *The Language of French Symbolism* (Princeton, NJ: Princeton University Press, 1969).

22. See chap. 1, note 42.

23. Georges Jean-Aubry, "Paul Verlaine et les musicians," in *La Musique française d'aujourd'hui* (Paris: Perrin, 1916), 237–238.

24. Ibid. Emphasis in original.

25. These were the words of P. Mansell Jones, who was introduced to de Souza while a student in Paris in 1914. See Jones, *The Background of Modern French Poetry* (Cambridge: Cambridge University Press, 1951), 152–153.

26. Robert de Souza, *La Poésie populaire et le lyrisme sentimental* (Paris: Mercure de France, 1899), 28–29.

27. Ibid., 34–35. De Souza offers as examples Jean Richepin's *Chanson des gueux* and Jean Rictus, *Soliloques du pauvre*.

28. Several poems appeared in 1885 in the literary journal *Lutèce* before being published in pamphlet form. See Gabriel Vicaire and Henri Beauclair, *Les Déliquescences: poèmes décadents d'Adoré Floupette* (Paris: H. Jonquières, 1923); also W. Kenneth Cornell, *The Symbolist Movement* (New Haven: Yale University Press, 1951), chap. 4, "Adoré Floupette, 1885," 35–44.

29. De Souza, *La Poésie populaire et le lyrisme sentimental*, 36. Emphasis in original. De Souza cites the passage without giving the source, but the words come from Vicaire's essay, "La Poésie populaire en Bresse et en Bugey," first published in *Le Nouvelle Revue* 94 (May-June 1895). That essay reappeared in Gabriel Vicaire, *Études sur la poésie populaire: légendes et traditions* (Paris: H. Leclerc, 1902), published posthumously by his brother Georges; for the passage in question, see pp. 146–147.

30. By the time of de Souza's writing in 1899, the name of Tiersot (1857–1936) was perhaps best known through the first volumes of his anthology, *Mélodies populaires des provinces de France* (Paris: Heugel, 1887–1928), and through his comprehensive *Histoire de la chanson populaire en France* (Paris: E. Plon, Nourrit, 1889). He had also brought out,

with Maurice Bouchor, a volume of *Chants populaires pour les écoles* (Paris: Librairie Hachette, 1895), as well as a series of more focused studies: *Les Types mélodiques dans la chanson populaire française* (Paris: Sagot, 1894); *Sur le Jeu de Robin et Marion d'Adam de la Halle, XIIIᵉ siècle* (Paris: Fischbacher, 1897); and *Trois chants du 14 Juillet sous la révolution* (Paris: Fischbacher, 1899).

31. Mauclair, "Le Sens du Lied," in *La Religion de la musique* (Paris: Fischbacher, 1938), 51–63.

32. De Souza, *La Poésie populaire et le lyrisme sentimental*, 102, note. The idea of *emotivité* harked back to Poe, and the emotive theory of language developed in his theoretical essay *Genesis of a Poem*. Mauclair conspicuously evoked Poe in his definition of the lied, saying that its "spontaneous, polyrhythmic, irregular form" reflected the principle of "brevity in intensity that Poe ascribed to all emotive works." That Poe's essay later turned out to be fraudulent did not seem to deter these French admirers. "What has been said, has been said," opined Mallarmé. See A. G. Lehmann, *The Symbolist Aesthetic in France, 1885–1895* (Oxford: Blackwell, 1968), 136–138.

33. De Souza, *La Poésie populaire*, 102. Among the twentieth-century critics who did get the ethos of the symbolists right, I should mention Marshall McLuhan. In his essay "The Aesthetic Moment in Landscape Poetry," he reminds us that "the great discovery of the nineteenth century was not this or that fact about nature but the discovery of the technique of invention so that modern science can now discover whatever it needs to discover. And Rimbaud and Mallarmé . . . made the same advance in poetic technique." Cited in Glenn Willmott. *McLuhan, or Modernism in Reverse* (Toronto: University of Toronto Press, 1996), 64.

34. De Souza, *La Poésie populaire*, 102.

35. Ibid., 159. De Souza's hierarchy comes from Julien Tiersot, *Histoire de la chanson populaire en France* (Paris: E. Plon, Nourrit, 1889).

36. De Souza, *La Poésie populaire*, 159.

37. "The most recent poetical writings do not tend to suppress the official verse; they tend rather to let a little more air into the poem, to create a kind of fluidity or mobility between long-winded verses, which has heretofore been lacking." Jules Huret, *Enquête sur l'évolution littéraire*. Cited and translated in William Austin, ed., *Debussy: Prelude to "The Afternoon of a Faun"* (New York: Norton, 1970), 109.

38. Smith, *Mallarmé's Children*, 25.

39. Ibid., 37–38.

40. Arthur Rimbaud, "Alchimie du verbe," in *Une Saison en enfer* (Paris: Arléa, 1997), 30.

41. By 1968, so many interpretations of the poem had been produced that a French commentator called Etiemble declared it was time to stop. See Etiemble, *Le Sonnet des voyelles* (Paris: Gallimard, 1968).

42. Which just might be the brow of a very significant V-person, the poet Verlaine, whose forehead was famously oversized. In that case, the V could be read as the last letter of P. V., which, in turn, may help to explain the incongruous pastoral image that shows up in the next line. The "peace of the pastures," seems to imply a *correspondance* not only with Verlaine's own pastoral poetry, "dotted with animals," but also, even more cleverly, with the older poet's first initial ("paix" = P). And that connection, in turn, may put a different spin on the blatantly sexual imagery of the first stanza, or the "lances" of the

second, with their pleasurable frissons followed by "penitential drunkenness" (also recalling the famously dissolute P. V., whom Rimbaud alluded to in *Une Saison en enfer* as a figure who "used to weep at the sight of those around us, in the hovels where we got drunk"). Indeed, one is tempted to read the sonnet as an encoded evocation of the intense homoerotic bond between the two poets. For an unembarrassed account of the affair, see Graham Robb, *Rimbaud* (New York: Norton, 2000).

43. Through the poem's organization, we see, in fact, how Rimbaud delivers on his claim from *Une Saison en enfer*. He *has* created a poetic language "accessible to all the senses," by his calculated move from the least poetic faculties—smell and touch—to the more evocative senses of taste, sight, and hearing. The stench of *A* modulates to the sharpness of *E*, which leads, in turn, to an unsavory *I* (having the bitter taste of "spit blood") and then to *U*, a pastoral vision that finally resolves in the clamorous sound of *O*.

44. "Car JE est un autre. Si le cuivre s'éveille clairon, il n'y a rien de sa faute. Cela m'est évident: j'assiste à l'éclosion de ma pensée: je la regarde, je l'écoute: je lance un coup d'archet: la symphonie fait son remuement dans les profondeurs, ou vient d'un bond sur la scène." Letter of 13 May 1871 to Paul Demeny. In Rimbaud, *Oeuvres*, ed. Suzanne Bernard and A. Guyaux (Paris: Garnier, 1987), 347. Cited in James Lawler, *Rimbaud's Theater of the Self* (Cambridge: Harvard University Press, 1992), 3.

45. In French, *une voix cuivrée* is a "resonant" or "sonorous" voice.

46. Usually classified in negative terms, timbre refers to the part of a musical score that is *not* contained by notation—representing neither pitch nor rhythm nor harmony. Dictionaries tend to describe it as a quality distinguishing the sound of one instrument from the next. Play the same note on flute or horn, we are told, and the resulting difference is the timbre. But this will hardly do, for the difference still remains unaccounted for. Adjectives can sometimes take up the slack but, in the end, prove no more helpful. By calling a sound dark or warm or sweet or sharp or even pungent, the aural experience is simply diverted to another realm. Timbre becomes, in this sense, just another form of synesthesia.

47. Jacques Derrida, "Tympan," in *Margins of Philosophy*, trans. Alan Bass (Chicago: University of Chicago, 1982), x. Originally published as *Marges de la philosophie* (Paris: Minuit, 1972).

48. Derrida's debt to French poetry is inherent in the whole deconstructive project and literally played out on the surface of this essay. The words of a former surrealist poet (the autobiographical essay "Perséphone" by Michel Leiris) fill the available margins, forming an alternative text that both comments on and performs this limit point, or tympanum, of Derrida's philosophical exposition. Like a typographic eardrum, the textual margin represents the confrontation of philosophy with its other. But that is not all. Like a *mise en abîme*, the margin re-produces that limit in yet another form, as Leiris's essay recalls the memory of a kind of alternative eardrum: the sound-collecting and sound-producing instrument from his childhood, the domestic gramophone.

49. "Timbre, style, signature are the same obliterating division of the proper. They make every event possible, necessary, unfindable." Derrida, "Tympan," xix.

50. Réné Ghil, *Traité du verbe* (Paris: Alcan Lévy, 1885).

51. Ghil, *Traité du verbe* (Paris: Alcan Lévy, 1887), 39–40.

52. Verlaine, "Conseils," from *Invectives*, in Verlaine, *Oeuvres complètes* (Paris: Leon Vanier, 1901), 22.

53. Ibid., 50, note xxvii. Capitalization in orginal.

54. "Un désir indéniable à l'époque est de séparer, comme en vue d'attributions différentes, le double état de la parole, brut ou immédiat ici, là essentiel." Mallarmé, Avant-dire, in Ibid., 7–8.

55. However surprisingly, Mallarmé was editor in chief of the short-lived Parisian fashion magazine *La Dernière Mode* between 1874–1875.

56. "A quoi bon la merveille de transposer un fait de la nature en sa presque disparition vibratoire selon le jeu de la parole, si ce n'est pour qu'en émane, sans la gêne d'un proche ou concret rappel, la notion pure?" I should perhaps explain my somewhat free translation of the parenthetical clause "sans la gêne d'un proche ou concret rappel." Following Mallarmé's idea of exchange, I want to take the word *rappel*, as well as *gêne*, in their more specifically monetary senses. For if *gêne* can mean financial trouble, then *rappel* can be read in the same vein: in accounting, *rappel* is not just a reminder but a remainder, a sum that must be repaid.

57. The lines were reproduced, almost word for word, in Mallarmé's later (and more celebrated) "Crise de vers" (1895). See Austin, *Debussy.*

58. "Je dis: une fleur! et, hors de l'oubli où ma voix relègue aucun contour, en tant que quelque chose d'autre que les calices sus, musicalement se lève, idée rieuse ou altère, l'absente de tous bouquets." Avant-dire, in Ghil, *Traité du* verbe, 8. I might point out that when this passage reappears at the end of "Crise de vers," Mallarmé has tinkered with it. In the later essay, the "idea" (*l'idée*) is now modified as "selfsame and suave" (*même et suave*) instead of "laughable or perverse" (*rieuse ou altère*).

59. Paul Valéry, "Poetry and Abstract Thought," trans. Jackson Matthews, in James Lawler, ed., *Paul Valéry: An Anthology.* Bollingen Series 15 (Princeton, NJ: Princeton University Press, 1977), 155–156.

60. Ibid., 156. Emphasis mine.

61. See David Code, "The Formal Rhythms of Mallarmé's Faun," in *Representations* 86 (Spring 2004): 73–119.

62. Robert Greer Cohn, *Mallarmé's Un Coup de dès: An Exegesis* (New Haven: Yale French Studies publication, 1949); Bertrand Marchal, *Lecture de Mallarmé: Poésies, Igitur, Le Coup de dès* (Paris: J. Corti, 1985); Christine Givry and Raoul Fabrègues, eds., *Les Échos de Mallarmé: du Coup de dès à l'informatique: Mallarmé et la typographie* (Sens: Musées de Sens, 1998).

63. Stéphane Mallarmé, "Observation relative au poème *Un Coup de Dès jamais n'abolira le Hasard*," *Cosmopolis* 4 (May 1897): 417–418.

64. Gustave Kahn, "Préface sur le vers libre," in *Premiers poèmes, avec une préface sur le vers libre* (Paris: Société du Mercure de France, 1897). The instructional preface was originally published as the introduction to an 1897 reprint of his first three volumes of poetry: *Les Palais nomades* (1887), *Chansons* d'amant (1891), *Domaine de fée* (1895).

65. "The lake of my eyes preserves the illusion of their faces." Note how, in French, the inverted syntax—which turns subject and object around the single verb *garde*—seems itself to imitate the effect of a glassy reflection.

66. In classic French prosody, of course, such syllables were always to be pronounced, retaining their full rhythmic value within the line whenever they were followed by a consonant. They remained mute only when followed by vowels, to which they would be elided, or when falling at the end of a line, where they would yield to the more important

sound of the rhyme. Kahn reasoned that, here, the words *mirage, visage,* and *garde* essentially functioned as end-rhymes within the smaller rhythmic measures, making the terminal *e* in each case rhythmically insignificant. By this logic, the syllable itself, no longer serving as an absolute value within the rhythm, lost all its former integrity. For an extended discussion of Kahn's argument, see Clive Scott, *Vers Libre: The Emergence of Free Verse in France, 1886–1914* (Oxford: Oxford University Press, 1990), chap. 3, 121ff.

67. De Souza was not alone in this pursuit. When Marinetti conducted his investigation into *vers libre* in 1909, Vielé-Griffin acknowledged that the poetic movement had acquired "a new positivistic spirit." The poet André Spire would later recall his own felicitous encounter with experimental phonetics in the same period, introduced to Rousselot (and to de Souza) by the playwright and musicologist Romain Rolland. See Marinetti, *Enquête internationale sur le vers libre* (1909), 33 (cited in Scott, *Vers Libre,* 171); and André Spire, *Plaisir poétique et plaisir musculaire: Essai sur l'évolution des techniques poétiques* (New York: S. F. Vanni, 1949), v.

68. Robert de Souza, *Du Rythme en français* (Paris: Librairie Universitaire, 1912), 15, 64.

69. Ibid., 14–15.

70. Michel Arnauld, "Du vers français," *La Nouvelle Revue française,* 1 January 1910.

71. Georges Lote, *Etudes sur le vers français: Première partie: l'alexandrin d'après la phonétique expérimental* (Paris: Editions de La Phalange, 1911; 2nd ed., rev., 1913). The project was comparable, in some ways, to the study of "parlers Parisiens" conducted by Koschwitz in 1895, as discussed in chapter 2.

72. De Souza, *Terpsichore* (Paris: Crès, 1920), 111–113.

73. Ibid.

74. Rosemary Lloyd, "Debussy, Mallarmé and 'Les Mardis,'" in *Debussy and His World,* ed. Jane Fulcher (Princeton, NJ: Princeton University Press, 2001).

75. Cited in Jean Pierrot, *The Decadent Imagination,* trans. Derek Coltman (Chicago: University of Chicago Press, 1981), 27.

76. It was Georges Servières who described the song thus: "Etrangetés et incorrections harmoniques, rythmes sans cesse brisés et décousus, intervalles inchantables, aucun souci des registre vocaux.... Les vers sont souvent mal déclamés, la prosodie violée, le sens détruit par la coupe de la mélodie, il y a aussi abus de chromatisme, de modulations heurtées." "Lieder français: Claude Debussy." *Le Guide musical* 15, no. 22 (September 1895). Camille Mauclair considered the settings "feverish." See "Le 'Lied' français contemporain," *Musica* 7, no. 74 (November 1908): 164.

77. According to a reviewer from 1895, they simply "scared off the publishers, as much by the choice of subject . . . as by the manner in which they were treated." Cited in Marcel Dietschy, *A Portrait of Claude Debussy,* trans. William Ashbrook and Margaret Cobb (Oxford: Oxford University Press, 1990), 56, n. 16. The composer eventually brought out the songs himself in 1890, with the help of friends, in a fancy presentation edition he would attempt to sell by subscription.

78. Graham Johnson and Richard Stokes, *A French Song Companion* (New York: Oxford University Press, 2000), 96–97.

79. This is the opening line of Baudelaire's "La Musique," the tenth poem of the *Fleurs du Mal.*

80. This is from the essay "Richard Wagner and Tannhäuser in Paris," in Charles Baudelaire, *Oeuvres complètes,* vol. 2, ed. Claude Pichois (Paris: Editions de la Pléiade,

1975), 790. Cited in Susan Bernstein, *Virtuosity of the Nineteenth Century* (Stanford, CA: Stanford University Press, 1998), 155.

81. Leo Bersani, *Baudelaire and Freud* (Berkeley: University of California Press, 1977).

82. The passage eventually made it into the introduction to Baudelaire's *Petits poëmes en prose.* Cited in Bernstein, *Virtuosity of the Nineteenth Century*, 175.

83. The term comes from an essay on *Pelléas*, where Laloy is describing the nature of the composer's prosody. Louis Laloy, "Le drame musicale moderne IV: Claude Debussy," *Le Mercure musical* (1 August 1905): 233–250. Essay translated in Deborah Priest, *Louis Laloy (1874–1944) on Debussy, Ravel and Stravinsky* (Aldershot, UK: Ashgate, 1999), 165–184. In an essay on the *Cinq poèmes* published in 1902, Laloy described Debussy's technique as follows: "No violence is done to the words: the melody is varied or repeated with them . . . according to whether the words are more or less emotional, the melody makes from them a coherent line, or a simple rhythmic declamation. . . . Monsieur Debussy's music is free, but there is nothing fantastic or incoherent about it." "Cinq poèmes de Baudelaire," *La Revue musicale* (October 1902): 404–408. Translated in Priest, *Louis Laloy*, 146–151.

84. The two forms of influence are not entirely incompatible. A writer like Dujardin (as noted in chapter 1) claimed Wagner as the inspiration for his own forays into *vers libre*. Debussy's much-discussed *wagnérisme* might be seen, then, as a manifestation of this literary phenomenon—that is, a musical influence once-removed. For another take on Wagner's literary significance for French composers, see David Code, "Hearing Debussy Reading Mallarmé: Music *après Wagner* in the *Prélude à l'après-midi d'un Faune." Journal of the American Musicological Society* 54, no. 3 (Fall 2001): 493–554.

85. Marcel Proust offers clear evidence of the mixed feelings surrounding the cycle in a letter from 1894. While he himself adored it, he noted with some impatience that "the young musicians [were] virtually unanimous in disliking [it]." Letter to Pierre Lavallée, September 1894. Cited in Carlo Caballero, *Fauré and French Musical Aesthetics* (Cambridge: Cambridge University Press, 2001), 149.

86. Johnson and Stokes, *A French Song Companion*, 167.

87. Mauclair, "Le 'Lied' français contemporain," 163.

88. See Laloy, "Le drame musical moderne: Claude Debussy," trans. Priest, *Louis Laloy*, 174. Also "Claude Debussy and Debussysme," in *S.I.M. Revue musicale* (August–September 1910): 507–519, trans., Priest, *Louis Laloy*, 85–98.

89. Huvelin, "Symbolistes et Impressionnistes," in *Pour la musique française: douze causeries* (Paris: Georges Crès, 1917), 319. Emphasis mine. This view of musical impressionism was not unique. It is likely, in fact, that Huvelin was glossing Laloy, who had discussed the connections between the "laws of sensation" that governed music and the "visual impression" of contemporary painters five years earlier in his "Claude Debussy and Debussysme." A critic named Paule de Lestang, writing for the *Revue musicale de Lyon* in 1906, spoke of Debussy's melodies in much the same way. Expressing bewilderment at the overly free form of the *Proses lyriques*, he described the music as an example of "pure impressionism," where the aim is "to illustrate each phrase, each word, with a [separate] musical idea." Paule de Lestang, "Les Chansons de Bilitis," *Revue musicale de Lyon* 4, no. 1 (October 1906): 235–239.

90. Huvelin, "Symbolistes et Impressionnistes," 319.

91. Jean-Michel Nectoux, *Gabriel Fauré: A Musical Life*, trans. Roger Nichols (Cambridge: Cambridge University Press, 1991), 187.

92. Louÿs later divulged that the name of the mystery professor was intended as a giveaway. When pronounced, G. Heim (or "Geheim") meant "mysterious." The whole hoax is described in loving detail in Jean-Paul Goujon's critical edition of Louÿs's *Les Chansons de Bilitis* (Paris: Gallimard, 1990). David Grayson offers a briefer account, based on Goujon's research, in "Bilitis and Tanagra: Afternoons with Nude Women," in *Debussy and His World*, ed. Fulcher, 117–139.

93. Susan Youens reports that "the German classical scholar Ulrich von Wilamo-witz-Moellenforff took the *Chansons* seriously enough to write a scathing review of Louÿs's 'translation,' which Louÿs, tongue-in-cheek, included in the bibliography appended to the revised edition of 1898." See her essay, "Music, verse, and 'prose poetry': Debussy's *Trois Chansons de Bilitis*," *Journal of Musicological Research* 7, no. 1 (1986): 93, n. 14. It is likely that this "review"—by a conspicuously hyphenated German—was a hoax, as well.

94. The generic title Louÿs assigned to the second edition of the *Chansons* (1898) sent the same message, while reversing the emphasis. He called the work a *roman lyrique*, a (prose) novel in lyric form.

95. Roger Nichols offers an alternative scansion of this poem in his chapter on "The Prosaic Debussy," in *Cambridge Companion to Debussy*, ed. Simon Trezise (Cambridge: Cambridge University Press, 2003), 97.

96. It is all the more significant to learn, as Goujon tells us, that the original manuscript of "La Chevelure," which Louÿs sent to Debussy in 1897, was actually laid out in *vers libre*.

97. Letter of 16 October 1898. Cited in *Debussy Letters*, ed. François Lesure, trans. Roger Nichols (Cambridge: Harvard University Press, 1987), 101.

98. Richard Strauss and Romain Rolland, *Correspondance: Fragments de journal*, ed. Gabriel Samazeuilh (Paris, 1951), 41. Cited in Nichols, "The Prosaic Debussy," 96. To hear a 1927 recording of Jane Bathori singing and playing "La Flute de Pan," see the companion Web site for this book ◐.

99. Gérold, "Monodie et Lied," in *Encyclopédie de la musique et dictionnaire du Conservatoire*, ed. Albert Lavignac and Lionel de la Laurencie (C. Delagrave, 1922), 2:2865.

100. Jean-Jacques Rousseau, "Essay on the Origin of Languages," in *The First and Second Discourses and Essay on the Origin of Languages*, trans. Victor Gourevitch (New York: Harper and Row, 1986), 282. I owe thanks to David Copenhafer, who reminded me of the frogs.

101. Koechlin would go so far as to say that Fauré "shows Leconte de Lisle for who he really is: a true *sensible*, contrary to the absurd reputation of the 'impassive Parnassian'" ("Mélodie," 3). To hear a 1930 recording of Reynaldo Hahn singing and playing "Le Parfum impérissable," see the companion Web site for this book ◐.

102. Marinetti, *Enquête sur le vers libre* (1909), p. 67. Cited in Scott, *Vers Libre*, 170.

103. Rousseau, "Essay on the Origin of Languages," 282.

104. Johnson has written: "Chausson's music . . . is pervaded by a note of profound melancholy and diffidence. It is this quality of a personality *en sourdine*, a muted and serious response to life itself, which . . . has prevented his automatic entry into the

pantheon of music's greatest heroes" (*A French Song Companion*, 78). I would say it is this quality that makes him a perfect example of the new idea of song that emerged in the 1890s.

105. Mauclair, "Un Lied d'Ernest Chausson," in *La Religion de la Musique*, 95–96.

106. Mauclair, "Le Sens du Lied," in *La Religion de La Musique*, 58.

107. "When compared to the opacity of the word *ombre*, the word *ténèbres* does not seem very dark; and how frustrating the perverseness and contradiction which lend dark tones to *jour* and bright tones to *nuit!*" Mallarmé, *Crise de vers* (1895), translated in Austin, ed., *Debussy: Prelude to "The Afternoon of a Faun,"* 118.

108. Graham Johnson takes "les heures" more literally to mean something like a ticking clock, calling the piece, "with its repeated octave As... a masterful musical description... of the lassitude associated with the slow passing of time." Pierre Bernac described the song in almost identical terms: "with its relentless pedal of A," Bernac wrote, "this mélodie attempts to give the impression of the monotony and fatality of the passing hours." See Pierre Bernac, *The Interpretation of French Song*, trans. Winifred Radford (New York: Norton, 1970), 100.

109. A similar downbeat event occurs at the end of the third quatrain, where the syllable "*Don*[-nent]" lands on a B♭ over a thickened piano chord that is itself strident and bell-like. In this case, the attack may remind us even more directly of the onomatopoeic terms for ringing bells in French: din dan *don*.

110. Mauclair, "Un Lied d'Ernest Chausson," in *La Religion de la musique*, 96.

111. Lawrence Kramer describes the rich range of song expression in his chapter on "Song," in *Music and Poetry: The Nineteenth Century and After* (Berkeley: University of California Press, 1984), 125–170. And yet because Kramer's focus is largely German music, the expressive possibilities he outlines usefully evade the one condition I am trying to articulate here. He speaks, on the one hand, of "the gestural continuity of the melodic line... *replacing* the phonetic/syntactic integrity of the text" in Schumann and, on the other, of the declamatory "alienation" of Schoenberg's *Sprechstimme* (131). The late songs of Fauré and Debussy or Chausson, as I show, avoid both of these outcomes by taking a third, more neutral path that lies obliquely between.

Chapter 4

1. Reynaldo Hahn, *Notes* (Paris: Plon, 1933), 4.

2. The complete Hahn recordings have been brought out on compact disc: Romophone 82015–2.

3. "Pourquoi Chante-t-on?" in Reynaldo Hahn, *Du Chant*, 7th ed. (Paris: Gallimard, 1957). The lectures, delivered at Université des annales in 1913 and 1914, were originally published in 1920.

4. Ibid.

5. Reynaldo Hahn, *On Singers and Singing: Lectures and an Essay*, trans. Léopold Simoneau (Portland, OR: Amadeus, 1990).

6. Barthes, "The Grain of the Voice," in *The Responsibility of Forms*, trans. Richard Howard (New York: Hill and Wang, 1985), 270–271.

7. Ibid.

8. Marcel Cohen maintains his idealistic position despite evidence to the contrary. As he puts it: "Malgré l'esprit routinier de beaucoup d'administration et de maints

professeurs de l'enseignement secondaire, malgré le manque de relations réguliere entre l'enseignement primaire et les membres de l'enseignement supérieure adonnés à la recherche, malgré l'ignorance de l'Académie française et de certains journalistes curieux de langue à l'égard de la linguistique, un souffle nouveau a commencé à se faire sentir dans l'enseignement." Cohen, *Histoire d'une langue: le français* (Paris: Editions sociales, 1967), 286.

9. From "Discours de M. René Viviani," 27 February 1914, cited in *Hommage des poètes à Sarah Bernhardt* (Paris: n.p., 1914). Unpaginated presentation edition.

10. Theodore Zeldin, "The National Identity," in *France, 1848–1945* (Oxford: Oxford University Press, 1977), 21.

11. To name just a few of the titles: Louis Becq de Fouquières, *Traité de diction et de lecture à haute voix : le rythme, l'intonation, l'expression* (Paris: Charpentier, 1881); Louis Favre, *Traité de diction à l'usage des écoles, des gens du monde, des étrangers, des professeurs, des avocats, des orateurs, des comédiens, et en general de tous ceux qui disent, déclament, lisent ou parlent en public* (Paris: n.p., 1894); Leon Brémont, *L'art de dire les vers* (Paris: Charpentier, 1903); Jean Blaize, *L'Art de dire: dans la lecture et la recitation, dans la causerie et le discours* (Paris: A. Colin, 1903); Ernest Coquelin *L'art de dire le monologue* (Paris: P. Ollendorff 1884); Alix Lenoël-Zévort, *Grammaire de la diction et du chant* (Paris: Ficker, 1910); Philippe Martinon, *Comment on prononce le français* (Paris: Larousse, 1913); and Maurice Grammont, *Traité pratique de prononciation française* (Paris: Delagrave, 1934).

12. This question seems to have been one of the chief motivations behind James Briscoe's 1999 collection, *Debussy in Performance* (New Haven: Yale University Press, 1999). Brooks Toliver takes up issues relating specifically to vocal performance in his essay, "Thoughts on the History of (Re)interpreting Debussy's Songs," 135–154.

13. "Comment chante-t-on?" in Hahn, *Du chant*, 40. The fascinating analogy was explored from a slightly different perspective by the symbolist poet Gustave Kahn in "De l'esthétique de verre polychrome," *La Vogue* 1, no.2 (18 April 1886): 54–65. Kahn doesn't quite make the link to the as yet unexplored area of free verse, but in his assertion that the Parisian fashion for such arts shows a "tendency toward the joy of color," we sense that he is not too far off.

14. And he knew Venice, too. The story is told of how he once entertained Proust and a throng of bystanders on the canals of Venice, singing in a gondola that was specially fitted out with a piano.

15. This is how Faure introduced himself on the only recording he ever made. According to Will Crutchfiled, Yale University holds this "unique original of his only known recording, a non-commercial cylinder in which the singer jovially announces himself as 'le grand-père des barytons.'" See "Grooves of the Academe," *Opera News* 48 (August 1983): 26–29. Recordings of de Reszké are equally rare. He apparently made the effort on a few occasions but destroyed the masters. The only record we have is a strange "bootleg" made in the rafters of the Met during a live performance in 1901, by the Met librarian, Lionel Mapelson. The Mapleson cylinders were issued as six LPs by the New York Public Library in 1985 and are now out of print.

16. Victor Matushevski, "Jean de Reszké as pedagogue: His ideas, their development, and the results," *Opera Quarterly*, 12, no. 1 (1995): 47–70.

17. He was immortalized by Manet in an 1877 portrait that captured him in the title role of Thomas's Hamlet (1868).

18. Hahn, *Du Chant*, 94.

19. Ibid., 95.

20. Among the other members were Auber, Félicien David, Théophile Gautier, Gevaert, Gounod, Guéroult, and Prince Poniatowski. See Jean-Baptiste Faure, *La Voix et le chant* (Paris: Heugel, 1886), 18.

21. Ibid.

22. He had had a very brief tenure as a professor at the Conservatoire between 1857 and 1860.

23. Faure, *La Voix et le chant*, 19.

24. "The art of song is not, like science, susceptible to endless enrichment by new discoveries. Everything on the subject has already been said, very well said, by [other] men." Ibid., 22.

25. Ibid. Jacques Isnardon tells the story of how, in one performance of *Faust*, Faure's Mephistophélès outsmarted the on-stage Valentin, who was apparently singing at the top of his lungs. Faure answered the zealous lead with a clear *mezza-voce* at every turn, a decision that gave him the upper hand, "redoubling the irony [of the scene] right to its final fermata." *Le Chant théatral* (Paris: Vieu, 1911), 9. That sense of triumph is somewhat flattened in modern accounts that stress Faure's acting ability as if apologizing for his lack of "voice." Hence, Elizabeth Forbes writes in the *New Grove*, "Although he possessed a fine, resonant, even and extensive voice, Faure was chiefly notable for the innate musicality and stylishness of his singing and for his great gifts as an actor." See "Faure, Jean-Baptiste," in *The New Grove Dictionary of Music Online*, ed. L. Macy (http://www.grovemusic.com).

26. Faure, *La Voix et le chant*, 88.

27. Ibid.

28. Faure, *Une Année d'études* (Paris: Heugel, 1890), 29.

29. Barthes, "The Grain of the Voice," 273–274.

30. Faure, *La Voix et le chant*, 97.

31. This was fairly standard advice by 1886, as we have seen. When Sarah Bernhardt dispensed the same dictum in *L'Art du théâtre* (1923), she could not resist wickedly parodying one of her female students who had never lost her *faubourien* accent ("'Oh, Médème,' she said to me one day, 'mon auteur préféré, cé Voltère!'"). See *The Art of the Theatre*, trans. H. J. Stenning (New York: Dial, 1925), 73.

32. Faure, *La Voix et le chant*, 87.

33. It is difficult to know specific details of de Reszké's "method," since he refused to write a treatise. But evidence comes in various testimonials. See Hahn, *Du chant*, 77; Clara Leiser, *Jean de Reszké and the Great Days of Opera* (New York: Minton, Balch, 1934); Dale Gilliand, *The Teaching of Jean de Reszké* (Minneapolis, MN: Pro Musica, 1993); and Victor Matushevski, "Jean de Reszké as pedagogue." Maggie Teyte described some of her experiences with him in her own autobiography, *A Star on the Door* (New York: Arno Press, 1977, originally published 1958).

34. Pierre-Jean Rousselot and Fauste Laclotte, *Précis de prononciation française* (Paris: Welter, 1902), 56.

35. There are interesting exceptions, however, especially among contemporary French singers, such as the ubiquitous François Le Roux, who can be heard using the more common French pronunciation (the *r grasseyé*) in his many recordings of French *mélodies*.

36. The other letter in this category was the *l*. The linguist Maurice Grammont would later complain that Rousselot's *vibrantes* represented a faulty category, preferring to identify the *r* and *l*, with their variable pronunciations, by the more general term *liquides*. But he nevertheless admitted that the term *vibrantes* was acceptable "if one understands the type of phoneme it refers to." *Traité de phonétique* (Paris: Delagrave, 1933), 72.

37. Legouvé, *The Art of Reading*, trans. Edward Roth (Philadelphia: Lippincott, 1879), 56.

38. Ibid., 58.

39. Reynaldo Hahn, *Thèmes varies* (Paris: Janin, 1946), 229.

40. Ibid., 229–230.

41. Charles Panzéra, *L'Art vocal* (Paris: Librairie Théatrale, 1959), 69.

42. Maurice Grammont, *Traité pratique de prononciation française*, eighth edition (Paris: Delagrave, 1934), 5. Originally published in 1914.

43. Ibid.

44. Hahn, *Du chant*, 86.

45. Georges Jean-Aubry, *La Musique française d'aujourd'hui* (Paris: Perrin 1916), 272–273.

46. Poem cited in Christine M. Crow, *Paul Valéry and the Poetry of Voice* (Cambridge: Cambridge University Press, 1982), 36–37. Italics in original.

47. Valéry was certainly not alone in feeling it. Henri de Régnier commented on Mallarmé's "marvelous diction," which had the power to "dispel the obscurities of the text, bringing forth its meaning without taking away any of its mystery." The Belgian Guy Rodenbach recalled the master's "savory voice" and the "luminous and flowering conversation" of the Tuesday salons over which he presided (usually as the sole speaker). He, in fact, suggested that it was not the content of Mallarmé's conversation but the delivery that transfixed the audience, uncovering "secret analogies, doors of communication, hidden contours in things." See Henri de Régnier, "Faces et profils," in Jacques Scherer, *Grammaire de Mallarmé* (Paris: Nizet, 1977), 68. Also Guy Rodenbach, "L'Elite," in Guy Michaud, *Mallarmé*, trans. Marie Collins and Bertha Hunez (New York: New York University Press, 1965), 123. Cited in Frantisek Deak, *Symbolist Theater: The Formation of the Avant-Garde* (Baltimore: Johns Hopkins University Press, 1993), 91.

48. Hahn, *Du Chant*, 69.

49. Legouvé, *The Art of Reading*, 52.

50. She died less than a year later, in March 1886, at the age of only thirty-five. Isnardon comments that "posterity has not been kind with regard to Mme Heilbron [*sic*]: you never hear her name cited any more, yet what a beautiful artist she was!" Isnardon, *Le Chant théatral*, 147.

51. Ibid. Italics in original.

52. Letter of 2 October 1893, in François Lesure, ed., *Debussy Letters*, trans. Roger Nichols (London: Faber and Faber, 1987), 56.

53. Albert Dauzat, *Le Génie de la langue française* (Paris: Payot, 1954), 15.

54. Ibid. Dauzat was by no means the only linguist interested in the properties of this elusive letter. To mention just two prominent examples, in 1929 Rousselot's protégé Hubert Pernot had published a ninety-page analysis of this vowel and its changing functions in poetry and prose, in the course of a serialized exposition of "Les voyelles Parisiennes," *Revue de phonétique* 6, no. 1 (1929): 64–151. And in 1956, just two years

after Dauzat's study, Jeanne Varney Pleasants, a professor at Columbia, published her *Études sur l'e muet* (Paris: Kincksieck, 1956), a dense little tome containing 152 figures, 117 tables, and 36 plates, designed above all to prove the uniqueness of this muted timbre within the French phonetic gamut.

55. Voltaire, Letter to Tovazzi, 24 January 1761. Cited in Léon Brémont, *L'Art de dire les vers, suivi d'une étude et d'une conférence sur l'adaptation musicale* (Paris: Charpentier et Fasquelle, 1903), 149.

56. Robert de Souza, "Le Role de l'e muet dans la poésie française," *Mercure de France* 13, no. 1 (1895): 23.

57. Brémont had advanced his position in a series of essays for *La Revue dramatique et musicale* and in *La Vie théâtrale*. In 1894, they were published separately by *La Revue dramatique* in a volume titled *Le Théatre et la poesie*.

58. See note 55.

59. Ibid., 39.

60. Ibid., 114.

61. This remark appeared in the *edition definitive* of Brémont's volume (Paris: Delamain Boutelleau, 1924), 111.

62. Brémont, *L'Art de dire les vers*, 1903 ed., 2.

63. The appendix to one edition of his treatise included transcripts of some of the experiments he conducted with Georges Lote, one of Rousselot's protégés.

64. Brémont offered as evidence an 1888 review of Brémont's own performance in Jule Amigue's *La Comtesse Frédégonde* by the drama critic Louis Ganderax. In it, Ganderax drew attention to the actor's brilliant declamation of the climactic alexandrine: "*L(e) morceau d(e) v(e)lour qui couvr(e) c(e) front pur.*" According to the critic, the line had caused the audience to gasp in pleasure at the sheer virtuosity of Brémont's articulated *e*'s, whose color and variety filled the line with a subtle and "melodious noise." Ibid., 144–150.

65. Ibid., 154.

66. De Souza, "Le Role de l'e muet dans la poésie française," 19. Emphasis in original.

67. Brémont, *L'Art de dire les vers*, 36. "Dans quels rapports les mots et les sons doivent-ils se présenter pour jouer les uns sur les autres, c'est tout l'art de dire; et comme c'est aussi tout l'art de chanter, nous percevons entre la poésie et la musique des affinités qu'il est plus facile de constater que de définir."

68. Brémont, *L'Art de dire les vers*, 1924 ed., 112.

69. She recorded more famous works in the same year, including the final monologue from Racine's *Phèdre*. That recording can also be heard at the Audiothèque of the BN and on *Le Théâtre parisien de Sarah Bernhardt à Sacha Guitry* EMI CD PM 664 France 1993. The Coppée performance appears on a 1971 compilation LP, *Actors and Actresses* (Rococo 4003), which included performances by the Coquelin brothers, along with Henry Irving and Adolf von Sonnenthal. I am extremely grateful to Janet Bochin, Head of the Music and Media Library at California State University, Fresno, for making a copy of the Bernhardt recording available to me. An excerpt can be heard on the companion Web site for this book ◐.

70. Including foreigners: the *Cours de gramophonie* got its start a few years earlier, in 1905, in a "live" course sponsored by the Alliance française. It is interesting to note that Saint-Génès was not the only one transcribing Bernhardt in 1911. In that same year,

Eugène Landry included a transcription of one of Bernhardt's readings in his *Théorie du rythme et le rythme du française déclamé* (Paris: Honoré Champion, 1911).

71. Marguerite de Saint-Génès, "Cours de gramophonie," *Revue de phonétique* 1, no. 1 (1911): 93–94.

72. She says not: "When they saw, in front of a poor shack, / A fisherman's widow...," but: "When they saw in front [of them], a poor shack, / A fisherman's widow...." Saint-Génès marks the slip in her transcription with a bracketed [oe].

73. Cited in Roger Shattuck, Review of Arthur Gold and Robert Fizdale, *The Divine Sarah: A Life of Sarah Bernhardt, The New Republic* 205, no. 16 (October 14, 1991): 39. It was a fairly standard judgment. Compare Sarcey's comment to the praise uttered by Réné Viviani in February 1914, on the occasion of Bernhardt's attaining the medal of the Legion of Honor: "You have made people love the noble ideas [our] language symbolizes, because by your voice you have made them hear the music hidden in each one of its words." *Hommage des poètes à Sarah Bernhardt* (Paris: n.p., 1914), 6.

74. For an excerpt of this imaginary song, see the companion Web site for this book ◐.

75. Recorded on *Reynaldo Hahn: Composer, Conductor, Singer and Accompanist. Recordings 1908–1935*. Pearl Gem 0003 [74.23].

76. See Brémont, *L'Adaptation musicale* (Paris: H. Lemoine, 1911).

77. Here is how he concludes his chapter on "The Bourgeois Mélodie": "However interesting these experiments may be, they cannot be said to have succeeded in establishing a new type of *mélodie*. Declaimed poetry needs highly colored surroundings, i.e., and orchestra or instrumental ensemble, and lacks warmth when sustained by a lone piano. Furthermore, the transition from song to declamation is always disturbing." Noske, *French Song from Berlioz to Duparc*, trans. Rita Benton (New York: over, 1970), 218.

78. Marcel Proust, *Les Plaisirs et les jours* (Paris: Calmann Lévy, 1896). Lithographic reproduction of Hahn's accompaniments begins on p. 122.

79. The premiere of the *Trois chansons* took place at a concert for the Société nationale de musique on March 17, 1900, at the Salle Pleyel, with Blanche Marot singing, accompanied by the composer. The second, staged performance of twelve *Chansons de Bilitis* took place on February 7, 1901, at the Salle des Fêtes of *Le Journal*, the newspaper that had serialized two of Louÿs's books. David Grayson sorts out all the fascinating details in his "Bilitis and Tanagra: Afternoons with Nude Women," in Jane Fulcher, ed., *Debussy and His World* (Princeton, NJ: Princeton University Press, 2001), 117–140.

80. Our sense of the piece as a mere sketch is helped along by the knowledge that Debussy went on to adapt some of the instrumental parts for his piano duo *Épigraphes antiques*.

81. *Debussy: Chansons de Bilitis*, Deutsche Grammophon 429 738–2, © 1990.

82. Which is essentially what happened, although from the other direction. The CD booklet indicates that the Ensemble Wien-Berlin recorded their parts in Abersee, in the Kirche St. Konrad in August of 1989. Deneuve read the poems seven months later in a studio at Radio France, in Paris.

83. Jules Renard, *Journal 1887–1910* (19 December 1906), ed. Léon Guichard (Paris: Gallimard, 1960), 1096.

84. Letter to Martha Bernays (8 November 1885). Cited in Shattuck, *Candor and Perversion: Literature, Education, and the Arts* (New York: Norton, 2001), 168. Tania and

James Stern render the translation slightly differently in their version of the *Letters*: "After the first words uttered in an intimate, endearing voice, I felt I had known her all my life. I at once believed everything about her." See Ernst L. Freud, ed. *Letters of Sigmund Freud*, trans. Tania and James Stern (New York: Dover, 1992), 180.

85. Roger Shattuck speaks to this very difficulty when he points up the irony that "Bernhardt, in the era of Ibsen and Strindberg and Zola avoided naturalism, and remained loyal to the classic tradition" and then admits that, for this reason, "her recordings can sound impossibly stilted to a contemporary ear." Shattuck, *Candor and Perversion*, 169. The question of whether this semi-sung diction represented an "avoidance" of naturalism is debatable, as should be clear from what has been said so far.

86. These are the final words to Brémont's appendix on *adaptation musicale*: "In several recent works—I will mention only *Pelléas et Mélisande*—some musicians seem to have sought a new *dosage* between the elements of the musical drama, between words and sounds, ideas and sensations. If these attempts are legitimate, one would not be able to refuse artists the right to allow these two muses to sing, as it were, in unison, two muses who were inseparable for the Greeks and for artists of the Renaissance—that is, the two eras when humanity reached highest in its efforts toward beauty!" *L'Art de dire les vers*, 311.

87. Laloy, "Claude Debussy and Debussyism," *S.I.M. Revue musicale* (August–September 1910). Translated in Deborah Priest, *Louis Laloy (1874–1944) on Debussy, Ravel and Stravinsky* (Aldershot: Ashgate, 1999), 85.

88. Laloy, "Le Drame musical moderne: Claude Debussy," in Priest, *Louis Laloy*, 171–174.

89. Romain Rolland, "Pelléas et Mélisande," in *Musiciens d'aujourd'hui*, 7th ed. (Paris: Hachette, 1917), 199. The first edition appeared in 1908, but this essay, Rolland notes, had been published originally in November 1907 in the Berlin review *Morgen*.

90. Ibid. It is striking how closely Rolland's argument follows the gist of Laloy's earlier essay on Pelléas, written for the *Mercure musicale* two years before (see note 87). The resemblance is so close in some places that one can imagine the *Mercure* sitting open in front of Rolland as he wrote.

91. Ibid., 202.

92. Lockspeiser writes: "[Rousseau's] theories had been discussed at the Conservatoire during Debussy's student years, in the courses of Bourgault-Ducoudray." *Debussy, His Life and Mind* (London: Cassell, 1962), 200.

93. David Grayson mentioned this reference to Antoine in his extensive and thorough study of *Pelléas*, although the immediate context of the remark (a chapter on "Revisions of the Vocal Parts") did not permit him to expound on it further. See his *The Genesis of Debussy's* Pelléas et Mélisande. Studies in Musicology, no. 88 (Ann Arbor, MI: UMI Research Press, 1986), 197.

94. See, for example, Jean Chothia, *André Antoine* (Cambridge: Cambridge University Press, 1991) and Michel Kovatchevitch, *La vie, l'oeuvre, l'influence et le prestige de André Antoine, fondateur du Théâtre-libre, dans le monde* (Clermont-Ferrand: Editions Mont-Louis, 1941).

95. André Antoine, *Le Théâtre-libre* (Geneva: Slatkin Reprints, 1979), 85. See also Antoine, *"Mes souvenirs" sur le Théâtre-libre*. (Paris: Arthème Fayard, 1921).

96. Claude Debussy, "Mes raisons de chosir Pelléas," in *Monsieur Croche et autres écrits*, ed. François Lesure (Paris: Gallimard, 1971), 62.

97. It is interesting to note that Vincent d'Indy—who despite his very different musical tastes approved of Pelléas—used a similar distinction to speak of the modern approach to text setting in his *Cours de composition musicale* (Paris: Durand, 1950). He identified what the younger composers were writing as a form of *lied dramatique*.

98. Debussy, *"Pelléas et Mélisande:* A Reply to the Critics," trans. Richard Langham Smith, in François Lesure, ed., *Debussy on Music* (Ithaca, NY: Cornell University Press, 1977), 80.

99. Mary Garden (and Louis Biancolli), *Mary Garden's Story* (London, 1952). Cited in Roger Nichols, *Debussy Remembered* (Portland, OR: Amadeus Press, 1992), 69.

100. Notes to *Mary Garden: The Complete Victor Recordings* (1926–1929), Romophone 81008–2, © 1994. Consider this remark by Camille Mauclair: "In order to interpret Mélisande one needs a slender young woman, without the domineering demeanor of an actress, an excellent musician, but having nothing of the hateful manner of a '*chanteuse.*' Mlle Garden seems to me to embody these qualities." *Revue universelle* (June 1902). Cited in Marcel Dietschy, *A Portrait of Claude Debussy*, trans. William Ashbrook and Margaret C. Cobb (Oxford: Clarendon, 1990), 111, note 4.

101. Laloy, *La Revue musicale* (15 April 1905), 244. Trans. in Priest, *Louis Laloy*, 185.

102. Désiré-Emile Inghelbrecht, "How Not to Perform *Pelléas et Mélisande*," trans. James Briscoe, in Briscoe, ed., *Debussy in Performance*, 163.

103. WLX 265–266; Columbia D 15206. Released on *Claire Croiza, Champion of the Modern French Mélodie*, Marston 52018–2, ©1999. Ward Marston gives March 1927 as the date in the CD booklet. Jean-Michel Nectoux lists it as 6 March 1928 in his catalogue, *Hommage à Claire Croiza* (Paris: Bibliothèque nationale, 1984), 41. The complete performance can be heard on the companion Web site for this book ◐.

104. Richard Langham Smith, "Debussy on Performance: Sound and Unsound Ideals," in Briscoe, ed., *Debussy in Performance*, 18–19.

105. Betty Bannerman, ed. and trans., *The Singer as Interpreter: Claire Croiza's Master Classes* (London: Gollancz, 1989), 51.

106. Croiza addressed this expressive elegance in a general way when she advised performers (as Hahn had done) to "sing . . . with a natural mouth, and a natural face—not with . . . the mouth of a singer deformed by the emission of sound." See Bannerman, *The Singer As Interpreter*, 30.

107. Hélène Abraham, *Un art de l'interprétation* (Paris: Office de centralisation d'ouvrages, 1954),193.

108. Bannerman, *The Singer as Interpreter*, 44. Brémont used the same metaphor in *L'Art de dire les vers*. While admitting that the "charm" of the word lay in the vowels, he noted how much the consonant could supply. Far from being the "cold skeleton" of words, the consonants were, in his words, "the living muscle," giving definition to the "flesh" of the vowel. *L'Art de dire les vers*, 120.

109. Ibid.

110. Isnardon, *Le Chant théâtral*, 155.

111. Ighelbrecht calls attention to the performance of these very letters (which he calls, somewhat tongue-in-cheek, "grammatical liquid dentals") in "How Not to Perform Pelléas," in *Debussy in Performance*, 160–161.

112. Smith, "Debussy on Performance: Sound and Unsound Ideals," 19.

113. Grayson, *The Genesis of Debussy's* Pelléas et Mélisande, 212, points out that in the 1902 vocal score for this phrase, Debussy included *tenuto* marks on the first syllable of <u>pleu</u>-re as well as on et <u>san</u>-<u>glo</u>-te. These disappeared in the 1904 orchestral score, in which he also offered a tiny rhythmic emendation, doubling the length of the original, sixteenth-note triplet approaching *sanglote*. In other words, he seems to have revised the rhythm of this passage to reflect how those values, with the *tenuto* marks, were actually sung in performance. What interests me, of course, is how Croiza, essentially singing the revised rhythm, has nonetheless retained the sense of the *tenuto*'s "pressure" by bending the relevant consonants.

114. The subject, which has memorable origins in Plato's *Cratylus*, was explored in essays and studies by many notable teachers and linguists of the nineteenth and early twentieth century, among them: Stéphane Mallarmé, *Les Mots anglais* (1878), in *Oeuvres complètes*, vol. 2 (Paris: Gallimard, 1998); Louis Favre, *Traité de diction* (Paris: Delagrave, 1894); Otto Jesperson, *Language: Its Nature, Development and Origin* (London: Allen and Unwin, 1922); Maurice Grammont, *Traité de phonétique* (Paris: Delagrave, 1933); see also, Jean-Michel Peterfalvi, *Introduction à la psycholinguistique* (Paris: Presses Universitaires de France, 1974); and Gérard Genette, *Mimologiques: Voyages en Cratylie* (Paris: Seuil, 1976). Finally, Robin Allott offers a detailed survey of the subject in her fine essay "Sound symbolism," in Udo L. Figge, ed., *Language in the Würm Glaciation* (Bochum: Brockmeyer, 1995), 15–38.

115. Grammont, *Traité de phonétique*, 377.

116. Grayson also points out the limitations of viewing Pelléas as "continuous recitative" or as a study in pure declamation, citing the conflicting views of a number of contemporary critics: "Boulez found an even greater range of vocal style in *Pelléas* and charged that, 'by dint of only seeing in *Pelléas* a continuous recitative, in reaction to Wagner's endless melody, its true novelty has been filched.'" *The Genesis of Debussy's* Pelléas et Mélisande, 198.

117. Carolyn Abbate, "Debussy's Phantom Sounds," *Cambridge Opera Journal* 10, no. 1 (Winter 1998): 89.

118. Ibid.

119. Huret, *Enquête sur l'évolution littéraire*, 70.

120. Mauclair, "Le sens du lied," in *La Religion de la musique*, 56.

121. As he wrote to Ernest Chausson in 1894, deep into the composition of *Pelléas*: "I have spent days in pursuit of the 'nothing' she is made of." In François Lesure, ed., *Debussy Letters*, trans. Roger Nichols (Cambridge: Harvard University Press, 1987), 62. For another view on what this symbolic "nothing" might stand for, see my essay "Mélisande's Hair, or the Trouble in Allemonde: A Post-Modern Allegory at the Opéra-Comique," in Mary Ann Smart, ed., *Siren Songs: Representations of Gender and Sexuality in Opera* (Princeton, NJ: Princeton University Press, 2000), 160–185.

122. The structural tones of this "mode" are built on Mélisande's own motive. See Bergeron, "Melisande's Hair," 174.

123. Mary Garden in Arias and Songs OASI 7001 (n.d.). See Margaret G. Cobb, *Discographie de l'oeuvre de Claude Debussy* (Geneva: Minkoff, 1975).

124. Laloy, "Le drame musical moderne IV: Claude Debussy," *Le Mercure musical* (1 Aug. 1905). Cited in Priest, *Louis Laloy*, 173.

125. The part was actually conceived for the very French voice type known as a *Baryton martin*, a kind of hyper-baritone, which added a lustrous top to its rich bottom. This was the voice type ascribed to Jean-Baptiste Faure, to Jean de Reszké (before he made the switch to tenor), Charles Panzéra, and Camille Maurane.

126. The scene is excerpted on *Charles Panzéra: Gabriel Fauré, Henri Duparc* LYS 003/4 (1992).

127. Her weightless, unaccompanied eighth notes actually embodied what French Benedictine theorists of Gregorian chant liked to call "free" rhythm. See my *Decadent Enchantments: The Revival of Gregorian Chant at Solesmes* (Berkeley: University of California Press, 1998), chap. 4.

128. The words, which form the epigraph to the present chapter, come from the end of Sarah Bernhardt's chapter on "Pronunciation" in *The Art of the Theater*, trans. H. J. Stenning (New York: Dial, 1925), 78.

129. Letter to Dufranne; cited in Orledge, *Debussy and the Theatre* (Cambridge: Cambridge University Press, 1982), 67.

Chapter 5

1. Deborah Priest, *Louis Laloy (1874–1944) on Debussy, Ravel and Stravinsky* (Aldershot, UK: Ashgate, 1999), 93.

2. Edward Lockspeiser and Harry Halbreich, *Claude Debussy*, trans. Léo Dilé (Paris: Fayard, 1980), 261.

3. Graham Johnson and Richard Stokes, *A French Song Companion* (New York: Oxford University Press, 2000), 99.

4. Verlaine's *Fêtes galantes* (1869) included twenty-two poems. For his first trio of songs, Debussy chose three equidistantly spaced poems from the collection, reading from back to front: the second-to-last (no. 21), the central (no. 11), and the first (no. 1). He followed the same process for the second set, though starting from the middle of the book and moving forward: nos. 7, 14, and 22. Hence he will close the first set with Verlaine's most innocent poem, *Clair de lune*; the last, with its most jaded, *Colloque sentimental*. This final poem of the book was, in fact, the last of Verlaine's poems he would ever set to music.

5. Debussy finished these songs and dedicated them to Mme Bardac in June 1904, a month before he left his wife.

6. Marcel Dietschy, *A Portrait of Claude Debussy*, trans. William Ashbrook and Margaret Cobb (Oxford: Oxford University Press, 1990), 98.

7. Johnson and Stokes, *A French Song Companion*, 99–100.

8. For a 1929 recording of Jane Bathori singing and playing "Colloque sentimental," see the companion Web site for this book ◐.

9. Susan Youens has read the diminished harmonies in this song as a symbolic manifestation of the passing of Romanticism. See "Debussy's Setting of Verlaine's 'Colloque sentimental': From the Past to the Present," *Studies in Music* 15 (1981): 93–105.

10. I owe this intriguing idea to the six students in my seminar on the music of Debussy, taught at Brown University in the fall of 2005. The idea that this song could be heard as a ghosted *Pelléas*, of course, calls into question a conventional performance practice that treats the first voice as male and the second as female; imagining the genders

the other way around changes the tone of the song considerably. The failed dialogue becomes less about malice than about misunderstanding, or a *malentendu.*

11. There is a hint of such demurral in Debussy's own remarks from 1903, for example, when he dedicated the *Ariettes oubliées* (which contained the song "C'est l'extase") to Mary Garden. Through the flowery salutation, he, too, admitted they were out-of-date: "For Miss Mary Garden, unforgettable Mélisande, this music (already somewhat old-fashioned) in affectionate and grateful homage."

12. Letter of 19 September 1904. In François Lesure, ed., *Debussy Letters*, trans. Roger Nichols (Cambridge: Harvard University Press, 1987), 149.

13. Charles Sowerwine offers a helpful summary in *France since 1870: Culture, Politics and Society* (Houndmills, Basingstoke, UK: Palgrave, 2001), 361–377.

14. Priest, *Louis Laloy (1874–1944)*, 250.

15. "It is as if Ravel himself is speaking to us." Johnson and Stokes, *A French Song Companion*, 404. Emile Vuillermoz was the first to point out the connection between the composer's speech habits and the melodies of *Histoires naturelles*:

> Ravel's friends were interested and amused to find in [these songs] the habitual inflections of the author reproduced with an amazing fidelity. . . . When he delivered himself of one of those perfectly fashioned ideas which were his specialty, he would make a very characteristic gesture: slipping the back of his right hand quickly behind his back, he would do a sort of ironical pirouette, lower his eyelids to conceal the malicious twinkle and end his little speech abruptly with a falling fourth or fifth. (Cited in Roger Nichols, *Ravel* [London: Dent, 1977], 54)

16. Michel Dimitri Calvocoressi, *Musicians Gallery: Music and Ballet in Paris and London* (London: Faber and Faber, 1933), 52.

17. Jane Bathori, "Souvenir," in *La revue musicale*, December (1938): 179–181.

18. Jules Renard, *Journal 1887–1910*, ed. Léon Guichard (Paris: Gallimard, 1960), 1101. Nichols (*Ravel*, 51) writes, expressing his own skepticism about the citation: "Was Renard reporting this conversation accurately? Some critics have doubted it."

19. Peter Kaminsky, "Vocal Music and the Lures of Exoticism and Irony," in *The Cambridge Companion to Ravel*, ed. Deborah Mawer (Cambridge: Cambridge University Press, 2000), 169; and Nichols, *Ravel*, 51.

20. Léon Guichard, *L'Oeuvre et l'âme de Jules Renard* (Paris: Libraire Nizet et Bastard, 1935), 40.

21. Renard, *Journal*, 759–760.

22. Johnson and Stokes, *A French Song Companion*, 404.

23. Nichols, *Ravel*, 49.

24. Released on *Jane Bathori, The Complete Solo Recordings*, Marston 51009 ©2001.

25. Interestingly, this was the only song that spoke to Debussy. In a slightly mean-spirited note to their mutual publisher, Jacques Durand, he described the score as "artificial and chimerical, rather like the house of a wizard!" But he conceded, "'Le Cygne' is very pretty music, even so." Letter of 25 February 1907, Cited in Lesure, *Debussy Letters*, 177.

26. For a 1929 recording of Jane Bathori singing and playing "Le Martin-Pêcheur," see the companion Web site for this book ◐.

27. Review published in *La Revue Pleyel* in February 1926. Cited in Arbie Orenstein, *A Ravel Reader* (New York: Columbia, 1990), 271.

28. Renard, *Journal* (Pléiade ed., 1960), 1101. Emphasis mine.

29. *La Revue musicale* 3 (October 1922): 22–27. Cited in Orenstein, *A Ravel Reader*, 387.

30. Ibid.

31. Philip Nord, *The Republican Moment: Struggle for Democracy in Nineteenth-Century France* (Cambridge: Harvard University Press, 1995), 230–231.

32. Ibid., 187.

33. Cited in T. C. W. Blanning, ed. *Oxford History of Modern Europe* (Oxford: Oxford University Press, 2000), 131.

34. Alexis de Tocqueville, *Democracy in America*, trans. Henry Reeve (New York: Pratt, Woodford, 1848), 232.

35. Legouvé, cited in Nord, *Republican Moment*, 230.

36. Nord, *Republican Moment*, 230–231.

37. See note 29.

38. Or Susan Sontag, who fraternized with Barthes in Paris during this period. I am thinking, for instance, of her 1964 essay "Against Interpretation," which ends with the following manifesto: "What is important now is to recover our senses. We must learn to *see* more, to *hear* more, to *feel* more." *A Susan Sontag Reader* (New York: Vintage, 1983), 104.

39. Jacques Rivière, "Sur les tendances actuelles de la peinture," *Revue d'Europe de d'Amérique* (March 1912): 397. Cited in T. J. Clark, *Farewell to an Idea: Episodes from a History of Modernism* (New Haven: Yale, 1999), 205. Emphasis mine.

40. Ibid.

41. T. J. Clark, who has influenced my thinking enormously on this point, would say that it did not. "Cubism and Collectivity," his remarkable account of the burden of cubist representation, is the fourth episode in his melancholy history of modernism, *Farewell to an Idea: Episodes from a History of Modernism*.

42. Richard Taruskin, "Getting Rid of Glue; Satie, Debussy, Fauré, Ravel, Lili Boulanger," in *The Oxford History of Western Music* (Oxford: Oxford University Press, 2005), 4:59–130.

43. Letter to Mme Alfred Casella, 2 April 1913. Cited in Vladimir Jankélévitch, *Ravel*, trans. Margaret Crosland (London: Calder, 1959).

44. Albert Thibaudet, *La Poésie de Stéphane Mallarmé: Etude littéraire* (Paris: Editions de la Nouvelle Revue Française, 1912).

45. Robert Greer Cohn reports that the vase, or *verrerie éphémère*, "as Mauron surmised . . . is probably a glass light fixture typical of the era." *Towards the Poems of Mallarmé* (Berkeley: University of Californi Press, 1965), 202. The Mauron he refers to is Charles Mauron, *Mallarmé l'obscur* (Paris: Denoël, 1941).

46. Cohn, *Towards the Poems of Mallarmé*, 203.

47. Although it may be perverse to say so, it seems entirely plausible to hear Rivière's cubist critique as a kind of adaptation of Mallarméan poetics. Rivière, a regular contributor to the *N.R.F.*, had proclaimed the modern irrelevance of symbolism in 1913 in "Le Roman aventure," an essay that (he later claimed) prophesied the coming of Proust. Still, his argument for symbolism's insignificance demonstrates an equally keen

awareness of its mechanics, an awareness Rivière seems to transfer onto the problem of understanding the new painting. See "Le Roman aventure," trans. Blache A. Price, in *The Ideal Reader: Selected Essays by Jacques Rivière* (London: Harvill, 1960), 35–81.

48. Johnson and Stokes, *A French Song Companion*, 408.

49. Olin Downes, "Maurice Ravel, Man and Musician," *New York Times* (August 7, 1927). Cited in Orenstein, *A Ravel Reader*, 450.

50. Roland-Manuel, "Lettres de Maurice Ravel," *Revue de musicology* 38 (July 1956), 53. Cited in Orenstein, *A Ravel Reader*, 38.

51. Robert Greer Cohn, "Mallarmé's Wake," in *New Literary History* 26, no. 4 (1995): 885.

52. Letter of 9 June 1913. Cited in Lesure, *Debussy Letters*, 272.

53. Letter of 8 August 1913. Lesure, *Debussy Letters*, 277.

54. Letter of 25 February 1912, to Vittorio Gui. Lesure, *Debussy Letters*, 256.

55. Lockspeiser and Halbreich, *Claude Debussy*, 643.

56. Although Elizabeth Leguin would still find its sighs impenetrable. See her "One Bar in Eight: Debussy and the Death of Description," in *Beyond Structural Listening? Postmodern Modes of Hearing*, ed. Andrew Dell'Antonio (Berkeley: University of California Press, 2004), 233–251.

57. An audio file of this famous recording can be found at http://www2.wheatonma. edu/Academic/AcademicDept/French/ViveVoix/Resources/pontmirabeau.html.🔊

58. In this speech from May 1926 (published in the *Figaro* literary supplement a month later), Valéry explained his belief that "one should start from song, put oneself in the attitude of the singer, tune one's voice to the fullness of musical sound, and from that point descend to the slightly less vibrant state suitable to verse." See Paul Valéry, "On Speaking Poetry," in *The Art of Poetry*, trans. Denise Folliot (Princeton, NJ: Princeton University Press, 1985), 162–163. To test his point, Valéry employed the great singer Claire Croiza and taught her to *dire* Ronsard. See also his encomium to Croiza, "Letter to Madame C.," in *The Art of Poetry*, 167–168.

59. This was a kind of parlor game, in which a group of participants created a poem collectively by writing a word or phrase on a sheet of paper and then folding it, to hide their contribution from the next player. The process gained its name from one such game, which resulted in the following line: *Le cadavre / exquis / boira / le vin / nouveau*, "the exquisite corpse will drink the new wine." In this passage of Debussy's *Eventail*, of course, the sense of a collective is virtual, because the song was, despite the multiple voices suggested by poem and music, actually in the hands of a single composer.

60. Mauclair considered this work the ultimate musical setting of Mallarmé. "*Un grand lied sans paroles*," he called it. See "Le 'lied' français contemporain," *Musica* 7, no. 74 (November 1908): 163–164.

61. Letter of 27 December 1915. Cited in J. Barrie Jones, ed., *Gabriel Fauré: A Life in Letters* (London: Batsford, 1988), 166.

62. Until 1917, that is, when his *Pavane* was used as the music for a new Spanish-tinged ballet by Massine, *Las Méninas*.

63. Robert Orledge, "A Voyage of Discovery into Fauré's Song Cycle *Mirages*," in *Regarding Fauré*, ed. Tom Gordon (Amsterdam: Gordon and Breach, 1999), 335.

64. Fauré had learned of the collection from his friend the journalist Gabriel Hanotaux and finished the four songs during a short month between July and August 1919. Robert Orledge summarizes the gestation in "A Voyage of Discovery," 333–368.

65. Letter of 12 March 1919. Cited in J. Barrie Jones, ed. *Gabriel Fauré: A Life in Letters*, 179.

66. Orledge points out that the premiere at a Société nationale concert on 27 December 1919 "was Fauré's last performance for the Société." Ibid., 366, n. 1.

67. Jean Cocteau, *Le Coq et l'arlequin* (Paris: Éditions de la Sirène, 1918). Brimont's preface was dated June 1918, though the poems were published in the following year.

68. The songs were written in Annecy-le-Vieux, near Vicomte, where Fauré had spent his summers in a villa rented by his friends, the Maillots. "I have before myself a wonderful, vast panorama," he wrote to Madeleine Grey in August, as he worked on the new songs. Letter of 10 August 1919 in Jones, ed., *Gabriel Fauré: A Life in Letters*, 183.

69. Undated letter 1918, in Ibid., 171–172.

Abbate, Carolyn. "Debussy's Phantom Sounds." *Cambridge Opera Journal* 10, no. 1 (Winter 1998).
———. *In Search of Opera*. Princeton, NJ: Princeton University Press, 2003.
Abraham, Hélène. *Un Art de l'interprétation: Claire Croiza*. Paris: Office de centralisation d'ouvrages, 1954.
Acquisto, Joseph. *French Symbolist Poetry and the Idea of Music*. Aldershot, UK: Ashgate, 2006.
Agulhon, Maurice. *La République de Jules Ferry à François Mitterrand: 1880 à nos jours*. Paris: Hachette, 1990.
Allott, Robin. "Sound symbolism." In *Language in the Würm Glaciation*, edited by Udo L. Figge, 15–38. Bochum, Germany: Brockmeyer, 1995.
Anderson, Kirsteen. *Paul Valéry and the Voice of Desire*. Oxford: Legenda, 2000.
André, Auguste. *Traité de prononciation française et de diction: accompagné de lectures en prose et en vers*. Lausanne: Leon Martinet, 1909.
Antoine, André. *"Mes Souvenirs"sur le Théâtre-libre*. Paris: Arthème Fayard, 1921.
———. *Le Théâtre-libre*. Geneva: Slatkin Reprints, 1979.
Arnauld, Michel. "Du vers français." *La Nouvelle Revue française*, 1 January 1910.
Austin, William, ed. *Debussy: Prelude to "The Afternoon of a Faun."* New York: Norton, 1970.
Bannerman, Betty, ed. *The Singer as Interpreter: Claire Croiza's Master Classes*. London: Gollancz, 1989.
Barlow, Michel. *Poésies: Verlaine*. Paris: Hatier, 1982.
Barraqué, Jean. *Debussy*. Paris: Éditions du Seuil, 1962.
Barre, André. *Le Symbolisme: Bibliographie de la poésie symboliste*. New York: Burt Franklin, 1968.
———. *Le Symbolisme: Essai historique sur le mouvement symboliste en France, 1885 à 1900*. New York: Burt Franklin, 1968. Originally published Paris: Jouve, 1911.
Barthes, Roland. *The Responsibility of Forms*. Translated by Richard Howard. New York: Hill and Wang, 1985.

Bathori, Jane. *On the Interpretation of the Mélodies of Claude Debussy.* Translated by Linda Laurent. Stuyvesant, NY: Pendragon, 1998.

———. "Souvenir." *La Revue musicale.* December 1938: 179–181.

———. *Sur L'Interprétation des mélodies de Claude Debussy.* Paris: Les Éditions Ouvrières, 1953.

Beaufils, Marcel. *Musique du son, musique du verbe.* Paris: Presses Universitaires de France, 1954.

Beaumont-James, Colette. *Le Français chanté ou la langue enchantée des chansons.* Paris: L'Harmattan, 1999.

Beauverd, J. *La Petite Musique de Verlaine: Romances sans paroles, Sagesse.* Paris: Societé d'édition d'enseignement supérieur, 1982.

Becq de Fouquières, Louis. *Traité de diction et de lecture à haute voix: le rythme, l'intonation, l'expression.* Paris: Charpentier, 1881.

———. *Traité général de versification française.* Paris: Charpentier, 1873.

Beltrando, Marie Claire. "La Mélodie à la recherche de sa forme et de son style." In *Autour de la mélodie française,* edited by Michelle Biget. Rouen: Université de Rouen, 1987.

Beltrando-Patier, Marie Claire. "Le Lied et la mélodie." In *Histoire de la musique,* 377–400. Paris: Bordas, 1982.

Bergeron, Katherine. *Decadent Enchantments: The Revival of Gregorian Chant at Solesmes.* Berkeley: University of California Press, 1998.

———. "Mélisande's Hair, or the Trouble in Allemonde: A Post-Modern Allegory at the Opéra-Comique." In *Siren Songs: Representations of Gender and Sexuality in Opera,* edited by Mary Ann Smart, 160–185. Princeton, NJ: Princeton University Press, 2000.

———. "A Bugle, a Bell, a Stroke of the Tongue: Rethinking Music in Modern French Verse. *Representations* 86 (Spring 2004): 53–82.

———. "Melody and Monotone: Performing Sincerity in Republican France." In *The Rhetoric of Sincerity,* edited by Ernst van Alphen, Mieke Bal, and Carel Smith, 44–59. Stanford, CA: Stanford University Press, 2009.

Berlitz, M. D. *Traité complet de la prononciation française, d'après les règles suivies à la Comédie-Française et au Conservatoire de Paris.* New York: Berlitz, 1893.

Bernac, Pierre. *The Interpretation of French Song.* Translated by Winifred Radford. New York: Norton, 1970.

Bernhardt, Sarah. *L'Art du théâtre: la voix, le geste, la prononciation.* Paris: Nilson, 1923.

———. *The Art of the Theatre.* Translated by H. J. Stenning. New York: Dial, 1925.

Bernstein, Susan. *Virtuosity of the Nineteenth Century.* Stanford, CA: Stanford University Press, 1998.

Bersani, Leo. *Baudelaire and Freud.* Berkeley: University of California Press, 1977.

Bert, Paul. *Discours parlementaires, 1872–1881.* Paris: G. Charpentier, 1882.

Beyers, Chris. *A History of Free Verse.* Fayetteville: University of Arkansas Press, 2001.

Blaize, Jean. *L'Art de dire: dans la lecture et la récitation, dans la causerie et le discours.* Paris: A. Colin, 1903.

Blanning, T. C. W., ed. *Oxford History of Modern Europe.* Oxford: Oxford University Press, 2000.

Blondel, Jules Edouard. *Phonologie esthétique de la langue française.* Paris: Guillaumin, 1897.

Boucher, Maurice. *Claude Debussy: Essai pour la connaissance du devenir.* Paris: Rieder, 1930.

Bourjéa, Serge. *Paul Valéry: le sujet de l'écriture*. Paris: L'Harmattan, 1997.

Boutan, Pierre. *La Langue des messieurs*. Paris: Armand Collin, 1996.

Brancour, Réné. "Melodie." In *La Grande Encyclopédie*, 23: 612–616. Paris: Société anonyme.

Braun, Marta. *Picturing Time: The Work of Etienne-Jules Marey*. Chicago: University of Chicago Press, 1992.

Bréal, Michel. *Quelques Mots sur l'instruction publique en France*. Paris: Hachette, 1872.

———. *Excursions pédagogiques*. Paris: Hatchette et Cie, 1882.

———. *De L'Enseignement des langues vivantes*. Paris: Hachette, 1900.

———. *Essai de sémantique*. Paris: Hachette, 1911.

Brémont, Léon. *Le Théâtre et la poésie; questions d'interprétation*. Paris: Bibliothèque de la Revue dramatique et musicale, 1894.

———. *Essai de sémantique*. Paris: Hachette, 1911 Brémont, Léon. *Le Théâtre et la poésie; questions d'interprétation*. Paris: Bibliothèque de la Revue dramatique et musicale, 1894.

———. *L'Art de dire les vers, suivi d'une étude et d'une conférence sur l'adaptation musicale*. Paris: Charpentier et Fasquelle, 1903. Edition définitive, Paris: Delamain, Boutelleau, 1924.

———. *L'Adaptation musicale*. Paris: H. Lemoine, 1911

Briscoe, James R. *Claude Debussy: A Guide to Research*. New York: Garland, 1990.

———. *Debussy in Performance*. New Haven: Yale University Press, 1999.

Brown, Rollo. *How the French Boy Learns to Write: A Study in Teaching the Mother Tongue*. Cambridge: Harvard University Press, 1922.

Bruézière, Maurice. *L'Alliance française: Histoire d'une institution*. Paris: Hachette, 1983.

Bruneau, Alfred. *La Vie et les oeuvres de Gabriel Fauré*. Paris: Charpentier, 1925.

Brunot, Ferdinand. "La Langue française de 1815 à nos jours." In *Histoire de la langue et de la littérature française des origines à 1900*, edited by L. Petit de Julleville, 8: 704–810. Paris: Colin, 1899.

———. *L'Enseignement de la langue française*. Paris: A. Colin, 1914.

———. *Méthode de langue française*. Paris: A. Colin, 1908–1924.

Brussel, Robert. "Les 'Lieder' de Fauré." *Musica* 77 (February 1909).

Buisson, Ferdinand. *Rapport sur l'instruction primaire à l'exposition universelle de Philadelphie en 1876*. Paris: Imprimerie nationale, 1878.

———. *Dictionnaire de pédagogie et d'instruction primaire*. Paris: Hachette, 1882.

Caballero, Carlo. *Fauré and French Musical Aesthetics*. Cambridge: Cambridge University Press, 2001.

———. "Fauré's Religion and *La Chanson d'Eve*." In *Regarding Fauré*, edited by Tom Gordon, 297–331. Amsterdam: Gordon and Breach, 1999.

Calvocoressi, Michel Dimitri. *Musicians Gallery*. London: Faber and Faber, 1933.

Cauvet, Alfred. *La prononciation française et la diction, à l'usage des écoles, des gens du monde et des étrangers*. Paris: P. Ollendorff, 1889.

Charle, Christophe. *Naissance des "intellectuels" 1880–1900*. Paris: Minuit, 1990.

———. *La République des universitaires 1879–1940*. Paris: Seuil, 1994.

Chevallier, Pierre. *La Séparation de l'église et de l'école: Jules Ferry et Léon XIII*. Paris: Fayard, 1981.

Chothia, Jean. *André Antoine*. Cambridge: Cambridge University Press, 1991.

Clark, T. J. *Farewell to an Idea: Episodes from a History of Modernism*. New Haven: Yale University Press, 1999.

Claude Debussy: Pelléas et Mélisande. Edited by Roger Nichols and Richard Langham Smith. Cambridge: Cambridge University Press, 1989.

Cobb, Margaret G. *Discographie de l'oeuvre de Claude Debussy*. Geneva: Minkoff, 1975.

———, ed. *The Poetic Debussy*. Translated by Richard Miller. Boston: Northeastern University Press, 1982.

Cocteau, Jean. *Le Coq et l'arlequin*. Paris: Éditions de la Sirène, 1918.

Code, David. "Hearing Debussy Reading Mallarmé: Music *après Wagner* in the *Prélude à l'après-midi d'un Faune*." *Journal of the American Musicological Society* 54, no. 3 (Fall 2001): 493–554.

———. "The Formal Rhythms of Mallarmé's Faun." *Representations* 86 (Spring 2004): 73–119.

Cohen, Marcel. *Histoire d'une langue: le français*. Paris: Editions sociales, 1967.

Cohn, Robert Greer. *Mallarmé's Un coup de dès; an exegesis*. New Haven: Yale French Studies Publication, 1949.

———. *Towards the Poems of Mallarmé*. Berkeley: University of California Press, 1965.

———. "Mallarmé's Wake." *New Literary History* 26, no. 4 (1995).

Combarieu, Christophe. *Le Lied*. Paris: Presses universitaires de France, 1998.

Compagnon, Antoine. *La Troisième République des lettres*. Paris: Seuil, 1983.

Coquelin, Ernest. *L'Art de dire le monologue*. Paris: P. Ollendorff, 1884.

Cornell, W. Kenneth. *The Symbolist Movement*. New Haven: Yale University Press, 1951.

Cotereau, Jean. *Laïcité, sagesse des peuples: anthologie des grandes textes de la laïcité, de Jules Ferry à nos jours*. Paris: Fischbacher, 1965.

Coubertin, Pierre de. *The Evolution of France under the Third Republic*. Translated by Isabel Hapgood. New York: Crowell, 1897.

Cresp, Joseph. *Essai sur la déclamation oratoire et dramatique, la diction et la prononciation, suivi d'une nouvelle méthode curative du bégaiement et de tous les vices de la parole*. Paris: Hachette, 1837.

Crow, Christine M. *Paul Valéry and the Poetry of Voice*. Cambridge: Cambridge University Press, 1982.

Crutchfiled, Will. "Grooves of the Academe." *Opera News* 48 (August 1983): 26–29.

Cuneo-Laurent, Linda. *The Performer as Catalyst: The Role of the Singer Jane Bathori (1877–1970) in the Careers of Debussy, Ravel, "Les Six," and Their Contemporaries in Paris 1904–1926*. Ann Arbor: University Microfilms International, 1982.

Darmesteter, Arsène. *Traité de la formation des mots composés dans la langue française comparée aux autres langues romanes et au latin*. Paris: A. Franck, 1874.

———. *De La Création actuelle de mots nouveaux dans la langue française, et des lois qui la régissent*. Paris: F. Vieweg, 1877.

Dauzat, Albert. *Le Génie de la langue française*. Paris: Payot, 1954.

Deak, Frantisek. *Symbolist Theater: The Formation of the Avant-Garde*. Baltimore: Johns Hopkins University Press, 1993.

Debussy, Claude. "Mes raisons de chosir Pelléas." In *Monsieur Croche et autres écrits*, edited by François Lesure. Paris: Gallimard, 1971.

————. "*Pelléas et Mélisande:* A Reply to the Critics." Translated by Richard Langham Smith. In *Debussy on Music*, edited by François Lesure, 79–82. Ithaca, NY: Cornell University Press, 1977.

Delafosse, Jules. "Les Evolutions du style." *La Nouvelle Revue* 18, no. 100 (May 1896): 42–69.

Derrida, Jacques. *Marges de la philosophie*. Paris: Minuit, 1972.

————. *Margins of Philosophy*. Translated by Alan Bass. Chicago: University of Chicago, 1982.

Dévigne, Roger. *Le Musée de la parole et du geste: les collections, le laboratoire, la phonothèque*. Paris: Musée de la parole, 1935.

DeVoto, Mark. *Debussy and the Veil of Tonality: Essays on His Music*. Hillsdale, NY: Pendragon Press, 2004.

Dictionnaire de l'Académie française, 6th ed. Paris: Didot, 1835.

Dietschy, Marcel. *La Passion de Claude Debussy*. Neuchâtel: A la Baconnière, 1962.

————. *A Portrait of Claude Debussy*. Translated by William Ashbrook and Margaret Cobb. Oxford: Oxford University Press, 1990.

Dorval, P. *L'Art de la prononciation appliquée au chant et manière facile d'augmenter les ressources de la voix par le secours de l'articulation*. Versailles: Chez l'auteur, 1850.

Duchen, Jessica. *Gabriel Fauré*. London: Phaidon, 2000.

Dujardin, Edouard. *Les Premiers Poètes du vers libre*. Paris: Société de Mercure de France, 1922.

Dumesnil, René. *Le Réalisme et le naturalisme*. Paris: De Gigord, 1955.

DuPont-Vernon, H. *Principes de diction*. 2nd ed. Paris: Ollendorff, 1882.

Dupuy, Fernand. *Jules Ferry, réveille-toi: souvenirs et réflexions d'un maître d'école*. Paris: Fayard, 1981.

Elliott, Martha. *Singing in Style: A Guide to Vocal Performance Practices*. New Haven: Yale University Press, 2006.

Elwitt, Sanford. *The Making of the Third Republic: Class and Politics in France 1868–1884*. Baton Rouge: Louisiana State University Press, 1975.

Emmanuel, Maurice, et al. *Pelléas et Mélisande de Claude Debussy: étude historique et critique*. Paris: Mellottée, 1926.

Esnault, Gaston. *Métaphores occidentales; essai sur les valeurs imaginatives concrètes du français parlé en basse-Bretagne comparé avec les patois, parlers techniques et argots français*. Paris: Presses universitaires de France, 1925.

Etiemble. *Le Sonnet des voyelles*. Paris: Gallimard, 1968.

Faure, Gabriel. *Gabriel Fauré*. Paris: Artaud, 1945.

Faure, Jean-Baptiste. *La Voix et le chant*. Paris: Heugel, 1886.

————. *Une Année d'études*. Paris: Heugel, 1890.

Fauré-Frémiet, Philippe. *Gabriel Fauré*. Paris: A. Michel, 1957.

Favre, Louis. *Traité de diction à l'usage des écoles, des gens du monde, des étrangers, des professeurs, des avocats, des orateurs, des comédiens, et en general de tous ceux qui disent, déclament, lisent ou parlent en public*. Paris: n.p., 1894.

————. *La Musique des couleurs et les musiques de l'avenir*. Paris, Schleicher, 1900.

————. *L'Esprit scientifique et la méthode scientifique*. Paris: Schleicher, 1903.

————. *La Réforme générale de l'enseignement*. Paris, A. Costes, 1923.

————. *La Métapsychique et la méthode scientifique*. Paris, 1925.

Fellot, Henri. "Lieder français." *Revue musicale de Lyon* 1, no. 23 (23 March 1904): 265–269.

Flothuis, Marius. "*...exprimer l'inexprimable...*": *essai sur la mélodie française depuis Duparc, en dix-neuf chapitres et huit digressions*. Amsterdam: Rodopi, 1996.

Forbes, Elizabeth. "Faure, Jean-Baptiste." In *The New Grove Dictionary of Music Online*, edited by L. Macy. http://www.grovemusic.com.

Foucambert, Jean. *L'Ecole de Jules Ferry*. Paris: Retz, 1986.

Fourrier, Charles. *L'Enseignement français de 1789 à 1945: précis d'histoire des institutions scolaires*. Paris: Institut Pédagogique National, 1965.

Friedman, Donald Flanell. *An Anthology of Belgian Symbolists Poets*. New York: Garland, 1992.

Freud, Ernst L., ed. *Letters of Sigmund Freud*. Translated by Tania and James Stern. New York: Dover, 1992.

Fulcher, Jane, ed. *French Cultural Politics and Music: From the Dreyfus Affair to the First World War*. Oxford: Oxford University Press, 1999.

———. *Debussy and His World*. Princeton, NJ: Princeton University Press, 2001.

Furet, François. *La Révolution: de Turgot à Jules Ferry: 1770–1880*. Paris: Hachette,1988.

———. ed. *Jules Ferry, fondateur de la république*. Paris: Editions de l'Ecole des hautes études en sciences sociales, 1985.

——— and Jacques Ozouf. *Lire et écrire: l'alphabétisation des français de Calvin à Jules Ferry*. Paris: Minuit, 1977.

———. *Reading and Writing: Literacy in France from Calvin to Jules Ferry*. New York: Cambridge University Press, 1982.

Gaiffe, Félix. "Les Petits Concerts." *Revue française de musique* 10, no. 2 (15 March 1912): 96–100.

Gaillard, Jean-Michel. *Jules Ferry*. Paris: Fayard, 1989.

Garcia, Gustave. *The Actor's Art: A Practical Treatise on Stage Declamation, Public Speaking, and Deportment*. London: Simpkin, Marshall, 1888.

Genette, Gérard. *Mimologiques: Voyage en Cratylie*. Paris: Seuil, 1976.

Gérold, Théodore. "Monodie et Lied." In *Encyclopédie de la musique et dictionnaire du conservatoire*, Part II, vol. 2, *Esthétique*. Edited by Albert Lavignac and Lionel de la Laurencie. Paris: Delagrave, 1930.

Ghil, Réné. *Traité du verbe*. Paris: Alcan Lévy, 1885; revised edition 1887.

———. *Les Dates des oeuvres: symbolisme et poésie scientifique*. Paris: Crès, 1923.

Giedion, Siegfried. *Mechanization Takes Command*. New York: Norton, 1969.

Gifford, Paul, and Stimpson, Brian, eds. *Reading Paul Valéry: Universe in Mind*. Cambridge: Cambridge University Press, 1998.

Gilliand, Dale. *The Teaching of Jean de Reszké*. Minneapolis, MN: Pro Musica, 1993.

Gilliéron, M. J. *Le Patois normand*. Paris: Champion, 1896.

Giolitto, Pierre. *Abécédaire et férule: maîtres et écoliers de Charlemagne à Jules Ferry*. Paris: Editions Imago, 1986.

Givry, Christine, and Raoul Fabrègues, eds. *Les Échos de Mallarmé: du Coup de dès à l'informatique: Mallarmé et la typographie*. Sens: Musées de Sens, 1998.

Goodkin, Richard E. "Zeno's Paradox: Mallarmé, Valéry, and the Symbolist 'Movement'." *Yale French Studies*, no. 74, Phantom Proxies: Symbolism and the Rhetoric of History (1988): 133–156.

Gordon, Tom, ed. *Regarding Fauré*. Amsterdam: Gordon and Breach, 1999.

Goubault, Christian. *Maurice Ravel, le jardin féerique*. Paris: Minerve, 2004.

Gourmont, Rémy de. *Esthétique de la langue française*. Paris: Mercure de France, 1913.

———. *Selected Writings*. Translated and edited by Glenn S. Burne. Ann Arbor: University of Michigan Press, 1966.

Grammont, Maurice. *Phonétique historique et phonétique expérimentale*. Bologna: N. Zanichelli, 1912.

———. *Traité de phonétique*. Paris: Delagrave, 1933.

———. *Traité pratique de prononciation française*. Paris: Delagrave, 1934.

———. *Le Vers français: ses moyens d'expression, son harmonie*. Paris: Delagrave, 1937.

———. *Petit Traité de versification français*. Paris: Armand Colin, 1949.

La Grasserie, Raoul de. *Des Parlers des différentes classes sociales*. Paris: P. Geuthner, 1909.

Grayson, David. *The Genesis of Debussy's* Pelléas et Mélisande. Studies in Musicology no. 88. Ann Arbor: UMI Research Press, 1986.

———. "Bilitis and Tanagra: Afternoons with Nude Women." In *Debussy and His World*, edited by Jane Fulcher, 117–139. Princeton, NJ: Princeton University Press, 2001.

Grévy, Jérôme, *La République des opportunistes, 1870–1885*. Paris: Perrin, 1998.

Guerlin de Guer, Charles. *Le Patois normand: introduction à l'étude des parlers de Normandie*. Caen: E. Lanier, 1896.

Guichard, Léon. *L'Oeuvre et l'âme de Jules Renard*. Paris: Libraire Nizet et Bastard, 1935.

Guizot, M., Jules Ferry, and Félix Pécaut. *Deux ministres pédagogues, M. Guizot et M. Ferry. Lettres adressées aux instituteurs par le ministre de l'instruction publique en 1833 et en 1883*. Paris: C. Delagrave, 1887.

Guyaux, André, and Bertrand Marchal, eds. *Les Fleurs du mal: Colloque du Sorbonne*. Paris: Presses de l'université de Paris, 2003.

Hagège, Claude. *Le Français et les siècles*. Paris: Odile Jacob, 1987.

Hahn, Reynaldo. *Du Chant*. Paris: Libraire Hachette, 1920.

———. Sarah Bernhardt. Translated by Ethel Thompson. London, 1932.

———. *Journal d'un musicien*. Paris: Plon, 1933.

———. *Notes*. Paris: Plon, 1933.

———. *L'Oreille au guet*. Paris: Gallimard, 1937.

———. *Thèmes variés*. Paris: Janin, 1946.

———. *On Singers and Singing*. Translated by Léopold Simoneau. Portland, OR: Amadeus, 1990.

Helmholtz, Hermann. *Die Lehre von den Tonempfindungen*. Braunschweig: F. Vieweg, 1863.

———. *On the Sensations of Tone as a Physiological Basis for the Theory of Music*. Translated by Alexander Ellis. London: Longmans, Green, 1875.

Hommage à Claire Croiza. Paris: Bibliothèque nationale, 1984.

Hommage des poètes à Sarah Bernhardt. Paris: n.p., 1914.

Honegger, Arthur. *Six Poésies de Jean Cocteau*. Paris: Éditions Maurice Senart, 1924.

Huebner, Steven. *The Operas of Charles Gounod*. Oxford: Oxford University Press, 1990.

———. *French Opera at the Fin de Siècle: Wagnerism, Nationalism, and Style*. Oxford: Oxford University Press, 1999.

———. "Laughter: In Ravel's Time." *Cambridge Opera Journal* 18, no. 3 (2006): 225–246.

Humbert, Gilbert. *Opéra, opéra comique, opérette, mélodie, romance et diction sur les disques à saphir Pathé (1911 à 1918)*. Fuveau, France: G. Humbert, 1998.

Huret, Jules. *Enquête sur l'évolution littéraire*. Paris: Charpentier, 1891.

Huvelin, Paul. "Symbolistes et impressionnistes." In *Pour la musique française: douze causeries*, 299–328. Paris: Georges Crès, 1917.

D'Indy, Vincent. *Cours de composition musicale*. Paris: Durand, 1950.

Isnardon, Jacques. *Le Théâtre de la Monnaie depuis sa fondation jusqu'à nos jours*. Bruxelles: Schott, 1890.

———. *Le Chant théatral*. Paris: Vieu, 1911.

———. *La Déclamation lyrique et la mise en scène de l'école au théâtre*. Paris: La Maison des arts, 1922.

Israel, Alexandre. *L'Ecole de la république: la grande oeuvre de Jules Ferry*. Paris: Hachette, 1931.

Ivry, Benjamin. *Maurice Ravel: A Life*. New York: Welcome Rain Publishers, 2000.

Jankélévitch, Vladimir. *Gabriel Fauré: ses mélodies, son esthétique*. Paris: Plon, 1938.

———. *Ravel*. Translated by Margaret Crosland. London: Calder, 1959.

———. *La Vie et la mort dans la musique de Debussy*. Neuchâtel: Baconnière, 1968.

———. *La Musique et l'ineffable*. Paris: Editions de Seuil, 1983.

Jarocinski, Stefan. *Debussy: Impressionism and Symbolism*. Translated by Rollo Myers. London: Eulenberg Books, 1976.

Jean-Aubry, Georges. *La Musique française d'aujourd'hui*. Paris: Perrin, 1916.

———. *French Music of To-Day*. Translated by Edwin Evans. London: Kegan Paul, Trench, Trubner, 1919.

Jesperson, Otto. *Language: Its Nature, Development and Origin*. London: Allen and Unwin, 1922.

Johnson, Graham, and Richard Stokes. *A French Song Companion*. New York: Oxford University Press, 2000.

Jones, Dora Duty. *Lyric Diction for Singers, Actors and Public Speakers*. New York; London: Harper & Brothers, 1913.

Jones, J. Barrie, ed. *Gabriel Fauré: A Life in Letters*. London: Batsford, 1988.

Jones, P. Mansell. *The Background of Modern French Poetry*. Cambridge: Cambridge University Press, 1951.

Kahn, Gustave. "De l'esthétique de verre polychrome." *La Vogue* (18 April 1886): 54–65.

———. *Premiers Poèmes, avec une préface sur le vers libre*. Paris: Société du Mercure de France, 1897.

Kale, Steven. *Legitimism and the Reconstruction of French Society 1852–1883*. Baton Rouge: Louisiana State University Press, 1992.

Kaminsky, Peter. "Vocal music and the lures of exoticism and irony." In *The Cambridge Companion to Ravel*, edited by Deborah Mawer, 162–187. Cambridge: Cambridge University Press, 2000.

Koechlin, Charles. "La Mélodie," In *Cinquante ans de musique française, de 1874 à 1925*, edited by Ladislav Rohozinski, 2: 1–62. Paris: Librarie de France, 1925.

———. "Tendances de la musique française moderne." In *Encyclopédie de la musique et Dictionnaire du conservatoire*, edited by Albert Lavignac and Lionel de la Laurencie, 56–145. Paris: Delagrave, 1925.

———. *Gabriel Fauré*. London: D. Dobson, 1945.

Koschwitz, Eduard. *Zur Aussprache des Französischen in Genf und Frankreich*. Berlin: Wilhelm Gronan, 1892.

————. *Les Parlers parisiens: anthologie phonétique*. Paris: H. Welter, 1893; rev. 1896.

————. *Les Plus Anciens Monuments de la langue française, publiés pour les cours universitaires*. Leipzig: O. R. Reisland, 1902.

Kovatchevitch, Michel. *La Vie, l'oeuvre, l'influence et le prestige de André Antoine, fondateur du Theatre-libre, dans le monde*. Clermont-Ferrand: Editions Mont-Louis, 1941.

Kramer, Lawrence. *Music and Poetry: The Nineteenth Century and After*. Berkeley: University of California Press, 1984.

Kravis, Judy. *The Prose of Mallarmé*. Cambridge: Cambridge University Press, 1976.

Laloy, Louis. "Cinq poèmes de Baudelaire." *La Revue musicale* (October 1902): 404–408.

————. "Le drame musicale moderne IV: Claude Debussy." *Le Mercure musical* (1 August 1905): 233–250.

————. "Claude Debussy and Debussysme." *S.I.M. Revue musicale*, August–September 1910.

Landry, Eugène. *La Théorie du rythme et le rythme du français déclamé*. Paris: H. Champion, 1911.

Langlois-Freville, Felix Constant Eugène. *Nouveau Traité de récitation et de prononciation*. Paris: Tresse, 1883.

Lavisse, Ernest. *Questions d'enseignement national*. Paris: Armand Colin, 1885.

————. *Etudes et étudiants*. Paris: Armand Colin, 1890.

Lawler, James R. *The Language of French Symbolism*. Princeton, NJ: Princeton University Press, 1969.

————. *Rimbaud's Theater of the Self*. Cambridge: Harvard University Press, 1992.

Legouvé, Ernest. *L'Art de la lecture*. Paris: Hetzel, 1877; rev. ed., 1897.

————. *Petit Traité de lecture à haute voix, à l'usage des écoles primaries*. Paris: Hetzel, 1878.

————. *The Art of Reading*. Translated by Edward Roth. Philadelphia: Lippincott, 1879.

————. *La Lecture en action*. Paris: Hetzel, 1881.

————. *Soixante Ans de souvenirs*. Paris: J. Hetzel, 1886–1887.

————. "Lecture à haute voix." In *Dictionnaire de pédagogie*, Ser. I, edited by Ferdinand Buisson, 2: 1551–1553. Paris: Hachette, 1887.

Leguin, Elizabeth. "One Bar in Eight: Debussy and the Death of Description." In *Beyond Structural Listening? Postmodern Modes of Hearing*, edited by Andrew Dell'Antonio, 233–251. Berkeley: University of California Press, 2004.

Lehmann, A. G. *The Symbolist Aesthetic in France, 1885–1895*. Oxford: Blackwell, 1968.

Leiris, Michel. *Biffures. La règle du jeu*, vol. 1. Paris: Gallimard, 1948.

————. "Alphabet." In *Biffures*, 40–76. Paris: Gallimard, 1975.

Leiser, Clara. *Jean de Reszké and the Great Days of Opera*. New York: Minton, Balch, 1934.

Lenoël-Zévort, Alix. *Grammaire de la diction et du chant*. Paris: Ficker, 1910.

Léon, Monique, and Pierre Léon. *La Prononciation du français*. Paris: Armand Colin, 2007.

Lesaint, M. A. *Traité complet de la prononciation française dans la seconde moitié du XIXe siècle*. Hambourg: W. Mauke, 1871.

De Lestang, Paule. "Les Chansons de Bilitis." *Revue musicale de Lyon* 4, no. 1 (October 1906): 235–239.

Lesure, François. *Debussy Letters*. Translated by Roger Nichols. Cambridge: Harvard University Press, 1987.

————. *Claude Debussy: biographie critique*. Paris: Fayard, 2003.

————, ed. *Lettres, 1884–1918/ Claude Debussy*. Paris: Hermann, 1980.

Liet, Albert. *Traité de prononciation française: théorie et pratique*. Paris: Boyveau et Chevillet, 1900.

Lockspeiser, Edward. *Debussy*. London: J. M. Dent; New York: E. P. Dutton, 1936.

———. *Debussy, His Life and Mind*. London: Cassell, 1962.

Lockspeiser, Edward, and Harry Halbreich. *Claude Debussy*. Translated by Léo Dilé. Paris: Fayard, 1980.

Lote, Georges. *Etudes sur le vers français: l'alexandrin d'après la phonétique expérimental*. Paris: Editions de La Phalange, 1911.

Louÿs, Pierre. *Les Chansons de Bilitis*. Edited by Jean-Paul Goujon. Paris: Gallimard, 1990.

Lloyd, Rosemary. "Debussy, Mallarmé and 'Les Mardis,'" in *Debussy and His World*, edited by Jane Fulcher, 255–270. Princeton, NJ: Princeton University Press, 2001.

Mallarmé, Stéphane. "Observation relative au poème *Un Coup de dès jamais n'abolira le Hasard*." *Cosmopolis* 4 (May 1897).

———. *Oeuvres complètes*. Paris: Bibliothèque de la Pléiade, 1945.

———. *Oeuvres complètes*. Paris: Gallimard, 1998.

Marage, René. *Contribution à l'étude des voyelles par la photographie des flammes manométriques*. Paris: Masson, 1898.

———. *Petit Manuel de physiologie de la voix, à l'usage des chanteurs et des orateurs*. Tours: n.p., 1911.

———. *Théorie de la formation des voyelles*. Tours: n.p., 1911.

Marchal, Bertrand. *Lecture de Mallarmé*. Paris: J. Corti, 1985.

———. *Lire le symbolisme*. Paris: Dunod, 1993.

Marey, Etienne-Jules. *La Méthode graphique dans les sciences expérimentales et principalement en physiologie et en médecine*. Paris: G. Masson, 1878.

Marichelle, H. *Phonétique expérimentale: la parole d'après le trace du phonographe*. Paris: Ch. Delagrave, 1897.

Martinon, Philippe. *Comment on prononce le français*. Paris: Larousse, 1913.

———. *Comment on parle en français*. Paris: Larousse, 1913.

Matushevski, Victor. "Jean de Reszké as Pedagogue: His Ideas, Their Development, and the Results." *Opera Quarterly* 12, no. 1 (1995): 47–70.

Mauclair, Camille. "Le 'Lied' français contemporain." *Musica* 7, no. 74 (November 1908): 163–164.

———. *La Religion de la musique*. Paris: Fischbacher, 1938.

Mauron, Charles. *Mallarmé l'obscur*. Paris: Denoël, 1941.

Maury, Liliane. *Les Origines de l'école laïque en France*. Paris: Presses universitaires de France, 1996.

Mawer, Deborah, ed. *The Cambridge Companion to Ravel*. Cambridge; New York: Cambridge University Press, 2000.

Mayeur, Françoise. *Histoire générale de l'enseignement et de l'éducation en France*, Vol. 3: "De la Révolution è l'école républicaine." Paris: Nouvelle Librairie de France, 1981.

McCombie, Elizabeth. *Mallarmé and Debussy: Unheard Music, Unseen Text*. Oxford: Clarendon Press; New York: Oxford University Press, 2003.

Meister, Barbara. *Nineteenth-Century French Song*. Bloomington: Indiana University Press, 1980.

"Mélodie," in *La Grande Encyclopédie*, 23: 613. Paris: Société Anonyme de la G.E., 1885–1902.

Meltzer, Françoise. "Color as Cognition in Symbolist Verse." *Critical Inquiry* 115, no. 2 (Winter 1978): 253–273.

Meschonnic, Henri. *De La Langue française: Essai sur une clarté obscure*. Paris: Hachette Littératures, 1997.

Meunier, Jean Marie. *Applications de la phonétique expérimentale à l'étude des langues vivantes et à la thérapeutique, c'est à dire à la correction des vices du langage et à la rééducation des sourds*. Coïmbra: Imprensa da universidade, 1927.

Michaelis, Hermann, and Paul Passy, *Dictionnaire phonétique de la langue française*. Hanover: Carl Meyer, 1897; rev. ed. 1914.

Michaud, Guy. *Mallarmé*. Translated by Marie Collins and Bertha Hunez. New York: New York University Press, 1965.

———. *Le Symbolisme tel qu'en lui-même*. Paris: Nizet, 1994.

Millet, Adrien. *Phonétique expérimentale*. Paris: H. Didier, 1925.

———. *L'Oreille et les sons du langage d'après l'Abbé Rousselot*. Paris: Librairie philosophique, 1926.

———. *L'Articulation des voyelles: Etudes expérimentales des conditions physiques et physiologiques de la résonance vocalique*. Paris: Vrin, 1937.

Mockel, Albert. "Charles Van Lerberghe." *Mercure de France* 4, no. 50 (April–June 1904): 32–33.

Moréas, Jean. "Un Manifeste littéraire: Le Symbolisme." *Le Figaro*, 18 September 1886.

Morin, Laurent Joseph. *Traité de prononciation*. Paris: Tresse, 1873.

Mott, F. W. *The Brain and the Voice in Speech and Song*. London: Harper, 1910.

Nadeau, Jean-Benoît, with Julie Barlow. *The Story of French*. New York: St. Martin's, 2006.

Nattiez, Jean-Jacques. *Wagner Androgyne: A Study in Interpretation*. Translated by Stewart Spencer. Princeton, NJ: Princeton University Press, 1993.

Nectoux, Jean-Michel. *Hommage à Claire Croiza*. Paris: Bibliothèque nationale, 1984.

———. *Gabriel Fauré: A Musical Life*. Translated by Roger Nichols. Cambridge: Cambridge University Press, 1991.

———, ed. *Gabriel Fauré: His Life through His Letters*. Translated by J. A. Underwood. London; New York: M. Boyars, 1984.

Niceforo, Alfredo. *Le Génie de l'argot: essai sur les languages spéciaux, les argots et les parlers magiques*. Paris: n.p., 1912.

Nichols, Roger. *Ravel*. London: Dent, 1977.

———. *Ravel Remembered*. New York: Norton, 1987.

———. *Debussy Remembered*. Portland, OR: Amadeus Press, 1992.

———. *The Life of Debussy*. Cambridge; New York: Cambridge University Press, 1998.

———. "The Prosaic Debussy." In *Cambridge Companion to Debussy*, edited by Simon Trezise, 84–100. Cambridge: Cambridge University Press, 2003.

Nora, Pierre, ed. *Les Lieux de Mémoire*, Quarto edition, vol. 1. Paris: Gallimard, 1997.

Nord, Philip. *The Republican Moment: Struggle for Democracy in Nineteenth-Century France*. Cambridge: Harvard University Press, 1995.

Noske, Frits. *La Mélodie française de Berlioz à Duparc: essai de critique historique*. Paris: Presses Universitaires de France, 1954.

Noske, Frits. *French Song from Berlioz to Duparc*. Translated by Rita Benton. New York: Dover, 1970.

Orenstein, Arbie. *A Ravel Reader*. New York: Columbia, 1990.

Orledge, Robert. *Gabriel Fauré*. London: Eulenberg Books, 1979.

———. *Debussy and the Theatre*. Cambridge: Cambridge University Press, 1982.

———. *Charles Koechlin (1867–1950): His Life and Works*. London: Harwood Academic, 1989.

Panzéra, Charles. *L'Art vocal*. Paris: Librairie Théâtrale, 1959.

———. *Cinquante Mélodies françaises: leçons de style et d'interprétation*. Paris: Schott, 1964.

Paris, Gaston. *Le Haut Enseignement historique et philologique en France*. Paris: H. Welter, 1894.

Parks, Richard S. *The Music of Claude Debussy*. New Haven: Yale University Press, 1989.

Pasler, Jann. *Writing through Music: Essays on Music, Culture, and Politics*. New York: Oxford University Press, 2008.

Passy, Paul. *Le Français parlé*. Heilbronn: Henninger, 1886.

———. *Etude sur les changements phonétiques et leurs caractères généraux*. Paris: Firmin-Didot, 1890.

———. *L'Ecriture phonétique*. Paris: Librarie Populaire, 1896.

———. *Les Sons du français*. Paris: Firmin-Didot, 1899; rev. ed. 1917.

———. *Premier Livre de lecture, méthode phonétique*. Paris: Firmin-Didot, 1896.

Pernot, Hubert. "L'Institut de phonétique de Paris." *Revue de phonétique* 5, no. 1 (1928).

———. *L'E muet*. Paris: H. Didier, 1929.

———. "Les Voyelles Parisiennes." *Revue de phonétique* 6, no. 1 (1929): 64–151.

———. *L'Intonation française*. Paris: H. Didier, 1930.

Pernot, Nicolette. *Recueil de textes phonétiques en transcription internationale*. Paris: H. Didier, 1929.

Peterfalvi, Jean-Michel. *Introduction à la psycholinguistique*. Paris: Presses Universitaires de France, 1970.

Petit de Julleville, L. *Histoire de la langue et de la littérature française des origines à 1900*. Vol. 8, *Dix-neuvième siècle, période contemporaine 1850–1900*. Paris: Colin, 1899.

Phillips, Edward R. *Gabriel Fauré: A Guide to Research*. New York: Garland, 2000.

Pierrot, Jean. *The Decadent Imagination*. Translated by Derek Coltman. Chicago: University of Chicago Press, 1981.

Pleasants, Jeanne Varney. *Études sur l'e muet*. Paris: Kincksieck, 1956.

Portebois, Yannick. *Les Saisons de la langue: les écrivains et la réforme de l'orthographe de l'exposition universelle de 1889 à la première guerre mondiale*. Paris: Honoré Champion, 1998.

Porter, Laurence. *The Crisis of French Symbolism*. Ithaca, NY: Cornell University Press, 1990.

Poujol, Geneviève. *L'Education populaire: histoires et pouvoirs*. Paris: Editions ouvrières, 1981.

Pour la musique française. Paris: Georges Crès, 1917.

Power, Thomas Francis. *Jules Ferry and the Renaissance of French Imperialism*. New York: King's Crown Press, 1944.

Priest, Deborah. *Louis Laloy (1874–1944) on Debussy, Ravel and Stravinsky*. Aldershot, UK: Ashgate, 1999.

Prod'homme, J. G. "Schubert's Works in France." *Musical Quarterly* 14, no. 4 (October 1928): 497–498.

Proust, Marcel. *Les Plaisirs et les jours.* Paris: Calmann Lévy, 1896.

Rambaud, Alfred. *Jules Ferry.* Paris: Plon-Nourrit, 1903.

Renard, Jules. *Journal 1887–1910.* Edited by Léon Guichard. Paris: Gallimard, 1960.

Revue de phonétique. Paris: Rousselot et Hubert Pernot, 1911–1930.

Rey, Alain. *L'Amour du français.* Paris: Editions Denoël, 2007.

Rimbaud, Arthur. *Oeuvres.* Suzanne Bernard and A. Guyaux, eds. Paris: Garnier, 1987.

———. "Alchimie du verbe." In *Une Saison en enfer*, 29–36. Paris: Arléa, 1997.

Rivarol, Antoine. *Discours sur l'universalité de la langue française.* Paris: Librairie Delagrave, 1929.

Rivière, Jacques. "Le Roman aventure." Translated by Blache A. Price. In *The Ideal Reader: Selected Essays by Jacques Rivière*, 35–81. London: Harvill, 1960.

Robb, Graham. *Rimbaud.* New York: Norton, 2000.

Rochelle, Ernest. *La Méthode directe dans l'enseignement des langues vivantes.* Bordeaux: G. Delmas, 1916.

Rohozinski, Ladislas, ed. *Cinquante ans de musique française de 1874 à 1925.* Paris: Librairie de France, 1925.

Roland-Manuel. *Maurice Ravel.* Translated by Cynthia Jolly. London: D. Dobson, 1947.

Rolland, Romain. *Musiciens d'aujourd'hui.* Paris: Hachette, 1912.

Ronsard et la musique. Special issue of *La Revue musicale.* Paris: Nouvelle Revue française, 1925.

Rostand, Claude. *L'Oeuvre de Fauré.* Paris: J. B. Janin, 1945.

Rousseau, Jean-Jacques. "Essay on the Origin of Languages." Translated by Victor Gourevitch. In Jean-Jacques Rousseau, *The First and Second Discourses and Essay on the Origin of Languages*, 239–295. New York: Harper and Row, 1986.

Rousselot, Pierre Jean. *Les Modifications phonétiques du language, étudiées dans le patois d'une famille de Cellefrouin (Charente).* Paris: H. Welter, 1891.

———. *Les Articulations parisiennes étudiées à l'aide du palais artificial.* Paris: H. Welter, 1899.

———. *Historique des applications pratiques de la phonétique expérimentale.* Paris: La Parole, 1899.

———. *Mélanges de phonétique expérimentale.* N.p., ca. 1900.

———. *Principes de phonétique expérimentale.* Paris: H. Welter, 1902.

———. "Phonétique expérimentale ou 'Instrumentalphonetik.'" *Revue de phonétique* 1, no. 1 (1911).

Rousselot, Pierre-Jean, and Fauste Laclotte. *Précis de prononciation française.* Paris: Welter, 1902.

———. *Premiers Eléments de prononciation française.* Paris: H. Welter, 1903.

———. "La Prononciation française." *La Revue phonétique* 1, no. 1 (1911).

Rousselot, Pierre-Jean, and Hubert Octave Pernot. *Revue de phonétique.* Paris: Rousselot et Hubert Pernot, 1911–1930.

Roy, Constant. *Le Livre de propagande de l'alliance française.* Paris: Armand Colin, 1894.

De Saint-Génès, Marguerite. "Cours de gramophonie." *Revue de phonétique* 1, no. 1 (1911).

Sartre, Jean-Paul. *Les Mots.* Paris: Gallimard, 1964.

Sartre, Jean-Paul. *The Words*. Translated by Bernard Frechtman. New York: George Braziller, 1964.

Saussure, Ferdinand de. *Recueil des publications scientifiques de Ferdinand de Saussure*. Geneva: Slatkine Reprints, 1984.

———. *Cours de linguistique générale*. Edited by Charles Bailly and Albert Séchehaye. Paris: Payot, 1995.

Scherer, Jacques. *Grammaire de Mallarmé*. Paris: Nizet, 1977.

Schuerewegen, Franc. *A distance de voix: essai sur les "machines à parler."* Villeneuve d'Ascq: Presses Universitaires de Lille, 1994.

Schwab, Catharine Mary. *The Mélodie Française Moderne: An Expression of Music, Poetry, and Prosody in Fin-de-siècle France and Its Performance in Recitals of Jane Bathori (1877–1970) and Claire Croiza (1882–1946)*. Thesis (PhD): University of Michigan, 1991.

Schwob, Marcel. *Études sur l'argot français*. Paris: Emile Bouillon, 1889.

Scott, Clive. *Vers Libre: The Emergence of Free Verse in France, 1886–1914*. Oxford: Oxford University Press, 1990.

Scripture, E. W. *The Study of Speech Curves*. Washington, DC: Carnegie, 1906.

Servières, Georges. "Lieder français: Claude Debussy." *Le Guide musical* 15, no. 22 (September 1895).

Shattuck, Roger. *The Banquet Years: The Arts in France, 1885 to 1918*. New York: Harcourt, Brace, 1958.

———. Review of Arthur Gold and Robert Fizdale, *The Divine Sarah: A Life of Sarah Bernhardt*. *New Republic* 205, no. 16 (14 October 1991): 34–38.

———. *Candor and Perversion: Literature, Education, and the Arts*. New York: Norton, 2001.

Shaw, Bernard. *Bernard Shaw and Mrs. Patrick Campbell*. New York: Knopf, 1952.

Smith, Richard Candida. *Mallarmé's Children: Symbolism and the Renewal of Experience*. Berkeley: University of California Press, 1999.

Smith, Richard Langham. *Debussy Studies*. Cambridge; New York: Cambridge University Press, 1997.

———. "Debussy on Performance: Sound and Unsound Ideals." In *Debussy in Performance*, edited by James Briscoe, 3-27. New Haven: Yale University Press, 1999.

Sontag, Susan. "Against Interpretation." In *A Susan Sontag Reader*. New York: Vintage, 1983.

Souza, Robert de. *Histoire de la chanson populaire en France*. Paris: E. Plon, Nourrit, 1889.

———. *Questions de métrique. Le rythme poétique*. Paris: Perrin et Cie, 1892.

———. *Rythme poétique*. Paris: Perrin, 1892.

———. "Le Role de l'e muet dans la poésie française." *Mercure de France* 13, no. 1, 1895.

———. *La Poésie populaire et le lyrisme sentimental*. Paris: Société de Mercure de France, 1899.

———. *Où nous en sommes : la victoire du silence*. Paris: Librairie H. Floury, 1906.

———. *Du Rythme en français*. Paris: Librairie Universitaire, 1912.

———. *Terpsichore*. Paris: Crès, 1920.

———. *Défense de la poésie vivante*. Paris: G. Cres, 1923.

Souza, Robert de, and Maurice Bouchor. *Les types mélodiques dans la chanson populaire française*. Paris: Sagot, 1894.

———. *Chants populaires pour les écoles*. Paris: Librairie Hachette, 1895.

————. *Sur le Jeu de Robin et Marion d'Adam de la Halle (XIIIe siècle)*. Paris: Fischbacher, 1897

Sowerwine, Charles. *France since 1870: Culture, Politics and Society*. Houndmills, UK: Palgrave, 2001.

Spire, André. *Plaisir poétique et plaisir musculaire: Essai sur l'évolution des techniques poétiques*. New York: S. F.Vanni, 1949.

Starobinski, Jean. *Words upon Words: The Anagrams of Ferdinand de Saussure*. Translated by Olivia Emmet. New Haven: Yale University Press, 1979.

Stimpson, Brian. *Paul Valéry and Music: A Study of the Techniques of Composition in Valéry's Poetry*. Cambridge: Cambridge University Press, 1984.

Stricker, Rémy. *La Mélodie et le lied*. Paris: Presses universitaires de France, 1975.

Sweet, Henry. "Phonetics." In *The Encyclopædia Britannica*, 11th ed., 11:466. New York: Encyclopædia Britannica, 1910–1911.

Talbert, Ferdinand. *De la prononciation en France au 16e siècle*. Paris: Thorin, 1887.

Talbott, John E. *The Politics of Educational Reform in France, 1918–1940*. Princeton, NJ: Princeton University Press, 1969.

Tarneaud, Jean. *Traité pratique de phonologie et de phoniatrie*. Paris: Librairie Maloine, 1941.

Taruskin, Richard. *The Oxford History of Western Music*. Oxford: Oxford University Press, 2005.

Tetel, Marcel, ed. *Symbolism and Modern Literature: Studies in Honor of Wallace Fowlie*. Durham, NC: Duke University Press, 1978.

Teyte, Maggie. *A Star on the Door*. New York: Arno Press, 1977.

Thibaudet, Albert. *La Poésie de Stéphane Mallarmé: Etude littéraire*. Paris: Editions de la Nouvelle Revue Française, 1912.

Thurot, Charles. *De La Prononciation française depuis le commencement du XVIe siècle: d'après les témoinages des grammairiens*. Paris: Impr. Nationale, 1881–1883.

Tiersot, Julien. de Tocqueville, Alexis. *Democracy in America*. Translated by Henry Reeve. New York: Pratt, Woodford, 1848.

Toliver, Brooks. "Thoughts on the History of (Re)interpreting Debussy's Songs." In *Debussy in Performance*, edited by James Briscoe, 135–154. New Haven: Yale University Press, 1999.

Tunley, David. "Mélodie." In *The New Grove Dictionary of Music and Musicians*, 16:356–360. London: Macmillan, 2000.

Valéry, Paul. *De La Diction des vers*. Paris: Emile Chamontin, 1933.

————. *Existence du symbolisme*. Maestricht: A. A. M. Stols, 1939.

————. *The Art of Poetry*. Translated by Denise Folliot. Princeton, NJ: Princeton University Press, 1985.

————. "Poetry and Abstract Thought." Translated by Jackson Matthews. In *Paul Valéry: An Anthology*, edited by James Lawler. Bollingen Series 15. Princeton, NJ: Princeton University Press, 1977.

————. "On Speaking Poetry." In *The Art of Poetry*. Translated by Denise Folliot. Princeton, NJ: Princeton University Press, 1985.

Villas, Léon. *Claude Debussy: His Life and Works*. Translated by Maire and Grace O'Brien. London: Oxford University Press, H. Milford, 1933.

Verlaine, Paul. *Oeuvres complètes* (Paris: Leon Vanier, 1901).

Vicaire, Gabriel. *Études sur la poésie populaire*. Paris: H. Leclerc, 1902.

Vicaire, Gabriel, and Henri Beauclair. *Les Déliquescences: poèmes décadents d'Adoré Floupette.* Paris: H. Jonquières, 1923.

Vielé-Griffin, Francis. "Jules Ferry: Père du symbolisme." *Mercure de France* (June 1896): 321–326.

Vigneron, Marcel Henri. *Recherches sur l'R anglo-américain d'après les procédés de la phonétique expérimentale.* Limoges: Imprimerie Commerciale Perrette, 1924.

Villemin, Emile. *Méthode naturelle de prononciation française et de phonétique pratique à l'usage des étrangers,* 5th ed. Paris: Larousse, n.d.

Vuillermoz, Emile. *Musiques d'aujourd'hui.* Paris: Crès, 1923.

———. *Claude Debussy.* Paris: Flammarion, 1962.

Watkins, Glenn. *Proof through the Night: Music and the Great War.* Berkeley: University of California Press, 2003.

Weber, Eugen. *Peasants into Frenchmen: The Modernization of Rural France, 1870–1914.* Stanford, CA: Stanford University Press, 1976.

———. *France: Fin de Siècle.* Cambridge: Harvard University Press, 1986.

———. *My France: Politics, Culture, Myth.* Cambridge: Harvard University Press, 1991.

Weisz, George. *The Emergence of Modern Universities in France, 1863–1914.* Princeton, NJ: Princeton University Press, 1983.

Wenk, Arthur B. *Claude Debussy and the Poets.* Berkeley: University of California Press, 1976.

White, Ruth L. *Verlaine et les musiciens.* Paris: Minard, 1992.

Whiting, Steven Moore. *Satie the Bohemian: From Cabaret to Concert Hall.* Oxford: Oxford University Press, 1999.

Willmott, Glenn. *McLuhan, or Modernism in Reverse.* Toronto: University of Toronto Press, 1996.

Woldu, Gail Hilson. "Fauré at the Conservatoire: Critical Assessments of the Years 1896–1920." In *Regarding Fauré,* edited by Tom Gordon, 97–118. Amsterdam: Gordon and Breach, 1999.

Youens, Susan. "Debussy's Setting of Verlaine's 'Colloque sentimental': From the Past to the Present." *Studies in Music,* no. 15 (1981): 93–105.

———. "Music, Verse, and 'Prose Poetry': Debussy's *Trois Chansons de Bilitis.*" *Journal of Musicological Research* 7, no. 1 (1986).

———. "*Le Soleil des morts:* A Turn-of-the-Century Portrait Gallery." In *Music at the Turn of Century: A 19th Century Music Reader,* edited by Joseph Kerman, 151–166. Berkeley: University of California Press, 1990.

Zeldin, Theodore. *France, 1848–1945.* Oxford: Oxford University Press, 1977.

Zund-Burguet, Adolphe. *Méthode pratique, physiologique et comparée de prononciation française.* Paris: Gymnase de la voix, 1902.

Musical scores are indicated with an italicized *e*, e.g., 74*e*.